Urban Politics

Urban Politics

Cities and Suburbs in a Global Age

Eighth Edition

Bernard H. Ross and Myron A. Levine

M.E.Sharpe
Armonk, New York
London, England

Library of Congress Cataloging-in-Publication Data

Ross, Bernard H., 1934–2010.
Urban politics : cities and suburbs in a global age / by Bernard H. Ross and Myron A. Levine. — 8th ed.
p. cm.
Includes bibliographical references and index.
ISBN 978-0-7656-2774-2 (pbk. : alk. paper)
1. Municipal government—United States. 2. Metropolitan government—United States.
I. Levine, Myron A. II. Title.

JS323.R67 2011
320.8'50973—dc22 2010053789

Printed in the United States of America

The paper used in this publication meets the minimum requirements of
American National Standard for Information Sciences
Permanence of Paper for Printed Library Materials,
ANSI Z 39.48-1984.

SP (p) 10 9 8 7 6 5 4 3 2

To Bernard H. Ross,

wonderful colleague, valued mentor, and kind friend.

Bernie loved cities, and he loved people. This book is dedicated to his memory, to his far-reaching scholarship, and to the joy that he found in his family and the city.

Contents

Preface

Metropolitan areas today are quite different than they were in the 1960s and 1970s, when the initial editions of *Urban Politics* first appeared. Since then, the United States has entered a suburban age: jobs, population, and voting power now lie in the suburban portions of the metropolis. Deindustrialization led to the decline of major manufacturing centers. Advances in transportation and telecommunications also facilitated a shift in population and economic activity to the Sunbelt. Today, economic restructuring continues with the outsourcing of jobs overseas.

In numerous ways, cities in the United States have "come back" and are no longer teetering on the edge of violent riots and bankruptcy, as they were in the 1960s and 1970s. The downtowns of many cities are booming. Inner-city neighborhoods are the sites of considerable gentrification and substantial upgrading. A "new immigration" from abroad, too, has brought life to once-declining neighborhoods. Community development corporations and other grassroots groups have built affordable housing and brought health care, job training, and other important services to the residents of inner-city neighborhoods.

Cities and suburbs, however, now face even more intense economic pressures and uncertainty than ever. Globalization exacerbates the competitive pressures on cities. In a global age, entire regions—not just individual communities—find that they are in competition with one another for businesses that have a choice of locations across the United States and around the world. Cities and suburbs offer major corporations substantial tax abatements and other inducements in an effort to "win" the location of attractive firms. The global competitive struggle has also awakened a new interest in regionalism, as government and private-sector leaders seek to find strategies that can cross local borders and build a region's economic competitiveness.

In numerous other ways, the urban crisis continues. Deindustrialization has resulted in the unabated decline of many former manufacturing centers. Numerous once-thriving cities and blue-collar suburbs continue their downward trajectory with little prospect of reversal. The problem of concentrated poverty remains. Public school systems have shown new levels of resegregation—not desegregation. The seemingly unending economic slowdown of the early years of the twenty-first century decreased municipal tax collections and saddled cities with new costs. A malfunctioning housing-finance market produced a wave of foreclosures and abandoned properties that marred communities in Phoenix and Las Vegas as well as Detroit and Cleveland. Federal and state aid reductions, coupled with voter resistance to new taxes, forced cities and suburbs to "tighten their belts" and find new ways to do more with less. Sprawled development continues to eat up green space and raises questions of sustainability. Indeed, a new generation of Americans schooled in environmental values has come to see the importance of "smart growth" alternatives to unconstrained suburban sprawl. The eighth edition of *Urban Politics* highlights the new attention that cities and suburbs are giving to sustainable development.

The 2008 election of Barack Obama brought new hopes that the national government would use its resources to target the problems of the nation's most distressed communities. But Obama worked within a system that imposes strict limits on urban action, confines that were soon reinforced by Republican congressional and gubernatorial victories in the 2010 midterm elections.

Urban Politics describes both the continuities and changes as U.S. cities and suburbs enter the twenty-first century. This volume pinpoints the many injustices and inequities that characterize contemporary urban America. But the book's assessment does not stop there. We also note the urban success stories, where policymakers have learned from the errors of the past, and where cities have changed for the better.

This book does not call for sweeping impossible-to-achieve policy changes. Instead, this book adopts a more pragmatic perspective, seeking to identify those more limited yet possible steps, policies, and strategies that can be undertaken to improve the urban condition.

There are a number of people whose contributions have added to the insights that this book has to offer. Robyne Turner wrote material on the gendered city that was included as a separate chapter in previous editions of this text. This book continues to recognize the importance of gendered perspectives on the exercise of power in the city. Bill Peterman and Janet Smith taught me a great deal about cities by allowing me to see firsthand the changes taking place in Chicago and in that city's community organizations. Jack Dustin, my colleague and chair at Wright State University, has been immensely supportive of this project. He continues to promote faculty engagement in the city arena and has generously shared his extensive knowledge of performance management and the evolving nature of city-suburban collaborations and regional strategies for economic development. I am also indebted to my colleagues in Wright State University's Department of Urban Studies who kept me up to date with their own fields of expertise: Jerri Killian and Enamul Choudhury for their knowledge of urban management; Mary Wenning for housing policy; Jennifer Subban for community development; and Marjory McLellan for urban history and her enthusiasm in using technology to bring the world of urban affairs into the classroom.

Special thanks go to Harry Briggs at M.E. Sharpe for his faith in this project. Indeed, there would be no eighth edition of *Urban Politics* were it not for Harry's continued support and patience. Special thanks also to go Ana Erlic at M.E. Sharpe for her excellent stewardship of various facets of production and to Elizabeth Granda Parker for her assistance with photo permissions

It is with great sadness that the publication of the eighth edition of *Urban Politics* also marks the passing of one of the volume's coauthors, Bernard Ross. Bernie's wealth of knowledge, especially in the fields of citizen participation, city management, and urban service delivery, continues to be reflected throughout the pages of this book. Bernie loved the texture of city life. He was a champion of cities. Bernie was also one of the founding organizers of the Urban Affairs Association, the nation's most prominent interdisciplinary forum for the study of cities and suburbs. The urban affairs profession has lost a cherished friend and scholar.

Myron A. Levine
Dayton, Ohio

Urban Politics

1 The Urban Situation

The Resilience of Cities: New York, Post-9/11

On the morning of September 11, 2001, Al Qaeda terrorists slammed a jetliner, loaded with passengers and fuel, into the ninety-first floor of the north tower of the World Trade Center (WTC) in Lower Manhattan. Eighteen minutes later, a second Boeing 767 hit the south tower. The resulting fire, fueled by massive amounts of office paper, reached 2,000 degrees Fahrenheit and effectively barred escape from the upper floors of the 110-story twin towers. Onlookers watched in horror as office workers jumped to their deaths. When the skyscraper's support structures melted, the towers crumbled to the ground.

More than 2,700 people died in the attacks at the World Trade Center.[1] All seven buildings in the complex, including the twin towers, collapsed. Nearby buildings suffered severe smoke, water, and structural damage. The fires and the massive dust cloud from the collapse spread asbestos, heavy metals, PCBs, and other toxins to the surrounding area,[2] a toxicity that would hamper rebuilding efforts.

In the months that followed the attack, economists and variety of commentators predicted that New York City would never recover. They predicted that the fear of terrorism would lead corporate executives to shift **secondary** or **back-office** functions to more secure sites in suburban office parks, small cities, and rural areas. The brokerage firm Goldman Sachs, which had suffered a terrible loss of life in its WTC offices, announced plans to move the firm's entire equity trading department across the river to Jersey City, a reversal of the company's earlier decision to cluster its employees in Manhattan. Morgan Stanley, the largest securities company in Manhattan, shifted part of its operations to suburban Westchester County, north of New York City. New York City officials responded by offering firms various tax breaks and other incentives in an effort to keep them downtown.[3] New York City lost 131,000 jobs in 2001, with three-fourths of the job loss occurring after the 9/11 attacks.[4]

Reconstruction efforts and even new construction in New York and other major cities increasingly began to take on characteristics of **urban fortresses**, with vehicular and pedestrian access strictly controlled through security-guarded entrances.[5] Cities across the nation spent large sums of money to protect bridges, airports, government buildings, and other vulnerable facilities. This was money that would no longer be available to support other much-needed public services.

Continuing concern about terrorism even led to major modifications in the design of the 1,776-foot Freedom Tower, the centerpiece of the rebuilding effort at Ground Zero. Architect Daniel Libeskind had proposed the construction of a monumental skyscraper that would be even taller than the twin towers. On top of the gigantic structure, Libeskind proposed a graceful off-center spiral, a parallel vision of the Statue of Liberty that faced it in New York harbor. The building was to embody the story and spirit of America. But the Freedom Tower would not be built as Libeskind had proposed. Security concerns led to a number of alterations in the building's design, hardening the base to shield it from a truck bomb and making the tower more symmetrical so as to withstand possible collapse. As revised, the Freedom Tower was no longer the architectural statement that Libeskind initially proposed. Instead, the building began to look more and more like a conventional skyscraper, although one that reached an amazing 1,776 feet into the air, with the number reflecting the Spirit of 1776, the founding of the nation.

Yet, despite the pessimistic predictions, New York City came back. The city's hotel rooms, vacant in the months immediately following the terrorist assault, soon filled again. Construction of the monumental Freedom Tower continued in spite of numerous delays. A new transit hub at the WTC site was opened, even though economic conditions forced a retreat from the original world-class design by Santiago Calatrava that had been originally chosen for the facility. Just five years after the attack, in 2006, the first major new building on the site, the forty-seven-story tower at 7 World Trade Center, opened despite a national economic recession that continued to depress the demand for prime office space.

Even the Goldman Sachs brokerage firm decided to stay in Lower Manhattan, taking advantage of low-interest Liberty Bonds and other governmental inducements to build a forty-three-story glass-and-steel headquarters building in Battery Park City, just across the street from the WTC site.[6] The corporation moved several thousand employees into its new headquarters, a decision that was a clear affirmation of the continuing economic primacy that Lower Manhattan and New York City had regained since the depths and gloom of 9/11.

New York's rebound shows that the prognostications that 9/11 marked the "end of cities" were vastly overstated. Cities like New York and Chicago serve important functions. Even in the midst of a global era, where technology enables decentralization, cities remain vital centers of commerce, knowledge, creativity, communications, and entrepreneurship.[7] Cities facilitate the idea sharing, research and development, and innovation critical to economic prosperity and society's advancement.[8] Given their importance, cities continue to endure, even amid the ongoing threat of terrorism.[9]

CITIES IN A GLOBAL SYSTEM: COMPARING THE RECOVERIES OF POST-9/11 NEW YORK AND POST-KATRINA NEW ORLEANS

Globalization denotes the eroding significance of national and local borders. Cities in a global age are affected by forces originating overseas that they cannot control.

Cities exist in a global system of interconnected relationships. The credit and investment decisions made by firms in one city can determine the opening and shutting down of a manufacturing plant half a world away. Political events, famines, and economic crises in one region of the globe can produce a human migration to cities in other countries. As the post-9/11 world clearly demonstrates, even political movements and ideologies from abroad can wind up influencing the spending decisions of U.S. cities.

Not all cities are equally central to the world economy: different cities occupy different positions in the global economy. New York was able to rebound from the disaster of 9/11 to a great extent because of its critical position as a **world city**, an international center of finance, banking, and corporate headquarters. Simply put, the global economy needed a restored New York.

Indeed, the terrorists chose the World Trade Center and New York as the targets of attack because of the importance of Wall Street and the Lower Manhattan financial district to the economies of Western nations. The gigantic towers of the World Trade Center were a symbol of American might and Western cultural and economic dominance. A highly advanced telecommunications network carried images of American wealth and power around the world, fueling the resentments that were unleashed in the WTC assault.

New York's financial leaders had built the World Trade Center in the decades following World War II, from fears that the industrial-rooted city of mid-century was losing its primacy in a new postindustrial global economy. (See Box 1.1, "The Global Challenge and the Decision to Build the World Trade Center.") In the wake of the 9/11 attacks, business leaders once again pushed for the construction of new office space, replacing the space lost in the attack, so that New York could maintain its position as a world economic capital.

New York, London, and Tokyo are generally regarded as the world's three top-tier cities. In the United States, Los Angeles is a rung or so below New York in terms of its reach on the world economic stage. While Los Angeles is a center of communications and Pacific Rim banking, the city still lacks the concentration of world-prominent corporate headquarters and financial services firms found in New York.

Chicago, Houston, Denver, Miami, and San Francisco are other U.S. cities with global connections. These cities are important national and regional commercial centers. They are not, however, critical command-and-control centers of the global economy.

In terms of a global hierarchy of cities, New Orleans falls below even these regional centers. New Orleans is a major tourist destination. But even before Hurricane Katrina hit, New Orleans' once-significant port activity and petroleum-related businesses had already faded. Miami, not New Orleans, emerged as the principal U.S. center of Caribbean finance and trade.[10]

The devastation wreaked by Hurricane Katrina in 2005 was substantial. The hurricane and subsequent flooding left 80 percent of the city underwater and destroyed 182,000 homes. Given the extensive scope of the devastation, New Orleans' recovery in the years that followed has, in many ways, been quite remarkable. Still, even with

Box 1.1

The Global Challenge and the Decision to Build the World Trade Center

By the middle of the twentieth century, New York's position as the world's most dominant city was beginning to slip. **Deindustrialization** (the disappearance of manufacturing and port-related jobs) and suburbanization eroded the city's economic foundations. Advances in transportation and telecommunications enabled corporate CEOs to shift production outside the city to low-tax, low-cost sites in the suburbs and in the Sunbelt. Federal subsidies for highway construction, home mortgages, and new business investment accelerated the decentralization of jobs and population.

The World Trade Center was the pet project of one man, Chase Manhattan Bank president David Rockefeller. Sitting in his office in Chase's headquarters building near Wall Street, he feared for the future of Lower Manhattan. No new skyscrapers had been erected in the area in the years following Chase's decision to build its own headquarters there. Rockefeller sought a dynamic megaproject that would kick-start Lower Manhattan's renewal. Rockefeller proposed to clear out the many small buildings and antiquated warehouses that dotted the area in order to make way for a modern new financial district. The construction of the World Trade Center commenced over the protests of the electronics storeowners of "Radio Row" who were evicted from the project site.

As president of Chase Manhattan, David Rockefeller was one of the most powerful financiers on the planet. Yet, as formidable a figure as he was, Rockefeller could not bring about the rebirth of Lower Manhattan by himself. The project needed public funds and the legal authority of government for evictions, land assembly, and various planning and construction approvals. David Rockefeller worked hand in hand with his brother, New York Governor Nelson Rockefeller. He also found another willing partner in the Port Authority of New York and New Jersey and its executive director Austin Tobin. Tobin and the Port Authority continued to provide financing for the project, even after the changes taking place in New York's economy made it clear that the towers would not be occupied by port-related trading companies but by the finance-related firms of Wall Street.

The construction of the World Trade Center was a critical element in New York's adaptation to a postindustrial economy. As the city's manufacturing and port-related jobs continued to disappear, New York reemerged as a center of multinational financial institutions and global corporate headquarters. The World Trade Center and the neighboring World Financial Center helped provide the prime office space that allowed the financial district of a growing global city to expand well beyond its old Wall Street confines.

Sources: Jameson W. Doig, *Empire on the Hudson* (New York: Columbia University Press, 2001); Eric Darton, *Divided We Stand: A Biography of New York City's World Trade Center* (New York: Basic Books, 2001); James Glanz and Eric Lipton, *City in the Sky: The Rise and Fall of the World Trade Center* (New York: Times Books, 2003).

the infusion of outside assistance, New Orleans has not been able to come all the way back, and obvious scars remain. New Orleans lost over a quarter of its population.[11] Large portions of the city outside of the center remain vacant. The local economy also proved sluggish, and the region continued to suffer high rates of poverty.[12] New Orleans does not occupy a critical position in the global economy. As a result, there was no equivalent urgency to restore the city—especially its low-lying, poor African-American neighborhoods—as there was to rebuild Lower Manhattan.

POWER AND THE STUDY OF URBAN GOVERNMENT

The particular focus of this book is on power and how it is exercised in the urban arena. The study of cities requires that we look behind the scenes, beyond public offices to private actors such as David Rockefeller who can influence a city's course of actions. The concept of globalization also serves to underscore the fact that many of the key decisions that affect a city's health are not always made by a city's elected leaders but by individuals and institutions from beyond a city's borders.

Power is too often viewed simply as **social control**, the ability of a political actor to force others to comply with his or her wishes. Under this elementary definition of power, an actor has "power over" others who fear sanctions or punishments if they fail to behave as expected.

In the study of cities, however, power does not refer only to situations of social control ("power over"). Rather, power also denotes **social production** or the "power to" get important things done. The exercise of power does not necessarily entail conflict and the use of overt or hidden threats. An actor also has power when he or she can get important projects accomplished, when he or she is successful in arranging coordination and joint action in the pursuit of goals.[13]

In the urban arena, we need to find out who has the power to get things done and who has the ability to stop or thwart proposed changes. Of course, we must look at a city's elected officeholders and the formal authority that they and the city possess. But our examination cannot stop there. A study of power must also go "behind the scenes" to find out whether governmental officials are highly constrained in their decision making.

As we shall see throughout this book, the formal structure of municipal government in the United States largely serves to limit local action and to fragment local authority. The United States Constitution makes no explicit mention of cities and their powers. States decide just what formal program authority a municipality may possess. In general, the states have fragmented local authority in the region, creating relatively autonomous local political bodies and only weak regional coordinating agencies. City officials also find that, given their limited ability to raise revenues, they are highly dependent on the program-funding decisions made by both state and national officials.

A brief review of the post-9/11 reconstruction of Lower Manhattan underscores the limited power of local government. New York's city council and even New York's mayor were not the key decision makers who determined what would be built at Ground Zero. The mayor enjoyed limited prerogatives, including the ability to determine how certain rebuilding funds were allocated. Yet, he and the City did not possess final approval over site design and other important reconstruction matters. Instead, as the following discussion shows, those decisions were made by private actors and by narrow-based special agencies that the state had created.

PUBLIC AND PRIVATE POWER IN THE REBUILDING AT GROUND ZERO

There was no consensus as to just what should be built at Ground Zero, a site that many Americans considered "holy ground." Enthusiasts urged that the twin towers be reconstructed or that an even taller skyscraper be built as a testament to America's perseverance and spirit. Wall Street interests, by contrast, were more focused on replacing the large volume of office space that was lost in the nation's financial heart as a consequence of the devastation. The business sector also generally opposed rebuilding visions that diminished the area's office space in order to set aside a large portion of the site as a memorial to the victims and heroes of 9/11.

Neighborhood advocates countered that there was no real demand for such a massive supply of office space in a weak economy, especially when the continuing threat of terrorism dampened the demand for prime office space in Lower Manhattan. Community activists sought to build a Lower Manhattan on a more human scale, with parks and a mix of residential and office developments, as opposed to the towering skyscrapers demanded by the business community.[14]

The families of the 9/11 victims demanded a proper memorial. They lobbied against projects that expanded the commercialization of the site to the detriment of a memorial to their lost loved ones.

As difficult as it may be to believe, New York City's government was not one of the key players when it came to some of the most critical rebuilding decisions. Neither the mayor nor the city council possessed the authority to decide what would be constructed at the WTC site. Instead, the decision making was lodged in the hands of narrow-based agencies and quasi-governmental bodies dominated by downtown corporate interests.

An independent body, the Port Authority of New York and New Jersey, owned the World Trade Center site. In existence for well over half a century, the Port Authority was established by bi-state agreement and was given considerable powers to develop the region's port facilities, road network, bridges, and airports. The Port Authority was not a city agency but its own independent entity, which does not operate under the direct command of the city and its mayor and council. The Port Authority even has its own police force separate from that of the better-known New York Police Department. On 9/11, thirty-seven Port Authority Police Department (PAPD) officers were killed, a number that was greater than the twenty-three fatalities suffered by NYPD officers. The PAPD deaths were the largest single-day loss "of any police force in history."[15]

Just weeks before the 9/11 attacks, the Port Authority made one of the more fateful decisions that would later complicate the rebuilding effort. The Port Authority leased the World Trade Center and its underground shopping complex to Larry Silverstein and his partners in return for $120 million per year in rental payments. Under the terms of the ninety-nine-year contract, Silverstein was legally obligated to continue payments even after the WTC's destruction.[16] The contract also gave Silverstein considerable say in the reconstruction process. As the WTC leaseholder, Silverstein stood to receive $4.6 billion or more in insurance money that would be essential to the rebuilding effort.[17]

Government power in the rebuilding was sharply limited by an American cultural and legal system of **privatism** that accords extensive deference to contractual obligations and other private property rights. The laws of contract made Silverstein—not New York's mayor—the prime decision maker in the rebuilding at Ground Zero. Yet, in a city where power is fragmented among a variety of municipal agencies, even Silverstein's power as leaseholder was far from absolute. For the rebuilding to proceed, Silverstein needed additional financial support and various approvals from the state, the Port Authority, and other public agencies.

Silverstein's position was most evident in the debate over the design of the new 1,776-foot Freedom Tower, the centerpiece of the reconstruction effort, a building that would be taller than the twin towers. Immediately after the attacks, New York governor George Pataki created the Lower Manhattan Development Corporation (LMDC) to oversee the postdisaster rebuilding in the broad WTC area. The LMDC sponsored an international competition to seek out the best possible design for the WTC site. Eventually, the proposal submitted by Daniel Libeskind, the celebrated architect of Berlin's Jewish Museum, emerged as the winner. Libeskind proposed a below-ground memorial and a number of tall office buildings, including the gigantic Freedom Tower with an off-center asymmetrical spire soaring above seventy floors of offices, reaching the symbolically significant height of 1,776 feet.

Silverstein, however, had little confidence in Libeskind's design and preferred the work of his own internationally renowned architect, Richard Childs. Silverstein, as leaseholder and the recipient of 9/11 insurance awards, was paying for much of the new construction. Acting under the rules of privatism, Silverstein was appropriately concerned with making a profit on his investment. Silverstein viewed Libeskind's proposal as lacking commercial viability; its twisting design failed to maximize leasable office space. Silverstein also believed that Libeskind lacked the experience and technical know-how to build a complex and gigantic skyscraper.

Silverstein, working in conjunction with the Port Authority, continued to advance the commercial aspects of the development, including plans for an expanded underground arcade of shops that would be connected to the new regional rail hub. The shops would provide the leaseholder with high-value commercial space. Critics argued that such an immense underground plaza would drain away pedestrian life from surface streets, diminishing the financial viability of stores in the surrounding area.

New York State gave the LMDC the authority to distribute federal aid, condemn land, and override local zoning ordinances that interfered with reconstruction. Critics charged that the new body was dominated by business representatives and more responsive to the concerns of Wall Street than to the desires of the residents of surrounding neighborhoods. The LMDC, however, could not control the actions of Silverstein and the Port Authority, as they continued to pursue their own rebuilding visions.

The LMDC initially did not select Libeskind's master plan as one of the first-round winners in its selection of a grand design to rebuild the WTC site. The selection process revealed the pro-business leanings of the LMDC as well as the Port Authority. The LMDC hosted numerous forums for public comment on a wide range of rebuilding plans. The process allowed extensive opportunities for public engagement. Yet, when it came to making the final decision, the LMDC retreated behind closed doors.[18] The

LMDC announced six finalists, architectural firms that proposed rather ordinary box-like business structures that would restore as much of the area's lost office space as possible. The proposals did not sufficiently memorialize the site. None offered the sort of grandiosity that would serve as testimony to America's spirit.

Public outcries over the choices led Governor Pataki to intervene. As a result, the LMDC reversed itself, rejecting the six proposals that it had earlier announced as finalists. The LMDC sponsored a second round of competition, announcing that it would give greater emphasis to innovation and architectural distinction. Daniel Libeskind's overall site design was selected in the second go-round.

As this brief retelling of post-9/11 decision making in New York underscores, the key agencies in the rebuilding effort gave considerable weight to the needs of the city's—and the nation's—business community. Despite the creation of an extensive process for citizen engagement, the actual decision making proved highly undemocratic.[19] The real planning decisions were made in a separate "parallel" process that was only "tenuously connected" to the numerous public meetings that took place throughout the city.[20] The principal actors had even made the decision to expand the rebuilding effort beyond the Ground Zero site and into neighboring Lower Manhattan before the matter was presented to the public.[21] A restored financial district was critical to the competitiveness of both the New York and the national economies. As a result, business voices occupied a privileged position in the reconstruction process.

The public's voice, though, was not entirely shut out. The concerns expressed in various participatory "Listening to the City" forums and the outrage over the LMDC's initial dismissal of the Libeskind master plan led to the intervention of Governor Pataki.[22] New York City's government, however, lacked any meaningful control over the rebuilding effort. Local elected officials could only hope to influence the decisions that were made by independent narrow-purpose bodies that largely responded to the concerns of various elements in the business community.

PRIVATISM: THE LIMITED POWER OF GOVERNMENT

As we have just described, post-9/11 decision making in New York gave great deference to private property rights and the profit-making activities of business. Decision makers failed to assert a "public interest" in identifying alternative, more balanced visions for renewing the Ground Zero site and the immediate surrounding area.[23]

Unlike cities in Europe, U.S. cities lack the strong authority and planning powers that can be used to assert the public interest, counterbalancing private power. In Europe, government officials guide private investment to ensure the achievement of public purposes. European planners enact strong measures to build affordable housing, preserve the city streetscape, curb urban sprawl, promote mass transit, and protect green areas, measures that are largely unthinkable in the United States. Planners in Europe even have the ability to insist that the developers of new commercial projects provide subsidized housing units for the poor.[24] In Europe, private developers and free-market forces do not dictate the geography of urban development.

The American culture of privatism, in contrast, keeps government planning and authority to a minimum while maximizing private-sector freedom. The privatist culture of the United States views cities narrowly as places where private profit-making activities take place. In the "private city,"[25] private-sector actors possess great leeway to develop and dispose of their property as they see fit. Americans resist urban planning requirements and land-use restrictions as violations of their freedoms and property rights.

In a privatist system, many of the most important decisions that affect a city's health are in the hands of private actors, not government officials. City officials cannot simply dictate to the private sector but must persuade or convince private actors to undertake actions in the public interest. Effective urban problem solving requires the forging of effective partnerships between public- and private-sector actors. However, as the tale of the rebuilding at Ground Zero indicates, such partnerships often wind up giving great respect to the demands of business actors and much less respect to "livability" concerns of residents of the city.

In both New York and New Orleans, business leaders and their political allies used the disaster as an opportunity to introduce market-led actions to enhance private profit making. Corporations building in the affected areas received generous tax exemptions, low-interest loans, and other assistance, with few guarantees that the new investment would provide a public benefit as well as corporate profits. In both New York and New Orleans, the state government created business-oriented agencies—the Lower Manhattan Development Corporation and the Louisiana Recovery Administration—to oversee the reconstruction effort, bypassing the authority of local elected officials. In both cases, the federal government waived the usual requirement that a portion of Community Development Block Grant assistance be used for projects that benefit lower- and moderate-income people.[26] In New York, private investors used the subsidies to build luxury housing; few, if any, affordable units were built. New York and New Orleans had engaged in a private-led rebuilding effort, where public monies subsidized corporate expansion with few guarantees that the new construction would produce public benefits.

THE THEMES OF THIS BOOK

The major focus of this book is on the interrelationship of private power and public authority in the modern metropolis. Six important subthemes further guide this book's study of America's cities and suburbs:

1. ***Globalization is a powerful force shaping cities.*** Global forces—including the cross-border flow of investment, the outsourcing of production to overseas sites, and heightened immigration—have had a great influence on urban development and city affairs (see Chapter 3). Advances in telecommunications and shipping have increased the mobility of businesses. As a result, municipal officials feel the need to win a competition for business that is increasingly national and global in its scope. The managers of a multinational corporation located in a particular city are often outsiders who move to a city on a corporation's orders. They do not even possess the civic loyalty and interest in municipal affairs that characterized an earlier generation of locally-rooted downtown business leaders (see Chapter 4).

2. *The formal rules and structure of local government continue to exert a great influence on city and suburban politics.* Cities do not have the powers to tax and spend as they wish. The formal structure of city governments details just what powers a local authority does and does not possess. The formal structure and processes of local government help determine just whose interests are represented in city hall.

3. *The state and federal governments play a critical role in urban affairs.* Cities are not autonomous actors in a self-contained, local political system. Instead, cities and suburbs exist in an intergovernmental setting where the decisions of the national government and especially those of the states help determine the powers and resources available to local governments. The ability of cities and suburbs to solve problems is highly dependent on decisions made by the state and national governments.

4. *In the contemporary United States, there is an important regional difference in urban patterns.* Over the past half century, Sunbelt communities in the South and the Southwest have generally prospered while Frostbelt communities in the Northeast and Midwest have suffered a long-term population and economic decline. The problems of growing communities—such as increased traffic, the lack of water, and land-use patterns that "eat up" the environment—differ markedly from the problems of declining communities. State and federal assistance that may target the problems of communities in one region may fail to target the problems of communities elsewhere in the country.

Of course, in talking about the differences between regions, we must be careful to avoid stereotypes. Not all Sunbelt communities are the same, just as Frostbelt cities are not all alike. Even before Hurricane Katrina, New Orleans was a Sunbelt community that experienced the sort of urban problems—deindustrialization and the loss of jobs, the concentration of inner-city poverty, and the racial segregation of schools and neighborhoods—that are typically associated with big cities in the Northeast and Midwest. Similarly, in the Frostbelt, New York and a number of other cities have experienced an economic rebound that has not been felt in cities like Detroit, Buffalo, and St. Louis.

Yet, despite the continuing significance of regional differences, the urban crisis is a national, not a regional, phenomenon. Home foreclosures, for instance, are not confined to the distressed neighborhoods of former industrial Rustbelt cities like Detroit, Indianapolis, and Cleveland. In fact, in 2009, four Sunbelt states—California, Florida, Nevada, and Arizona—reported the highest rates of foreclosures. The twenty-five cities with the highest rates of foreclosures were all in the Sunbelt.[27] Previously the site of a property boom, Sunbelt communities were centers of property abandonment when the real estate markets went bust. In troubled economic times, communities in the Sunbelt as well as the Frostbelt have great difficulty in finding the resources to provide basic services.

5. *Questions of economic development have come to dominate local politics.* City after city and suburb after suburb have sought new strategies in the competition for industry and jobs. Postindustrial dislocation and advances in telecommunications that increase business mobility have intensified the economic vulnerability of cities. An underperforming national economy and cutbacks in national and state aid programs have further led local communities to emphasize programs aimed at job creation and economic development.

6. *Race remains an important but often unacknowledged part of urban and metropolitan politics.* In the United States, city politics remains intertwined with the politics of race. Patterns of residential imbalance and ghettoization persist. School integration is not improving; instead, the evidence in recent years points to heightened levels of racial *resegregation* in the nation's public schools (see Chapter 9). Yet, public authorities have been able to do relatively little to confront continuing racial disparities. A "new immigration" from Latin American and Asia (see Chapter 2) has added to the diversity found in U.S. communities, compounding the complexity of ethnic and race relations in the contemporary city.

GLOBALIZATION

Globalization denotes the increased permeability of cities to international economic forces, global corporate decision making, new population movements, and other forces outside their borders—even to terrorist attacks plotted from abroad. As this chapter has already shown, New York City adapted to globalization and deindustrialization, including the loss of manufacturing jobs to the Sunbelt and to low-cost sites overseas, by strengthening its position as a world financial center. New York is also one of a large number of communities that have become tourist cities and entertainment cities, with new activities in tourism, sports, and convention-related business replacing the industrial jobs of old.[28] Such cities, however, run the risk of providing a good level of services for visitors while neglecting the conditions of the city's poorer residential neighborhoods (see Chapter 4).

Not all cities are able to find a niche in the new global economy. Advances in transportation, communications, and computerization allow corporations to shift manufacturing, data processing, and record-keeping activities to low-wage, low-cost sites overseas. Good-paying manufacturing jobs, once the backbone of central-city economies, have largely disappeared, only to be replaced by unstable, low-paying service work. Advances in information technology have also freed national and global corporations from central-city locations, enabling firms to site branch-office production in **edge cities**, the concentration of office parks and technology-related centers that have sprung up along the suburban rim of the metropolis.[29]

As middle-class families moved to suburbia, they left behind a **dual city** that is home to both America's "haves" and "have-nots," with a great gulf separating the lives of the two. Young professionals and technologically competent workers, well-rewarded for their skills, live in doorman-guarded luxury condominiums and take advantage of fine shopping, dining, and the best that the city has to offer. The urban poor live in much different sectors of the city, in neighborhoods with poorer-quality housing, malfunctioning schools, and much less opportunity. The most pessimistic scenarios portray America's big cities as slipping toward a **Blade Runner future**, where, as portrayed in the science fiction movie *Blade Runner*, daily life entails an ever-present and increasingly violent clash between the technologically skilled and affluent "haves" and the low-skilled, superfluous urban poor.

Urban poverty, though, is no longer confined to central cities. By the early years of the twenty-first century, the number of poor families living in the nation's suburbs actually surpassed the number living in central cities.[30] The Great Recession of the early twenty-first century had brought urban dualism to America's suburbs.

Globalization entails the transborder flow of populations, not just of jobs and capital. Advances in transportation and liberalized immigration laws have altered the demography of U.S. cities. According to the 2002 U.S. Census estimates, 36 percent of New York's population was born outside the United States. In a global age, New York City, like other port-of-entry cities, is more than ever a city of immigrants. A brief look at a listing of the victims of the WTC attacks underscores the diversity of population of a global city. The homelands of the victims ranged from the Dominican Republic to Canada to Poland.[31] The dead on 9/11 included both legal and undocumented immigrants, many from Mexico, who worked as window washers, custodial staff, and food-service personnel in the WTC's below-ground eateries and its top-floor world-renowned Windows on the World restaurant. Mexicans had become New York's fastest growing minority.

Immigration is redefining urban politics. Twenty-four large- and medium-size cities have a population that is more than one-fifth foreign born (see Table 1.1). Over 60 percent of the population in Miami was born outside the United States, as was nearly half the population of Santa Ana and over 40 percent of the Los Angeles and Anaheim populations. In immigration gateway cities such as Los Angeles, New York, San Francisco, Miami, Chicago, Washington, Houston, San Diego, Boston, Dallas, Philadelphia, and Seattle, newcomers represent both a source of urban vitality and a strain on local resources.

The arrival of the new immigrants helps to mask the continuing weakness of cities. Some observers looked at the 2000 U.S. Census and took satisfaction in the small population gains reported by central cities, gains that, in many cases, stood in sharp contrast to decades of central-population decline. Yet, suburban growth continues to outstrip that of central cities (see Figure 1.1). Were it not for the arrival of new immigrants, the decline of central cities would be even more apparent, with many continuing to report population decline. Rustbelt cities in the nation's old industrial core—Detroit, Toledo, Cleveland, Akron, Pittsburgh, Scranton, Buffalo, and Syracuse—continued to lose population throughout the first decade of the twenty-first century.[32]

The Formal Rules and Structure of Municipal Government

The fifty states determine the formal powers and reach of their local governments. As we saw in our case study of the reconstruction at Ground Zero, neither the mayor of New York nor the city council possessed the legal authority to decide what would be built. Instead, a bi-state agreement between the states of New York and New Jersey had created The Port Authority, the special-purpose governing body that enjoyed numerous prerogatives as the owner of the WTC site. In the wake of 9/11, New York Governor Pataki created a second body, the LMDC, to control the overall rebuilding of Lower Manhattan. In New Orleans, State of Louisiana officials distrusted the city and set up their own bodies to direct the post-Katrina rebuilding effort, denying the city control over reconstruction monies.[33]

In New York, as elsewhere across the nation, the creation of numerous units of government leads to the **fragmentation of governmental authority**. No government possesses the authority to govern a metropolitan region. Instead, governing authority

Table 1.1

Cities Ranked by Percent of Population That Is Foreign Born, 2002, Top 30 Cities

Rank	Place	Percent
1.	Miami, FL	60.6
2.	Santa Ana, CA	48.4
3.	Los Angeles, CA	41.3
4.	Anaheim, CA	40.3
5.	San Francisco, CA	36.7
6.	San Jose, CA	36.5
7.	New York, NY	36.0
8.	Long Beach, CA	30.9
9.	Houston, TX	28.1
10.	San Diego, CA	27.9
11.	Oakland, CA	27.1
12.	Boston, MA	27.0
13.	Dallas, TX	26.5
14.	Sacramento, CA	26.4
15.	Honolulu CDP, HI	25.5
16.	El Paso, TX	24.9
17.	Stockton, TX	24.2
18.	Riverside, CA	23.9
19.	Fresno, CA	22.7
20.	Chicago, IL	22.6
21.	Newark, NJ	22.4
22.	Phoenix, AZ	21.1
23.	Las Vegas, NV	21.1
24.	Denver, CO	20.2
25.	Austin, TX	19.6
26.	Aurora, CO	17.7
27.	Minneapolis, MN	17.6
28.	Seattle, WA	17.2
29.	Arlington, TX	16.6
30.	St. Paul, MN	16.3

Source: Extracted from U.S. Census Bureau, American Community Service Office, "Percent of Population that Is Foreign Born," September 2, 2003; available at www.census.gov/acs/www/Products/Ranking/2002/R15T160.htm.

is chopped up into many small pieces and dispersed among a variety of cities, counties, townships, and independent districts, authorities, and quasi-governmental bodies such as the Port Authority and the LMDC. The public is quite unaware that so many narrow-based specialized bodies possess many of the powers that we commonly associate with local governments. Mayors and other elected officials find it difficult to lead when formal authority is divided among so many autonomous bodies.

THE INTERGOVERNMENTAL CITY

The concept of the **intergovernmental city** points to the significant impact that state and national government actions have on local affairs. The states can grant or deny municipalities the ability to tax and borrow money. Cities are also greatly reliant on state and local financial assistance. National and state aid accounts for nearly

Figure 1.1 **Suburban Population Is Growing Twice as Fast as Cities** (Percent Change in Metropolitan Population and Families, 1990–1997)

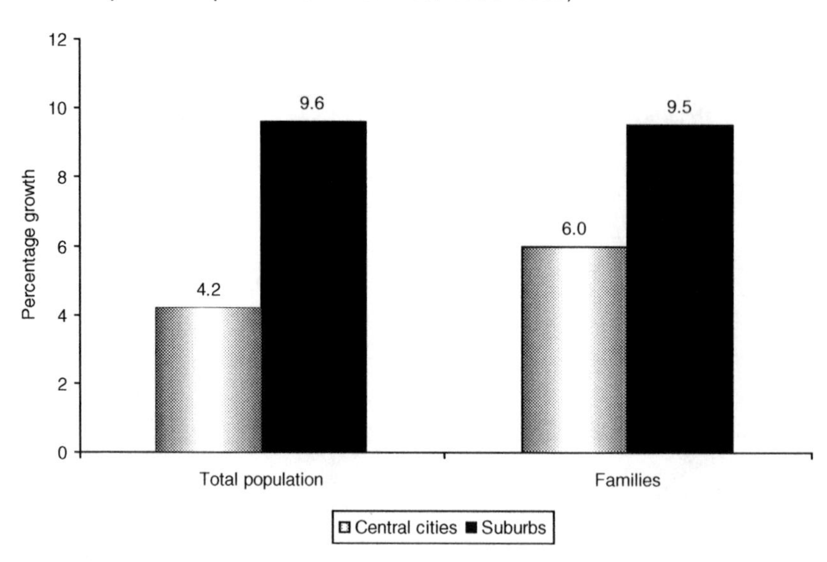

Source: U.S. Department of Housing and Urban Development (HUD), *The State of the Cities*, 1998, p. 7; available at www.huduser.org/Publications/PDF/soc_98.pdf.

Note: The HUD figure is based on the U.S. Bureau of the Census Current Population Study.

40 percent of local government revenues.[34] More financially strapped communities are dependent on intergovernmental assistance that allows for basic service provision.

State and federal mandates can also burden a city with the cost of providing specified services. New York State law, for instance, mandated that New York City pay for half the state share of the federal Medicaid program for poor people. This was the largest Medicaid burden that any state in the nation imposed on its local governments. In 2002 alone, this mandate cost New York City taxpayers $3.1 billion.[35] The attacks of 9/11 added to the burdens placed on local governments, as federal Homeland Security legislation did not fully reimburse cities for their new responsibilities in policing and safeguarding federal facilities, bridges, the municipal water supply, and other possible targets of terrorist attacks.

The federal government promised New York $21 billion in rebuilding assistance, with another $5 billion going to victims' families. The money was a great help but still fell far short of compensating the city for the economic losses that it sustained as a result of the attacks, which through 2004 were estimated at $83 billion to $95 billion.[36]

Federal and state action can be quite helpful to cities. The federal government created tax-exempt Liberty Bonds that encouraged private investment to aid post-9/11 Lower Manhattan recovery projects, leading to a boom in upscale residential construction as well as the creation of new office space.[37]

Yet, as we shall see in Chapter 2, federal and state actions have not always been that helpful to cities. Too often, federal and state programs constitute a "hidden" urban policy that has worked to exacerbate urban ills.

REGIONAL PATTERNS: SUNBELT AND FROSTBELT

The 2000 Census documented the continuing shift of population to the **Sunbelt**, that is, to the South, the Southwest, and the West (see Figure 1.2). Phoenix, San Diego, San Antonio, Los Angeles, Houston, and Dallas all reported the greatest population gains. The nation's most quickly growing communities—Gilbert, Chandler, and Peoria (Arizona), North Las Vegas and Henderson (Nevada), and Irvine, Rancho Cucamonga, and Chula Vista (California)—are all in the Sunbelt. In contrast, the six counties suffering the most extensive population losses—Baltimore, Philadelphia, Allegheny (Pittsburgh), Wayne (Detroit), St. Louis, and Washington, DC—were all in the **Frostbelt**, the once-industrial Northeast and Midwest.[38]

Sunbelt growth, as we shall see in Chapter 2, is not simply the result of a favorable climate and the modernization of transportation. Ann Markusen uses the term **gunbelt** to underscore the importance of defense-related expenditures to Sunbelt communities, especially in California, Texas, Florida, and the Southwest. The "gunbelt," however, clearly goes beyond the more traditional borders of the Sunbelt to include Seattle, Colorado Springs, Washington, DC, the high-tech suburbs of Boston, and other areas that have benefited from defense-related spending.[39]

Yet, there is a great analytical danger in dividing the United States into two such large and loosely defined regions. Such a rough regional division may hide and distort as much as it reveals.

Data from the 2007 Census underscore the extent to which poverty is a fact of life for fading industrial cities in the Frostbelt. One-third (33.8 percent) of Detroit's population was below the poverty line. Other Frostbelt cities showed nearly as high and debilitating poverty rates: Cleveland (29.5 percent), Buffalo (29 percent), Newark (24 percent), Philadelphia (24 percent), Milwaukee (24 percent), Cincinnati (23.5 percent), Toledo (23 percent), St. Louis (22 percent), Pittsburgh (21 percent), Columbus (21 percent), Chicago (20.5 percent), Minneapolis (20 percent), Baltimore (20 percent), and Boston (20 percent). The poverty rates of America's disaster cities are almost unbelievable: Benton Harbor, Michigan (56.7 percent); Camden, New Jersey (38.2 percent); and East Cleveland (37.7 percent).[40]

While the Frostbelt was certainly a region of urban distress, a number of Sunbelt cities also had large concentrations of poverty: El Paso (27 percent), Memphis (26 percent), Miami (25.5 percent), Fresno (22 percent), Dallas (21 percent), New Orleans (21 percent), Atlanta (21 percent), and Houston (21 percent). In a number of Old South states, new local growth and dynamism are largely confined to resort and retirement communities. While Sunbelt communities have generally fared better than Frostbelt communities, as we can readily see, the Sunbelt is not a region of uniform urban growth and prosperity.

THE DOMINANCE OF LOCAL ECONOMIC DEVELOPMENT

In the 1960s, school busing, community control, urban riots, civilian-police review boards, and battling inner-city poverty were all issues that dominated urban politics. A half century later, the agenda of local governments is vastly different. Issues

Figure 1.2 **The Regional Shift: Percent Change in Population by State, 1990–2000**

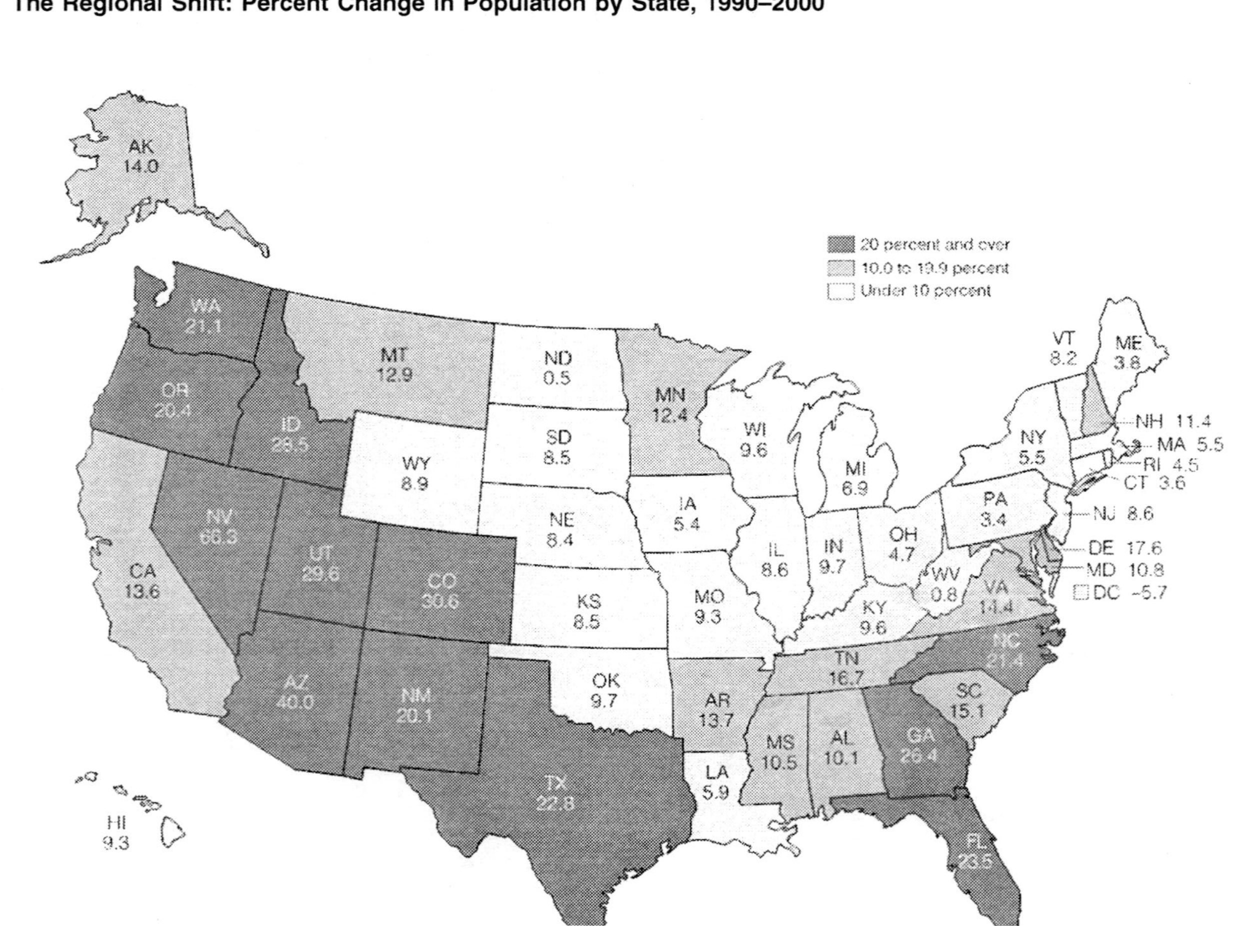

Source: U.S. Census Bureau.

regarding race, equity, and neighborhood empowerment have been displaced by a heightened concern for jobs and local economic development. Virtually all competing concerns have fallen on the agenda as local officials devote their attention to attracting new industries.

Of course, "crime" is still a salient issue in many communities, especially in the inner city. Younger and more upscale voters also tend to be interested in preserving the natural environment. Cities in the arid West are particularly concerned with "water," as the limited availability of water imposes severe constraints on industrial and residential development. By 2010, the debate over immigration and the status of undocumented workers also gained new prominence in local arenas, especially in communities in the Southwest.

Economic development is not the only important issue on the agenda of every community. Still, a cumulative sense of economic insecurity has reshaped local politics across the nation. Deindustrialization and a badly fluctuating national economy have led local voters and municipal officials alike to give enhanced attention to policies aimed at local industrial and job growth.

THE CONTINUING RELUCTANCE TO CONFRONT RACIAL DISPARITIES IN THE METROPOLIS

Hurricane Katrina revealed the continuing significance of race in urban affairs. The maintenance of the levees that protected New Orleans' low-lying black neighborhoods just did not occupy a very prominent place on the agendas of the state and national government. New Orleans' neighboring white communities were also quite unwilling to cooperate in disaster-preparedness drills for the evacuation of New Orleans' poor.[41] The Superdome, the city's emergency shelter, was poorly supplied with food and water, an inadequacy that proved deadly once the storm and flooding hit. In the midst of the storm, vigilantes, and in some cases even the police, in the surrounding suburbs barred the entry of black New Orleanians as they attempted to flee their disaster-plagued city. Despite the important gains that had been made in racial progress over the years, America's cities had not quite entered the post–civil rights era.[42]

The evidence on racial segregation in the metropolis is mixed (see Chapter 9). There is clearly quite good news: recent decades have seen increases in residential integration and the virtual disappearance of the all-white suburb. However, more subtle forms of racial discrimination still mar the housing market, and residential neighborhoods continue to be stratified by race. The continuing significance of race is readily apparent in cities like Chicago where even the most casual observer will easily see that African Americans make up nearly all the patrons on the platforms of the city's South Side "El" train stations, while the patronage turns overwhelmingly white on the platforms on the North Side of the city.

In schools, the evidence is not only mixed but increasingly disappointing. While the most extreme forms of school segregation have disappeared, recent data point to the rise of **resegregation**, a return to higher levels of racial separation in public school systems.

Americans, especially white Americans, are quite ambivalent when it comes to racial desegregation. Americans overwhelmingly condemn **de jure segregation**, that is, segregation mandated by law, as existed in the South through the early 1960s. In 1954, the Supreme Court in the ***Brown v. Board of Education*** decision began the prolonged process of bringing an end to the *de jure* segregation of public schools. Americans similarly endorse federal fair housing laws that bar the most blatant forms of discrimination in housing.

Yet, despite this endorsement of the ideal of racial integration, Americans are largely unwilling to back measures to undo the school and housing discrimination that continue to exist. Despite Brown, many big cities continue to have schools with either no white enrollment or with only a handful of white students. While some suburbs have integrated schools, others have only a quite minimal African-American enrollment.

These disparities go largely unchallenged. Americans disapprove of de jure segregation but show no equivalent willingness to eliminate **de facto segregation**, patterns of residential and school segregation that continue to exist "in fact" even though separation is not mandated by law. The racial imbalance of schools is a reflection of the racial imbalance of neighborhoods.

The Supreme Court has made it nearly impossible for cities to effectively combat continuing patterns of school segregation. In its 1974 ***Milliken v. Bradley*** decision, the Court ruled that Detroit's suburbs did not have to participate in a metropolitan busing plan even if their participation was necessary to desegregate central-city schools. According to the Court, a suburb must be found guilty of having intentionally kept racial minorities out before it can be ordered to participate in a desegregation effort. While it is easy to demonstrate that racial imbalance exists in the metropolis, it is quite another thing for a plaintiff to prove conclusively that a suburb intentionally excluded racial minorities. Suburbanites argue that their policies have no racial motivation whatsoever, that they just reflect the natural desires of taxpayers to finance schools and services for their own residents.

The Milliken ruling effectively doomed most big-city school desegregation efforts to failure. Except for the most exceptional circumstances, a suburb does not have to participate in a desegregation plan. Desegregation efforts confined to the central city accomplish little; white families can also escape racial integration efforts by moving to the suburbs. In the years since Milliken, the Court has retreated still further from its earlier insistence on school desegregation, even allowing cities found guilty of *de jure* segregation new leeway to terminate desegregation plans even when patterns of segregation persist. More recent Court rulings have also limited the ability of local school districts to use magnet schools as a tool for voluntary school integration.

In looking at the underlying causes of the riots that swept U.S. cities in the 1960s, the **President's National Advisory Commission on Civil Disorders** (popularly known as the **Kerner Commission**) warned against a future where the United States continued as "two societies, one black, one white—separate and unequal."[43] A half century later, the Kerner Commission's assessment remains largely accurate. Today, the Kerner Commission's "two societies" warning appears deficient only in that it does not capture the complexity of tensions in metropolises experiencing new racial and ethnic diversity. The racial cleavage is no longer simply "black" versus "white." In Los Angeles, new arrivals from Asia, Mexico, and Central America—Salvadorans, Caribbean blacks, Chinese, Japanese, Iranians, Indians, Filipinos, Vietnamese, Koreans, and others—contend with established Latino and African American populations for a piece of the shrinking inner-city economic pie. In Los Angeles, in the wake of the city's 1992 riots, African Americans, Hispanics, Asians, and whites all fought over jobs at the central-city rebuilding sites. Many of the Korean-owned liquor stores that were burned during the disturbances never reopened. A number were denied planning permissions, as African American activists objected that the liquor stores were a blight on their community.[44] New York and Los Angeles both experienced tense confrontations between Korean shop owners and African Americans.[45]

Not too long ago, the phrase **"chocolate city, vanilla suburbs"**[46] provided a shortcut that accurately pinpointed the racial imbalance and inequities of the American metropolis. Today, the metaphor seems sorely antiquated because a simplistic black/white dichotomy does not capture the complexities of ethnic and racial populations, the full range of "flavors," of urban America. It even fails to denote the heterogeneity of America's black population. New arrivals from the Caribbean (from Jamaica, Haiti, and the Dominican Republic) and West Africa and sub-Saharan Africa (including Nigeria and Senegal) have their own history and cultural norms that make the members of these groups different from African Americans who have grown up in the United States.[47] The chocolate-city/vanilla-suburb dichotomy also does not point to the growing numbers of racial minorities who have taken up residence in suburbia in recent years (see Chapter 9).

CONCLUSION: THE URBAN SITUATION

In the age of terrorism, cities have assumed new and costly homeland security responsibilities. Faced with an unstable national economy, shrinking tax revenues, cutbacks in federal and state aid, and the anti-tax sentiment of voters, cities found it quite difficult to perform all that was expected of them. Across the nation, cities and suburbs alike instituted new managerial systems for performance improvements, but, nonetheless, still had to reduce public services and lay off municipal workers.

Despite downtown revivals, gentrification, and the fragments of an urban renaissance, the urban crisis continues. Job growth in central cities lags behind that of the suburbs. Despite a central-city rebound, core cities continue to lose private-sector employment market share to the suburbs.[48] The poverty rate in primary cities (18.2 percent) in 2007 was nearly twice that found in suburbs (9.5 percent).[49] One of every six central-city families lives in poverty.

The urban crisis is national in scope and exists in all regions. The deindustrialized cities of the Frostbelt suffer the largest concentrations of poverty. Nevertheless, big cities in the Sunbelt also have extremely large pockets of poverty. Sunbelt communities have also been hard-hit by property foreclosures and abandonment.

The urban crisis has also spread to suburbia. In the early years of the twenty-first century, poverty was growing at a faster rate in suburbs than in primary cities. From 2000 to 2008, suburbs experienced a 25 percent increase in the number of people living in poverty.[50] The nation's older or inner-ring suburbs also exhibited economic weakening, with a shutdown of aging manufacturing plants and a rise in the number of housing vacancies, a vulnerability exacerbated by the collapse of housing finance beginning in the early twenty-first century. Younger homebuyers preferred new homes with modern conveniences in exurban communities: they did not want the smaller floor plans and antiquated kitchens of homes in America's older or "first" suburbs.

The urban crisis is not new. As we discuss in greater detail in Chapter 2, the loss of population and tax base to the suburban rim has been a fact of life for many big cities since the end of World War II. The transition to postindustrialism and the emergence of a global economy have further weakened the economic position of many cities and older suburbs.

The homeland security costs borne by local governments constitute just one more burden that compounds the already difficult choices faced by cities. How cities and suburbs respond to the challenges they face depends on power—the power allocated to cities and the power exercised by both public and private actors in the metropolitan arena. The focus of this book is on power: Who has the power to get things done in the local arena? Whose cooperation is essential for effective governance? Whom do cities serve?

NOTES

1. The death toll for the World Trade Center, reported as of January 2004. See "Rebuilding At a Glance," *Gotham Gazette*, www.gothamgazette.com/rebuilding_nyc/at_a_glance.shtml.

2. Megan D. Nordgren, Eric A. Goldstein, and Mark A. Izeman, "The Environmental Impacts of the World Trade Center Attacks: A Preliminary Assessment" (Report of the National Resources Defense Council, February 2002), www.nrdc.org/cities/wtc/wtc.pdf.

3. Charles V. Bagli, "Seeking Safety, Manhattan Firms Are Scattering," *New York Times*, January 29, 2002; Leslie Eaton, "Attack Gave a Devastating Shove to the City's Teetering Economy," *New York Times*, September 8, 2002.

4. Fiscal Policy Institute, "The Employment Impact of the September 11 World Trade Center Attacks: Updated Estimates Based on the Benchmarked Employment Data," New York, March 8, 2002, www.fiscalpolicy.org/Employment%20Impact%20of%20September%2011_Update.pdf. Not all businesses from Lower Manhattan fled New York. Over two-thirds of the former World Trade Center tenants relocated to other parts of Manhattan; others found sites in the city's outer boroughs. See Jack Lyne, "NYC Report: Most Displaced Tenants Pick Manhattan, but Available Space Up in All Markets," *Online Insider*, November 26, 2001, www.conway.com/ssinsider/snapshot/sf011126.htm.

5. In the pre-9/11 city, the fear of crime had already led businesses and residents to retreat into "defensible enclaves." See Mike Davis, "Fortress Los Angeles: The Militarization of Urban Space," in *Variations on a Theme Park: The New American City and the End of Public Space,* ed. Michael Sorkin (New York: Hill and Wang, 1992), pp. 154–180; and Peter Marcuse, "The Enclave, the Citadel, and the Ghetto: What Has Changed in the Post-Fordist City," *Urban Affairs Review* 33, no. 3 (November 1997): 228–264; and Edward I. Blakely and Mary Gail Snyder, *Fortress America: Gated Communities in the United States* (Washington, DC: Brookings Institution Press, 1997).

6. Paul Goldberger, "Shadow Building: The House that Goldman Built," *New Yorker*, September 8, 2010.

7. Edward Glaeser, *Triumph of the City: How Our Greatest Invention Makes Us Richer, Smarter, Greener, Healthier, and Happier* (New York: Penguin, 2011). In "Why Cities Matter," *New Republic*,

January 19, 2010, Glaeser focuses on Chicago as he observes the important roles that cities continue to play, even in a postindustrial, globalized age.

8. Nikos Komninos, *Intelligent Cities: Innovation, Knowledge Systems and Digital Spaces* (London, New York: Routledge/Spon Press, 2002). For an argument that New York City must build on its universities and other resources to maintain its position as an innovation center and economic leader, see Jim O'Grady and Jonathan Bowles, "Building New York City's Innovation Economy," a report of the Center for an Urban Future, September 2009, available at www.nycfuture.org.

9. Alice Rivlin and Alan Berube, "The Potential Impacts of Recession and Terrorism on U.S. Cities," report of the Brookings Institution Center on Urban and Metropolitan Policy, Washington, DC, 2002, http://www.brookings.edu/reports/2002/01terrorism_rivlin.aspx

10. Ramon Grosfugel, in "Global Logics in the Caribbean City System: The Case of Miami," *World Cities in a World-System*, ed. Paul L, Knox and Peter J. Taylor (New York: Cambridge University Press, 1995), 164.

11. Campbell Robertson, "Smaller New Orleans After Katrina, Census Shows," *New York Times*, February 3, 2011.

12. Amy Liu and Allison Plyer, "An Overview of Greater New Orleans: From Recovery to Transformation," in *The New Orleans Index at Five* (Washington, DC: Brookings Institution and Greater New Orleans Community Data Center, 2010), https://gnocdc.s3.amazonaws.com/NOIat5/Overview.pdf.

13. The distinction between power as "social production" and "social control" is based on Claren N. Stone, *Regime Politics: Governing Atlanta, 1946–88* (Lawrence: University Press of Kansas, 1989), pp. 8–9, 222–226, and 289.

14. Michael Sorkin and Sharon Zukin, ed., *After the World Trade Center: Rethinking New York City* (New York: Routledge, 2002).

15. *The 9/11 Commission Report: Final Report of the National Commission on Terrorism Attacks Upon the United States* (New York: Norton, 2004), 311.

16. Charles V. Bagli, "A Memorial, Yes, but Battle Lines Form for Everything Else," *New York Times*, February 29, 2003.

17. Silverstein argued that he should receive not just $3.5 billion in insurance awards; as two attacks occurred, one on each tower, he argued that his insurance companies were obligated to pay up to $7 billion in compensation for two attacks. In December 2004, a federal jury ruled that the insurance companies were indeed obligated to compensate Silverstein for two separate incidents. The ruling awarded Silverstein $4.65 billion in insurance funds, money that was critical to paying for new construction at Ground Zero. Silverstein later raised additional insurance claims, seeking over $12 billion in awards. See Devin Leonard, "Freedom Tower: Tower Struggle," *Fortune*, January 26, 2004; Charles V. Bagli, "Towers' Insurers Must Pay Double," *New York Times*, December 7, 2004; and Anemona Hartocollis, "Developer Sues to Win $12.3 Billion in 9/11 Attack," *New York Times*, March 27, 2008.

18. "Six Months Later," *Gotham Gazette*, March 11, 2002, www.gothamgazette.com/iotw/911_six-months/; Herbert Muschamp, "An Agency's Ideology Is Unsuited to Its Task," *New York Times*, July 17, 2002; Michael Sorkin, "Bring It On: In Search of Democracy at Ground Zero," *Slate*, January 15, 2003, www.slate.com/id/2077010.

19. John Mollenkopf, ed., *Contentious City: The Politics of Recovery in New York City* (New York: Russell Sage Foundation, 2005).

20. Robert A. Beauregard, "Mistakes Were Made: Rebuilding the World Trade Center, Phase I," *International Planning Studies* 9, nos. 2/3 (May 2004): 45.

21. Lynne B. Sagalyn, "The Politics of Planning the World's Most Visible Redevelopment Project," in *Contentious City*, ed. Mollenkopf, 30.

22. Arielle Goldberg, "Civic Engagement in the Rebuilding of the World Trade Center," in *Contentious City*, ed. Mollenkopf, 112–139.

23. Beauregard, "Mistakes Were Made: Rebuilding the World Trade Center, Phase I," 139–153.

24. Pietro S. Nivola, *Laws of the Landscape: How Policies Shape Cities in Europe and America* (Washington, DC: Brookings Institution Press, 1999); H.V. Savitch and Paul Kantor, *Cities in the*

International Marketplace: The Political Economy of Urban Development in North America and Western Europe (Princeton, NJ: Princeton University Press, 2002); Michael Keating, "Local Economic Development Politics in France," *Journal of Urban Affairs* 13, no. 4 (1991): 443–459.

25. For the classic statement identifying privatism as a limit on the reach of U.S. local government, see Sam Bass Warner Jr., *The Private City* (Philadelphia: University of Pennsylvania Press, 1968).

26. Kevin Fox Gotham and Miriam Greenberg, "From 9/11 to 8/29: Post-Disaster Recovery and Rebuilding in New York and New Orleans," *Social Forces* 87, no. 2 (December 2008): 1039–1062.

27. Alex Finkelstein, "Highest Foreclosure Rates Remain in CA, FL, NV and AZ, Says Mid-year Reality Trac Report," Real Estate Channel, July 30, 1998, www.realestatechannel.com/us-markets/residential-real-estate-1/realtytrac-mid-year-foreclosures-james-j-saccacio-alex-finkelstein-1158.php.

28. Dennis R. Judd and Susan R. Fainstein, eds., *The Tourist City* (New Haven, CT: Yale University Press, 1999); Dennis R. Judd, *Building the Tourist City* (Armonk, NY: M.E. Sharpe, 2002); Heywood T. Sanders, "Convention Center Follies," *Public Interest* 132 (Summer 1998): 58–72; Heywood T. Sanders, "Convention Myths and Markets: A Critical Review of Convention Center Feasibility Studies," *Economic Development Quarterly* 16, no. 3 (August 2002): 195–210.

29. Joel Garreau, *Edge City: Life on the New Frontier* (New York: Doubleday, 1991).

30. Elizabeth Kneebone and Emily Garr, "The Suburbanization of Poverty: Trends in Metropolitan America, 2000 to 2008," Washington, DC, Brookings Institution Metropolitan Policy Program, January 2010, www.brookings.edu/~/media/Files/rc/papers/2010/0120_poverty_kneebone/0120_poverty_paper.pdf.

31. Steven Greenhouse and Mireya Navarro, "The Hidden Victims," *New York Times*, September 17, 2001.

32. Brookings Institution, *State of Metropolitan America: On the Front Lines of Demographic Transformation* (Washington, DC: Brookings Institution Metropolitan Policy Program, 2010), 28, www.brookings.edu/~/media/Files/Programs/Metro/state_of_metro_america/metro_america_report.pdf

33. Peter F. Burns and Matthew O. Thomas, "A New New Orleans? Understanding the Role of History and the State-Local Relationship in the Recovery Process," *Journal of Urban Affairs* 30, no. 3 (2008): 259–271.

34. Figures for 2006. See *The Tax Policy Briefing Book—State and Local Tax Policy: What Are the Sources of Revenue for Local Government?* an electronic publication of the Urban Institute and the Brookings Institution, 2008, www.taxpolicycenter.org/briefing-book/state-local/revenues/local_revenue.cfm.

35. William C. Thompson Jr., New York City Comptroller, remarks presented at the "State of the City's Economy Conference," Federal Reserve Bank, New York, January 14, 2003.

36. William C. Thompson, remarks presented at the "State of the City's Economy Conference"; Erica Pearson, "Money for Rebuilding," *Gotham Gazette*, February 3, 2003, www.gothamgazette.com/article/issueoftheweek/20030203/200/271.

37. David W. Dunlap, "Liberty Bonds' Yield: A New Downtown," *New York Times*, May 30, 2004.

38. U.S. Census Bureau, "County and City Data Book: 2000," Table B-1; U.S. Census Bureau, "Large Suburban Cities in West Are Fastest-Growing, Census Bureau Reports" (Press release, July 10, 2003), www.census.gov/Press-Release/www/2003/ch03–106.html; U.S. Census Bureau, "Large Suburban Cities in West Are Fastest-Growing, Census Bureau Reports" (Press release, July 10, 2003), www.census.gov/Press-Release/www/2003/cb03–106.html.

39. Ann Markusen, Peter Hall, Scott Campbell, and Sabina Diedrick, *The Rise of the Gunbelt: The Military Remapping of Industrial America* (New York: Oxford University Press, 1991).

40. U.S. Census Bureau, *The 2010 Statistical Abstract of the United States,* Table 692: "Household Income, Family Income, and Per Capita Income and Individual and Family Below Poverty Level by City: 2007." The Benton Harbor, Camden, and East St. Louis figures are also 2007 U.S. Census estimates, as reported by City-Data.com.

41. John J. Kiefer and Robert S. Montjoy, "Incrementalism Before the Storm: Network Performance for the Evacuation of New Orleans," *Public Administration Review* 66, S1 (December 2006): 122–130.

42. Clarence Taylor, "Hurricane Katrina and the Myth of the Post-Civil Rights Era," *Journal of Urban History* 35, no. 5 (July 2009): 640–655, argues that institutional racism continued to define the federal government's response even as it sought to aid the victims and rebuild the city after the storm. See also Thomas Craemer, "Evaluating Racial Disparities in Hurricane Katrina Relief Using Direct Trailer Counts in New Orleans and FEMA Records," *Public Administration Review* 70, 3 (May 2010): 367–377; and Camilla Stivers, "So Poor and So Black: Hurricane Katrina, Public Administration, and the Issue of Race," *Public Administration Review* 67, S1 (December 2007): 48–56; Jeremy I. Levitt and Matthew C. Whitaker, eds. *Hurricane Katrina: America's Unnatural Disaster* (Lincoln: University of Nebraska Press, 2009); and Robert D. Bullard and Beverly Wright, eds., *Race, Place, and Environmental Justice after Hurricane Katrina: Struggles to Reclaim, Rebuild, and Revitalize New Orleans and the Gulf Coast* (Boulder, CO: Westview Press, 2009).

43. *Report of the National Advisory Commission on Civil Disorders* (New York: Bantam Books, 1967).

44. Pyong Gap Min, *Caught in the Middle: Korean Communities New York and Los Angeles* (Berkeley: University of California Press, 1996), 91–92; Raphael I. Sonenshein, "The Battle over Liquor Stores in South Central Los Angeles: The Management of an Interminority Conflict," *Urban Affairs Review* 31, no. 6 (July 1996): 710–737.

45. Claire Jean Kim, *Bitter Fruit: The Politics of Black-Korean Conflict in New York City* (New Haven, CT: Yale University Press, 2000).

46. Reynolds Farley et al., "Continued Racial Residential Segregation in Detroit: 'Chocolate City, Vanilla Suburbs' Revisited," *Journal of Housing Research* 4, no. 1 (1993): 1–38.

47. John R. Logan and Glenn Deane, "Black Diversity in Metropolitan America" (Report of the University of Albany's Lewis Mumford Center for Comparative Urban and Regional Research, Albany, NY, August 2003), http://mumfordl.dyndns.org/cen2000/BlackWhite/BlackWhite.htm.

48. Annette Steinacker, "Economic Restructuring of Cities, Suburbs, and Nonmetropolitan Areas, 1977–92," *Urban Affairs Review* 34, no. 2 (November 1998): 229; John Brennan and Edward W. Hill, "Where Are the Jobs? Cities, Suburbs, and the Competition for Employment," Brookings Institution Survey Series, Washington, DC, November 1999.

49. Kneebone and Garr, *The Suburbanization of Poverty*, 11, Fig. 4.

50. Kneebone and Garr, *The Suburbanization of Poverty*.

2 The Evolution of Cities and Suburbs

The free choices made by homebuyers, developers, and business investors all help to determine which communities grow and which decline. Yet, the "free market" does not tell the full story as to why certain cities and suburbs have grown over the years while others have declined. Differences in income and buying power, for instance, only partially explain why people of different races tend to live in different communities. As this chapter shows, "hidden" governmental policies have also, often inadvertently, dictated patterns of urban growth and decline. At times, private-sector actors, too, have manipulated actions, interfering with the free-market growth and decline of American cities.

Natural Factors and the Shape of the Evolving Metropolis

In a classic essay on urban development, political scientist Edward C. Banfield pointed to the importance of three natural forces or "imperatives" in determining urban growth and decline.[1] The first force is **demographic**: increases in population force a city to expand outward. The second is **technological**: the available transportation and communications technology determine just how far outward residents and businesses can move. The third is **economic**: people with the necessary financial means can buy the "good life" away from the congestion, cramped housing, and crime of the central city, while people of lesser wealth are left behind in the less desirable areas of the city.

The oldest portion of most American cities can be found by a major locus of transportation—a harbor, river, canal, or important railroad or trail junction that, during the earlier history of the United States, provided the transportation necessary for a community's economic growth. Cities such as Fort Worth (Texas) and Fort Collins (Colorado) are exceptions: they sprouted under the protection of army outposts in a hostile environment.

Commercial centers in the 1700s and early 1800s were relatively small in size. As walking was a major form of urban transportation, historian Kenneth Jackson has labeled these preindustrial communities **walking cities**.[2]

Steam Trains and Electric Trams, The Bowery, New York City, 1896. In the pre-automobile age, cities were the center of economic activity, with trains and electric streetcars providing the essential transportation lifelines. Originally published in 1896 in *The New York Times*. http://commons.wikimedia.org/wiki/File:The_Bowery,_New_York_Times,_1896.JPG.

Primitive transportation technology limited the geographical size of the walking city. Workshops and residential spaces were often located in the same neighborhood. Wealthy merchants, shippers, manual workers, and the poor all lived inside the city, close to work. During this early era, cities had not yet lost population and wealth to suburbs. The hamlets and farm villages outside the city were rural, not suburban, and residents of the countryside had little interaction with the city.

Cities grew in a process called **urbanization**: migrants left the poverty and economic vagaries of life in the countryside for the promise of jobs and educational opportunity found in the city. Cities, however, were not always prepared to cope with the sudden surge of new arrivals. With overcrowded housing and primitive sanitation, cities were the sites of major public health epidemics. The 1793 yellow fever outbreak killed 5,000 people in Philadelphia. St. Louis in 1849 lost one-tenth of its population to cholera. Four years later, yellow fever killed 11,000 in New Orleans.[3]

The industrial age, with its smoke-belching factories and cinder-throwing train engines, further compounded the environmental and health problems of urban living. The job opportunities of the industrial city attracted immigrants both from the countryside and from overseas, adding to the population pressures that would force the city to expand.

Suburbs were not a significant part of the American landscape until the latter half of the nineteenth century.[4] The population movement away from the center city had to await progress in transportation technology. During the early 1800s, workers could move only as far out as a horse-pulled streetcar could take them. Successive transportation innovations—the electric trolley, the steam railroad, electric commuter trains, and the automobile—each enabled more and more residents to move farther and farther away from the city center.

But even during the age of the electric streetcar, urban areas were relatively compact, quite unlike the sprawling megalopolises of today. Advances in building technology, including the introduction of the elevator, reinforced the urban core, with the first skyscrapers constructed in the late 1880s. The American city expanded upward before it greatly expanded outward.

For a long while, permissive state laws enabled the city to extend its political boundaries to reflect the outward movement of population. Cities used the power of **annexation** to adjoin neighboring areas to the city, with the city swallowing up an abutting community and making it part of the city. The residents of underdeveloped outlying communities, where streets were barely paved and service provision was quite poor, often looked to the larger city for road paving, street lighting, and the provision of municipal water and gas.

A turning point came in 1893 when the growing suburb of Brookline, Massachusetts, spurned annexation by the city of Boston, despite being surrounded on three sides by the city. Brookline residents saw their community as a "refuge" from the dirt and corruption of the industrial city. They also feared that joining the city would lead to higher taxes. Ethnocentrism, also played a role in the suburban rejection of the city. Opponents of annexation "frankly stated that independent suburban towns could maintain native American life free from Boston's waves of incoming poor immigrants."[5] Suburbs, after the Brookline revolt, began to fight to maintain their independence from the city.

Changes in state laws began to favor the suburbs, making major annexations increasingly difficult. The population continued to move outward, but cities could no longer easily extend their boundaries. **Streetcar suburbs** sprouted along the electric trolley tracks, beyond the borders of the central city. As historian Sam Bass Warner Jr. summarized, "the metropolitan middle-class abandoned their central city."[6]

At the same time that the middle class began its move to the suburbs, the rural poor continued to pour into cities in search of economic opportunity. In the **Great Migration** (from 1910 through the 1940s), millions of poor African Americans—and whites—from the rural South made their way to Chicago, Detroit, Pittsburgh, and other big cities of the North. The mechanization of agriculture and the end of the sharecropper system in the South pushed the rural poor to migrate. The production needs of both World Wars I and II also led city factories to send recruiters to the South in search of workers, Appalachian and rural whites as well as African Americans moved northward in search of economic opportunity and social freedoms.[7]

The automobile revolutionized urban form, as suburbanites no longer needed to live in close proximity to streetcar and railway lines. New suburban housing spread to fill in the spaces between the "fingers" or spokes of the streetcar and rail systems. With the automobile, commuters could also live at considerable distance from the central city.

Industrial and commercial enterprises followed the shift to suburbia. Manufacturers, seeking the space for assembly-line production, were attracted by the relatively low price of undeveloped suburban land. The rise of the trucking industry soon led to an exodus of warehousing and distribution activities out of the central city. Older manufacturing and warehousing sections of the core city, areas such as New York's SoHo and Lower East Side, suffered a steep decline. Beginning in the 1970s, advances in cargo containerization further accelerated the suburbanization of warehousing and distribution, as narrow, congested city streets and old central-city warehouses with their small loading docks could not handle the new shipping technologies.

Retail and entertainment establishments followed the middle class and its buying power to the suburbs. Suburban residents did not want to be bothered with long commutes, traffic jams, and the search for parking downtown. Commercial developers responded with open-air plaza-type shopping centers and, later, enclosed shopping malls. By the 1950s and 1960s, retail sales in the central city plummeted. In 1983, Hudson's department store, long associated with Detroit, closed the doors of its downtown flagship store, having opened new stores in various suburban shopping malls. Detroit gained the dubious distinction of being the largest city in the country not to have a major department store within its borders. Baltimore, Toledo, and Fort Worth are only a few of the major cities that soon followed, where the closing of department stores signified the decline of the downtown core.

During the latter years of the twentieth century, advances in telecommunications freed white-collar offices from the need to be located in the central city's downtown. They, too, moved to the suburbs. Orange County, California, witnessed an office boom south of Los Angeles. Outside Chicago, the office towers of Schaumburg comprise the region's second downtown. Similar growth occurred in the **edge cities** on the rim of virtually every major metropolitan area: Route 128 outside of Boston; White Plains (New York) and the New Jersey suburbs of New York City; Rosslyn and Crystal City, Virginia (just across the Potomac River from Washington, DC); Troy and Southfield just north of Detroit; the Houston Galleria; the Perimeter Center north of Atlanta's beltway, and the Silicon Valley peninsula lying between San Francisco and San Jose, to name only a few. High-technology-oriented suburbs or **technoburbs** mushroomed as the sites of globally oriented and foreign-owned firms.[8] The **multicentered metropolis** emerged as the new urban reality; the central city and its downtown no longer dominated the urban region.

The newer developments redefined suburbia. In the 1950s, when the mass movement to the urban rim was just beginning to reshape metropolitan areas, suburbia was stereotyped as the land of relatively tranquil **bedroom communities** where residents—that is, husbands—commuted to the city for work. An occasional industrial or factory community did little to mar the overall portrait of a serene, predominantly white, middle-class suburbia. Today, by contrast, suburbia has matured and is clearly much more diverse and dynamic, the site of high-tech industry, office campuses, entertainment venues, cultural centers, universities, and fine dining. Life on the city's rim no longer seems "sub" to central cities.

Over the past few decades, the all-white suburb, which had no African American residents, has largely disappeared. The racial integration of suburbia has increased. Yet, it must be noted that suburbia is not fully open to minority citizens and the poor, populations that continue to be disproportionately found in the central city and in declining inner-ring suburbs. Conditions in the most troubled inner-ring suburbs, including East Cleveland, East St. Louis (Illinois), and East Palo Alto (California), are in many ways indistinguishable from those of the urban core.

The latter half of the twentieth century also saw a major shift of population and economic activity from the older **Frostbelt** cities of the Northeast and the Midwest to the growing **Sunbelt** communities of the South and West. By 1980, the shift to the Sunbelt was already well apparent. The nation's most dynamically growing cities were in the South and the West, while cities in the Northeast and North Central regions, by contrast, continued to lose population (see Table 2.1). In the early years of the twenty-first century, the nation's fastest-growing metropolitan areas—Las Vegas, Austin, Phoenix, Boise, and Santa Ana (California), to name just a few—continued to be found in the Southwest and the West.

A number of natural factors help to explain Sunbelt growth. Jet travel and other advances in transportation and telecommunications allowed citizens and firms to move to Sunbelt communities with their warm weather, sunny skies, good beaches, and promise of escape from the congestion and social ills of northern communities. Businesses were also attracted to the region's relatively cheap land. The introduction of air-conditioning was essential for the growth of cities in the torridly hot South. Without the marvel of machine-cooled air, northerners would have been very reluctant to move to Miami, a city built on a mangrove swamp.

Fax machines, satellite communication, and new digital technology freed businesses to move to small towns across the country and even out of the country. Business CEOs (chief executive officers) moved data entry and other clerical and support operations out of the nation's big cities to less costly sites in far-off small towns or even overseas. Rosenbluth Travel, one of the nation's largest travel agencies, relocated its 200-employee reservations center from downtown Philadelphia to low-wage Linton, North Dakota. American Airlines moved its ticket-processing center from Tulsa to Barbados. New York Life and a number of other insurance companies shifted their insurance processing operations to Ireland, where workers are well educated but are paid less than workers in the United States.[9]

Not every business, of course, has the ability to relocate to the suburbs or to move overseas. As we will describe more fully in Chapter 3, major corporations still find considerable advantage in locating in close proximity to one another and close to firms that provide essential financial, legal, and support services.

A number of former manufacturing centers have also completed their transformation into **post-industrial global cities**, the office and financial centers of the knowledge-based world economy. New York, Los Angeles, Chicago, and San Francisco, no longer the factory towns of old, have reemerged as centers of corporate headquarters, banking, conventions, trade shows, and tourism.

Table 2.1

Growing and Declining Cities by Region: Cities over 100,000 Population, 1980

U.S. region	Number of cities with 100,000+ population	Number of cities gaining population	Number of cities losing population
Northeast	23	—	23
North Central	39	8	31
South	60	46	14
West	47	39	8
Total	169	93	76

Source: Bureau of the Census, *U.S. Department of Commerce News* (Washington, DC, June 23, 1981), x.

Other former manufacturing centers, however, continued on their downward trajectory. These cities lack a healthy economic diversity and the highly educated, professional workforce that global firms value. These cities suffered such extensive population losses that inner-city neighborhoods are littered with abandoned housing and vacant lots. Cleveland has already lost over half of its population, dropping from 915,000 in 1950 to 438,000 in 2017. Estimates forecast that Cleveland's population will plummet even further, to just 387,000 by the year 2017. Cities like Cleveland, Detroit, Dayton, Buffalo, and Atlanta no longer expect that they will ever recover their former status. Instead, they have begun to cope creatively with their decline, turning to extensive **greening strategies**—plans to turn vacant properties into side lots, expanded parks, bikeways, natural swales that aid storm-water retention and filtering, and even community gardens and urban farms—in order to create a new living environment that will be more appealing to residents and corporate investors.[10]

HIDDEN URBAN POLICY: GOVERNMENTAL INFLUENCES ON METROPOLITAN DEVELOPMENT

As we have just seen, natural factors—population pressures, technology, and affluence—have had a great impact on determining where people live and where businesses locate. But contrary to Edward Banfield's claim, these forces are not "imperatives" that dictate the exact patterns of urban growth and decline. Rather, government policies and the actions of powerful private actors—including banks, lending institutions, real estate firms, and land developers—have intruded on and distorted the operations of the market, accelerating the disinvestment in older cities and the shift of activity to the suburbs and the Sunbelt.[11]

The federal programs that have had the greatest effects on metropolitan development actually did not have an explicit urban orientation. These programs had quite laudable objectives: building the interstate highway system; helping Americans to buy homes of their own; rewarding returning veterans for their service; promoting the construction of much-needed hospitals and sewage plants; and incentivizing investment and expansion by business. Yet, these programs also constituted a **hidden urban policy** as they had a tremendous, albeit often unintended, influence on the growth and decline of American communities.

THE FHA AND VA: HOMEOWNERSHIP PROGRAMS SHAPE URBAN GROWTH

Were it not for federal assistance, a great many middle- and working-class families would not have been able to buy homes of their own. The 1934 Housing Act, which established the **Federal Housing Administration (FHA)**, committed the nation to helping families become homeowners. The FHA was intended to expand home ownership by inducing banks and other mortgage lending institutions to give loans to people who, in the program's absence, would have been seen as too great a financial risk to deserve credit.

FHA loan insurance provided protection for up to 80 percent of the value of an approved property. The FHA essentially guaranteed that credit institutions would be repaid 80 percent of a loan if an FHA-certified homeowner defaulted on payments. By eliminating most of the financial risk that a lender faced in issuing a home loan, FHA insurance spurred financial institutions to give mortgages to millions of Americans who would not have received credit on their own. Facing less risk of loss with FHA-backed loans, lenders could also lower down-payment requirements and interest rates, putting home ownership more easily within the reach of the working and middle classes.

The **GI Bill of Rights of 1944** extended similar assistance through the **Veterans Administration (VA)** to millions of soldiers returning home from World War II. As "the VA very largely followed FHA procedures and attitudes . . . the two programs can be considered as a single effort."[12] Together, the VA and FHA programs offered prospective homebuyers a very attractive package of low or no down payment,[13] easy credit, and a twenty-five- to thirty-year period of very manageable monthly payments.

These credit insurance programs accelerated suburban development. The government programs backed the purchase of new homes, not the purchase of apartments or the renovation of older housing stock in the central city. The FHA was also guilty of **redlining** large portions of the city, refusing to insure a loan in the inner city even to an otherwise qualified homebuyer. FHA redlining meant that bank loans for home renovation or home buying in the central city were not readily forthcoming. The FHA redlined large portions of cities, including the entire city of Camden, New Jersey, "as unacceptably risky, and consequently mortgage money dried up almost completely."[14] FHA redlining guaranteed the downward spiral of neighborhoods that had already begun to exhibit weaknesses.

The anti-city bias of the FHA was written into the agency's 1939 *Underwriting Manual.* The *Manual* instructed FHA underwriters to minimize credit risks and homeowner defaults by looking for "economic stability" when making neighborhood evaluations. As the *Manual* continued, "crowded neighborhoods lessen desirability."[15] The FHA wrote off the "graying" areas of the inner city, choosing, instead, to finance suburban development.

FHA bias was even more crude and pernicious when it came to maintaining racial segregation. Until the agency's policy was effectively changed in the 1950s and 1960s, the FHA—an arm of the federal government—explicitly endorsed a policy of racial segregation as a means of protecting the value of government-insured homes. As the

The Working-class Suburban Paradise: Levittown, Pennsylvania (1952). FHA- and VA-insured loans enabled the lower-middle class and the working class to flee the cities for the suburbs. The mass-produced tract housing of Levittown further helped to put the suburban dream within the reach of the working class. Levittown, however, was racially restricted in order to maintain the community's attractiveness to white buyers. In the community's early years, African Americans were denied the right to buy homes in Levittown. http://commons.wikimedia.org/wiki/File:LevittownPA.jpg.

agency's *Underwriting Manual* warned, "If a neighborhood is to retain stability, it is necessary that properties shall continue to be occupied by the same social and racial classes."[16] The *Manual* instructed federal underwriters to give a low rating to mortgage applications that would lead to the "infiltration of inharmonious racial or nationality groups" into a neighborhood.[17] The FHA even endorsed the use of **restrictive covenants**, legally binding agreements that prohibited a buyer from reselling a home to someone of a different race.[18] This was government-mandated segregation.

FHA **racial steering** sent black and white homebuyers to different neighborhoods. The FHA did not approve loans to minority applicants who sought to buy homes in all-white suburbs. Only 2 percent of the homes built with FHA mortgage insurance in the post–World War II era were sold to minorities, and half of that was for homes in all-minority subdivisions where the presence of a new black family only served to reinforce local segregation.[19] Just outside Detroit, the FHA in the 1940s even required the developer of an all-white subdivision to build a six-foot-high, half-mile-long concrete fence—a wall—to seal off his property from a nearby black neighborhood.[20]

"The Wall," Detroit, 1941. A half-mile long concrete wall constructed along Detroit's outer boundary was designed to keep African Americans from the city out of a new housing development that was built in the suburban community on the other side. From the Library of Congress Prints & Photographs Division, Washington, DC 20540, http://hdl.loc.gov/loc.pnp/pp.print.

The FHA, an important federal agency, practiced segregation. FHA administrators feared that racial integration would jeopardize local property values, maybe even leading white families to flee changing neighborhoods and default on their loans. The FHA also reflected a point of view that was popular at the time. The National Association of Real Estate Boards in its code of ethics similarly encouraged practices to preserve the racial homogeneity of a neighborhood.

Outcries from the civil rights community eventually led the FHA to change its discriminatory practices. By 1949, the agency deleted from its manual the references to "racial groups" and "infiltration." Discriminatory patterns in loan approvals took a bit more time to root out. By then, however, the harm had already been done. The FHA had helped to underwrite the growth of racially homogeneous suburban communities and the decline of the central cities. The agency's lending policies also promoted sprawl. In Los Angeles and other metropolitan areas, the FHA examiners approved home loans for leap-frog development that ate up the natural environment.[21]

Much to its credit, the FHA eventually reversed course and began to aggressively approve home loans in the inner-city areas it had once ignored. Unfortunately, even this action inadvertently hastened inner-city decline. In its zeal to serve inner-city communities, the FHA approved loans to applicants who lacked a strong work and credit history. The agency also failed to monitor the practices of unscrupulous lenders and real estate firms that suckered marginally qualified people into applying for loans they could not repay. As a result, many FHA-insured properties wound up in default, boarded up and abandoned, accelerating the decline of core urban neighborhoods. Once again, the FHA was forced to clean up its act.

Critics blamed the credit decisions of the FHA for much of the home loan defaults that led to the collapse of the mortgage market in the early 2000s. Yet, the evidence shows that this time the FHA was not really at fault. The FHA actually did a better job than private lenders in ensuring that borrowers had a good credit history and an ability to repay.

FHA-backed loans were not at the root of the initial defaults that plagued housing markets in the early 2000s. Instead, the Republican-inspired deregulation of the credit industry allowed new lenders to offer non–FHA-backed loans at quite advantageous terms. As a result, the FHA's share of the home-mortgage market actually shrank considerably (before reversing and increasing again in 2008). The unscrupulous, predatory lending practices of unregulated lenders—not the FHA—led to the rash of foreclosures and the collapse of the housing market.[22] This time, the "bad guys who stuck up the cities were not using federal mortgage insurance to 'FHA' entire neighborhoods with vacant foreclosed homes." Instead, the housing crisis of the early years of the twenty-first century was the result of "high-cost, abusive, and often fraudulent transactions designed to trap homeowners and homebuyers into usurious obligations." [23] "Unregulated loans, not FHA-backed loans, were at the heart of the foreclosure crisis.

FHA-backed lending has also served to promote Sunbelt development. The FHA sees its job as helping a family to obtain a mortgage wherever it wishes to buy a home. As a result, California, Florida, Texas, and Arizona continue to be the four states with the most loans backed by FHA guarantees. In the absence of FHA insurance, many fewer families would have been able to buy homes in the Sunbelt.

THE FEDERAL TAX CODE AND ITS SUBSIDIES FOR HOMEOWNERS: A HIDDEN URBAN PROGRAM WITH A HUGE EFFECT

The federal tax code encourages homeownership, allowing homeowners to deduct mortgage interest and property taxes from their taxable gross income. This is a huge subsidy for homeownership that, between 2009 and 2013, cost the federal government a whopping $700 billion.[24] In 2011 the estimated $120 million in federal tax subsidies awarded to homeowners vastly dwarfed the amount that the government spent that year on all low-income housing programs.

The tax write-offs have helped millions of Americans to buy a home of their own. But the deductions also wound up fueling suburban development, subsidizing the flight of the middle class to the suburbs. As the tax advantages are not given to renters, the program did not offer a similar level of assistance to central cities. Nor does the program aid the inner-city poor: even when the poor families own homes, their incomes are so low that they rarely itemize deductions. The mortgage deduction offers them little.

The tax favors given homeowners fail to target government assistance to the families most in need of help. Instead, the program is often criticized as being **Robin Hood**

in reverse, a **mansion subsidy** that offers **welfare for the rich**. Nearly two-thirds of the program's subsidies go to people who make more than $200,000 a year.[25] Wealthier families buy the most expensive houses, pay the biggest mortgages, and hence receive the biggest subsidies. The tax credits give $7,200 to a person making more than $200,000. A lower-middle-class taxpayer earning between $50,000 and $75,000 receives only a mere fraction of that amount, a paltry $1,150.[26] Renters, of course, get no tax subsidy.

The tax deductions for homeownership have also been a factor in stimulating **condominium and cooperative apartment conversions** in the city. As a tenant receives a subsidy only for buying—and not for renting—a dwelling unit, the tax credits help to create the demand that leads landlords to convert apartment buildings into condominiums and cooperatives, displacing tenants who cannot afford to buy and hold onto their units in a building that is "going condo."

The Anti-urban Bias of Federal Highway Programs

During the Cold War, the government committed itself to completing a national highway network that would enable the quick and efficient transport of military personnel and materiel. The National Defense Highway Act of 1956 increased the federal share of funding for highway construction projects from 50 percent to 90 percent.

The new highways opened outlying areas in a metropolis to development and suburbanization. Retail soon followed the middle class to the suburbs. Developers built huge shopping centers—and later enclosed malls and office parks—at the intersections of major highways and the "beltway" road encircling the city.

Federal highway construction also destroyed the vitality of numerous inner-city neighborhoods.[27] The new highways divided communities, displacing tenants and erecting physical barriers that made it difficult for area residents to reach neighborhood stores. The stores closed, residents moved to the suburbs, and neighborhoods declined.

In numerous cities, local decision makers also used highway construction as a tool of racial removal, a means of removing the black population from developable areas near the city center. In Miami, the building of I-95 "ripped through the center of Overtown," a large African American community of at least 40,000 people, displacing residents who were forced to resettle in more distant black neighborhoods, most notably Liberty City. The new expressway destroyed much of Overtown, once renowned for its vitality as the "Harlem of the South."[28]

The black poor were not the only victims of highway construction. In some cases, the new highways also displaced the working and middle classes. In New York in the 1950s, construction of the Cross Bronx Expressway uprooted a solid working-class, Jewish neighborhood. Many of the residents left the city, never to return.

The Influence of Military and Aerospace Spending

Government military and defense spending also promoted the growth of suburbs and the Sunbelt. During World War II, decision makers sought spread-out production sites that could not easily be bombed by the enemy. The War Production Board (WPB) "did no less than reconstruct America's capital plant by investing enormous sums of federal monies to build new production facilities for America's industries."[29] Rather than expand production in Detroit, the war planners built new plants outside the city, a shift in geography that would continue to promote suburban development even after the war's end.[30]

The corporate executives who served on the WPB also preferred cheap-labor Sunbelt locations that had none of the labor unions found in the manufacturing centers in the North. Warm-weather locations also provided ideal sites for port activities, troop training, and airplane testing. World War II production contributed to the economic dynamism of Los Angeles, San Diego, Phoenix, Fort Worth, San Antonio, Oklahoma City, New Orleans, and Atlanta.[31]

Even with the end of World War II, Cold War military and aerospace production continued to fuel Sunbelt economies. From 1951 to 1981, Defense Department spending on prime contracts increased by 810 percent in the South and 402 percent in the West, but fell by 1.5 percent in the Midwest.[32] The Defense Department closed the New York and Philadelphia naval yards, deciding to retrofit its Atlantic and Pacific fleets in lower-cost Norfolk (Virginia) and San Diego. Massive governmental expenditures on space exploration provided the basis for the economic boom of communities in Florida (the Cape Canaveral launch site) and Texas (with NASA's Johnson Space Center located in Houston). Government contracts for missile-guidance systems and other high-tech computerized and electronic components propelled the dynamic growth of California's Silicon Valley and the Pacific Northwest (with Boeing's headquarters at the time located in Seattle). Defense contracts even helped pay for the recruitment and relocation of engineers to Silicon Valley.[33]

The Urban Effects of Other Federal Programs and Tax Credits

Generous **federal grant programs for hospitals and sewage processing facilities** helped to underwrite the infrastructure costs of new development in the suburbs and the Sunbelt. Federal **tax incentives to businesses** to promote private investment in more modern machinery and physical plant similarly served as a spur to new commercial construction in suburbia and the Sunbelt; the government did not give a similar array of tax benefits to firms that chose to stay and rehabilitate the aging manufacturing plants in the cities of the Northeast and Midwest. Critics derisively referred to the government's investment tax credit as the **urban disinvestment tax credit**, as the tax incentives led businesses to abandon older central-city plants.[34]

Federal tax incentives for the oil and gas industries similarly catalyzed economic development in the South and West. Houston's dynamic growth can be attributed at least in part to the quite favorable tax treatment accorded the petrochemical industry. Federal grants for port development and highway construction also helped pay for Houston's growth.[35]

The federal **urban renewal** program of the 1950s and 1960s, a program that was intended to help troubled cities, also had the unfortunate, even if unintended, effect of pushing businesses and residents out of cities and into the suburbs. Urban renewal cleared large parcels of land, razing homes and businesses in poor, working-class, and even, at times, middle-class neighborhoods. Urban renewal tore down more housing than it built. Forced from their homes, families with the financial means often chose to move outside the city, leaving the city's ills behind.

The urban renewal program also gained the nefarious reputation of being **Negro removal**: local governments used federal renewal assistance for construction programs that forced African Americans out of areas that were located too close to a city's central business district or privileged white neighborhoods. Hispanics, too, were sometimes the victims of urban renewal. In 1997, the Chicago suburb of Addison agreed to pay $1.8 million to Hispanic families who had been pushed out of a designated renewal area. The city had razed a number of structures that could not be considered blighted: "It was Mexican removal in the guise of urban renewal," said the lead attorney representing the Leadership Council for Metropolitan Open Communities.[36]

The Actions of Local Government

The actions of local governments, especially their exercise of **land-use and zoning powers**, also contribute to the imbalances of metropolitan development. As we discuss in more detail in Chapter 9, the vast majority of suburbs use these powers to exclude subsidized housing for the poor. Upper-income, more exclusive communities even seek to restrict the construction of apartment buildings and townhouses, housing that would be within the financial reach of working- and lower-middle-class families. A suburb can drive up the price of entry into a community by requiring that new homes be built on excessively large lots of land and that homes meet expensive construction requirements that exceed concerns for health and safety. (See Box 2.1, "The Uses and Misuses[?] of Zoning: The New York Metropolitan Area.") These actions by more exclusive suburbs serve to concentrate a region's poorer and minority citizens in the central city and in the more distressed, inner-ring suburban communities.

Low-density zoning adds to the racial imbalance of communities in the metropolis.[37] Yet, in a way, it is a bit hypocritical for central cities to focus on the segregative action of America's suburbs. For much of their history, big cities similarly took action to maintain racial segregation in residential neighborhoods and public housing.

In Chicago, various governmental bodies pursued actions that reinforced residential segregation in the decades following World War II. The Chicago Housing Authority (CHA) did not award a vacant public housing unit to the next family on a waiting list. Instead, the CHA considered the race of an applicant when deciding whether a prospective tenant would be compatible with the population of the surrounding neighborhood. Each member of the Chicago city council also maintained a veto over the placement of new public housing in his or her ward, and white council members effectively barred the construction of any public housing projects that would introduce racial minorities into their neighborhoods. Chicago pursued a policy of racial segregation, building public housing for racial minorities only in areas that already had large minority populations. In an effort to keep blacks from moving into white areas of the city, Chicago constructed a new or **second ghetto** of high-rise public

Box 2.1

The Uses and Misuses(?) of Zoning: The New York Metropolitan Area

In 1916, New York became the first city in the United States to adopt a zoning ordinance, a move so revolutionary that it was hailed as opening "a new era of civilization."[1] The New York ordinance regulated the use, height, and bulk of all new buildings, an effort to protect residential neighborhoods against the intrusion of new skyscrapers.

Zoning helps to assure orderly land development by preventing incompatible land uses. No homeowner wants to see a factory or an automobile repair station built next to his or her home. Zoning prevents such incongruous development by designating different sections of a community for different uses. Certain land parcels are designated for industrial and commercial uses; other parcels are reserved for residential development. Light industry can be kept separate from heavy industry. Apartment buildings may be allowed in certain areas while other sections of the city are zoned for only single-family homes.

Suburbs deploy their zoning and land-use powers in an attempt to keep out both nuisance industrial activities and lower-income people. Communities in Westchester County, just north of New York City, for example, have relied on zoning and other land-use restrictions in an effort to prevent the "Bronxification" of their area; they did not want their communities to become like the neighboring borough of New York City. Suburban ordinances typically restrict (or even ban) the construction of apartment buildings. Local regulations typically require that new homes be built on large lots with large-size rooms and other expensive construction features. In many communities, such local ordinances wind up shutting out middle- and working-class families, not just the poor.

What would happen if a locality could not use zoning and land-use laws to constrain new development? One hint of the answer is provided by the 1964 opening of the Verrazano Narrows Bridge, which connected Staten Island to the rest of New York City. Staten Island was a part of New York City and hence was not a suburb with the legal authority to enact zoning and other land-use controls. As a result, new construction on Staten Island differed from that in the suburbs of nearby New Jersey: "Compared with the region's typical suburb, Staten Island has been a paradise for the home building industry." A typical home on Staten Island is "smaller, less expensive, more crowded, and less attractive than that built during the same period in the suburbs of the New York region."[2] New construction threatened green space and "the suburban neighborhood character" of Staten Island.[3]

Zoning and land-use plans have obvious virtues. They are important tools to prevent incompatible land uses. As evident in the Staten Island case, they can also prevent levels of overdevelopment that diminish the quality of life in a community. Yet, such local controls also diminish the production of affordable housing of good quality. Suburbs too often use zoning as a potent weapon of exclusion, a means of keeping less-advantaged people out of more privileged communities.

[1]Robert M. Fogelson, *Downtown: Its Rise and Fall, 1880–1950* (New Haven, CT: Yale University Press, 2001), 160. See Fogelson's larger discussion, 160–166.

[2]Michael N. Danielson and Jameson Doig, *New York: The Politics of Urban Regional Development* (Berkeley: University of California Press, 1982), 79, 106–107.

[3]"New York City Council Stated Meeting Report, December 3, 2003," *Gotham Gazette,* December 3, 2003, www.gothamgazette.com/searchlight/council.2003.12.03.shtml.

"We Want White Tenants in Our White Community," sign opposite the Sojourner Truth Housing Project, Detroit, 1942. Racism and segregated housing were found in northern cities, not just in the South. In Detroit, a riot by white neighbors prevented African Americans from moving into a federal housing project. From the Library of Congress Prints and Photographs Division, Washington, DC 20540, http://hdl.loc.gov/loc.pnp/pp.print.

housing located in minority neighborhoods.[38] A half century later, living conditions in the high-rise projects proved so awful that the city, with the financial assistance of the federal government, finally decided to tear down much of the high-rise ghetto it had previously constructed.

Chicago is not alone in its history of segregation by public agencies. New York City, for instance, violated the federal Fair Housing Act, setting racial quotas on certain public-housing projects and steering black and Hispanic applicants away from projects with largely white populations. The city also gave preferential treatment to applicants who lived in the area surrounding a housing project, a practice that served to prevent black families from gaining public housing in predominantly white neighborhoods.[39]

In the Sunbelt, local growth was not entirely the result of the workings of a free market. Rather, local governments provided vast subsidies for growth. Los Angeles, Houston, San Antonio, and San Jose all incurred huge debts in order to provide the sewer, street, highway, and other infrastructure improvements demanded by business. During the years following World War II, Houston boosted its debt eightfold in order to finance the municipal construction boom. In Houston, the "public sector actively fueled and sustained the urban development process with public dollars."[40] In Los Angeles, the "local state" similarly invested heavily in the region's port, airport, and rail facilities, allowing the region to emerge as a center of global trade.[41] It was not an unfettered free market that by itself attracted business to the South. Quite the contrary! Corporations in the Sunbelt received the vast benefits of a business-oriented municipal socialism!

SUMMING IT UP: THE GOVERNMENT'S ROLE ASSESSED

In his review of American urban development, historian Kenneth Jackson asks, "Has the American government been as benevolent—or at least as neutral—as its defenders claim?"[42] The answer must be a resounding "No!" Urban problems are not purely the result of natural ecological evolution—they are clearly also the consequences of government policies and actions.

Government policy—especially government's "hidden" urban policy—has played a great role in shaping the metropolis. An urban advocate may reasonably argue that the government has an obligation to remedy the urban problems it helped to create.

THE IMPORTANCE OF CORPORATE AND PRIVATE POWER

Private decision makers—oftentimes working hand in hand with government officials—also played a critical role in dictating patterns of urban growth and decline. As Joe R. Feagin and Robert Parker observe, "the most powerful players on the urban scene" include the "array of visible real estate decision makers in industry, finance, development, and construction."[43]

Even the Great Migration was not entirely the result of the aspirations of African Americans who sought a new life in the cities of the North. Rather, industrial owners promoted the migration for their own purposes. In need of labor, the mills and foundries of the North in the early 1900s sent recruiters to the South to hire poor black tenant farmers. The recruiters promised the migrants an ideal life, which, in reality, was nowhere to be found, especially as the new arrivals were often shunted into segregated worker dormitories: "Poor rural blacks with little understanding of industrial conditions and no experience with unions were recruited in the South and transported directly to northern factories, often on special trains arranged by factory owners."[44] The mill owners found a particular advantage in hiring African Americans who could also be employed as **strike breakers** in an effort to contain labor organizing.

PRIVATE POWER, SUBURBAN GROWTH, AND THE SHIFT TO THE SUNBELT

The movement of industry to the suburbs was similarly prompted, at least in part, by an effort to contain labor militancy. The movement was not simply a natural or free-market process where industry followed its workforce to the suburbs. In fact, in the early twentieth century, a number of industrial giants actually decided to move their manufacturing facilities to suburban areas that had no existing large residential population.

> Between 1899 and around 1915, corporations began to establish factory districts just beyond the city limits. New suburban manufacturing towns were being built in open space like movie sets. Gary, Indiana, constructed from 1905 to 1908, is the best-known example. Other new industrial satellite suburbs included Chicago Heights, Hammond, East Chicago, and Argo outside Chicago; Lackawanna outside Buffalo; East St. Louis and Wellston across the river from St. Louis; Norwood and Oakley beyond the Cincinnati limits; and Chester and Norristown near Philadelphia.[45]

These industries did not move to areas to take advantage of a skilled workforce that already lived in suburban communities. Instead, these manufacturers built **company towns** to house their workers.

Why would business giants seek to locate plants in such inaccessible sites, before advances in transportation had even opened the suburbs to the masses? Quite simply, business owners found a considerable strategic advantage in locating their production facilities in relatively remote locations that would allow them to **contain labor militancy**. Central cities in the 1880s and 1890s were sites of labor conflict and unrest. Factory owners sought suburban plant sites that would allow their plants to escape trade union organizing: "Employers quickly perceived an obvious solution. Move!"[46]

The establishment of company towns gave factory owners additional power to control workers and contain labor militancy. In the manufacturing suburb of Pullman, at the time just south of Chicago, industrial magnate George Pullman, inventor of the railway sleeping car, exerted strict control over his workforce. He offered good-quality company-owned cottages as a reward to cooperative workers. As the owner of all housing in the community, Pullman was also able to evict union organizers and other "troublemakers," ousting them from their homes as well as their jobs.

The natural-growth theory looks to the impact of the automobile in explaining the sprawled character of development in the Los Angeles region. In contrast to the older cities of the Northeast and Midwest, Los Angeles's rapid growth took place during the age of the automobile. Yet, a closer look at the region's history reveals that such an automobile-focused explanation is incomplete. Los Angeles actually took its "spread city" shape *before* the automobile gained popularity, before the region's famed freeways were built.

Los Angeles' fringe development actually began in the early years of the twentieth century. It was largely the result of the manipulations of local real estate developers, including Henry Huntington who also owned a private streetcar company, the Pacific Electric Railway. Huntington sought to make a fortune in real estate. He built his system of electric interurban streetcars as a means of bringing potential buyers to his newly developed suburban home sites. The finest mass transit system of its day, Huntington's Red Cars (featured in the cartoon movie *Who Framed Roger Rabbit?*) traveled along at speeds of forty-five to fifty-five miles per hour. Huntington's streetcars operated at a loss, but the monetary losses did not matter. They were the subsidy that Huntington was willing to pay to generate the demand for new suburban homes, a demand that was not there until Huntington helped to create it:

> The Pacific Electric lost millions of dollars extending lines far ahead of demands for service, but the loss was compensated many times over by the profits from land sales gained by the Huntington Land and Improvement Company. The streetcar system was built not to provide transportation but to sell real estate.[47]

Los Angeles's sprawled development was the product of the manipulations of real estate speculators who sought quick profits.[48]

Private real estate interests in greater Los Angeles and across the nation vigorously promoted the ideal of suburban living. The Irvine Company touted the rural tranquility of its new community, Irvine, California, located forty miles south of Los Angeles: "Come to Irvine and hear the asparagus grow." The company, interested in profits, marketed a highly exaggerated and idealized picture of life in suburbia. As one company executive recalled, "When you live between two highways, it's hard to hear the asparagus grow."[49]

PRIVATE INSTITUTIONS, RACIAL STEERING, AND CORE CITY DISINVESTMENT

Differences in group buying power only explain part of the reason for the racial imbalance of urban neighborhoods. As we shall see, private institutions also undertook a series of actions that served to prevent minority families from moving to neighborhoods they had the means to afford.

During the first half of the twentieth century, **restrictive covenants** or binding deed restrictions prohibited a property owner from selling or renting a housing unit to the members of specified ethnic and racial groups. Local real estate boards insisted that racial restrictions be included in sales contracts. The Chicago Real Estate Board even formulated a model restrictive covenant to be included in property contracts.[50] In different parts of the country, restrictive covenants banned home sales to African Americans, Chinese, Jews, and Japanese. Racial ghettos and Chinatowns expanded as minorities were barred from housing markets in other parts of the city. Restrictive covenants produced a segregated city, a legacy that would continue beyond 1948 when the Supreme Court ruled that racial covenants could no longer be enforced by the courts.[51]

In a set of practices commonly referred to as **racial steering**, real estate agents, mortgage lenders, and insurers failed to show homes in a white neighborhood to a minority buyer or approve the sale of a home to a minority; instead, the agents of these institutions directed minority home seekers to different neighborhoods. As we have already observed, the Federal Housing Administration endorsed racial steering, advising home-loan examiners only to approve loans that preserved neighborhood racial homogeneity.

Not all segments of the local real estate community endorsed racial steering. Instead, some hoped to profit from the quick sales of homes in neighborhoods facing the prospect of racial transition. As late as the mid-twentieth century, in a process known as **blockbusting** or **panic selling**, an employee of a real estate firm would secretly help a black family move into an all-white neighborhood. Real estate agents would then go door to door, preying on the fears of white owners and the elderly, pushing owners to sell their homes before the neighborhood changed and the value of their homes plummeted. The real estate dealers profited from the sales fees they earned in the turnover.

Blockbusting did not lead to stable integration; instead, the creation of a panic led to white flight and ultimately to a neighborhood's **resegregation**. All-white areas of the city quickly became all-black areas as the whites fled. Other real estate speculators profited by buying houses cheaply amid the panic, and then **subdividing single-family homes** into small, shabby apartments that could be rented at a high price to black families. The overcrowded and poorly maintained structures quickly deteriorated.

The **1968 Fair Housing Act** made racial steering, blockbusting, and other similar techniques illegal. Yet, as we discuss in greater detail in Chapter 9, the more subtle and less-easy-to-detect forms of racial steering continue to exist. Home seekers who feel that they are the victims of discrimination have a very difficult time proving in court that racial steering actually occurred. A minority home seeker does not know what exact houses an agent has shown white buyers, nor is it easy to prove that any differences were the result of race and not the size of a family or its buying power.

Redlining was a major contributor to core-city disinvestment and decline: banks and other credit institutions simply refused to make loans in large areas of the city that credit officers viewed as posing greater-than-desired financial risks. Even good applicants with excellent job histories and credit records found that they could not get loans for properties in redlined neighborhoods. At one time, banks, insurance companies, and other financial institutions literally drew a red line on a map around the areas of a city where the company would not make loans or insure properties. The result was neighborhood **disinvestment** and decline, as redlining cut off the economic blood for new construction, major structural repairs, and a community's rejuvenation.

Since the 1970s, federal law has prohibited redlining. Banks and other financial institutions can no longer crudely draw a line on a map or otherwise refuse credit to an entire section of a city. The **Community Reinvestment Act (CRA) of 1977** further sought to pressure lending institutions to advance credit to homebuyers and small business owners in underserved areas of the city. Under the CRA, banks must make loans in communities, including poorer communities, from which they receive deposits.

Yet, despite federal law, redlining persists, albeit in modified form. A financial institution may offer financing for condominium and cooperative conversions while denying loan applications to groups seeking to renovate older buildings for affordable housing. Race continues to be a factor in lending decisions."[52]

A Richmond, Virginia, jury in 1998 ordered Nationwide Insurance to pay more than $100 million in damages as a result of the company's reluctance to insure homes in black neighborhoods. Nationwide's practices were not as blatant as the crude redlining of the 1950s and 1960s. The company did not reject all applications from inner-city black neighborhoods. Instead, the company instructed its agents to avoid "black urbanite households with many children."[53]

Credit institutions, of course, are allowed to deny loans to applicants with low credit scores. Similarly, the CRA does not require private insurers to reveal how they came to a judgment on an applicant's credit score. As a consequence, state departments of insurance seldom give priority to fighting insurance redlining.[54]

The CRA, however, does require mortgage-finance institutions to disclose the geographical area of each loan. Community groups have used this information to document the areas of a city that are underserved, putting pressure on banks to extend credit to applicants in disadvantaged communities. The CRA even gave community organizations the right to challenge bank mergers if they could prove that a bank failed to meet its lending obligations under the Act. ACORN (the Association of Community Organizations for Reform Now) and various other community groups used the threat to oppose bank mergers as leverage to convince financial institutions to commit millions of dollars in new loans to inner-city businesses and affordable housing mortgages. Republican Senator Phil Gramm of Texas criticized the Act for allowing "professional protest groups" to extort benefits from financials institutions.[55]

The threat that the CRA poses to banks is largely overplayed. Banks have had little difficulty in meeting the requirements of the CRA. In 1998, only 15 of the 772 banks examined—just 2 percent—received less than a satisfactory grade from regulators.[56] To meet CRA requirements, a bank must simply take positive steps in advertising its lending services in disadvantaged neighborhoods. Banks work with community groups that help identify potential homebuyers and counsel prospects in how to budget funds for home repairs and the other demands of homeownership.

Overall, the CRA has been an amazing urban success story, producing tens (if not hundreds) of billions of dollars in loans to homeowners and businesses in low-income and minority neighborhoods. In Cleveland, Chicago, Pittsburgh, and other cities, the CRA led banks to "'rediscover' the inner city as a viable and profitable market."[57]

Despite the CRA's record of success, credit officers and free-market conservatives continue to complain about the intrusiveness of the legislation. The 1999 Gramm-Leach-Bliley Act limited the scope of the CRA, exempting many credit institutions—especially smaller banks and savings institutions—from compliance. The amendments severely weakened the CRA, allowing an increasing number of home loans to be issued by businesses that do not have to meet CRA requirements.[58]

Talk-radio hosts and prominent political conservatives blasted the CRA and its lending requirement for producing the foreclosure crisis of the early years of the twenty-first century.[59] But their attempt to blame the crisis on the CRA lacks merit, especially as the Act had been in operation for a quarter of a century before the housing finance crisis flared. The waves of home loan defaults involved condominium projects and single-family homes and properties in well-to-do Sunbelt areas, not just properties in inner-city neighborhoods covered by the CRA. (See Box 2.2, "Did the CRA Produce the Housing Foreclosure Crisis?")

Unscrupulous **predatory lenders**, not the CRA, undermined the operations of a truly free and fair mortgage market. Numerous small, private firms in search of a quick profit relied on deceptive practices to market "exotic" high-risk loans. Some loans required no down payment. Other loans entailed monthly mortgage payments that barely covered interest on the money borrowed, never reducing the principal on the loan. Low- and

Box 2.2

Did the CRA Produce the Housing Foreclosure Crisis?

When the nation's housing markets collapsed in the early 2000s, conservatives blamed one of their favorite bogeymen, the Community Reinvestment Act. The conservatives charged that CRA requirements led businesses to make loans to unworthy applicants in inner-city neighborhoods. The accumulation of bad loans, they argued, led the bankers to panic, which affected the housing market nationwide. The conservatives argued for further **deregulation**, that the government needed to repeal the harmful provisions of the CRA that intruded on proper business decisions.

The evidence, however, does not support the conservatives' charges. The CRA had been in effect for a quarter of a century before the housing crisis. It is a bit absurd to put the blame on a policy twenty-five years after its enactment and not give credit to the policy for the revival of inner-city neighborhoods and the boom in housing markets and the national economy that took place during the intervening twenty-five years.

Core urban neighborhoods in cities such as Cleveland and Detroit did suffer extensive foreclosures. Yet, the housing crisis was not confined to the inner city. In fact, most defaults did not involve properties in the inner city. Overextended borrowers walked away from the loans they had taken to finance Florida condominiums, $300,000 Arizona villas, and luxury dream houses. The home foreclosures and distress sales in these areas cannot be attributed to the provisions of the CRA.

CRA-covered banks were actually less likely to make the high-cost and risky loans than the newer entrants to the credit industry that did not have to abide by CRA regulations. Loans subject to CRA supervision suffered fewer defaults than did comparable non-CRA loans. "Bad" loans were disproportionately issued by the smaller credit institutions and speculators who entered the housing field when the previous era of Republican **deregulation** removed large chunks of the home mortgage industry from CRA supervision.

It was not CRA regulation but deregulation that led to the rash of ill-advised mortgages and subprime loans that resulted in the housing finance crash. The most seamy or abusive **predatory lending practices**—loans that incurred outrageously high placement fees; loans with super-low monthly payments but with an excessively high final **balloon payment** that buyers could not meet; high prepayment penalties that prevented homeowners from refinancing with a loan at a lower rate of interest—were all the work of lenders not subject to the CRA's provisions.

Sources: Gregory D. Squires, "Predatory Lending: Redlining in Reverse," *Shelterforce Online* 139 (January/February 2005), www.nhi.org/online/issues/139/redlining.html; Traiger & Hinckley LLP, "The Community Reinvestment Act: A Welcome Anomaly in the Foreclosure Crisis—Indications that the CRA Deterred Irresponsible Lending in the 15 Most Populous U.S. Metropolitan Areas," January 7, 2008, www.traigerlaw.com/publications/traiger_hinckley_llp_cra_foreclosure_study_1–7–08.pdf; and Traiger & Hinckley LLP, "The Community Reinvestment Act of 1977: Not Guilty—Mortgage Data Refute Charge that the CRA Is at the Root of the Financial Crisis," January 26, 2009, http://traigerlaw.com/publications/The_community_reinvestment_act_of_1977-not_guilty_1–26–09.pdf.

moderate-income owners lost their homes, life savings, and good credit rating. Renters were evicted from foreclosed apartment buildings. The resulting flood of boarded-up structures had a particularly devastating impact on marginal communities.[60]

PRIVATE INSTITUTIONS AND THE MISSHAPING OF URBAN RENEWAL

Private power also explains how **urban renewal**, a mid-twentieth-century program aimed at the elimination of slums and urban blight, could have brought such great harm to core urban neighborhoods. Private-sector interests, working with the assistance of government planners, shaped the program to achieve their own ends. Downtown merchants used the program to modernize and expand central business districts in an effort to compete with suburban shopping centers. Local hospitals and universities used urban renewal to gain room for expanded campuses. Corporate and institutional elites used the urban renewal program to clear the poor and minorities out of the path of commercial and institutional expansion. Urban renewal did not fully replace the housing stock it tore down. Instead, downtown business leaders fought for the construction of upscale housing that would attract people with good buying power back to the city.

In Chicago, downtown leaders sought redevelopment efforts that would strengthen the city's then-ailing central business district. Michael Reese Hospital, the Illinois Institute of Technology, and the University of Chicago also used the program to obtain land for institutional expansion. The minority residents displaced by urban-renewal projects were shunted off into newly built high-rise ghettoes, areas that were kept separate from the city's white ethnic neighborhoods.[61]

PRIVATE INTERESTS AND THE GROWTH OF THE SUNBELT

The move of industry to the Sunbelt was not simply a search for a sunny climate and warm-weather ports. Factory owners were motivated more by their worries about labor costs and militancy than by a concern about climate. Manufacturers saw Sunbelt locations as an escape from the high-wage, high-tax, pro-union regulatory environment of northern cities.

In the mid-1900s, clothing and textile manufacturers left the mill towns of New England and the Northeast and moved south in an effort to escape the militancy of unionized workforces in the northern cities. **Right-to-work laws** in the South undermined labor organizing. As workers in right-to-work states could not be forced to join a union, employers could undermine unionization efforts by hiring only nonunion workers.

States and municipalities in the South offered a pro-business climate. Taxes on business were kept low as welfare benefits and social services were kept to a minimum. Business owners in the South also did not have to comply with the extensive and costly regulations for worker benefits and environmental protection that were typical of northern states.

PUBLIC AND PRIVATE POWER AND THE RISE OF HOMELESSNESS

There are complex reasons why people are homeless. Some individuals are drug users and alcoholics who cannot hold steady employment. Others have developmental disabilities. Young people may be seeking escape from abusive homes. Still others wind up homeless because they can no longer pay the monthly rent due to a disruption of income caused by the loss of a job or a marital breakup.

Yet personal failings are not the sole cause of homelessness. Homelessness also stems from the "shortage of low-income housing, the impact of changing technology on work, the globalization of the economy, and the labor market that dooms certain kinds of workers to economic marginality,"[62] all factors that are beyond the control of any individual. Government programs that deinstitutionalize psychiatric patients and reduce social welfare and public housing assistance also serve to increase the number of the homeless.

Homelessness increases when low-cost housing disappears. Both private interests and local governments share the blame for the virtual disappearance of the **single room occupancy (SRO) hotel**, the cheap by-the-night or by-the-week housing that offered the poor a last-chance refuge from the streets. An SRO is not what any tourist would deem an acceptable hotel. Most SROs are rather run-down and are located in undesirable parts of town. Still an SRO offers a place where a poor person with a few dollars can find a place to sleep for the night or the week.

Today, the SRO hotels and the flophouses of **skid row** have all but disappeared. Private developers and public redevelopment officials have built new office and retail complexes, convention centers, and luxury apartment buildings in areas where SRO housing once stood. Private developers and public officials rebuilt the inner city. In the process, the poorest and most vulnerable residents of the city lost their last alternative to the municipal-provided shelters and the streets.[63]

CONCLUSION: PRIVATE POWER, HIDDEN POLICIES, AND THE URBAN SITUATION

Natural forces—population pressures, technological advances, and affluence—have had a great influence on the shape of U.S. cities and suburbs. Yet, by themselves, these forces did not dictate the urban crisis. Government policies—often hidden policies—and the exercise of private-sector power also had a great influence on urban-development patterns. Their actions helped to produce extensive suburban sprawl, deep city-suburban fiscal disparities, metropolitan racial imbalance, and a regional shift in jobs and population—all beyond what can be explained by reference to natural forces and the workings of a free market. Simply put, government policies and private-sector actions exacerbated urban problems such as the decline of older manufacturing centers, central cities, and core residential neighborhoods.

Natural forces, hidden governmental policies, and private-sector power helped to produce a contemporary metropolis characterized by three overwhelming problems:

1. The Separation of Resources from Need

In a process of **dual migration**, the poor and racial minorities continue to move into cities while the well-to-do middle class moves out to the suburbs. Government policies, especially the tax code, continue to encourage the outflow of middle-class families to the suburbs. As we discuss in Chapter 3, the "back to the city" movement of young professionals does little to offset the prevailing pattern. Populations that are in need of services remain concentrated in the cities while taxable wealth is largely found in the suburbs. Suburban land-use and zoning practices and continued discrimination in housing markets reinforce the inequalities that characterize metropolitan America.

Uneven development also characterizes suburbia. The suburbs are not uniformly white and prosperous. While some suburbs are bastions of wealth and prosperity, other suburbs are the sites of overcrowded schools, aging infrastructure, vacant housing, and populations in need of assistance. The most troubled suburbs find that their situation resembles that of central cities: they, too, lack the resources to strengthen schools and neighborhoods and to reverse urban decline.

2. Racial Imbalance in the Metropolis

Dual migration, exclusionary land-use practices, racial steering, and discriminatory lending practices have created a metropolitan America marred by severe racial imbalance. Some communities have large concentrations of ethnic and racial minorities, while others have little diversity. Racial imbalance in the metropolis is not simply the result of group differences in income and education. Statistical evidence shows that increased income and education do not allow African Americans to move to better neighborhoods to the same degree that income and schooling enhance the neighborhood choices available to whites and even to Latinos.[64] Discrimination remains.

National and state fair housing laws have corrected many of the most odious practices of the past. Residential integration has increased, most notably in the suburbs. Yet, the provisions of the Fair Housing Act are vague and difficult to enforce. A lack of political will has also undermined enforcement. In a suburban America, where suburban residents outnumber city residents, elected officials are especially reluctant to combat the segregative practices of suburbia.[65]

3. The Dominance of Sprawled Development and Related Environmental Problems

The American metropolis is marked by extreme **sprawl**. Germany and other European nations, by contrast, have strong policies that limit the extent of suburban development outside of major cities.[66] The United States has no such policy.[67] Compared to the compact development of Europe, urban-settlement patterns in the United States eat up extensive green space and farmland. Shaped by both property developers and consumer choice, the American metropolis is automobile-dominated. The exclusionary zoning and land-use practices of better-off communities serve to drive new development farther out toward the edges of the metropolis. In the spread American metropolis, effective mass transit is all but impossible: relatively few citizens live close enough to a bus or train stop to take mass transit on a regular basis.

Communities on the metropolitan rim seek new residential and commercial development to add to the local tax base. The paved roads and impervious parking surfaces of suburban shopping malls and offices accelerate water runoff and exacerbate groundwater contamination and the pollution of streams and rivers. Each community in the fragmented metropolis enacts policies that promote its own advantage, with little consideration given to protecting the natural environment or the sustainable growth of the region.

. . . . .

Public and private power continues to alter the shape of the U.S. cities and suburbs. In recent years, private corporations have continued to shift production and support activities overseas, especially to low-wage Latin America and Asia, a shift that has added to the vulnerability of cities. Some cities have responded by carving out a place for themselves in the global economy. As we shall see in the next chapter, both local governments and private businesses share an interest in building a city attractive to global corporations and their upper-status workforces. In the next chapter, we explore just how globalization and programs aimed at neighborhood gentrification and upgrading are continuing to reshape the American metropolis.

NOTES

1. Edward C. Banfield, *The Unheavenly City Revisited* (Boston: Little, Brown, 1974), 25–51.

2. Kenneth T. Jackson, *Crabgrass Frontier: The Suburbanization of the United States* (New York: Oxford University Press, 1985), 14–15.

3. David R. Goldfield and Blaine A. Brownell, *Urban America: A History*, 2d ed. (Boston: Houghton Mifflin, 1990), 152.

4. Jackson, *Crabgrass Frontier*, 12–45, esp. 13.

5. Sam Bass Warner, Jr., *Streetcar Suburbs: The Process of Growth in Boston, 1870–90,* 2nd ed.. (Cambridge, MA: Harvard University Press, 1978), 164–165. Also see Ronald Dale Karr, "Brookline Rejects Annexation, 1873," in *Suburbia Re-examined*, ed. Barbara M. Kelly (New York: Greenwood Press, 1989), 103–110.

6. Warner, *Streetcar Suburbs*, 165.

7. Joe William Trotter Jr., ed., *The Great Migration in Historical Perspective: New Dimensions of Race, Class, and Gender* (Bloomington: University of Indiana Press, 1991); James N. Gregory, *The Southern Diaspora: How the Great Migrations of Black and White Southerners Transformed America* (Chapel Hill: University of North Carolina Press, 2007).

8. Joel Garreau, *Edge City: Life on the New Frontier* (New York: Doubleday, 1991); Robert Fishman, *Bourgeois Utopias: The Rise and Fall of Suburbia* (New York: Basic Books, 1987).

9. Robert D. Atkinson, "Technological Change and Cities," *Cityscape: A Journal of Policy Development and Research* 3, no. 1 (1998): 135–136.

10. Cleveland City Planning Commission, "Re-Imagining Cleveland: A More Sustainable Cleveland: Citywide Strategies for Reuse of Vacant Land," adopted 2008; John Gallagher, *Reimagining Detroit: Opportunities for an American City* (Detroit: Wayne State University Press, 2010).

11. Janet Rothenberg Pack, ed., *Sunbelt/Frostbelt: Public Policies and Market Forces in Metropolitan Development* (Washington, DC: Brookings Institution Press, 2005), traces the continuing effects of government spending and regulatory actions on the regional population and job shift, and on the health of local communities.

12. Jackson, *Crabgrass Frontier*, 204.

13. The VA program offered no-money-down loans to veterans. In more recent years, the FHA has required down payments of around 3 percent or 3.5 percent.

14. David L. Kirp, John P. Dwyer, and Larry A. Rosenthal, *Our Town: Race, Housing, and the Soul of Suburbia* (New Brunswick, NJ: Rutgers University Press, 1997), 27.

15. Quoted in Jackson, *Crabgrass Frontier*, 207.

16. Ibid., 208.

17. Citizens Commission on Civil Rights, "A Decent Home . . . A Report on the Continuing Failure of the Federal Government to Provide Equal Housing Opportunity" (Washington, DC: 1983), reprinted in *Critical Perspectives on Housing*, ed. Rachel G. Bratt, Chester Hartman, and Ann Myerson (Philadelphia: Temple University Press, 1986), 299.

18. For a good overview of the evolution of FHA anti-city actions and various other practices that produced the racial segregation of the American city, see Douglas Massey, "Origins of Economic Disparities: The Historical Role of Housing Segregation," in *Segregation: The Rising Costs for America*, ed. James H. Carr and Nandinee K. Kutty (New York: Routledge, 2008), 39–80.

19. Citizens Commission on Civil Rights, "A Decent Home," 301.

20. Thomas J. Sugrue, *The Origins of the Urban Crisis: Race and Inequality in Postwar Detroit* (Princeton, NJ: Princeton University Press, 1996), 64.

21. Mike Davis, "How Eden Lost Its Garden: A Political History of the Los Angeles Landscape," in *The City: Los Angeles and Urban Theory at the End of the Twentieth Century,* ed. Allen J. Scott and Edward J. Soja (Berkeley and Los Angeles: University of California Press, 1996), 169.

22. Gregory D. Squires and Charis E. Kubrin, *Privileged Places: Race, Residence, and the Structure of Opportunity* (Boulder, CO: Lynne Rienner, 2006); Dwight M. Jaffee and John M. Quigley, "Housing Policy, Mortgage Policy, and the Federal Housing Administration," paper presented at the NBER Conference on Measuring and Managing Fiscal Risk, Evanston, Illinois, February 2007, updated May 2009, http://faculty.haas.berkeley.edu/jaffee/Papers/MS_ch5_DwightJaffeeJohnQuigley_p163–213.pdf.

23. Jeff Crump et al., "Cities Destroyed (Again) for Cash: Forum on the U.S. Foreclosure Crisis," *Urban Geography* 29, no. 8 (2008): 749.

24. Joint Committee on Taxation, "Estimates of Federal Tax Expenditures for Fiscal Years 2009–2013" (Washington, DC: U.S. Government Printing Office, 2010), 33.

25. Joint Committee on Taxation figures, reported by Jeanne Sahadi, "Mortgage Deduction: America's Costliest Tax Break," CNNMoney.com, April 18, 2010, http://money.cnn.com/2010/04/14/pf/taxes/mortgage_interest_deduction/index.htm.

26. Peter Dreier, "Will President Bush Reform the Mansion Subsidy?" *Shelterforce Online* 144 (November/December 2005), table titled "Distribution of Tax Benefits for Mortgage Deduction, FY2004," www.nhi.org/online/issues/144/mansionChart1.html.

27. See, for instance, Joseph F.C. DiMento, "Stent (or Dagger?) in the Heart of Town: Urban Freeways in Syracuse, 1944–1967," *Journal of Planning History* 8, no. 2 (2009): 133–161.

28. Raymond A. Mohl, "Race and Space in the Modern City: Interstate-95 and the Black Community in Miami," in *Urban Policy in Twentieth-Century America*, ed. Arnold R. Hirsch and Raymond A. Mohl (New Brunswick, NJ: Rutgers University Press, 1993), 102.

29. Paul Kantor with Stephen David, *The Dependent City: The Changing Political Economy of Urban America* (Glenview, IL: Scott, Foresman, 1988), 99.

30. John H. Mollenkopf, *The Contested City* (Princeton, NJ: Princeton University Press, 1983), 103–109.

31. Richard M. Bernard and Bradley R. Rice, "Introduction," in *Sunbelt Cities: Politics and Growth Since World War II*, ed. Richard M. Bernard and Bradley R. Rice (Austin: University of Texas Press, 1983), 12.

32. Virginia Mayer and Margaret Downs, "The Pentagon Tilt: Regional Biases in Defense Spending and Strategy," Northeast-Midwest Institute, Washington, DC, January 1983, 9.

33. Mia Gray, Elyse Golob, Ann R. Markusen, and Sam Ock Park, "The Four Faces of Silicon Valley," in *Second Tier Cities: Rapid Growth Beyond the Metropolis*, ed. Ann R. Markusen, Yong-Sook Lee, and Sean DiGiovanna (Minneapolis: University of Minnesota Press, 1999), 293–299.

34. Michael P. Smith, *City, State, and Market* (New York: Blackwell, 1988), 55, cited by Benjamin Kleinberg, *Urban America in Transformation* (Thousand Oaks, CA: Sage, 1995), 114, 237.

35. Joe R. Feagin, *Free Enterprise City: Houston in Political and Economic Perspective* (New Brunswick, NJ: Rutgers University Press, 1988), 54–55, 63–71, 186–188, 203–204.

36. Melita Marie Garza and Flynn McRoberts, "Addison Settles with Hispanics," *Chicago Tribune*, August 8, 1997.

37. Jonathan Rothwell and Douglas S. Massey, "The Effect of Density Zoning on Racial Segregation in U.S. Urban Areas," *Urban Affairs Review* 44, no. 6 (June 2009): 779–806.

38. Arnold R. Hirsch, *Making the Second Ghetto: Race and Housing in Chicago, 1940–60* (Chicago: University of Chicago Press, 1983 and 1998).

39. Robert Pear, "New York Admits to Racial Steering in Housing Lawsuit," *New York Times*, July 1, 1992.

40. Heywood T. Sanders, "The Political Economy of Sunbelt Urban Development: Building the Public Sector," paper presented at the annual meeting of the American Political Science Association, New York, September 2–5, 1994.

41. Steven P. Erie and Scot A. MacKenzie, "The L.A. School and Politics Noir: Bringing the Local State Back In," *Journal of Urban Affairs* 31, no. 5 (2009): 545–552; Steven P. Erie, *Globalizing L.A.: Trade, Infrastructure, and Regional Development* (Stanford, CA: Stanford University Press, 2004).

42. Jackson, *Crabgrass Frontier*, 191,

43. Joe R. Feagin and Robert Parker, *Building American Cities: The Urban Real Estate Game,* 2d ed. (Englewood Cliffs, NJ: Prentice Hall, 1990), 16.

44. Massey, "Origins of Economic Disparities," 48.

45. David M. Gordon, "Capitalist Development and the History of American Cities," in *Marxism and the Metropolis*, 2d ed., ed. William K. Tabb and Larry Sawers (New York: Oxford University Press, 1984), 40.

46. Ibid., 41.

47. David L. Clark, "Improbable Los Angeles," in *Sunbelt Cities: Politics and Growth Since World War II,* ed. Richard M. Bernard and Bradley R. Rice (Austin: University of Texas Press, 1983), 271–272. See also David Brodsly, *L.A. Freeway* (Berkeley: University of California Press, 1981), 68–71.

48. Martin Wachs, "The Evolution of Transportation Policy in Los Angeles: Images of Past Policies and Future Prospects," in Scott and Soja, *The City*, 107–112.

49. William Fulton, *The Reluctant Metropolis: The Politics of Urban Growth in Los Angeles* (Baltimore: Johns Hopkins University Press, 1997, 2001 [paperback]), 15.

50. Massey, "Origins of Economic Disparities," 56.

51. *Shelley v. Kraemer*, 334 U.S. 1 (1948).

52. Even one of the most prominent business periodicals has recognized the continued existence of racial disparities in mortgage lending and home insurance. See "The New Redlining," *U.S. News & World Report,* April 17, 1995, 51–58.

53. Joseph P. Treaster, "Insurer Must Pay $100.5 Million in Redlining Case," *New York Times*, October 27, 1998.

54. Gregory D. Squires, "Prospects and Pitfalls of Fair Housing Efforts," in Carr and Kutty, *Segregation,* 317.

55. Christi Harlan, "Why Gramm Strangled Bank Bill," *Austin American-Statesman,* October 23, 1998.

56. Allan J. Fishbein, general counsel for the Center for Community Change, testimony before the Senate Committee on Banking, Housing, and Urban Affairs, Hearings on the "Financial Services Act of 1998," June 24, 1998.

57. Alex Schwartz, "The Limits of Community Reinvestment: The Implementation of Community Reinvestment Agreements in Chicago, Cleveland, New Jersey, and Pittsburgh," paper presented at the annual meeting of the Urban Affairs Association, Fort Worth, Texas, April 22–25, 1998.

58. William C. Apgar and Mark Duda, "The Twenty-Fifth Anniversary of the Community Reinvestment Act: Past Accomplishments and Future Regulatory Challenges," *Economic Policy Review* (June 2003): 174. See also Michael S. Barr, "Credit Where It Counts: Maintaining a Strong Community Reinvestment Act," Brookings Institution Research Brief, Washington, DC, May 2005, www.brookings.edu/~/media/Files/rc/reports/2005/05metropolitanpolicy_barr/20050503_cra.pdf.

59. Rush Limbaugh, in his February 11, 2010, nationally syndicated radio broadcast, blamed the CRA for the housing finance meltdown: "The Community Reinvestment Act was hatched by Carter, it was expanded by Clinton, it was used by ACORN and their allies to wreck the housing market by wrecking the mortgage market, by demanding that mortgages be given to people who could no way pay them back. Ergo, the sub-prime mortgage crisis. . . . I don't defend AIG [the giant mortgage insurance institution that was unable to pay its obligations on defaulted loans], but they were treating loans—derivatives, if you will—that was based fundamentally on loans developed by liberal policies." See Greg Lewis, "Limbaugh Resurrects CRA Falsehoods, Claims Affordable Housing Was Designed To Wreck The Whole System," MediaMatters for America, February 11, 2010, http://mediamatters.org/limbaughwire/2010/02/11.

60. Dan Immergluck, *Foreclosed: High-Risk Lending, Deregulation, and the Undermining of America's Mortgage Market* (Ithaca, NY: Cornell University Press, 2009), esp. 55–58, 162–163, and chap. 3.

61. Hirsch, *Making the Second Ghetto*, 100–170.

62. Doug A. Timmer, D. Stanley Eitzen, and Kathryn D. Talley, *Paths to Homelessness: Extreme Poverty and the Urban Housing Crisis* (Boulder, CO: Westview Press, 1994), 5.

63. Charles Hoch and Robert A. Slayton, *New Homeless and Old: Community and the Skid Row Hotel* (Philadelphia: Temple University Press, 1989).

64. Rachael A. Woldoff and Seth Ovadia, "Not Getting their Money's Worth: African-American Disadvantages in Converting Income, Wealth, and Education into Residential Quality," *Urban Affairs Review* 45, no. 1 (September 2009): 66–91.

65. Charles M. Lamb, *Housing Segregation in Suburban America since 1960: Presidential and Judicial Politics* (New York: Cambridge University Press, 2005).

66. Anne Power, Jörg Ploger, and Astrid Winkler, *Phoenix Cities: The Fall and Rise of Great Industrial Cities* (Bristol, UK: Policy Press, University of Bristol, 2010).

67. Portland's Urban Growth Boundary is a noteworthy exception, as we note in Chapters 9 and 10.

3 Recent Trends

Gentrification and Globalization

Since the1970s, numerous large- and medium-size U.S. cities experienced a renaissance or "rebirth" that was unimaginable only twenty or so years previous. Global as well as national firms located their headquarters in the downtowns of big cities. Upscale *gentrifiers* moved in and "resettled" once-declining inner-city areas. Once ignored inner-city neighborhoods became the sites of boutique stores, coffeehouses, and sidewalk cafés.

Yet, the extent of the urban rebound is often exaggerated. While certain downtowns and inner-city neighborhoods have come back, others suffer property abandonment and continued decline. While some cities have found a new position in the global economy, others face a downward spiral, suffering the loss of manufacturing and clerical jobs to the suburbs and to low-wage sites overseas. The national economic recession and mortgage finance crises of the early years of the twenty-first century underscored the vulnerability of cities, with a flood of foreclosures and "For Sale" signs pinpointing local distress.

This chapter looks at two of the more important recent trends in the evolution of cities: gentrification (the so-called back-to-the-city movement) and globalization. In an era of globalization, cities are vulnerable to forces from beyond their borders and from beyond the nation's borders.

Gentrification, as we shall see, is, in part, a reaction to globalization. The well-paid workers in global headquarters and service firms search for quality housing near work, with their buying power serving to push out the poor residents who live there. Local governments have promoted gentrification as a means of luring top firms. Charlotte, North Carolina, is just one of a great many cities where civic leaders pursued a conscious strategy of gentrification in an effort to alter perceptions of the city's decline. Local leaders feared that corporations would move elsewhere if Charlotte did not change its policies in order to create a living environment attractive to professional, upscale workers.[1]

The Gentrification of Core City Neighborhoods

A Partial Urban Comeback

As far back as the late 1970s and early 1980s, journalists began to report the beginnings of a "back to the city" movement as urban "pioneers" bought and renovated housing in distressed inner-city neighborhoods. **Gentrification** refers to the upgrading of core neighborhoods that occurs when young professionals—especially singles and childless couples—place new value on city living. Gentrification denotes that movement of a relatively well-to-do urban "gentry" into areas close to the work and entertainment opportunities of an active downtown. In the beginning phases of gentrification, home seekers are also attracted to the relatively low property values that make the purchase of a home in the inner city a "good buy."

Writers have used many terms and phrases as synonyms for gentrification: urban regeneration, the back-to-the-city movement, inner-city revitalization, neighborhood renewal and rehabilitation, neighborhood reinvestment, and urban reinvasion and resettlement.[2] When the term is used very precisely, gentrification refers to a transformation process that "operates in the residential housing market"[3] and results in class (and often racial) succession: upscale home seekers displace the poor. Today, however, the term gentrification is also used to refer to nonresidential investment in the core city, such as the opening of a luxury shopping galleria or a new multiplex cinema.

Gentrification is often viewed as a market-driven process where a few urban "pioneers" take advantage of low prices to buy and rehabilitate property in troubled neighborhoods. Artists similarly seek lofts, vacant warehouses, and other large workspaces offered at low rents. As these early gentrifiers "open" a neighborhood, they are soon followed by other buyers interested in taking up residence in the newly "hip" and discovered areas of the city.

The above description, however, ignores the pivotal role that developers and real estate agents play in a neighborhood's transformation, especially in their efforts to "brand" and aggressively market a "new" neighborhood to upscale buyers, changing an area's social composition.[4] In Cincinnati, the Over-the-Rhine (OTR) area just north of the downtown was one of the city's poorest districts. Developers sold condominiums in what they called the "Gateway District," the southern part of Over-the-Rhine, as if it were a separate area not attached to the OTR ghetto.

In SoHo in Lower Manhattan, artists had previously converted empty manufacturing lofts into working and living spaces. The artists themselves were later displaced as landlords and developers sought more profitable land uses in such a "hot" neighborhood.[5] "Supergentrified" SoHo became the site of upscale residences and retail chain stores, losing much of the "artsy" flavor that had drawn so much attention to the neighborhood during the early days of its revival.

Loretta Lees uses the terms **financifiers** and **supergentrifiers** to denote the quite different character of the second invasion wave that took place in hot areas such as New York's SoHo.[6] Many of the first-wave urban pioneers valued the racial and ethnic diversity and the "authentic" character of the neighborhood in which they settled.[7] (See Box 3.1, "A Neighborhood Changes, and So Do Its Coffeehouses.") But the well-off homebuyers who followed them did not place a similar value on urban authenticity. The supergentrifiers moved to a neighborhood because of its upscale trajectory and its convenient location. The supergentrifiers did not seek to preserve the character of a neighborhood; instead, they welcomed the introduction of upscale cafés, trendy boutiques, and strip shopping malls with convenient in-front parking. In some cases,

Box 3.1
A Neighborhood Changes, and So Do Its Coffeehouses

In the Wicker Park section of Chicago, the opening and closing of coffeehouses stands as evidence of how different waves of gentrification have altered the neighborhood. When Wicker Park was a Polish working-class neighborhood, local residents gathered at Sophie's Busy Bee, the local "greasy spoon" that had a photograph of the Pope prominently displayed on its walls. The first wave of gentrification saw the introduction of a new coffeehouse, the neo-bohemian Urbus Orbis, which served as a hangout for artists and young "hipsters." The new arrivals changed the image of Wicker Park, and the area was soon "discovered" by newcomers who were less fond of preserving the area's gritty urban texture. Developers built new housing for young professionals who sought residences near Chicago's downtown offices and nightlife. Unlike the first wave of gentrification pioneers, the newest arrivals did not value art and hipness. They frequented the new Starbucks. The Busy Bee and Urbus Orbis both closed.

Source: Richard Lloyd, *Neo-Bohemia: Art and Commerce in the Postindustrial City* (New York: Routledge, 2006), 107–112.

supergentrifiers built supersized, fortified modern homes that were clearly incongruent with an area's existing housing stock and character.

How Extensive Is Gentrification?

Initially, gentrifying neighborhoods were seen as interesting exceptions to the general story of central-city decline: gentrified neighborhoods were "islands of renewal in seas of decay."[8] Over the years, however, gentrification has become more widespread, with neighborhoods in cities across the nation experiencing various aspects of revival. To some urban observers, gentrification has become so commonplace that it is now troubled neighborhoods that should be treated as the exceptions, as "islands of decay in seas of renewal."[9]

While gentrification is quite commonplace, not all cities across the United States have enjoyed such a rebound. Gentrified neighborhoods are more typically found in corporate headquarters cities with downtowns that offer good-paying jobs and an abundance of cultural and nightlife opportunities. Cities with dying downtowns, by contrast, have not attracted a similar scale of investment in nearby inner-city areas. Detroit, Cleveland, Newark, Buffalo, and a number of cities of the old South have experienced only the most minimal gentrification.[10] Gentrification is also least likely to occur in those neighborhoods with the greatest concentrations of poverty and the highest rates of social disorganization.[11]

Critics often charge that gentrification constitutes a white "invasion" into poor black and Hispanic neighborhoods. A number of cities, however, have also begun to experience black gentrification. Black professionals have moved into New York's

Harlem and Clinton Hill (Brooklyn) and Chicago's Bronzeville, near the lakeshore on the city's South Side, areas that were once exclusively the domain of the black poor.[12] While South Side activists in Chicago saw black gentrification as more acceptable than white resettlement, nonetheless even black gentrification altered the social composition of the neighborhood, marginalizing poorer and more vulnerable residents.[13] In New York and Chicago, the opening of a Starbucks signaled the change in the class structure of black areas.

THE BENEFITS AND COSTS OF GENTRIFICATION

Gentrification brings a number of benefits to cities.[14] New investment helps to stabilize declining neighborhoods, upgrading residential structures and making an area more attractive to future investment. Gentrified areas also give a city a supply of workers with advanced technological and specialized skills, the sort of workforce that a city needs in order to be successful in its efforts to attract high-tech, legal, and financial service firms. Neighborhood upgrading expands the municipal tax base, yielding higher property-tax revenues and, where state law permits, higher local income-tax revenues as well.

Once-declining neighborhoods exhibit a new sense of vitality. New shops and restaurants add to the quality of daily urban life. Even the African American residents of transition areas generally say that they like how the area is changing.[15] Gentrification provides an area's poor and minority residents with higher-quality shops, greater public safety, improved municipal services, and new cultural opportunities and career paths. Gentrification brings once-overlooked neighborhoods more into the mainstream of American life.[16]

But critics counter that the focus on such benefits overstates gentrification's positive impacts while slighting the process's more harmful effects. Most troubling, gentrification results in **displacement** as poor families and racial minorities are "pushed out" to make way for newcomers with more buying power. Soaring property values and rents make a suddenly "discovered" neighborhood unaffordable to the working class and the poor.[17] Unscrupulous developers fail to maintain properties or, in extreme cases, resort to arson and other illegal actions in their efforts to oust existing tenants in order to make way for more profitable land uses.[18]

Urban geographer Neil Smith sees gentrification as a process of neighborhood "invasion," where the city's better classes expropriate poorer and minority areas of the city.[19] Gentrification is "a process that is fundamentally rooted in class" and "class transformation."[20] Cultural clashes occur when the lifestyles of newcomers and long-term residents come into conflict. Gentrifiers demand policies to "manage neighborhood behaviors"[21] such as public drinking, the blaring of loud music, and playing basketball at night. The "creative class" and other gentrifiers also demand better police protection and a variety of other service improvements, demands that may lessen the resources available for service provision in poorer sections of the city.[22]

Gentrification does not mark the end of the urban crisis. Compared to the continuing outmigration of population and wealth to suburbia, gentrification is a relative trickle.[23] Despite the back-to-the-city movement, suburbia, not the inner city, remains the locus of growth. Over 80 percent of new homes are built in the suburbs, not in central cities.[24]

Promoting Gentrification: The Role of Public and Private Actors

Gentrification is not entirely the product of a free market where homebuyers find bargain-priced properties in the inner city.[25] Instead, private business elites and governmental actors also play a clear role in promoting neighborhood transformation.

The turnaround of Philadelphia's Society Hill was produced by the joint actions and marketing efforts of the city's downtown real estate community and governmental planners. A civic elite willed a revitalized Society Hill area into being. The city expelled all but a few of the residents already living in the area to make way for a new neighborhood that was marketed to a higher class of tenant.[26] Similarly, real estate interests vigorously promoted the lifestyle virtues of "Silicon Alley," a newly branded "technobohemian" district in New York's Lower Manhattan. Real estate interests recognized the profits that they could make from the "selling of a new media district," repositioning an area of relatively low-value small offices and warehouses as a new high-tech paradise.[27]

The City of Chicago supported the transformation of the Wicker Park neighborhood by granting the area a historic landmark status, a designation that helped developers and real estate firms to rebrand and market the area. Designation also provided tax credits for housing rehabilitation, helping to attract newcomers who wished to buy into the neighborhood.[28] Realtors and developers opposed the efforts of a nonprofit group to rehabilitate nearby housing units for the poor, fearing that new housing for poor people would diminish the area's attractiveness to market-rate homebuyers.[29]

Limiting the Ill Effects of Gentrification

In some cities, **grassroots organizing efforts** have succeeded in combating gentrification, or at least curtailing some of the ills brought about by unfettered gentrification. In the Washington Heights neighborhood of New York's Upper Manhattan, a multiethnic coalition of community groups fought to ensure that housing opportunities for the poor were included in plans to bring new development to the area. By contrast, grassroots groups were weakly organized in the Park Slope section of Brooklyn. As a result, property developers in Park Slope enjoyed greater freedom to convert apartments into cooperatives and condominiums, actions that led to substantial displacement.[30]

In San Francisco, grassroots groups fought for restrictions to limit the conversion of single room occupancy (SRO) hotels, minimizing the displacement of the large transient population that lives in the city's Tenderloin area.[31] The action effectively throttled plans by the city's business community to extend the adjoining financial district into the Tenderloin. In the southern part of San Francisco, in Bernal Heights, progressive community organizations lobbied the city to acquire land for public housing so that the neighborhood would be able to retain its income diversity in the face of gentrifying pressures.[32] Similarly in San Diego, a coalition of community groups threatened to fight the construction of Ballpark Village, a bayfront development next to the new Padres stadium, dropping their opposition only after the developer and city council agreed to expand the number of affordable housing units to be built on-site and elsewhere in the downtown.[33]

Yet, despite the occasional success of grassroots groups, gentrification continues. Local governments have only the most limited ability to control private investment and property upgrading. Most cities do not even try to limit residential change. Quite the opposite! Municipal officials tend to promote and assist gentrification as part of a strategy to attract new businesses and jobs to a city. Homeowner associations in working-class and lower-middle-class areas of the city also tend to support gentrification as a means of upgrading neighborhoods, raising the value of their property, and removing problem residents from a community.[34]

In a privatist nation, local governments possess only the most limited ability to curtail property conversion and investment. Still, cities can take a number of actions to minimize residential displacement and to promote the balanced development of neighborhoods undergoing change. Cities can tame—but not stop—gentrification.

Cities can aid the activities of **community development corporations (CDCs)** that seek to provide affordable housing in neighborhoods experiencing rebirth. As we describe in greater detail in Chapter 7, CDCs are neighborhood-based groups that work with bankers, public officials, and other partners to produce quality housing units for poor and working-class tenants. In Chicago, the Bickerdike Redevelopment Corporation worked with various partners to pull together the funds to rehabilitate older apartment buildings in order to maintain good-quality low-income housing in neighborhoods undergoing transformation. In Atlanta, the Reynoldstown Redevelopment Corporation (RRC) pursued a similar course of action, building both new rental units and affordable owner-occupied homes. RRC kept new home prices low by building on vacant lots.[35]

Municipalities can assist the housing efforts of CDCs by giving them government-held properties at greatly reduced cost. Affordable housing advocates also argue for **mandatory set asides**, legislative requirements that new residential developments include a certain percentage of affordable units. Boston and San Francisco utilized an alternative strategy, imposing **linkage fees** on the construction of new office buildings, with the collected funds used to support affordable housing projects elsewhere in the city. Boston's program provided assistance for more than 5,000 units of affordable housing located throughout the city.[36] Seattle has a special **housing levy** that provides funding for a variety of balanced development efforts, including the preservation of rental apartments, the construction of affordable rental units, and the development of mixed-income residential projects.[37]

Seattle's housing efforts are commendable but also quite expensive. Most cities, especially in periods of hard economic times and local budget constraints, are reluctant to commit to expensive program efforts or impose development restrictions that may deter private investment.

GLOBALIZATION OR GLOBAL CITIES?

GLOBAL CITIES: THE CENTERS OF A WORLD ECONOMY

Global cities have a dense concentration of corporate headquarters, and banks and other financial institutions. Global cities are the **command-and-control centers** of

Miami's downtown has grown as a global corporate finance center for Central and South America. Copyright © by Tom Schaefer. http://commons.wikimedia.org/wiki/File:Miami_downtown_by_Tom_Schaefer_-_Miamitom.jpg.

an economy where corporate decisions reach into cities located elsewhere around the world. Global cities are also the centers of telecommunications technology.

Why do major multinational corporations continue to congregate their headquarters and front offices in major cities when advances in transportation and telecommunications seemingly give corporations the freedom to move facilities to smaller towns and suburban areas? Corporations seek the advantages of **agglomeration** or dense sectoral development. Firms in an industrial sector find it advantageous to locate close to those businesses that provide the specialized financial, legal, and other support services that the members of an industry require. Similar firms also draw from the same pool of professional talent in specialized labor markets. It just makes sense for a computer firm, for instance, to locate in an area that has other computer firms and an existing pool of experienced, qualified labor.

New York, London, and Tokyo each have such a great concentration of corporate headquarters and financial offices that they are generally recognized to be the world's three preeminent global cities. Still, other cities below this tier also merit attention as important corporate and financial centers and as cities that exhibit other aspects of internationalization.[38]

Los Angeles, Chicago, and Washington, DC, rank just below New York in terms of global significance. Los Angeles is an important center of Pacific Rim banking and multicultural communications. The growth of textile manufacturing in the city has also been fueled by the immigration of low-wage workers from Mexico and Asia. (See Box 3.2, "Is Los Angeles a Global City?") Chicago similarly enjoys great "global

Millennium Park, Chicago. Chicago leaders built Millennium Park on the downtown lakefront site of the old commuter railyards. The construction of Millennium Park was part of the effort by civic leaders to transform the image of the city, to promote Chicago as an attractive "world class" city. Millennium Park, Pritzker Pavilion band shell. From Wikimedia Commons via user Adrian104. http://commons.wikimedia.org/wiki/File:Jay_Pritzker_Pavilion_Chicago.jpg.

connectivity" as the headquarters of a number of major national and international firms.[39] Chicago's emergence as a global corporate center is reflected in the dynamic expansion of the city's downtown office district and the new shops and upscale residences of the South Loop, West Loop, University Village, North Park Village, and River North developments.[40] Washington, DC, of course, represents an important center of government activities.

Other big cities occupy more specialized or limited positions in the global economic hierarchy. Third-tier global cities include Houston (with its connections to Mexico and Latin America), Miami (with its Cuban enclave and its emergence as a center of Caribbean banking and finance), and San Francisco (which stands as a competitor to Los Angeles as a Pacific Rim financial center). Boston, Dallas, and Philadelphia can be considered fourth-tier cities, clearly important in their regions but with more limited international ties. A fifth tier would likely include Atlanta, Rochester, Columbus, and Charlotte (an important regional banking center), cities where aggressive entrepreneurs have just begun to carve out global connections.

Box 3.2

Is Los Angeles a Global City?

New York, London, and Tokyo clearly meet anyone's definition of global cities. But is Los Angeles, the second largest city in the United States, a global city?

To a great many observers, the answer is an obvious "Yes!" Los Angeles' downtown is a center of banking where decisions are made that influence development on both sides of the Pacific Ocean. Corporations in Japan have invested heavily in real estate in the city, an investment promoted by Los Angeles mayors who have led trade missions overseas to tout L.A. as the "gateway for the Pacific Rim." Los Angeles also expanded the region's port and airport facilities to accommodate increased international commerce. City leaders even encouraged immigrants to maintain business contacts in their countries of origin, in order to promote new cross-border investment in Los Angeles.[1] It is also a multicultural mecca, where the local culture and economy have been enriched by new arrivals from Mexico, El Salvador, Guatemala, India, Pakistan, China, Korea, Japan, as well as other Latin American and Pacific Rim nations.

Yet urban sociologist Michael Peter Smith argues that despite the city's obvious internationalization, Los Angeles should *not* be regarded as a global city. Smith observes that Los Angeles is "a receiver rather than a sender of global commands and controls."[2] It lacks the denseness of headquarters and banking firms of a command-and-control city such as New York. Decisions made by firms in Los Angeles do not really have that great an impact on the economies of cities overseas. Instead, L.A. is more typically the victim of, than a master of, global forces. The financial decisions made by corporations in Japan, for instance, had a great impact on L.A. real estate prices and the "boom" and "bust" of the downtown Los Angeles office economy at the end of the twentieth century and the beginning of the twenty-first century.

Yet, Smith's conceptualization of a global city may be too narrow. Urban geographer Edward Soja argues that many of the lists and rankings of global cities give too much consideration to the presence of command-and-control industries in downtown financial districts. Soja argues that other aspects of globalization are just as important. Los Angeles, with more than 40 percent of its population foreign born, is a global city where citizens maintain bicultural identities and where issues of multiculturalism often dominate the local arena.[3]

Los Angeles is not one of the world's top-tier command-and-control centers. But in other ways, it is clearly a global city.

[1]Steven P. Erie, *Globalizing L.A.: Trade, Infrastructure, and Regional Development* (Stanford, CA: Stanford University Press, 2004), 224–227.

[2]Michael Peter Smith, "Looking for Globality in Los Angeles," in *Articulating the Global and the Local*, ed. Ann Cvetkovich and Douglas Kellner (Boulder, CO: Westview, 1997), 55–71, here, 55.

[3]Edward W. Soja, *Postmetropolis: Critical Studies of Cities and Regions* (Maiden, MA: Blackwell, 2000), 222–232.

GLOBALIZATION: THE PERMEABILITY OF CITY BORDERS

Even communities not commonly regarded as global cities are influenced by globalization, by forces from beyond their borders and from overseas. **Globalization** denotes the permeability of local borders.

International flare-ups, changes in currency exchange rates, and the attractiveness of investment opportunities in other countries all affect the well-being of U.S. cities. *New York Times* columnist and globalization expert Thomas Friedman uses the label "the electronic herd" to underscore the rapid speed and relative uncontrollability of the global transactions that have such a great influence on national and local economies.[41] In an age of multinational corporate giants, instantaneous communications, and high-speed transportation, decisions and events from overseas can have a great effect on U.S. cities.

What are the changing aspects of the global system that have made cities so vulnerable to overseas influences? A few of the more important ones include:

1. Advances in Transportation and Telecommunications

Fax machines, satellite communications, computer technology, fiber optics, teleports (which make advanced telecommunications technology available to a variety of firms and customers), and jet travel all give a corporation the ability to locate its headquarters and financial services divisions at some distance from its production facilities. A multinational firm can choose the prestige addresses of New York, London, Tokyo, Paris, Frankfurt, Hong Kong, Seoul, or any big city as the site of its headquarters while simultaneously choosing to locate its manufacturing plants and support operations in lower-cost smaller cities and suburbs, or even overseas. Advances in transportation and shipping, for instance, allow automobile companies to develop supply chains where parts manufactured in Mexico, Brazil, or even South Africa and Central Europe can be shipped to the United States for assembly.

Not all firms have the freedom to shift production overseas: many firms must maintain locations close to suppliers, customers, and skilled labor markets in the United States. Yet, while the mobility of capital can be overstated, it is undeniable that a great many firms have a greater variety of geographic options today than at any time in the past. As a consequence, U.S. localities find they are in competition not just with one another but also with communities overseas.

2. The Growing Importance of Advanced Technology and the Knowledge Industry

In a postindustrial global age, U.S. cities can no longer stake their economic future on "smokestack chasing." To a great extent, knowledge work has displaced factory work. Confronted by the decline of manufacturing, cities have upgraded their telecommunications infrastructure and provided the levels of education, training, and housing necessary to attract global headquarters and service firms.

A concentration of highly educated professionals with advanced mathematical, computer programming, and other digital-related skills provided the basis for the sustained economic growth of California's **Silicon Valley**, the area centered on Stanford University. San Francisco, just to the north, responded with its own efforts to assist the start-up of entrepreneurial "dot-com" firms. Austin, Texas, built on the advantages the city possessed as the home of the University of Texas and Dell Computer Corporation. New York City similarly upgraded its teleport facilities and other telecommunications infrastructure in order to promote the development of **Silicon Alley**, the warehouse area of the old Garment District that became the takeoff site for software, Web advertising, and other digital and "new media" firms.[42]

3. The New Value that Professionals Place on Leisure, Artistic, and Cultural Activities

Municipal leaders have come to realize that a strategy of tax inducements is no longer sufficient to attract industries that have so great a choice of locations. **Smart cities** offer more than just tax advantages; they also offer a good quality of life, an attractive living environment that will serve as a lure to a corporation's top executives and technology-oriented workers.

4. The Rise of a New Immigration

If capital in a global age is increasingly mobile, so too is labor. The media and transportation revolutions have heightened immigration pressures, as laborers from Latin America, South Asia, East Asia, the Near East, and Africa have come to the United States seeking opportunity. U.S. foreign policy has also resulted in immigration from Korea, Vietnam, the Philippines, Russia, Cuba, and El Salvador. In New York, Los Angeles, and other port-of-entry cities, postindustrial economic restructuring has been characterized by the **informalization** or **casualization of work**, with immigrant labor hired to perform low-wage, off-the-books work.[43]

5. The Vulnerability of Cities to Terrorism, International Political and Economic Crises, and Disease

One often unrecognized characteristic of globalization is the increased vulnerability of cities.[44] The horror of 9/11 serves as witness to the potential impact that terrorism can have on cities. Even cities that have not been victimized by a terrorist attack have had to increase spending for activities related to homeland defense. A city's economy can also be subject to computer network failure and to digital attacks by malcontents and enemies who seek to inflict serious harm.[45]

In an age of cities without borders, there are still other global factors that have an impact on the well-being of U.S. cities. International crises—including famine, civil wars, and political turmoil—create waves of immigration that bring new workers and entrepreneurs to a city but also add to municipal service burdens. The banking and currency actions taken in one country can have a sudden detrimental effect on a local economy an ocean away. With modern jet travel, diseases such as AIDS, too, can quickly cross from one continent to another.[46]

MindSpace Campus, HiTec City, Hyderabad, India. U.S. cities are losing jobs as American firms digitalize and outsource work to well-educated workers in lower-wage nations. From Wikimedia Commons via Flickr and user peculiar235. http://commons.wikimedia.org/wiki/File:Hydabada.jpg.

Back-Office Development and Outsourcing

While some cities have emerged as global centers of the new economy, other cities continue to suffer deindustrialization and economic decline. While major firms often choose to congregate their headquarters in global cities, advances in technology have freed corporations from the necessity of siting facilities in a central city. Numerous national and multinational corporations have chosen to locate headquarters and branch offices in the office parks of "self-contained high-end suburbs," the **nerdistans**, as Joel Kotkin has labeled them, where the "raw material is not ports, coal, iron, or even highway locations, but concentrations of skilled workers."[47]

The new technology further allows cities in the heartland to compete for jobs with major metropolitan centers. A corporation may choose to maintain its central headquarters in a global city but seek to save money by moving production and support operations to **back offices** situated in lower-cost small cities. American Express moved its back offices from New York to Salt Lake City; Metropolitan Life relocated back-office operations to Greenville (South Carolina), Scranton (Pennsylvania), and Wichita (Kansas).[48]

Salt Lake City and fifteen other Utah communities joined together to begin work on the UTOPIA (Utah Telecommunication Open Infrastructure Agency) fiber-optic network, which the region's economic boosters claim is one of the largest capacity ultra-high-speed digital networks in the world. Utah's civic leaders hope that the $470 million investment will make the region attractive to technology-oriented businesses: "The best network in the U.S. will be in Utah—not in New York, not in Chicago, not in Los Angeles."[49]

Increasingly, multinational firms are engaged in **offshoring**, the move or contracting of support activities to subsidiaries or support firms located in low-cost areas overseas. The shift of customer service **call centers** to English-speaking Bangalore and Hyderabad, India, provides a most visible illustration of the private outsourcing of jobs overseas. India, China, Mexico, the Philippines, and the former communist countries of Eastern Europe all offer low-wage alternatives to U.S. cities. Cities and metropolitan areas with large concentrations of information technology jobs—including San Francisco, San Jose, Lowell (Massachusetts), and Boulder (Colorado)—may find that they are especially vulnerable in an industry where corporations have the ability to contract computer- and communications-related work to firms overseas.[50]

THE NEW IMMIGRATION

Immigration is changing the demography of U.S. cities. Phoenix's population grew by more than two-thirds between 1980 and 2000, with the increase coming primarily as a consequence of immigration from Mexico. Between 2007 and 2009, however, the number of immigrants living in Phoenix actually dropped, as the city, in the face of a continuing economic recession, had fewer job opportunities to offer new arrivals.[51]

Immigration is redefining local politics even in cities beyond the Southwest. In 1970, 17 percent of the population of New York City was foreign born. By 1980, the immigrant population had doubled: over a third of the city's population were immigrants.[52] New York's Chinese population spilled well beyond the traditional borders of Chinatown into neighboring Little Italy and the Lower East Side. New Chinatowns also emerged in the city's outer boroughs, in Jackson Heights and Flushing (Queens) and in Sunset Park (Brooklyn).[53] Similarly in Chicago, the city's burgeoning Chinese population spread beyond the city's traditional South Side Chinatown and into the adjoining Bridgeport neighborhood. A second Chinatown expanded on the city's North Side, along Argyle Street and Broadway, a port-of-entry center for new arrivals from China, Vietnam, and Southeast Asia.[54]

Since the 1960s, a series of changes in U.S. law effectively opened the country's doors to a **new immigration** from the Caribbean, Latin America, the Pacific Rim, and Africa, a sharp contrast to the much earlier waves of immigration that came primarily from Europe. By 1980, reforms abolished the old system of per-country quotas that had sharply limited immigration from countries outside of Europe.[55] The revised law also eased family reunification, allowing family members from overseas to join a breadwinner working in the United States. Amnesty provisions, which sought the humane goal of regularizing the status of undocumented residents, also served to spur new arrivals, especially from Mexico.[56] U.S. political commitments led to the welcoming of Soviet Jews and Vietnamese, Cambodian, Laotian, and Cuban refugees.

The new immigration has reshaped small cities and suburbs, not just the nation's biggest cities. The foreign-born population has increased in heartland cities such as

Denver, Nashville, Oklahoma City, Wichita, and St. Paul.[57] One-fifth of Denver's population is foreign born, with immigrants from Mexico accounting for virtually all of the city's population growth during the 1990s. Over the same decade, Kansas City saw its immigrant population double.[58] A number of smaller cities in Minnesota (Rochester) and Wisconsin (Wausau, Green Bay, Sheboygan, Appleton, LaCrosse, and Eau Claire) saw the growth of a local Hmong population, an ethnic group from Laos that resettled in the United States as a result of the Vietnam war.[59]

The new immigration has occurred in a metropolitan era when jobs and population had already shifted from central cities to the suburbs. In contrast to the earlier arrival of immigrants from Europe, many of the new immigrants have skipped the central city and moved directly to the suburbs, especially when welcomed by members of their extended family. Contemporary Los Angeles is ringed by various Mexican, Korean, Chinese, and Vietnamese communities. Westminster, south of Los Angeles in Orange County, is popularly known as "Little Saigon." On New York's Long Island, Hempstead and Hicksville are suburban centers of the region's Indian population; Hicksville is often referred to as "Little India."[60] In greater Chicago, Naperville, Schaumburg, Skokie, Hoffman Estates, Glendale Heights, Hanover Park, and Palatine are only a few of the suburbs with a large concentration of Asian Indians.[61]

While a growing number of immigrants can be found in suburbia, the nation's new arrivals are still disproportionately concentrated in central cities. As a result, immigration imposes a special burden on cities. Immigrants are an especially large portion of the population of **port-of-entry** or **gateway cities**. Over 60 percent of Miami's population is foreign born, as is nearly half the population of Santa Ana, California.[62] Los Angeles (41 percent), New York (37 percent), and San Francisco (35 percent) in 2007 reported figures that are nearly as large. Boston (29 percent); Houston (28 percent); Dallas, El Paso, and Phoenix (26 percent each); San Diego (25 percent); and Chicago (22 percent) are other cities with large immigrant concentrations.[63]

In port-of-entry cities, low-paid clerical and assembly jobs, often held by women, have replaced the good-paying jobs of the docks and factories of the late industrial city. The new **informalization of the urban economy** is marked by the rise of small migrant-owned shops and even the reemergence of **piecework** (where workers are paid by the piece of work they finish, not by the hour), sweatshops, and manufacturing at home.[64] In Los Angeles, a large labor force of Asian American and Latina immigrants contributed to the city's resurgence as a low-wage, textile manufacturing center. (See Box 3.3, "Film Images of the City.")

Critics often point to the costs that cities and local school systems incur in absorbing the new immigrants. Yet, the new arrivals also contribute to the local economy. Immigration also brings life to urban neighborhoods that might otherwise suffer abandonment and steep decline. (See Box 3.4, "Are Cities Better Off as a Result of Immigration? Chicago's Killer Heat Wave and 'Little Village.'")

Advances in transportation and communications have altered what it means to be an immigrant. Unlike the earlier arrivals from Europe, contemporary immigrants do not sever relations with their old homelands and become totally "American." E-mail, Skype, cheap telephone calling cards, and relatively affordable transportation allow the new immigrants to keep in constant contact with family and friends back home,

Box 3.3

Film Images of the City—Immigrant Los Angeles:
Real Women Have Curves* and *Bread and Roses

Director Patricia Cardoso's *Real Women Have Curves* (2002) focuses on the struggles of Ana, an eighteen-year-old Latina (played by America Ferrera), as she juggles the conflicting demands of her Mexican and U.S. worlds. Should she defy the expectations of her family, leave Los Angeles, and take a scholarship to attend Columbia University in far-off New York City? Or should she remain in L.A. and play the traditional supportive role expected of Latina women in the home and the workplace? Initially, Ana bows to her family's wishes and helps out in the small dressmaking business run by her sister.

The film points to the feminization and the low-wage nature of work in the "casual" side of Los Angeles' new global economy. The small factory is literally a sweatshop where the ladies strip down to their underwear in order to cope with the suffocating heat. Ana rails against the exploitation of the immigrant women; corporations sell the women's hand-crafted gowns for hundreds of dollars but pay the women only a pittance for their work.

Ken Loach's *Bread and Roses* (2000) is a more strident, unvarnished indictment of the social and work conditions suffered by immigrants who occupy the bottom-rung positions in Los Angeles' global economy. Loach starts by showing the dangers that the migrants face in crossing the border, even the possibilities of rape. The undocumented migrants pay a "coyote" high fees to smuggle them across the U.S. border. The coyotes abandon their human cargo when things go wrong; the smugglers often "rip off" their paying customers.

Maya (played by Pilar Padilla) escapes the coyotes and, with the help of her sister, finds a job cleaning offices in one of Los Angeles' gleaming downtown office towers. The film reveals the low-wage, no-benefits, insecure jobs that make up the underside of the city's glitzy global economy. The women put up with all sorts of abuse on the job for fear of losing their livelihood. The city's downtown corporations contract with smaller firms to clean their offices. The contracted firm stands as a buffer between the women and the city's giant corporations which, by outsourcing the janitorial tasks, deny responsibility for the low pay and poor work conditions of the largely Latina workforce. Even though the cleaning firm is run by Mexican Americans, it, too, exploits the women, with the men in charge demanding a portion of the women's wages and even sexual favors in return for giving them work. The film underscores the **dualism** of the global city, contrasting the harsh lives of the workers with the flamboyant excesses of a lavish Hollywood party.

feeding a sense of bicultural loyalty and identity. Even the seemingly far-off reaches of the world are no longer all that far off. By nonstop jet, Chicago is only eleven hours to Turkey and eighteen hours to India.[65]

In an age of globalization, immigration no longer entails "the crossing of rigid, territorial national boundaries." Instead, in a shrinking global world where technology and transportation enable a "back-and-forth migration," new immigrants come to the United States for economic opportunity but do not relinquish their home ties.[66] Even in communities far from the border, in Chicago's Pilsen and Little Village neighbor-

Box 3.4

Are Cities Better Off as a Result of Immigration?
Chicago's Killer Heat Wave and "Little Village"

Does immigration help or hurt a city? In some cases, immigration can actually add to a city's well-being, as demonstrated by a review of the death toll of Chicago's 1995 killer heat wave. That summer, over 485 people died in Chicago from heat-related causes. The elderly were especially vulnerable.

But the deaths were not distributed equally throughout the city. As a study of the city map readily revealed, people in certain neighborhoods were more likely to die than the residents of other neighborhoods.

The mortality rate was actually fairly low in the predominantly poor Mexican American community of South Lawndale, commonly called "Little Village." Public-health authorities began to ask why the death rate in Little Village was so low, especially when the death rate in neighboring North Lawndale, a poor African American area, was so high.

Continuing immigration from Mexico had made Little Village a lively neighborhood, with an active shopping district and a well-supported network of churches. The elderly in Little Village were able to escape the heat of their old apartments by frequenting the area's air-conditioned stores. The elderly were not scared to venture into the busy 26th Street shopping district, with its stores, bakeries, restaurants, and pushcart vendors selling juices and churros. The community's well-financed and socially active churches also provided outreach services, with church members visiting homes and tending to the needs of the elderly.

North Lawndale, by contrast, was a distressed community pockmarked by boarded-up buildings, abandoned lots, and drug dealing on the streets. North Lawndale had few air-conditioned stores for the elderly to frequent in order to escape the blast-furnace conditions of their apartments. The elderly in North Lawndale lived in fear; even in the heat, they were reluctant to open first-floor windows, venture out into the streets, or even unchain the door when municipal officials inquired as to their health. They were afraid to open the door to strangers. Many died in their apartments, behind locked doors and windows bolted shut. Even the churches of North Lawndale exhibited advanced distress; they lacked the membership to provide the home visits and networks of support evident in Little Village.

Both Little Village and North Lawndale are poor neighborhoods, and both suffer serious problems of gang activity. Yet there is a vast difference between the two communities. Continuing immigration gave Little Village a vital street life and an active network of churches. North Lawndale experienced no such immigration and, as a result, suffered an exodus of population that emptied streets, closed stores, and diminished residents' sense of personal safety. Without new arrivals, North Lawndale suffered abandonment and steep decline.

Source: Eric Klinenberg, *Heat Wave: A Social Autopsy of Disaster in Chicago* (Chicago: University of Chicago Press, 2002), chap. 2.

hoods and in Detroit's Mexicantown, migrants can send a part of their paychecks to families back home and return home for frequent visits. Globalization has created **transnational communities**.

The diversity brought by the new immigration is apparent in racial voting patterns. Politics in the contemporary U.S. city does not fall neatly along racial fault lines. Racial "block voting" is undermined as newcomers to a community do not share the same history and political attitudes of longer-term residents. In New York, African Americans and African Caribbeans have not been able to form a sturdy political alliance. The two groups have clashed over just which group is most deserving of the next open council seat or any step up the political ladder.[67]

CONCLUSION: GLOBALIZATION, POWER, AND DEMOCRACY

Confronted by the pressures of globalization, cities emphasize programs aimed at local economic development, slighting social welfare and housing policies that do not help win the competition for business: "Economic pressures can force cities into a competitive mode within which economic goals dominate social goals and locally expressed aspirations succumb to wider forces."[68] Thomas Friedman phrases it even more provocatively, that in the face of global pressures, "Your politics shrinks." Countries and communities put on a "Golden Straightjacket," pursuing wealth by ceding to investor demands and ignoring community and poor-people's needs.[69] Cities offer subsidies and tax abatements in an effort to lure businesses, even though such efforts divert resources away from social policy and other neighborhood goals.

A number of U.S. cities, however, have attempted to break out of the Golden Straightjacket and find more balanced approaches to their future development.[70] In Seattle, neighborhood groups have played a vigilant role in the local arena. Their presence helps to ensure that business interests will not dictate the exact shape of Seattle's postindustrial transformation.[71]

A city can no longer hope to win businesses by relying on a simple strategy of tax cuts and subsidies, as hundreds of competitor communities can offer a prospective firm essentially the same, or even a better, package of benefits.

"Smart" communities do not rely on tax cuts but instead invest heavily in their telecommunications infrastructure, upgrading fiber-optic networks, teleports, and wireless access to the Internet in an effort to improve their competitive position. Rather than cut business taxes across the board, municipalities have begun to see the wisdom of targeting assistance to small businesses and to business start-ups, where the city's favors are likely to make the greatest difference.

Local leaders have begun to see the importance of building on the competitive advantages that exist in a region. No city can reasonably expect to "win" the competition for businesses in all industrial sectors. Rather, cities in a region will likely get better results by seeking to expand an existing industry cluster.

The economic-growth literature underscores the importance of **industry clusters**. A cluster is a group of "linked" or interconnected firms that will tend to locate in the same region as they share specialized supply networks and support services, recruit form the same pool of skilled labor, and benefit by exchanging knowledge with one

Box 3.5
Responding to Globalization:
The Arts- and Technology-Based Strategy of Tacoma, Washington

Tacoma, Washington, has undertaken a renewal strategy that is both technology-oriented and arts-based. Suffering deindustrialization, this old port and lumber city had to find a way to diversify its economic base. The central business district could not compete with suburban retail.

Local planners sought a novel strategy to bring people back to the city by developing the downtown as an arts, cultural, and education center. Planners changed the ambience of the center city, bringing in educational and cultural facilities hospitable to technology-oriented development.

The city revitalized its aging theaters and took advantage of tax credits for the rehabilitation of buildings. The city core became the site of new art galleries. The city redeveloped its downtown waterfront, an area that had become an eyesore and a barrier to new investment. The State of Washington helped by expanding the University of Washington campus in the city and establishing a Technology Institute to aid technology-related businesses. Tacoma Power vigorously sold businesses on the capacity of its new fiber-optic system. Tacoma's arts and education strategy, focused on nonpolluting industries, gained widespread public approval.

Sources: Susan E. Clarke and Gary L. Gaile, *The Work of Cities* (Minneapolis: University of Minnesota Press, 1998); Paul Sommers and Deena Heg, "Spreading the Wealth: Building a Tech Economy in Small and Medium-Sized Regions," a discussion paper prepared for The Brookings Institution Center on Urban and Metropolitan Policy, Washington, DC, October 2003, www.brookings.edu/es/urban/publications/200310_Sommers.htm.

another.[72] Clustering allows the members of an industry to share ideas. This process, known as **knowledge transfer**, underscores the fact that businesses in a region cooperate as well as compete with one another. Knowledge transfer leads to innovation, greater productivity, and spinoffs that further enhance a region's economic competitiveness and growth.

Local universities often serve as a regional economic anchor, providing the research that is critical to the expansion of a high-tech industry in the region. The communities of Silicon Valley, anchored by Stanford University, became the center of computer and software development.[73] Even the economy of California's wine country, concentrated in the Napa, Sonoma, and neighboring valleys, is aided by the work of the viticulture and enology programs of the University of California at Davis.[74]

Industry clusters are "the new engines of metropolitan economies."[75] States, cities, and suburbs must first figure out just what industries they are—and are not—capable of attracting. A region will then enjoy its greatest chance of success when it builds on or seeks to expand an existing local cluster. Interlocal collaboration is essential, as no community has the capacity to build an industry cluster from scratch.[76]

Once "the rubber capital of the world," Akron, Ohio, reversed its long decline by reestablishing its position as a new center of polymer chemistry and technology.

Despite the loss of thousands of manufacturing jobs, the city remains the corporate headquarters of B.F. Goodrich. The University of Akron's nationally ranked polymer science and engineering program supports the city's economic restructuring.[77]

Numerous communities have also seen the wisdom of **investing in human resources**, not just in physical infrastructure. Cities with an educated, technologically competent, and adaptable workforce have the best chances of attracting knowledge-based industry.

Finally, the local quality of life also helps to make a community attractive to both professional workers and high-tech firms.[78] (See Box 3.5, "Responding to Globalization: The Arts- and Technology-Based Strategy of Tacoma, Washington.") Parks, bicycle trails, and quality cultural and entertainment facilities help to attract high-end workers. Cities have also begun to stress **sustainable development**, pursuing only growth that is compatible with environmental values.

Competitive pressures constrain local choices. Yet, no city is the mere prisoner of global economic forces.[79] As we will discuss in Chapter 4, neighborhood groups, inner-city minorities, taxpayer associations, and environmentalists have begun to challenge business-led urban-growth agendas.

NOTES

1. Heather Smith and William Graves, "Gentrification as Corporate Growth Strategy: The Strange Case of Charlotte, North Carolina and the Bank of America," *Journal of Urban Affairs* 127, no. 4 (2005): 403–428.

2. Bruce London, "Gentrification as Urban Reinvasion: Some Preliminary Definitions and Theoretical Considerations," in *Back to the City*, ed. Shirley Bradway Laska and Daphne Spain (New York: Pergamon Press, 1980), 77–92. See also Japonica Brown-Saracino, ed., *The Gentrification Debates: A Reader* (London and New York: Routledge, 2010); and Loretta Lees, Tom Slater, and Elvin Wyly, eds., *The Gentrification Reader* (London and New York: Routledge, 2010).

3. Neil Smith and Peter Williams, "Alternatives to Orthodoxy: Invitation to a Debate," in *Gentrification of the City*, ed. Neil Smith and Peter Williams (Boston: Allen and Unwin, 1986), 1.

4. Jason Hackworth, "Post-Recession Gentrification in New York City," *Urban Affairs Review* 37, no. 6 (2002): 815–843; John J. Betancur, "The Politics of Gentrification: The Case of West Town in Chicago," *Urban Affairs Review* 37, no. 6 (July 2002): 780–814.

5. Neil Smith, "Gentrification Generalized: From Local Anomaly to Urban Regeneration as Global Urban Strategy," paper presented at the conference on Upward Neighbourhood Trajectories: Gentrification in a New Century, Glasgow, Scotland, September 26–27, 2002.

6. Loretta Lees, "A Reappraisal of Gentrification: Towards a 'Geography of Gentrification,'" *Progress in Human Geography* 24, no. 3 (2000): 389–408. See also Hackworth, "Post-Recession Gentrification in New York City"; Betancur, "The Politics of Gentrification."

7. Japonica Brown-Saracino, "Social Preservationists and the Quest for Authentic Community," *City and Community* 3, no. 2 (2004): 135–147. Gentrifiers clearly are not a homogeneous group when it comes to their political attitudes.

8. Brian J.L. Berry, "Islands of Renewal in Seas of Decay," in *The New Urban Reality,* ed. Paul E. Peterson (Washington, DC: Brookings Institution Press, 1985), 72–95.

9. E.K. Wyly and D.J. Hammel, "Islands of Decay in Seas of Renewal: Housing Policy and the Resurgence of Gentrification," *Housing Policy Debate* 10, no. 4 (1999): 711–771. Rowland Atkinson and Gary Bridge, in "Introduction," in *Gentrification in a Global Context: The New Urban Colonialism*, ed. Atkinson and Bridge (New York: Routledge, 2005), 1–17, argue that gentrification is quite widespread and that gentrified neighborhoods are found in cities around the globe.

10. Maureen Kennedy and Paul Leonard, "Dealing with Neighborhood Change: A Primer on Gentrification and Policy Choices," discussion paper prepared for the Brookings Institution Center on Urban and Metropolitan Policy, Washington, DC, 2001, www.brookings.edu/es/urban/gentrification/gentrification.pdf.

11. George C. Galster, Roberto G. Quercia, Alvaro Cortes, and Ron Malega, "The Fortunes of Poor Neighborhoods," *Urban Affairs Review* 39 (November 2003): 205–227.

12. For descriptions and competing perspectives on the gentrification of Harlem and the South Side of Chicago, see: Rivka Gerwitz Little, "The New Harlem," *Village Voice,* September 18–24, 2002; Monique M. Taylor, *Harlem between Heaven and Hell* (Minneapolis: University of Minnesota Press, 2002); Gina M. Pérez, *The Near Northwest Side Story: Migration, Displacement, and Puerto Rican Families* (Berkeley: University of California Press, 2004); Timothy Williams and Tanzina Vega, "As East Harlem Develops, Its Accent Starts to Change," *New York Times*, January 21, 2007; Derek S. Hyra, *The New Urban Renewal: The Economic Transformation of Harlem and Bronzeville* (Chicago: University of Chicago Press, 2008). For a description of the arrival of middle-class blacks in Brooklyn's Clinton Hill neighborhood, see Lance Freeman, *There Goes the 'Hood: Views of Gentrification from the Ground Up* (Philadelphia: Temple University Press, 2006), 40–48.

13. Michelle Boyd, "Defensive Development: The Role of Racial Conflict in Gentrification," *Urban Affairs Review* 43, no. 6 (July 2008): 751–776.

14. Atkinson and Bridge, "Introduction," 4–5, present a brief overview of the pros and cons of gentrification.

15. Daniel Monroe Sullivan, "Reassessing Gentrification: Measuring Residents' Opinions Using Survey Data," *Urban Affairs Review* 42, no. 2 (March 2007): 583–593.

16. Freeman, *There Goes the 'Hood,* esp. 62–74, 92–94, and 190–202.

17. Tom Slater, "The Eviction of Critical Perspectives from Gentrification Research," *International Journal of Urban and Regional Research* 30, no. 4 (December 2006): 737–757; Kathe Newman and Elvin K. Wyly, "The Right to Stay Put, Revisited: Gentrification and Resistance to Displacement in New York City," *Urban Studies* 43, no. 1 (January 2006): 23–57.

18. Betancur, "The Politics of Gentrification."

19. Neil Smith, "New City, New Frontier: The Lower East Side as Wild, Wild West," in *Variations on a Theme Park*, ed. Michael Sorkin (New York: Hill and Wang, 1992), 61–93. See also Neil Smith, *The New Frontier: Gentrification and the Revanchist City* (London: Routledge, 1996).

20. Wyly and Hammel, "Islands of Decay in Seas of Renewal," 716.

21. Mary Pattillo, *Black on the Block: The Politics of Race and Class in the City* (Chicago: University of Chicago Press, 2007), 284.

22. Jamie Peck, "Struggling with the Creative Class," *International Journal of Urban and Regional Research* 29 (December 2005): 740–770.

23. Kennedy and Leonard, "Dealing with Neighborhood Change," 1.

24. Elvin K. Wyly, Norman J. Glickman, and Michael L. Lahr, "A Top 10 List of Things to Know about American Cities," *Cityscape: A Journal of Policy Development and Research* 3, no. 3 (1998): 21.

25. Hackworth, "Post-Recession Gentrification in New York City," 835–838; Betancur, "The Politics of Gentrification," 806–808.

26. Roman A. Cybriwsky, David Ley, and John Western, "The Political and Social Construction of Revitalized Neighborhoods: Society Hill, Philadelphia, and False Creek, Vancouver," in Smith and Williams, *Gentrification of the City*, 119. See also Smith, *The New Frontier*, 119–139.

27. Michael Indergaard, *Silicon Alley: The Rise and Fall of a New Media District* (New York: Routledge, 2004), 26–27, 102–112.

28. Susan J. Popkin, Bruce Katz, Mary K. Cunningham, Karen D. Brown, Jeremy Gustafson, and Margery A. Turner, *A Decade of Hope VI: Research Findings and Policy Challenges* (Washington, DC: Urban Institute and Brookings Institution, 2004), 44–45; Betancur, "The Politics of Gentrification," 790.

29. Betancur, "The Politics of Gentrification," 787–789, 801–803.

30. Joyce Gelb and Michael Lyons, "A Tale of Two Cities: Housing Policy and Gentrification in London and New York," *Journal of Urban Affairs* 15, no. 4 (1993): 345–366.

31. Tony Robinson, "Gentrification and Grassroots Resistance in San Francisco's Tenderloin," *Urban Affairs Review* 30, no. 4 (1995): 483–513.

32. Kennedy and Leonard, "Dealing with Neighborhood Change," 30.

33. Murtaza H. Baxamusa, "Empowering Communities through Deliberation: The Model of Community Benefits Agreements," *Journal of Planning and Education Research* 27, no. 3 (March 2008): 261–276.

34. Christopher Niedt, "Gentrification and the Grassroots: Popular Support in the Revanchist Suburb," *Journal of Urban Affairs* 28, no. 2 (2006): 99–120.

35. Diane K. Levy, Jennifer Comey, and Sandra Padilla, "In the Face of Gentrification," *Journal of Affordable Housing and Community Development Law,* 32–42.

36. Rolf Pendall, "From Hurdles to Bridges: Local Land-Use Regulations and the Pursuit of Affordable Rental Housing," paper prepared for the conference Revisiting Rental Housing: A National Policy Summit, November 2006, www.jchs.harvard.edu/publications/rental/revisiting_rental_symposium/papers/rr07–11_pendall.pdf.

37. Levy, Comey, and Padilla, *In the Face of Gentrification*, 59–82.

38. The ranking of global cities that is described in the paragraphs that follow draws on the work of Paul K. Knox, "Globalization and Urban Economic Change," *Annals of the American Academy of Political and Social Science* (May 1997), 22–23. See also Anthony M. Orum and Kiangming Chen, *The World of Cities* (Oxford: Blackwell, 2003), 98–99.

39. Peter J. Taylor and Robert E. Lang, "U.S. Cities in the 'World Cities Network,'" report of the Brookings Institution Survey Series, February 2005, www.brookings.edu/~/media/Files/rc/reports/2005/02cities_taylor/20050222_worldcities.pdf. Taylor and Land rank U.S. cities solely according to their global connectivity. Their hierarchy, as a result, differs slightly from the tiers of rankings of global cities presented in this chapter.

40. Charles S. Suchar, "The Physical Transformation of Metropolitan Chicago," in *The New Chicago: A Social and Cultural Analysis,* ed. John P. Koval et al. (Philadelphia: Temple University Press, 2006), 56–76.

41. Thomas L. Friedman, *The Lexus and the Olive Tree: Understanding Globalization* (New York: Anchor Books, 2000), 13–14, 112–142.

42. Indergaard, *Silicon Alley.*

43. Saskia Sassen, *The Global City*, 2d ed. (Princeton, NJ: Princeton University Press, 2001), 294–300.

44. Hank V. Savitch and Paul Kantor, *Cities in the International Marketplace: The Political Economy of Urban Development in North America and Western Europe* (Princeton, NJ: Princeton University Press, 2002), 14–15.

45. William J. Mitchell and Anthony M. Townsend, "Cyborg Agonistes: Disaster and Reconstruction in the Digital Electronic Era," in *The Resilient City: How Cities Recover from Disaster,* ed. Lawrence J. Vale and Thomas J. Campanella (New York: Oxford University Press, 2005), 313–334.

46. Randy Shilts, *And the Band Played On: Politics, People, and the AIDS Epidemic* (New York: St. Martin's Press, 1987).

47. Joel Kotkin, *The New Geography: How the Digital Revolution Is Reshaping the American Landscape* (New York: Random House, 2000), 9.

48. Leonard I. Ruchelman, *Cities in the Third Wave: The Technological Transformation of Urban America* (Chicago: Burnham, 2000), 91.

49. Matt Richtel, "In Utah, Public Works Project in Digital," *New York Times,* November 17, 2003.

50. Robert Atkinson and Howard Wial, "The Implications of Service Offshoring for Metropolitan Economies," report of the Brookings Institution's Metro Economy Series, February 2007, www.brookings.edu/~/media/Files/rc/reports/2007/02cities_atkinson/20070131_offshoring.pdf.

51. Brookings Institution, "Phoenix in Focus: A Profile from Census 2000," Washington, DC,

November 2003, www.brookings.edu/reports/2003/11_livingcities_Phoenix.aspx; Audrey Singer and Jill H. Wilson, "The Impact of the Great Recession on Metropolitan Immigration Trends," report of the Brookings Institution, Washington, DC, December 2010, www.brookings.edu/~/media/Files/rc/papers/2010/1216_immigration_singer_wilson/1216_immigration_singer_wilson.pdf.

52. Nancy Foner, "Introduction: New Immigrants in a New New York," in *New Immigrants in New York*, ed. Foner (New York: Columbia University Press, 2001), 1.

53. Min Zhou, "Chinese: Divergent Destinies in Immigrant New York," in Foner, *New Immigrants in New York,* 152–167.

54. Yvonne M. Lau, "Chicago's Chinese Americans: From Chinatown and Beyond," in Koval et al., *The New Chicago,* 168–181.

55. James M. Lindsay and Audrey Singer, "Changing Faces: Immigrants and Diversity in the Twenty-First Century," in *Agenda for the Nation*, ed. Henry J. Aaron, James M. Lindsay, and Pietro S. Nivola (Washington, DC: Brookings Institution Press, 2003), esp. 217–225; Ellen Percy Kraly and Ines Miyares, "Immigration to New York: Policy, Population, and Patterns," in Foner, *New Immigrants in New York*, 33–43.

56. Robert C. Smith, "Mexicans: Social, Educational, Economic, and Political Problems and Prospects in New York," in Foner, *New Immigrants in New York*, 280.

57. Richard C. Jones, ed., *Immigrants Outside Megalopolis: Ethnic Transformation in the Heartland* (Lanham, MD: Lexington Books, 2008).

58. See the November 2003 reports of the *Living Cities Project: Denver in Focus: A Profile from Census 2000; Kansas City in Focus: A Profile from Census 2000*, both published in Washington, DC, by the Brookings Institution.

59. Jeremy Hein, *Ethnic Origins: The Adaptation of Cambodian and Hmong Refugees in Four American Cities* (New York: Russell Sage Foundation, 2006); Karl Byrand, "The Quest for Home: Sheboygan's Hmong Population," in Jones, *Immigrants Outside Megalopolis*, 189–211.

60. Janet L. Abu-Lughod, *New York, Chicago, Los Angeles: America's Global Cities* (Minneapolis: University of Minnesota Press, 1999), 374; Karin Aguilar-San Juan, "Staying Vietnamese: Community and Place in Orange County and Boston," *City and Community* 4, no. 1 (March 2005): 37–65; Madhulika S. Khandelwal, *Becoming an American, Being Indian: An Immigrant Community in New York City* (Ithaca, NY: Cornell University Press, 2002), 20–21 and 56.

61. Padma Rangaswamy, "Asian Indians in Chicago," in Koval et al., *The New Chicago*, 130–131.

62. Franklin J. James, Jeff A. Romine, and Peter E. Zwanzig, "The Effects of Immigration on Urban Communities," *Cityscape: A Journal of Policy Development and Research* 3, no. 1 (1998): 174–176; Abu-Lughod, *New York, Chicago, Los Angeles,* 413.

63. U.S. Census Bureau, *2007 American Community Survey*, Table 41.

64. Saskia Sassen, *Cities in a World Economy*, 3d ed. (Thousand Oaks, CA: Pine Forge Press, 2006), chap. 6.

65. John P. Koval and Kenneth Fidal, "Chicago: The Immigrant Capital of the Heartland," in Koval et al., *The New Chicago*, 102.

66. Jerome Straughan and Pierrette Hondagneu-Sotelo, "From Immigrants in the City, to Immigrant City," in *From Chicago to L.A.: Making Sense of Urban Theory*, ed. Michael J. Dear (Thousand Oaks, CA: Sage, 2002), 199–203, here 201.

67. Reuel R. Rogers, "Race-Based Coalitions Among Minority Groups: Afro-Caribbean Immigrants and African-Americans in New York City," *Urban Affairs Review* 39, no. 3 (January 2004): 283–317.

68. Robin Hambleton, Hank V. Savitch, and Murray Stewart, "Globalism and Local Democracy," in *Globalism and Local Democracy: Challenge and Change in Europe and North America*, ed. Hambleton, Savitch , and Stewart (London: Palgrave Macmillan, 2003).

69. Friedman, *The Lexus and the Olive Tree*, 104–106; see also Friedman's discussion, pp. 13–14 and 112–142.

70. Susan E. Clarke and Gary L. Gaile, "Local Politics in a Global Era: Thinking Globally, Acting Locally," *Annals of the American Academy of Political and Social Science* 551 (May 1997): 28–43; idem, *The Work of Cities* (Minneapolis: University of Minnesota Press, 1998), 107–214.

71. Mark Purcell, *Recapturing Democracy: Neoliberalization and the Struggle for Alternative Urban Futures* (New York: Routledge, 2008), 109–152.

72. Michael E. Porter, *The Competitive Advantage of Nations* (New York: Free Press, 1990); idem, "Location, Competition, and Economic Development: Local Clusters in a Global Economy," *Economic Development Quarterly* 14, no. 1 (2000): 15–34; Yasuyuki Motoyama, "What Was New about Cluster Theory? What Could It Answer and What Could It Not Answer?" *Economic Development Quarterly* 22, no. 4 (2008): 353–363.

73. Martin Kenney, ed., *Understanding Silicon Valley: The Anatomy of an Entrepreneurial Region* (Palo Alto, CA: Stanford University Press, 2000).

74. Porter, "Location, Competition, and Economic Development," 17.

75. Robert J. Stimson, Roger R. Stough, and Brian H. Roberts, *Regional Economic Development: Analysis and Planning Strategy*, 2d ed. (Berlin and New York: Springer, 2006), 252.

76. Mark Muro and Bruce Katz, "The New 'Cluster Moment': How Regional Innovation Clusters Can Foster the Next Economy," report of the Brookings Institution, Washington, DC, September 2010, www.brookings.edu/~/media/Files/rc/papers/2010/0921_clusters_muro_katz/0921_clusters_muro_katz.pdf.

77. Larry Ledebur and Jill Taylor, "Akron, Ohio: A Restoring Prosperity Case Study," report of the Metropolitan Policy Program of the Brookings Institution, Washington, DC, September 2008, www.brookings.edu/~/media/Files/rc/reports/2007/05metropolitanpolicy_vey/200809_Akron.pdf.

78. Kotkin, *The New Geography*, 7.

79. Savitch and Kantor, *Cities in the International Marketplace*, 313–345, esp. 344–345.

Who Has the Power?

Decision Making, Economic Development, and Urban Regimes

How democratic are U.S. cities and suburbs? To whom does local government respond?

A simple review of the actions of city officials—mayors, managers, and council members—will not provide a meaningful answer to these questions. We must also look "behind the scenes" to determine the extent to which off-stage actors influence the decisions made by municipal officials.

MOVING BEYOND THE "POWER ELITE VERSUS PLURALISM" DEBATES

For too many years, two schools of thought dominated the debate over urban power. **Power elite** theorists argued that big business and other behind-the-scenes notables effectively controlled the local arena. City council votes and other decisions made by public officials merely affirmed courses of action that had already been decided in private. The power elite theory perceives the local arena as highly undemocratic, as essentially closed to competing voices.[1] Popular commentary, including movies like *Roger and Me*, continues to portray corporate chief executive officers (CEOs) as having a fateful hold on local affairs. (See Box 4.1, "Urban Films—A Corporate Power Elite: *Roger and Me*.")

For much of their history, Sunbelt communities were dominated by established families and powerful local merchants. Throughout the early and mid-twentieth century, a "commercial-civic elite" effectively ruled many Sunbelt cities. Local politics reflected "the close relationship between the private economic community and the public decision-making community."[2] Business-led civic associations, including the Citizen's Charter Association in Dallas, the Good Government League in San Antonio, and the Phoenix 40, guided local affairs. In Houston, the borderline between business and government was not even easily discernible. Oscar Holcombe, a real estate dealer and developer, served twenty-two years as mayor. The city's planning commission was populated by developers and appointees with ties to the real estate

Box 4.1
Urban Films—Corporate Power Elite: *Roger and Me*

Michael Moore's "guerilla" documentary, *Roger and Me* (1989) provides a clear statement of the power that corporate elites wield in a city's affairs. Moore, a native of Flint, Michigan, traces the decline of his beloved city as it passed from an auto factory worker's paradise to a destitute city marred by joblessness, extensive poverty, housing foreclosures, evictions, and property abandonment. Moore points to the villains he sees as responsible for Flint's decline: General Motors (GM) and its then-CEO Roger Smith, who closed automobile plants in the city while shifting production to low-wage plants in Mexico and overseas. Thousands of workers in Flint lost their jobs as a result of plant closings.

Moore shows Smith as accountable to his stockholders, not to the people of Flint. Smith and other corporate executives do not even possess the civic loyalty once exhibited by a previous generation of homegrown managers. Instead the new executive elite work in security-guarded corporate boardrooms and play in private clubs; they have lost all meaningful contact with the people of Flint and their daily lives and sufferings. Moore contrasts scenes of Smith and other GM leaders as they celebrate the Christmas season with pictures of a poor Flint family in the process of eviction because they can no longer pay the rent.

Moore's message is clear, albeit lacking in nuance and very one-sided. The people have no meaningful control over what happens in Flint. The decisions made by Smith and other corporate boardroom leaders have doomed the city and its hard-working people.

industry.[3] Houston's priorities reflected those of its business community: the city sought to provide the physical infrastructure necessary for growth while keeping tax rates and social service provision to a minimum.

Clearly, major businesses are powerful actors in the city arena. Still, power elite theory does not provide an accurate description of power relations in most cities. The adherents of a competing school of thought, **pluralism**, point to the many flaws and overstatements of power elite theory. The pluralists do not contend that city politics is perfectly fair and democratic. Still, the pluralists observe that local political systems are not closed but are open to a diversity of (that is to "plural") voices and interests. Even racial minorities and the poor are not shut out. Instead, they, like other groups, have the ability to organize, vote, and be "effectively heard," that is, to gain a meaningful response when situations prompt them to action.[4]

The pluralists also argue, quite correctly, that the business community in a city is seldom a unified or monolithic group capable of overbearing action. Different factions in the business community have different interests. Center-city merchants may support the construction of a new downtown sports arena or convention center, an expensive course of action that will likely be opposed by business owners from other parts of the city who do not wish to pay higher taxes to support a development agenda that provides them no direct benefit.[5]

Globalization has further served to pluralize or diversify a city's business community. San Jose and Charlotte are examples of cities where multinational firms have brought in managers from the outside who did not share the perspective of local leaders.[6] The corporate managers of a multinational firm often stay in a city on a short-term basis. They do not have the depth of experience in, and commitment to, the city that locally-rooted business leaders so often possess. The results of a national survey of corporate CEOs underscore their lack of local engagement:

> [L]ocal executives are now less engaged in civic life, are rotating cities more frequently and consequently less knowledgeable about their communities, and possess less autonomy to make local civic and financial commitments.[7]

The new national and global managers do not always have the interest, time, or willingness to take charge of municipal affairs. Contrary to elite theory, businesses do not form a cohesive block, nor do corporate leaders always possess a willingness to take an active part in local affairs.

In Sunbelt cities, dramatic demographic changes have altered traditional patterns of power. The growth of the Latino population, coupled with the heightened activism of racial minorities, middle-class homeowners, taxpayer associations, and environmentalists, have presented new challenges to elite rule by powerful business interests.[8]

Yet, pluralism, too, provides a sorely deficient interpretation of local politics. The local political system is not nearly as open as the pluralists contend. The poor are not "effectively heard," as municipal officials can ignore their demands and even outwait protest action that is difficult to sustain over time.[9] While local political systems are not closed and business leaders cannot simply dictate to a city, nonetheless the local agenda is heavily tilted toward business needs. Business possesses an influence in local affairs that is quite a bit more extensive than pluralists admit.

Even activist, progressive mayors cannot be insensitive to the concerns of the local business community. Business leaders hold the keys, determining investments that are critical to the success of major development projects and a city's financial well-being.

Business, then, is not simply one of a number of contending pluralist groups. Even though corporate leaders cannot simply dictate to city hall, business interests occupy a special place in the local arena.

"CITY LIMITS": ECONOMIC COMPETITION SHAPES LOCAL POLITICS

ECONOMIC COMPETITION: THE ROOTS OF CITY LIMITS

Why is it that cities give so much respect to business needs even when there is no small cabal of business leaders with the power to manipulate city decision making from offstage? Paul Peterson, in his important book *City Limits*, articulates one possible explanation.[10] According to Peterson, business influence in the local arena is the product of the **mobility of capital**. The owners of a business can locate their facilities in another town or state. Municipal officials, fearing the loss of a city's job and tax base, will take whatever actions are necessary to attract businesses in an effort to ensure the city's economic and fiscal health. Business leaders threaten to locate facilities elsewhere in order to leverage substantial tax abatements and other municipal subsidies and considerations.

Business leaders are not concerned with every aspect of municipal affairs. In some areas, local officials can freely act without considering the concerns of business. Peterson argues that businesses are primarily concerned with **developmental policy**, those municipal decisions that directly affect business investment and growth. Municipalities tend to provide subsidies, land-use plans, and the roads and physical infrastructure improvements as demanded by business. Each suburb or city strives to maintain the reputation for being a place that is "good for business."

Redistributive policy, which encompasses social welfare, health, housing, and other programs of assistance to the poor, is also important to business, as it indirectly affects the city's business climate. Generous social welfare spending will require tax levels that businesses do not wish to bear. Consequently, municipal officials face a harsh set of constraints when they examine the possibilities of providing more extensive housing and social benefits to people in need of assistance:

> [T]he pursuit of a city's economic interests, which requires an efficient provision of local services, makes no allowance for the care of the needy and unfortunate members of the society. Indeed, the competition among local communities all but precludes a concern for redistribution.[11]

For Peterson, New York City's mid-1970s flirtation with bankruptcy underscores the disastrous consequences that can result when a municipality ignores "**city limits**" and imposes a high level of taxes to fund a broad range of social welfare and housing programs.

Still, large portions of municipal action are of no real concern to business. Business leaders have no direct concern with **allocational policy**, decisions that deal with how a city distributes various services—such as fire stations or library books and computer facilities—throughout its neighborhoods. In the allocational arena, a city is free to act in response to the demands of citizens, as decisions do not really affect a city's standing with the business community.

WHY CITIES BUILD NEW SPORTS STADIUMS

Intercity competition and a city's concern for its "business climate" help to explain why local authorities are willing to use taxpayer money to help build new sports arenas with luxury skyboxes. Local authorities often sign stadium deals that give the team owner generous tax abatements and allow sports franchises to retain the revenues from stadium-naming rights, parking, and other concessions. Team owners secure these generous terms by pointing to the "better deal" that they can obtain from other cities. The results, too often, are legally binding contracts that are extremely one-sided. Such contracts leave the local taxpayer, not the team owners, "on the hook" when a project fails to pay for itself.

Cincinnati area voters found that they still had to provide sizable subsidies for the construction of the city's riverfront football and baseball stadiums, even at a time when public school budgets and the funding of public services were experiencing sharp cutbacks. A decade earlier, citizens in Cincinnati and Hamilton County had voted to increase the local sales tax in order to fund two new stadiums. To help gain voter approval, the measure also contained the promise of additional funding for local schools. But when the economy declined and the sales tax failed to deliver the revenues that stadium backers had projected, it was only the public schools and county services—and not the stadium subsidies—that were placed in jeopardy. The subsidies given the stadium could not be touched even though deep cutbacks were being made in service provision throughout the county. The one-sided contract that public officials had earlier signed even barred the county from placing a tax on stadium tickets, parking, and concessions, revenue sources that the local government could have used to help defray the costs of its obligations.[12]

When faced with the possible threat of losing a sports franchise, municipal action can be embarrassingly quick. In the late 1990s, Ross Perot Jr., then-majority owner of the Dallas Mavericks basketball team, began aerial tours with suburban officials to explore possible sites for a new arena. The City of Dallas immediately responded by sweetening its own offer for the construction of a downtown facility.[13]

Cities continue to provide financing for new stadiums and arenas despite evidence that such investments are a very expensive and inefficient way to create new jobs.[14] Why do most cities pursue such an unwise investment? It is not just that local officials fear the wrath of fans if a team leaves town. A city also gains prestige from hosting a major sports franchise, a presence that tells the global business community that the city itself is "major league" and worthy of big-league investment. New stadiums provide "intangible benefits," adding to community pride and refashioning the image of a city so that it will be more attractive to business.[15] The loss of a sports franchise, in contrast, signals the decline of a city, jeopardizing future investment.

Not all stadium deals are bad for a city. Cities like Indianapolis show that there can be "major league winners," that a city can invest in sports facilities as part of a strategic plan to raise the profile of a city and increase its economic competitiveness. In San Diego, public authorities and sports team owners formed a public–private partnership to share the costs of constructing a new downtown ballpark for the Padres.[16] Petco Park helped to kick off a resurgence of investment in the surrounding neighborhood.

Even though it is often portrayed as a model of success, the San Diego ballpark deal has also been the subject of intense criticism. Taxpayers paid the up-front costs of the stadium, but the contract terms gave the private developers—not the public—the ability to control land uses and development in, and reap the benefits from, the surrounding twenty-six-block Ballpark Village development area. The developers scaled back their earlier promise to build affordable housing. The developers also built a smaller green park than the one that was envisioned when the project was brought before voters. The city's share of the project's costs also increased, as the development did not yield the tax revenues that the project's backers had projected.[17]

State authorities have also stepped in to enable the completion of stadium projects in instances where local governments or voters denied funds for a stadium project. In Chicago, Cleveland, Milwaukee, Phoenix, Pittsburgh, San Jose, and Seattle, the respective state governments set up independent special authorities to formulate creative arrangements to provide the funding for a stadium project after local voters had previously turned down funding measures. The state's interest was in economic development; the concerns of local groups opposed to stadium development were given much less consideration.[18]

Our quick review of new sports stadium development is consistent with Peterson's theory. Municipal officials fear that the loss of a sports team can adversely affect a city's image. Public officials often prove responsive to demands of team owners, overriding the opposition of neighborhood and taxpayer groups. When local officials prove too responsive to antigrowth forces and in cases where local voters reject stadium funding measures, state officials step in to create new public entities with the authority to get the project back on track.

Seattle is the rare exception, a city where citizens are so concerned with project affordability, environmental protection, and neighborhood preservation that voters said "No!" to the owners of a National Basketball Association team, leading the team to move to Oklahoma City. In Minnesota, the state legislature and voters had exhibited similar reluctance over the years to fund a number of sports arena projects. But Minnesota soon rejoined the urban mainstream, finally agreeing to help pay for the construction of Target Field for the baseball Twins, but without the expensive retractable roof that the team owners had initially sought.[19]

Do Local Officials Possess Greater Freedom to Act than Peterson Admits?

Peterson points to the constraints that interlocal competition imposes on urban decision making, leading city and suburban leaders to give primacy to economic development agendas. Yet, critics charge that Peterson overstates his case, especially in his contention that local leaders must keep taxes low and disdain major welfare, health, and social and housing policy initiatives in order to maintain a city's attractiveness to business.

A strategy of tax cuts and reduced social services provides one possible route for attracting new investment. But it is not the only route that local leaders can choose.

In fact, the promise of tax cuts may no longer provide a winning local strategy. Firms do not always look favorably on low-tax, low-service communities. "Knowledge" firms prefer communities that offer the quality schools and community amenities that can attract a skilled and technologically capable labor force. Rather than keep taxes low, municipalities may find that continued investment in public education, job training programs, and ample parks and recreational activities may actually have a positive influence on economic development.[20]

Peterson also overstates the ability of businesses to pick up and leave a community. Not every business is freely able to relocate to whatever community offers the most advantageous package of tax reductions and other subsidies. Numerous studies show that tax rates are *not* the number one factor in a business-siting decision. Businesses give greater consideration to the transportation infrastructure, the quality of the local labor force, and accessibility of a site to suppliers and markets.[21] A business may also be hesitant to uproot families, as a geographical move may lead to the loss of top executives.

If businesses are not always free to move, cities may have more bargaining room than Peterson avers and civic leaders imagine. Cities and suburbs can pursue subsidized housing, health care, education, and social services without having to worry that every such action will lead to the outmigration of business.

REGIME THEORY: GETTING THINGS DONE BY BUILDING GOVERNING COALITIONS

Clarence Stone asks, "Why, when all of their actions are taken into account, do officials over the long haul seem to favor upper-strata interests, disfavor lower-strata interests, and sometimes act in apparent disregard of the contours of electoral power?"[22] For Stone, the answer lies in the dependence of municipal leaders on private business to get things done. Private business leaders may not be able to dictate to a city, but their cooperation is nonetheless needed if a mayor and other public officials are going to be successful in their own development plans for the city. Ultimately, business leaders possess the final say, deciding if they will invest in a city's downtown, participate in a neighborhood renewal program, and establish mentoring programs for at-risk youth. In these and a great many other policy areas, the decisions made by private actors can act to further—or to frustrate—city objectives.

City officials and private business leaders do not always share the same perspectives. At times, they may even vigorously oppose each other on salient public issues. Yet, despite any frictions that may arise, public officials and private business leaders sooner or later recognize that they need one another. The city cannot prosper and get important things done without the cooperation of corporate leaders. In some cities, business cooperation is so crucial to the success of public projects that the business community can be seen to possess **preemptive power**.[23] In other words, their reluctance to cooperate can effectively doom a civic project. Business officials, in turn, find that they require government approval and subsidies for many of their plans. As a result, in many cities, private and public officials forge a working relationship that enables each to achieve more of their objectives.

THE IMPORTANCE OF GOVERNING COALITIONS

According to Clarence Stone, *power* is not simply the control of A over B; rather, **power** denotes the ability to get things done. As we have just noted, public and private actors often find that they need each other and that it is in their mutual interest to work together to get things done. As a result, informal governing alliances often emerge in a city over time. The long-term, informal public-private governing arrangement that can be found in many cities is known as an *urban regime*.

A **governing regime** exists when an informal public–private alliance, based on mutual cooperation, carries over from one administration to the next. Regime theory points to the importance of looking at **governance**, not just at election results and who holds formal positions of authority in the city: Just whose cooperation is essential to get important things done?

The members of a city's governing regime may be quite different from the electoral coalition that put the mayor and city council into office. Once in office, a mayor must reach out beyond his or her electoral base to forge a working alliance with whoever has the resources necessary to help carry his plans to fruition. A city's governing coalition frequently includes actors who were not enthusiastic supporters of the mayor during the previous election. Regime theory points to the importance of looking beyond election results when seeking to assess just who governs a city.

The mere election of an African American or Latino mayor and council does not guarantee that a city's government will be capable of pursuing policies that will work to the advantage of the city's African American, Hispanic, and poor populations. Instead, black and Latino mayors often find that they must reach an accommodation with business officials who control investment resources critical to the city's future health.[24]

In Atlanta, the city's black majority has dominated municipal elections. Uninformed observers too quickly rushed to the conclusion that *Black Power* had displaced the old civic business elite that once ran the city. A closer examination of decision making in Atlanta, however, reveals that local business leaders were still able to maintain their privileged position in the biracial regime that governed Atlanta. (See Box 4.2, "Atlanta's Biracial Governing Regime.")

Different Regime Types

As we have already observed, the business community typically enjoys a privileged position in most cities. Said another way, corporate-oriented governing regimes are the norm in most big cities.

Broadly speaking, there are three basic types of local governing regimes.[25] A **corporate regime** (also called a **development regime**) reflects the growth-oriented policies preferred by major businesses, slighting equity concerns and programs that would provide assistance to a city's more distressed neighborhoods. In a great many suburbs, too, the local agenda reflects the growth-oriented policies preferred by real estate and development interests.

Not all cities and suburbs, however, aggressively pursue growth. Especially in smaller and medium-size communities, a **caretaker regime** (also called a **maintenance regime**) may be reluctant to make the financial commitments to support large-scale development projects. In the caretaker city, the small-business community and homeowners join together to oppose projects that require tax increases and that will disrupt established patterns of local life. Caretaker regimes focus on the provision of routine services, not the initiation of major renewal and development projects. In well-off bedroom suburbs, caretaker regimes seek to keep taxes low and bar development that will add to local congestion and bring new populations to the community.[26]

The least commonly found governing arrangement is the **progressive regime** committed to advancing the interests of a city's lower- and middle-class residents and homeowners.

Box 4.2
Atlanta's Biracial Governing Regime

For most of the mid- and late 1900s, Atlanta was governed by a biracial regime, an alliance between local businessmen and the leaders of the city's middle-class African American community. In this city of the Deep South, while the two groups did not always see eye to eye, they nonetheless found mutual advantages in working together.

The existence of an informal, biracial alliance helps to explain why Atlanta, amid the civil rights turmoil of the 1950s and 1960s, responded with more moderation and less racial violence than did other southern cities. The city's downtown merchants worked with leaders of the middle-class African American community to avoid protest marches and civil unrest. Atlanta proclaimed itself to be the "City Too Busy to Hate." Downtown merchants did not want the sort of conflict that would scare off customers and tarnish the city's good-place-for-business image.[1]

In more recent decades, Atlanta has gained a black mayor and a black majority on the city council. Yet, the business community has been able to maintain a position of influence despite the change in governing officials. The city's first black mayors, Maynard Jackson (elected in 1973) and Andrew Young (1981), recognized the importance of working with the city's business community.

Maynard Jackson was a political outsider who at first challenged Atlanta's traditional system of elite-led accommodation. Much to the horror of white business leaders, Jackson insisted on strong affirmative-action hiring policies, including that 20 percent of the contracts on development projects be awarded to minority firms. He also reformed the police department.

Many business leaders greatly disliked Jackson, but recognized that they had to maintain a working relationship with city hall. Jackson, in turn, discovered that he could not afford to dismiss the business community, that he needed their assistance and cooperation. Despite initial antagonism, the mayor and the local business elite eventually reached an accommodation. The city approved the construction of a new international airport, the business community's number-one priority. In return, they accepted the affirmative-action requirements in hiring and contracting that Jackson had demanded. As part of the accommodation he reached with business leaders, Mayor Jackson backed off from his earlier commitment to neighborhood-oriented planning. He also opposed the wage increases demanded by municipal labor unions.

Andrew Young, Jackson's successor, was even more supportive of economic growth and biracial governance. Young enthusiastically backed the business community's effort to bring the 1996 Summer Olympics to Atlanta. The concerns of black neighborhood groups were largely ignored, as the city demolished homes and small businesses in a low-income section of town, clearing the area for a new park that was to serve as a gathering place for visitors to the Olympic games. Construction of a new ballpark (which, after the Olympic games, became the home of the Atlanta Braves) commenced despite protests regarding the displacement of inner-city homeowners and the homeless.[2] The mayors who succeeded Jackson and Young—Bill Campbell, Shirley Franklin, and Kasmin Reed—all similarly sought to forge a working partnership between the city and local business leaders.[3]

(continued)

Box 4.2 *(continued)*

As this brief review reveals, for much of its contemporary history, a biracial coalition in Atlanta coalesced around economic development projects of mutual interest. At times, severe tensions marred the working relationship. Globalization weakened the partnerships, as corporate managers newly assigned to Atlanta have not built the levels of trust essential to maintaining a smooth alliance with local black leaders. The African American community has also splintered, with representatives from the city's poor neighborhoods calling into question the policy commitments of the city's large black professional community.

Atlanta's biracial regime has evolved. It no longer possesses the ability to guide the city to the extent it did in the past.[4]

[1]Clarence N. Stone, *Regime Politics—Governing Atlanta: 1946–88* (Lawrence: University of Kansas Press, 1989), esp. 77–159.

[2]Drew Whitelegg, "Going for the Gold: Atlanta's Bid for Fame," *International Journal of Urban and Regional Research* 24, no. 4 (2000): 801–817, esp. 806 and 810.

[3]Cynthia Horan, "Racializing Urban Regimes," *Journal of Urban Affairs* 24, no. 1 (2002): 25–27; Harvey K. Newman, "Race and the Tourist Bubble in Downtown Atlanta," *Urban Affairs Review* 37, no. 3 (January 2002): 301–302; Matthew J. Burbank, Charles H. Heying, and Greg Andranovich, "Antigrowth Politics or Piecemeal Resistance? Citizen Opposition to Olympic-Related Economic Growth," *Urban Affairs Review* 35, no. 3 (January 2000): 334–357; Matthew J. Burbank, Gregory D. Andranovich, and Charles H. Heying, *Olympic Dreams: The Impact of Mega-events on Local Politics* (Boulder, CO: Lynne Rienner, 2001); Larry Keating, *Atlanta: Race, Class and Urban Expansion* (Philadelphia, PA: Temple University Press, 2001).

[4]Clarence Stone and Carol Pierannunzi, "Atlanta's Biracial Coalition in Transition," paper presented at the annual meeting of the Americ\an Political Science Association, Washington, DC, August 31–September 3, 2000.

In a progressive regime, nonprofit entities, community-based organizations, community development corporations (CDCs), and nonprofit organizations have access to city hall that is more normally the preserve of business and development interests.[27]

There are actually two variants of the progressive regime: a **middle-class progressive regime** represents the concerns of environmentalists and homeowners opposed to the costs and ecological damage inflicted by growth projects. The second type of progressive regime, a **regime devoted to lower-class opportunity expansion**, does not similarly emphasize environmental preservation and a slow-growth agenda. Instead, such a progressive regime seeks to steer job development and targeted assistance to a city's poorer neighborhoods.

Progressive coalitions built around resource redistribution are politically unstable. The progressive coalition often withers because middle-class homeowners, environmentalists, and minority activists do not share a common agenda. Progressive regimes also lose support when voters, in hard times, demand local policies for economic growth and job creation.

Harold Washington, the first African American to be elected mayor in Chicago, embraced a program of neighborhood equity and empowerment.[28] Mayor Washington held his lower-class-opportunity coalition together through the force of his own charisma and leadership skills. But when Washington died in office, the progressive regime in Chicago dissolved. The election and long tenure of Richard M. Daley marked the return of growth coalition interests to city hall.[29]

Boston's progressive regime was similarly short-lived. In 1983, community activists helped to elect the self-styled progressive Raymond Flynn as mayor. Flynn was committed to growth restrictions, affordable housing, and job training for the poor. But faced with a national economic recession and federal aid cutbacks, Flynn in the 1990s—and his successor, Thomas Menino—soon gave renewed priority to growth as opposed to neighborhood projects.[30] African American activists accused both mayors, especially Menino, of co-opting black influence while failing to challenge the racial hierarchy of Boston politics.[31]

Some cities have no governing regime or stable governing alliance. With no effectively organized working coalition, such cities often lack the capacity to get important things done. In mid-century Milwaukee, continuing frictions between the municipal officials and downtown business leaders thwarted efforts to revitalize the city's declining downtown.[32] In New Orleans, the failed response to Hurricane Katrina revealed that the city had no set of stable working relationships to assure effective disaster preparedness. The lack of long-standing cooperative relations between the city, suburban officials, and private and nonprofit providers impeded the development of an emergency ride-sharing program to evacuate the city's car-less poor, and the provision of food, water, and medicine to people trapped in the city.[33] There was no governing regime in New Orleans.

THE TRANSFORMATION OF SAN FRANCISCO: POLITICAL POWER AND LOCAL ECONOMIC DEVELOPMENT

Modern San Francisco would seem to be the perfect example of a pluralist city open to emergent political voices, including environmentalists, neighborhood activists, Chinese Americans, African Americans, Hispanics, and gays and lesbians. In 2011, an Asian American was selected to serve as mayor, filling out the term of Gavin Newsom who was elected as California's Lieutenant Governor. Clearly, no business elite controls modern San Francisco. Over the years, the city gained national attention for having enacted numerous growth-control measures over the objections of development interests.

Yet, such a pluralist assessment seriously understates the influence of progrowth forces. As a brief review of contemporary San Francisco reveals, activist neighborhood groups have won numerous victories, but corporate influence is still evident in the major development projects that have altered the face of the city.

The construction of the Yerba Buena Center, a large development project centered around the new Moscone Convention Center, was advanced "by the city's ruling forces to expand the city's downtown boundaries" across Market Street into the low-income South of Market area. The project contained important cultural facilities. It entailed much more than a mere convention center. Yet, the overwhelming purpose of the project was to lure businesses and visitors to San Francisco and, more specifically, to generate new hotel, office, and residential development in the warehouse area lying just south of the city's central business district.

The Manhattanization of San Francisco: The Transamerica Pyramid and the New Downtown. Copyright © Jesse Garcia. http://commons.wikimedia.org/wiki/File:San_Francisco_skyline_-a.jpg.

The project failed to deliver the full number of jobs that the city's growth coalition had predicted. Growth advocates also glossed over the project's displacement of 723 businesses and 7,600 jobs. Rising land values and rents led to further displacement in the surrounding areas. Even the operation of the convention center did not prove to be self-sustaining; instead, city taxpayers had to provide the center with annual subsidies.[34]

Mayor Dianne Feinstein, who would later be elected to the U.S. Senate, gave the project her endorsement. She argued that economic growth was good for the city. She also had a campaign war chest that "came primarily from downtown corporations and big business."[35]

Grassroots neighborhood and environmental groups objected to the "Manhattanization" of their city. Antigrowth forces were able to scale back development projects,

Yerba Buena Gardens and Center, San Francisco. This major urban redevelopment project extended the city's downtown into the South of Market neighborhood, opening an area of old warehouses and low-income housing to new corporate and convention-related development. Courtesy of Sebastian Wallroth through Wikimedia Commons. http://commons.wikimedia.org/wiki/File:San_Francisco_Yerba_Buena_Gardens_006.jpg.

limit building heights, control rents, restrict condominium conversion, and protect much of the city's stock of low-income residential hotels. Yet, as the construction of the Yerba Buena project reveals, despite the antigrowth measures, the corporate-led transformation of the city continued.

Community groups seemed to gain control of city hall when, in 1987, they helped elect a mayor, Art Agnos, who promised to protect the city's neighborhoods from unfettered development. Agnos was a progressive who, in office, "turned over the keys of City Hall to people who in the past often had the door slammed in their face."[36] Yet Agnos soon disappointed many of his grassroots supporters by endorsing a number of growth projects favored by business elites, including new waterfront development and the construction of a downtown ballpark for the baseball Giants.[37]

Agnos was succeeded by the more conservative Frank Jordan, who promised to reverse the city's "anything goes" philosophy. He even initiated efforts to take back the city's streets from panhandlers. Liberals regained control of city hall in 1995 with the election of legendary California house speaker Willie Brown, an African American and a Democrat, as mayor. But Brown, an old-style politician, had ties to development interests and construction unions that favored growth projects. The growth coalition succeeded in its push for new commercial intrusions into the Presidio (a large green area and former army base on San Francisco Bay), a major-league ballpark that opened a new area of the city to development, and the huge Mission Bay project that created an entirely new office and upscale residential section of the city beyond the ballpark.[38]

Brown quashed a 1999 challenge from antigrowth populist Tom Ammiano, who had promised to "declare war" on gentrification and the city's continued transformation. Contributions from business interests and labor unions allowed Brown to outspend Ammiano by more than 10 to 1. Faced with the antibusiness stance of Ammiano, even the Republican Party threw its support to Brown in the city's nonpartisan mayoral contest.[39]

In 2003, "socially connected entrepreneur" Gavin Newsom won a runoff election for mayor, defeating the "[s]haggy-haired Matt Gonzalez, darling of the young, the hip and the non-propertied classes."[40] Gonzales, a member of the Green Party, emphasized tenants' rights and neighborhood preservation. He won endorsements from Ammiano and the actor and political activist Martin Sheen. Newsom, in contrast, promised a balanced approach to growth, allowing various downtown and waterfront projects to continue, but increasing requirements for affordable housing. Newsom had the backing of the city's growth coalition, including the construction unions.[41]

In office, Newsom won the support of a number of progressive groups as a result of his high-profile actions in favor of legalizing same-sex marriage. Other grassroots groups, however, remained quite critical of the mayor's tolerance for development. These groups sought—but failed—to find a strong progressive to run against the mayor in 2007.

The vibrant activity of neighborhood and antigrowth groups serves to make San Francisco quite different from the vast majority of U.S. cities.[42] Yet, as this brief review of San Francisco's contemporary political history reveals, progressive forces were not able to establish a governing regime with the capacity to act in the pursuit of their pro-neighborhood, anti-growth agenda. Instead, the progressive voices on the San Francisco Board of Supervisors (the body that functions as the city council) found that they were working with a series of mayors who endorsed new growth projects. Overall, the development and transformation of San Francisco continues, despite the occasional modifications and regulations that antigrowth forces have succeeded in imposing on new growth projects.

In sum, in San Francisco, neither growth interests nor community groups were able to establish a stable governing regime committed to their overall vision of the city. Instead, San Francisco was an **anti-regime city** where a loose alliance of activist groups was able to block a number of the projects it disliked but could not effectively take control of government and steer the city toward neighborhood preservation.[43]

CONCLUSION: CONSTRAINED LOCAL POLITICS

Local political systems are not as closed as elite theory asserts, nor are they as open as the pluralists presume. Even in San Francisco, a city that is hospitable to the voices of neighborhood activists, gays and lesbians, racial minorities, and environmentalists, the influence of business is still clearly felt.

Business elites are not all-powerful. Nor is the business community a monolith that is always united in its actions. Still, cities find that they are not in a very strong position to challenge business. As Paul Peterson has observed, capital mobility imposes severe constraints on municipal officials. Elected officials are hesitant to challenge a firm's demands: municipal leaders do not wish to risk losing a business that may leave a city. Businesses ask for generous tax abatements and other concessions. Cities are seldom even in the position where they can accurately assess just what concessions a business really requires in order to locate, or to stay, in a city.[44]

Corporate regimes dominate most big cities and many suburbs. Yet, political leaders with the will and skill can build an alternative political regime committed to neighborhood interests and minority empowerment. Progressive regimes, however, are difficult to sustain. Even progressive mayors in office recognize the necessity of working with business leaders.

Overall, regime theory constitutes a severe challenge to the pluralist view of political power. While no closed elite controls a city, few cities have a political system that is as open and penetrable as the pluralists contend. Success in the electoral arena by neighborhood constituencies and racial minorities does not guarantee the ability to govern. "At best," electoral empowerment "reaches only part of the process of shaping public policy in a city."[45]

Regime analysis points to the "weakness in the foundation for democratic politics" in the American city.[46] Regime theory tells the urban observer to look beyond election results in order to find out how things really get done in a city.

Mayors and other local leaders find that the completion of key development projects and a city's economic future require that municipal officials enlist the support of business leaders. Even progressive mayors find that they cannot give a "priority position"[47] to an agenda that emphasizes social policy and neighborhood preservation and fails to respond to the concerns of business. In office, even progressive mayors find that they must build a governing coalition that gives a prominent voice to business. Business interests do not command city officials but nonetheless still enjoy a privileged position in city and suburban governing coalitions.

The next chapter explores how the formal structure of local government affects the possibilities of leadership and just whose interests are represented in city hall.

NOTES

1. For the classic statement of power elite theory, see Floyd Hunter's study of mid-century Atlanta (which, in his study, he called "Regional City"), *Community Power Structure* (Garden City, NY: Anchor Books, 1963, originally published in 1953). A quarter of a century later, Hunter updated the study and came largely to the same conclusions. See his *Community Power Succession: Atlanta's Policymakers Revisited* (Chapel Hill: University of North Carolina Press, 1980).

2. Peter A. Lupsha and William J. Siembieda, "The Poverty of Public Services in a Land of Plenty: An Analysis and Interpretation," in *The Rise of the Sunbelt Cities,* ed. David C. Perry and Alfred J. Watkins (Beverly Hills, CA: Sage, 1977), 185.

3. Arnold Fleischmann and Joe R. Feagin, "The Politics of Growth-Oriented Urban Alliances: Comparing Old Industrial and New Sunbelt Cities," *Urban Affairs Quarterly* 23 (December 1987): 216.

4. The phrase "effectively heard" is from Robert A. Dahl's classic statement of pluralism, *Who Governs? Democracy and Power in an American City* (New Haven, CT: Yale University Press, 1961); Robert J. Waste, ed., *Community Power: Future Directions in Urban Research* (Newbury Park, CA: Sage, 1986) presents a capable overview of the competing viewpoints of pluralism and power elite theory.

5. Heywood T. Sanders, "The Politics of Development in Middle-Sized Cities," in *The Politics of Urban Development*, ed. Clarence N. Stone and Heywood T. Sanders (Lawrence: University of Kansas Press, 1987), 182–198.

6. Stephen Samuel Smith, "Hugh Governs? Regime and Education Policy in Charlotte, North Carolina," *Journal of Urban Affairs* 19, no. 3 (1997): 247–274; Philip J. Trounstine and Terry Christensen, *Movers and Shakers: The Study of Community Power* (New York: St. Martin's Press, 1982), 127 and 162–192.

7. Royce Hanson, Harold Wolman, David Connolly, Katherine Pearson, and Robert McManmon, "Corporate Citizenship and Urban Problem Solving: The Changing Civic Role of Business Leaders in American Cities," *Journal of Urban Affairs* 22, no. 1 (2010): 8.

8. For a discussion of the degree to which population changes and a changed economic situation have altered Houston's elite rule and commitment to growth agenda, see Igor Vojnovic, "Governance in Houston: Growth Theories and Urban Pressures," *Journal of Urban Affairs* 25, no. 5 (December 2003): 589–624.

9. Michael Lipsky, *Protest in City Politics* (Chicago: Rand McNally, 1972), is the classic statement as to why political protest provides "relatively powerless" groups with only the most fragile of political resources.

10. Paul E. Peterson, *City Limits* (Chicago: University of Chicago Press, 1981).

11. Ibid., 37–38.

12. Sharon Coolidge, "Plans to Bail Out Stadium Funds All Have Problems," *Cincinnati Enquirer*, July 8, 2010; Ken Benson, "Stadium Boom Deepens Municipal Woes," *New York Times*, December 24, 2009.

13. Todd J. Gillman, "Dallas Boosts Offer for Arena," *Dallas Morning News*, September 12, 1997.

14. The literature on this subject is vast. See Mark S. Rosentraub, *Major League Losers: The Real Cost of Sports and Who's Paying for It* (New York: Basic Books, 1997), esp. 129–170; David Swindell and Mark S. Rosentraub, "Who Benefits From the Presence of Professional Sports Teams? The Implications for Public Funding of Stadiums and Arenas," *Public Administration Review* 58, no. 1 (1998): 11–20; Ian Hudson, "Bright Lights, Big City: Do Professional Sports Teams Increase Employment?" *Journal of Urban Affairs* 21, no. 4 (1999): 397–408; Phillip A. Miller, "The Economic Impact of Sports Stadium Construction: The Case of the Construction Industry in St. Louis, MO," *Journal of Urban Affairs* 24, no. 2 (2002): 159–173.

15. Mark S. Rosentraub, "The Local Context of a Sports Strategy for Economic Development," *Economic Development Quarterly* 20, no. 3 (August 2006): 278–291; Costas Spirou and Larry Bennett, *It's Hardly Sportin': Stadiums, Neighborhoods, and the New Chicago* (DeKalb: Northern Illinois University Press, 2003), 21–28.

16. Mark S. Rosentraub, *Major League Winners: Using Sports and Cultural Centers as Tools for Economic Development* (Boca Raton, FL: CRC Press, 2010).

17. Steven P. Erie, Vladimir Kogan, and Scott A. MacKenzie, "'Redevelopment, San Diego Style': The Limits of Public-Private Partnerships," *Urban Affairs Review* 45, no. 5 (2010): 644–678.

18. Peter Eisinger, "The Politics of Bread and Circuses: Building the City for the Visitor Class," *Urban Affairs Review* 35, no. 3 (January 2000): 316–333.

19. Jay Weiner, *Stadium Games: Fifty Years of Big League Greed and Bush League Boondoggles* (Minneapolis: University of Minnesota Press, 2000).

20. Robert J. Waste, "City Limits, Pluralism, and Urban Political Economy," *Journal of Urban Affairs* 15, no. 5 (1993): 445–455. Peterson, *City Limits*, 52, acknowledges that education policy is difficult to classify, as it spills over into more than one policy area.

21. Todd Swanstrom, "Semisovereign Cities: The Politics of Urban Development," *Polity* 21, no. 1 (1988): 88–96.

22. Clarence N. Stone, "Systemic Power in Community Decision Making: A Restatement of Stratification Theory," *American Political Science Review* 74 (December 1980): 978.

23. Unless otherwise noted, the details of regime theory are taken from Clarence N. Stone's classic work, *Regime Politics—Governing Atlanta: 1946–88* (Lawrence: University of Kansas Press, 1989), 242.

24. Cynthia Horan, "Racializing Urban Regimes," *Journal of Urban Affairs* 24, no. 1 (2002): 23.

25. Clarence N. Stone, "Summing Up: Urban Regimes, Development Policy, and Political Arrangements," in Stone and Sanders, *The Politics of Urban Development*, 272–273.

26. John R. Logan and Kyle D. Crower, "Political Regimes and Suburban Growth, 1980–1990," *City & Community* 1, no. 1 (December 2002): 113–135; John Rennie Short, *Urban Theory: A Critical Assessment* (New York: Palgrave Macmillan, 2006), 147.

27. David L. Imbroscio, *Reconstructing City Politics: Alternative Economic Development and Urban Regimes* (Thousand Oaks, CA: Sage, 1997), 97–138. Imbroscio advocates decentralized community-based economic development initiatives, as he details in his *Urban America Reconsidered: Alternatives for Governance and Policy* (Ithaca, NY: Cornell University Press, 2010). Also see Richard C. Hula, Cynthia Y. Jackson, and Marion Orr, "Urban Politics, Governing Nonprofits, and Community Revitalization," *Urban Affairs Review* 32, no. 4 (March 1997): 459–489.

28. Pierre Clavel and Wim Wiewel, eds., *Harold Washington and the Neighborhoods: Progressive City Government in Chicago, 1983–87* (New Brunswick, NJ: Rutgers University Press, 1991).

29. John J. Betancur and Douglas C. Gills, "Community Development in Chicago: From Harold Washington to Richard M. Daley," *Annals of the American Academy of Political and Social Science* 594, no. 1 (2004): 92–108; Dan Immergluck, "Building Power, Losing Power: The Rise and Fall of a Prominent Community Economic Development Coalition," *Economic Development Quarterly* 19, no. 3 (August 2005): 211–224.

30. Alan DiGaetano, "Urban Governing Alignments and Realignments in Comparative Perspective: Developmental Politics in Boston, Massachusetts, and Bristol, England, 1980–96," *Urban Affairs Review* 32, no. 6 (July 1997): 852–854, 856–860, and 864–866.

31. William E. Nelson Jr., *Black Atlantic Politics: Dilemmas of Political Empowerment in Boston and Liverpool* (Albany: State University of New York Press, 2000), 72–78.

32. Joel Rast, "Governing the Regimeless City: The Frank Zeidler Administration in Milwaukee, 1948–1960," *Urban Affairs Review* 42, no. 1 (2006): 81–112.

33. Peter Burns and Matthew O. Thomas, "The Failure of the Nonregime: How Katrina Exposed New Orleans as a Regimeless City," *Urban Affairs Review* 41, no. 4 (2006): 517–527.

34. Chester Hartman and Rob Kessler, "The Illusion and Reality of Urban Renewal: San Francisco's Yerba Buena Center," in *Marxism and the Metropolis*, ed. William K. Tabb and Larry Sawers (New York: Oxford University Press, 1978), esp. 154 and 168. See also Chester Hartman, *The Transformation of San Francisco* (Totowa, NJ: Rowman and Littlefield, 1984) and Chester Hartman with Sarah Carnochan, *City for Sale: The Transformation of San Francisco*, rev. ed. (Berkeley: University of California Press, 2002).

35. Hartman, *The Transformation of San Francisco*; the quotation appear, respectively, on pp. 169 and 174.

36. Dawn Garcia, "Who Holds the Keys to Power in S.F. Under Agnos?" *San Francisco Chronicle*, July 11, 1988.

37. Richard Edward DeLeon, *Left Coast City: Progressive Politics in San Francisco, 1975–91* (Lawrence: University of Kansas Press, 1992), 12.

38. G. William Domhoff, "Why San Francisco Is Different: Progressive Activists and Neighborhoods Have Had Big Impact," September 2005, http://sociology.ucsc.edu/whorulesamerica/local/san_francisco.html.

39. Richard E. DeLeon, "San Francisco: The Politics of Race, Land Use, and Ideology," in *Racial*

Politics in American Cities, 3d ed., ed. Rufus P. Browning, Dale Rogers Marshall, and David H. Tabb (New York: Longman, 2003), 168–169, and 186–193.

40. John Ritter, "Green Win Could Have Impact Beyond City Race," *USA Today*, December 4, 2003.

41. "Election 2003, On the Issues: How the Candidates Deal with Business Concerns," *San Francisco Chronicle*, editorial, December 2, 2003; Rachel Gordon, "Newsom's Housing Initiative Warms Up: Mayor-elect Plans Strategy to Pass March Measure," *San Francisco Chronicle*, December 12, 2003.

42. Domhoff, "Why San Francisco Is Different."

43. DeLeon, *Left Coast City*, 7–8, 132–133, and 142–149.

44. Bryan D. Jones and Lynn W. Bachelor, "Local Policy Discretion and the Corporate Surplus," in *Urban Economic Development: Urban Affairs Review,* vol. 27, ed. Richard D. Bingham and John P. Blair (Beverly Hills, CA: Sage, 1984), 265.

45. Clarence N. Stone, "Looking Back to Look Forward: Reflections on Urban Regime Analysis," *Urban Affairs Review* 40, no. 3 (January 2005): 309–341. The quotation presented in this paragraph can be found on pp. 310–312.

46. Ibid., 326.

47. Ibid., 332.

5 Formal Structure and Leadership Style

Local government is not a small-scale replica of the national government in Washington. As we shall see, the power of local government is vastly more limited. Constitutionally speaking, cities are created by the states. Each state determines just what powers a locality may and may not possess and what a city may and may not do. States also define local taxing and borrowing authority, quite often denying cities and suburbs the revenue sources necessary to tackle urban ills.

Each state establishes the requirements for **incorporation**, the conditions that an area must meet for citizens to establish a village or municipality with certain limited powers of self-governance. A state-issued **city charter** is the rough equivalent of a city constitution. The charter spells out the structure of a city's government (whether a city will have a weak-mayor, a strong-mayor, or a council-manager system of government) and the powers that are allocated to a city. Local governments are given much less capacity to act as compared to the states and to the national government in Washington. City charters also serve to fragment local power, forcing the mayor to share executive-branch authority with independently elected executives, professional managers, and numerous boards and commissions whom the mayor does not directly control.

Mayors and other local officials cannot depend on the formal authority of their offices to get important things done. To lead, local officials must mobilize the assistance and resources commanded by others. As we shall see, African American and Latino mayors have difficult choices to make as they seek to build effective governing coalitions without compromising the promises made to their primary electoral base.

Dillon's Rule, Home Rule, and Preemption

The United States Constitution recognizes only two levels of government, the national government and the states. It contains no mention of local governments and their powers. In terms of constitutional law, localities are the administrative subunits of a state. Each state creates local governments and decides just what powers local governments may exercise.

Iowa Judge John F. Dillon in 1868 clearly articulated the quite limited constitutional position of municipal governments, setting forth a doctrine of public law that, over the years, has become known as **Dillon's Rule**. As Judge Dillon pronounced, municipalities are the mere "creatures of the states" and possess only those powers expressly delegated to them by the states.

Dillon's Rule denotes a hierarchical, superior–subordinate relationship between a state and its local governments. A state possesses total legal authority over local governments, even enjoying the power of life and death over cities, counties, and other forms of local government. As Judge Dillon observed, as a state creates local governments, it also possesses the right to destroy them. The state's power is so complete that "the Legislature might, by a single act, if we can suppose it capable of so great a folly and so great a wrong, sweep from existence all municipal corporations in a state."[1] A state may abridge, amend, or revoke any power that it has given to a city.

Under Dillon's Rule, the powers delegated to local government are strictly construed, that is, narrowly interpreted. Local governments do not have a right to expansive powers. Instead, if there is a dispute as to whether or not a local government possesses a particular power, that power is denied to the locality. As Judge Dillon articulated, "Any fair, reasonable substantial doubt concerning the existence of power is resolved by the courts against the [municipal] corporation and the power is denied."[2]

In its own decisions, the United States Supreme Court affirmed the logic of Judge Dillon's ruling.[3] Constitutionally speaking, local governments are the subunits of the states and have only those powers given to them by the states.

As we have already noted, a state issues a city charter that spells out the powers that it gives a city. Until the mid-1800s, state legislatures wrote **special-act charters** that detailed the exact structure and unique set of powers given to each newly incorporated municipality.

But the states eventually found it too burdensome to write a detailed individual charter for each city. Consequently, the states shifted to **general-act charters** (also called **classified charters**) that divide cities into different classes based on population (and, in some cases, on the value of the local tax base as well). The state then metes out different powers and service responsibilities to the different classes of local government. Larger cities are granted a fuller range of powers and taxing authority than are smaller cities, towns, and villages.

Grouping cities by class also helps to protect a city against arbitrary treatment by a state legislature: the state cannot simply pass a law that imposes special service responsibilities on an individual city. Yet, the classification system does not fully assure protection.[4] The history of state–city relations is filled with instances where a state legislature has been able to single out the state's largest city for special action. When a state has only one city in the largest class (a Baltimore, Boston, Chicago, Des Moines, New Orleans, or New York), the legislature can target that city simply by imposing new obligations on its highest class of cities. A state can also seek to help major urban centers by giving their highest class of cities new powers. The State of Maryland, for instance, enacted a quick-take law that enabled Baltimore to acquire tax-delinquent, abandoned properties in an effort to prevent the free-fall decline of blighted neighborhoods.[5]

States also possess the power of **preemption**, the authority to bar localities from taking specified actions or from acting in specified policy areas. Fewer than half of the states allow localities to levy an individual income tax; the majority of states prefer to preserve this lucrative source of revenue to support their own affairs. Similarly, only thirteen states permit local governments to tax fuel, and only eleven allow local taxation of cigarettes.[6]

States often enact preemptive legislation at the behest of powerful interest groups. The National Rifle Association succeeded in getting forty-six states to prohibit or otherwise restrict local gun-control ordinances. Efforts by the tobacco lobby led more than half of the states to preempt local restrictions on smoking, including local measures designed to restrict tobacco use by minors.[7] Influential pesticide manufacturers and agricultural interests similarly fought for state laws that barred local regulation of pesticide use. In Massachusetts, California, Georgia, and Tennessee, landlords pushed for state measures that effectively barred local rent-control laws.[8]

At times, states preempt local action in response to public sentiment. Arizona, Oklahoma, and a number of other states passed measures that restricted various local actions in support of immigration. States can prohibit local sanctuary laws or other local actions that have the effect of impeding the enforcement of laws aimed at restricting illegal immigration. More than forty states have passed laws to curb local government's use of **eminent domain** powers, the ability of government to take land for public use.[9] The legislation, which protects the rights of property owners, winds up limiting the ability of cities to initiate economic revitalization projects. Some states have even passed legislation that prohibits local governments from banning cell phone use while driving. Other states bar local governments from using red-light cameras to enforce traffic laws.

Provisions for home rule can ease much of the tightness of Dillon's Rule. Virtually every state has enacted some version of **home rule**, which empowers cities (and, in most cases, counties as well) to make numerous decisions without having to go to the state for explicit permission to act. However, the extent of local home-rule authority varies greatly from state to state.[10] In a handful of states, the state supreme court has declared that home rule language in a state's constitution requires that the powers given local government be liberally construed. In these states, cities and counties possess expansive power and can initiate a broad range of actions not otherwise prohibited by state law.

But even in states with a strong home-rule tradition, the state government still maintains an ability to intrude in local affairs and, depending on the exact provisions of a state's constitution, even reverse a municipal action. In Michigan, public-sector labor unions lobbied to have the state legislature overturn a City of Detroit **residency law** that required municipal workers to live in the city. In Ohio, the state legislature similarly barred localities from enforcing any locally enacted residency law. The Ohio Supreme Court ruled in 2009 that such a state ban on local action was not a violation of the protections offered cities by the home-rule provisions of the Ohio constitution.[11]

Despite home rule, Dillon's Rule remains the dominant doctrine of municipal law in four-fifths of the states.[12] State constitutions and statutes define—and limit—the reach of city governments. A brief review of state actions in key areas will serve to underscore the dependent nature of municipal authority.

ANNEXATION AND SECESSION

Each state sets forth the criteria and procedures that a city must meet in order to expand via **annexation**, that is, to grow by extending its borders, making adjoining territory a part of the city. The State of North Carolina gave Charlotte and other cities liberal powers of annexation; Charlotte was even able to swallow up certain parcels of land without the owner's consent.[13] In more recent years, however, protests from suburban areas have led state legislatures to change the rules in order to make annexation more difficult (see Chapter 10).

State constitutions and statutes also detail the requirements for **secession**, the conditions that must be met for the residents of an area to separate or detach from a city. California statutes put severe obstacles in the path of San Fernando Valley residents who sought to break away from Los Angeles and establish what, in terms of population, would have been the sixth largest city in the United States. California state law requires approval by **dual-majorities,** that the larger city and the seceding area both give their consent for a detachment to proceed. State law also required secession to be "revenue neutral," that secession must not hurt the larger city financially. Enthusiasm for secession declined as residents discovered that this requirement meant that a new Valley city would likely have to pay millions of dollars in "alimony" to Los Angeles, compensating L.A. for past services provided and for the revenue losses it would suffer as a result of detachment. On the East Coast, efforts by Staten Island to secede from New York City were similarly stymied by provisions of the state constitution that gave the city the power to veto detachment efforts.[14]

LIMITS ON LOCAL TAXING AND BORROWING

Unlike the national and state governments in the United States, localities are not free to tax, impose fees, and borrow money as they wish. Once again, Dillon's Rule applies: each state determines what a local jurisdiction may (and may not) tax, the maximum taxes that a locality may levy, the fees that a locality may (and may not) impose on citizens and businesses, and the amount of money that a local government may borrow for construction projects and other purposes.

Depending on the provisions of a state's constitution, a state legislature may even "grab" locally imposed taxes and use them for the state's own purposes! In 2003, the California legislature faced a quite severe financial crisis and had difficulty passing a state budget. The state "solved" its immediate budgetary dilemma by taking half of the municipal sales tax revenues, promising to repay the cities in the future. The legislature acted without local approval. Arizona in 2008 similarly reached into local budgets, ordering cities to donate $30 million to the state's general fund. The Arizona Supreme Court reversed the money grab on a technicality: the state had the power to take the locals' money but in this case had not followed the necessary procedures.[15]

Figure 5.1 **Municipal General Fund Revenue Composition, 2009**

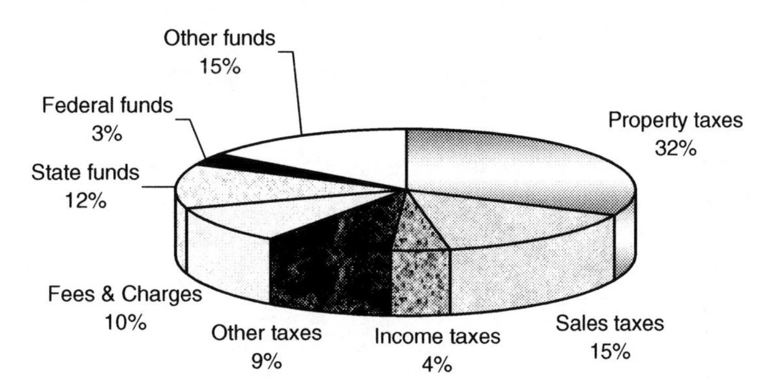

Source: Christopher W. Hoene and Michael A. Pagano, "City Fiscal Conditions in 2009," Research Brief on America's Cities, March 2009 (Washington, DC: National League of Cities), 3, fig. 3, www.nlc.org/ASSETS/E1BD3CEFA8094BD097A04BD10CBB785B/CityFiscalConditions_09%20(2).pdf.

Across the nation, state laws that preclude local access to more expansive revenues sources have served to make cities reliant on the local property tax. Property levies are cities' most important source of revenues, constituting 45 percent—nearly half—of local tax collections.[16] Even when state and federal aid is factored in, property taxes still make up nearly a third of the monies that local governments have for general fund operations (see Figure 5.1). School districts are especially reliant on the property tax, which constitutes 97 percent of the locally collected tax revenues for K–12 education.[17] State aid for public education, however, serves to temper some of schools' dependence on the property tax. In more recent years, state aid to public education surpassed property tax collections.

Thirty-eight states allow localities to levy a sales tax, which is often piggybacked atop the state-imposed sales tax. Sales taxes account for 10 percent of local own-source revenues, a figure that is less than a fourth of the amount that cities collect in property taxes.[18]

Municipal individual income taxation yields even less money, a paltry 4 percent of local own-source revenues. State laws keep localities from making more extensive use of the income tax. Only eighteen states allow localities to levy an income tax, and only a small handful permit a local income tax of any significant size.[19] State laws also sharply cap municipal income-tax rates even when such taxation is permitted. Michigan law, for instance, limits cities to a maximum 1 percent tax on residents and only a half of a percent tax on nonresidents who work in the city. Only in a very small handful of states (most notably Ohio and Pennsylvania) do cities rely on a local income or earnings tax to any significant degree. Localities, themselves, are often reluctant to impose or increase income taxes that they fear will drive residents and economic activity to neighboring communities and states.

City-to-city variations in taxing reflect the provisions of state law. Dallas, Oklahoma City, and Shreveport are cities where state law permits greater reliance on a local sales tax. New York, Philadelphia, Baltimore, and Louisville, by contrast, are cities that collect substantial income taxes.[20] Ohio cities—including Columbus, Cleveland,

Cincinnati, and Dayton—benefit from a unique provision of state law that allows a municipality to impose a local earnings tax, with commuters being able to use the amount paid as a credit that reduces their income tax obligations where they live. The system effectively allows the state's cities to tax the income of local workers who reside outside a city's borders.[21]

The property tax remains the backbone of the tax systems of most cities. However, it suffers major shortcomings. In "property poor" jurisdictions and during troubled economic times when property values are not rising, the property tax may fail to generate sufficient revenues to meet the demand for municipal services. Citizen ballot initiatives to roll back property taxes further make the property tax a less-than-reliable revenue source for public education and other important local services.

Numerous critics charge that the property tax is unfair as it is a **regressive tax**; the amount paid in property taxes by low- and moderate-income homeowners may represent a greater percentage of their annual income than the percentage paid by upper-income homeowners. Poor homeowners who live in housing markets that suddenly become "hot" may find also that they face extreme difficulty in coping with soaring property values and tax bills.[22] Local sales taxes, too, are often attacked for being regressive.

Denied the ability to use more lucrative forms of taxation, cities wind up levying a miscellany of small **nuisance taxes** (on items such as entertainment and hotel room occupancy), licensing fees (to operate a taxicab, sell alcohol, etc.), **user charges** (for instance, for the use of the public swimming pool or picnic shelter), and **special assessments** (where property owners pay an additional fee to support nearby street paving, lighting, and other infrastructure improvements). Revenues from nuisance taxes and user fees and charges make up a quarter of local own-source collections.[23]

An expanded income tax would offer local governments a more reliable and fair source of revenues. An income tax levy can also be a **progressive tax** based on an individual's ability to pay; if structured like the federal income tax, people in the higher income brackets would pay a higher tax rate than the rates imposed on the middle class and the poor. But, as we have seen, the states do not allow cities a greater use of the income tax. State laws also generally bar sharply graduated income brackets. Rather than being a graduated or progressive tax, the municipal income tax is generally a **flat-rate tax**, where people of all income levels pay essentially the same rate of taxation.[24]

State laws also restrict not only the amounts of money that a locality can tax but also how much a municipality may borrow. State law often requires voter approval through a public referendum before a city or school district can borrow money through the issuance of bonds. Such referenda are not easily won.

Even home-rule cities are constrained by state-imposed limitations on local taxing, borrowing, and spending. This is most clearly seen in the citizens' **tax revolt** that started in California in 1975 and touched off an anti-tax movement that swept the nation. Voters in state after state revised the state constitution, and state legislatures responded to voter sentiment by enacting new laws to place severe restrictions on local taxing and spending authority.

California's 1975 **Proposition 13** rolled back property taxes to much lower levels, limited any annual increase to just 2 percent, and required a two-thirds vote by the citizens for new local taxes, fees, and user charges. The measure eased the burdens suffered by homeowners who had been facing a rapid escalation in their property tax obligations. But by so strictly capping local taxation, Proposition 13 impaired the ability of California cities to fund key programs.

Constrained by state-imposed tax limitation measures, per-pupil school spending in California plummeted. Parents protested, and the California legislature responded by mandating that local governments reallocate billions of dollars in local property taxes to help fund the schools. Despite the shift in aid, California lost its national preeminence in K–12 education. Once "number one" in the nation in terms of money spent per child in the public schools, California in 2008 ranked only twenty-first, spending just about the national average on education.[25]

The forced reallocation of property tax revenue helped to cushion the impact that Proposition 13 had on the state's schools. But it also worsened the fiscal position of cities, diverting the funds that municipalities had available for nonschool services. Constrained by tax limitation measures and new state mandates for spending on schools and other services, California cities lost much of their autonomy. In California, home rule has a "hollow ring" as localities lack both the revenues and the flexibility to make meaningful program choices.[26] Despite the seeming protections of home rule, even major governments like Los Angeles County have lost meaningful autonomy and have become little more than the "embattled 'service delivery arm' of the State."[27]

In California and other states, local leaders desperate to find ways to support local services needed by residents have searched for loopholes in state-imposed taxing and borrowing limitations. One strategy has seen municipalities shift service provision responsibilities to special districts, independent bodies not subject to the same taxing and borrowing restrictions placed on cities and counties.[28]

Such subterfuges are not restricted to California. In Ohio, independent port districts have issued revenue bonds and otherwise helped to provide the capital necessary for the construction of sports arenas, museum extensions, the Cleveland Rock and Roll Hall of Fame, and various other economic development projects not directly relate to port activities.[29] Such subterfuges raise important questions of local accountability and democratic control, especially as borrowing and spending decisions are increasingly being placed in the hands of unelected and politically invisible public officials.

In California, Florida, and other states across the nation, localities have desperately searched for sources of revenue that have not been strictly banned by tax limitation measures. Cities have resorted to imposing special assessments, user charges, and service fees for solid waste disposal, street improvements, fire protection, and other such services.[30] Local governments levy **impact and developer fees** that charge developers for the costs of roads, sewers, schools, and other infrastructure provided new subdivisions.[31] The developers, in turn, shift the fees to homebuyers, adding thousands of dollars to the cost of a home.

Caught between state-imposed tax limitations and the continuing demand for public services, a number of localities have engaged in the high-risk strategy of borrowing money to invest in what they hope will be high-yield opportunities. If things go well, the money earned from such investments is used to repay the loans and to support improved service provision, without necessitating an increase in local taxation. But should the value of an investment suddenly decline, the municipality may find itself in a position of extreme fiscal distress, unable to repay its creditors as the loans become due.

Orange County, California, in 1994, gambled and lost nearly $2 billion in its investment pool by undertaking just such a creative, high-risk financing strategy. The result was a fiscal crisis that led to emergency measures. The county filed for bankruptcy, closed library branches, cut school programs, reduced social programs and policing, and even stopped testing for fecal coliform bacteria on its beaches.[32]

Caught in a similar financial squeeze, a number of local school districts have also gambled in an effort to find the money to support services. School districts in Denver and the greater Milwaukee area borrowed money to fund investments that administrators hoped would yield earnings to help the districts meet their quite sizable pension obligations. The school districts ended up in a crisis situation when, in the underperforming recession economy of the early twenty-first century, the investments wound up losing money.[33]

State Law and "Academic Bankruptcy": The Takeover of Schools in Crisis

School districts are units of local governments. Like other units of local government, they are subject to Dillon's Rule. A locally elected school board possesses only the authority that a state chooses to allow. Normally, states give school districts considerable decision-making powers, a reflection of the American grassroots orientation toward K–12 education. In recent years, however, states have breached that autonomy in an effort to turn around failing school districts.

By the beginning of the twenty-first century, twenty-four states had **academic bankruptcy laws** that allowed for direct state intervention in, and even the state takeover of, poorly performing school systems.[34] In some cases, the state transferred control of school operations to a state-appointed manager, removing authority from the hands of locally elected school officials. Other states placed troubled city schools under the direct control of a mayor with the political clout to challenge vested interests and shake up established ways of doing things. This, too, diminished the power of the locally elected school board.

The list of instances where the state stepped in and forced a change in local school governance is fairly long. It includes New Jersey (which took control of the Newark, Jersey City, and Paterson schools), Connecticut (Hartford), Maryland (where the state in 1997 assumed broad oversight power over a state-appointed Baltimore school board), California (Compton, Oakland, and West Fresno), New York (where the state appointed a management team to run the Roosevelt, Long Island, schools, reducing the elected school board to an advisory role), Massachusetts (Lawrence), Louisiana (where the state took charge of eighteen failing high schools), South Carolina (Allendale), Pennsylvania, Massachusetts, and Michigan.

Pennsylvania took charge of Philadelphia's schools, replacing the school board with a School Reform Commission and a chief executive officer who turned to private firms and nonprofit managers to run city schools.[35] The State of Massachusetts similarly gave Boston University managerial authority in running the troubled Chelsea school district. Michigan took over Detroit's public schools and gave extensive power to the city's mayor. But in the face of bitter criticism from local activists, the state reversed course and began to resurrect the authority of the elected school board, only later to reverse course again when continuing episodes of mismanagement and corruption led the state to appoint an emergency financial manager.[36]

The states have also given extensive authority for school operation to mayors in New York, Chicago, Boston, Cleveland, Harrisburg, Providence, New Haven, Trenton, Hartford, Oakland, Jackson (Mississippi), and a number of other cities.[37] In Washington, DC, too, the mayor gained the authority to shake up school operations by appointing a reform-oriented schools superintendent. In these cities, the conditions of inner-city schools had deteriorated to the point that state legislators, governors, and school reformers were all willing to break with the long-standing American tradition that kept the public schools separate from the more normal realm of politics. The poor condition of public schools in Chicago even caused a Republican-led Illinois legislature to put new powers in the hands of Democratic mayor Richard M. Daley. He was given the ability to name the Chicago schools' chief executive, the chief financial officers, and a five-member board of trustees. Daley also received control over the schools' $3 billion annual budget.[38]

Critics decry that such state takeovers undermine local democracy by demeaning the authority of locally elected school officials. In cities where African Americans control the school board, local activists charge that a takeover initiated by a white-dominated state government, amounts to a reversal of hard-fought civil rights victories. Municipal unions, in particular, object to state efforts to undermine hard-fought-for bargaining rights and to dismiss large numbers of teachers in inner-city schools.

State intrusion in local school affairs resulted in bitter controversy in 2011 when the newly elected Republican governments in Wisconsin, Michigan, and Ohio rewrote the rules for K–12 school operations, limiting collective bargaining by teachers, requiring teachers and administrators to pay a greater share of their health coverage, and tying teachers' pay raises to the improvement that their students showed on standardized exams. Advocates of the reforms argued that they were necessary to cut costs, as the states' dire fiscal situations required that it reduce its support to schools. Critics charged that the measures went beyond cost savings to "union busting."

Whatever the merits and criticisms of state school reform efforts, one thing is pristinely clear: Dillon's Rule remains the operative constitutional doctrine. Except where state constitutions contain provisions to the contrary, state governments have the power to abridge and even to suspend the powers of locally elected school boards.

THE FORMAL STRUCTURE OF CITY GOVERNMENT

In the United States, there are three basic forms of city government: the mayor-council plan (with its weak-mayor and strong-mayor variants), the commission arrangement (which is no longer widely used) and the council-manager plan (which places executive authority in the hands of a professional city manager, not an elected mayor).

Over half of U.S. communities are governed by the council-manager arrangement with its professional city manager.[39] The council-manager form of government is particularly popular among midsized communities and in cities in the Pacific West. The nation's big cities (including New York, Los Angeles, Chicago, Houston, Philadelphia, and Detroit), however, continue to place authority in the hands of an elected mayor as opposed to an appointed manager. Small towns, too, tend to be governed by the mayor-council arrangement.[40] In this case, small communities often see little need to pay for a full-time professional manager.

WEAK-MAYOR SYSTEM

The earliest American cities had mayors who possessed little authority. The country still regarded its colonial experience under England's King George III as sound enough reason to distrust executive power.

But the growth of urban populations led to the demand for new municipal services and the need to increase the capacities of municipal government. In the early 1800s, state legislatures did so, but without increasing the authority of the mayor. Instead, the states created independently elected positions and various appointed boards and commissions to oversee the operations of the police and fire departments and other important municipal operations. The existence of such independent bodies is the defining characteristic of the weak-mayor system, which denies the mayor meaningful authority, even effective control over the executive branch of a city's government.

In the **weak-mayor system**, the mayor possesses only the most limited administrative authority and lacks the power to appoint and dismiss key administrative personnel. Unlike the president of the United States, the mayors in weak-mayor cities do not possess equivalent authority to appoint the heads of major executive departments. Instead, the mayor governs with a variety of other executives whom he or she does not appoint or control: independently elected executives (such as the local prosecutor, the city's chief administrative officer, and the city's financial controller), appointees made by the city council (and, in some cases, appointees made by the state's governor), and the members of numerous independent boards and commissions (see Figure 5.2).

In a weak-mayor city, the members of independent boards and commissions serve long, rotating fixed terms of office that effectively insulate the boards from direct mayoral control. In the absence of resignations, a mayor may be able to appoint only one member a year to a public board or commission. In many cities, mayoral appointments are also subject to confirmation by the city council. The mayor cannot dismiss such an appointee without first gaining council approval. In the classic weak-mayor city, the mayor also plays a quite limited legislative role and does not even possess the power to veto council-passed legislation.

Weak-mayor systems were created to shield city operations from improper political intrusion by the mayor. But weak-mayor systems suffer considerable deficiencies. Just like private corporations, big cities and suburbs find that they need a central executive with the authority to provide clear policy direction and effective program coordination. The weak mayor lacks such leadership prerogatives. In the majority of

Figure 5.2 **Two Variants of the Weak-Mayor Structure**

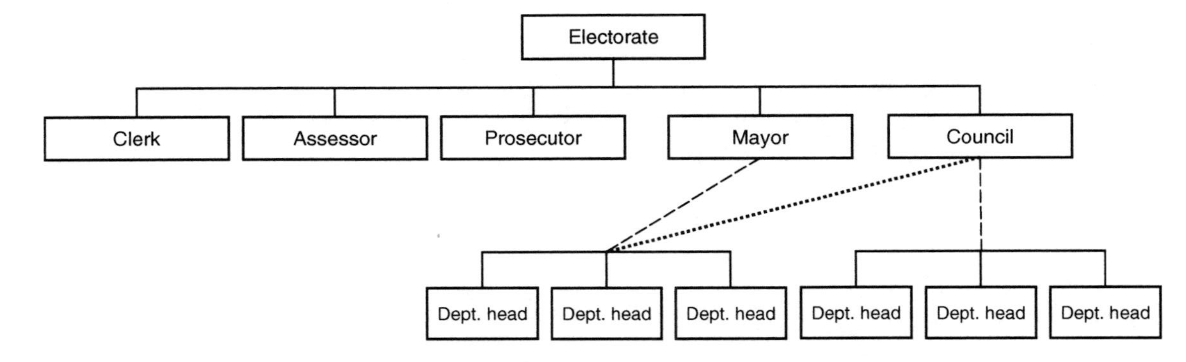

(a) The mayor does not possess total control over the executive branch but shares it with independently elected officials. Other departmental heads are subject to city council confirmation or are appointed directly by the council.

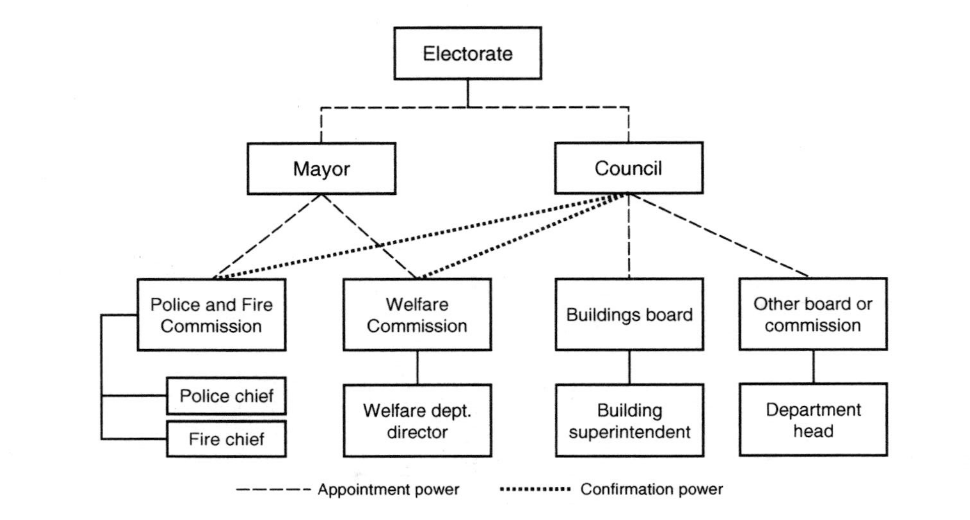

(b) Departmental heads are appointed not by the mayor but by the independent boards and commissions. The members of these boards and commissions serve long, fixed terms, and are appointed directly by the council or by the mayor,

U.S. communities, the mayor does not even control the preparation of the city budget, an important vehicle for setting policy direction that is often placed in the hands of an independent administrator.[41] The existence of multiple independent executives, boards, and commissions adds to policy confusion: without mayoral direction, boards and commissions can pursue their own agendas, often working at cross-purposes.

On the whole, the weak-mayor form of government is seen as incapable of providing the strong leadership that bigger cities need. Critics of Minneapolis' government, for instance, continue to argue for reform of the city's weak-mayor system.[42] Over the years, cities across the country have increased the authority given to the mayor or city manager.

Strong-Mayor System

The strong-mayor system is the dominant form of government in big cities, including Baltimore, Boston, Denver, Detroit, New York, Philadelphia, Pittsburgh, and St. Louis. The **strong-mayor system** gives the elected mayor substantial authority over city departments. Similar to the president of the United States, the mayor is chief of the executive branch, with the ability to appoint department heads and top agency officials (see Figure 5.3).

But even a "strong" mayor is subject to numerous checks. Top mayoral appointments typically require city council confirmation. City councils vote on the city's budget and appropriations (spending) bills. Councils generally also possess the power to review proposed purchases and contracts. In cities where the mayor possesses the power to veto new laws, the council can vote to override the mayor's veto. Civil service and merit systems (discussed in Chapter 6) and provisions of collective bargaining contracts further impose limits on the mayor's ability to command executive-branch personnel.

A strong-mayor charter, then, does not guarantee a mayor the ability to lead. Much depends on a mayor's leadership skills and ability to build effective governing coalitions.

Where mayors have abused their powers, reformers have advocated that the powers of the mayor's office be reduced. Detroit's reputation for mismanagement was

Figure 5.3 **Strong-Mayor Structure**

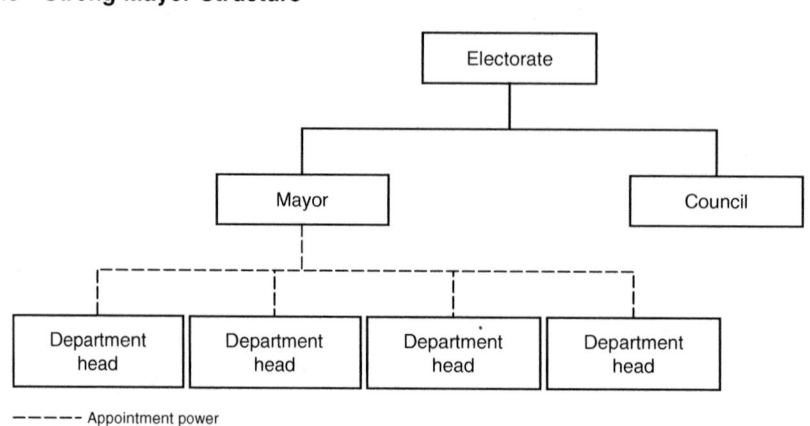

only compounded by the virtual paralysis that existed at city hall as a result of the scandals that swirled around Mayor Kwame Kilpatrick. The International City/County Management Association in 2010 called on Detroit to abandon its strong-mayor system for a new system that would add the professionalism of a city manager. But the proposal failed to gained much backing. The election of Mayor Dave Bing, the popular former NBA Detroit Pistons player and local businessman, began to instill new confidence in the mayoralty. Bing took on the municipal unions, cut city expenditures, and even dismissed unnecessary municipal workers in an attempt to balance the city's budget.[43]

COMMISSION GOVERNMENT

When Galveston, Texas, proved incapable of responding to the disastrous hurricane and flood of 1900, the State of Texas allowed local citizens to create a new form of government, the city commission. The new government initially proved quite successful and, for a time, was widely imitated. However, Houston and other cities eventually abandoned the commission arrangement, given the plan's obvious shortcomings.

Tulsa and Portland (Oregon) are the two largest cities that have retained the commission structure of government. Forest Park, Illinois, a suburb of Chicago, is another notable community with a commission system. Variants of the commission system can also be found not just in numerous small towns but also in the nation's counties, where more than one-third are run under the commission arrangement.[44]

Under the **commission system**, a five- to nine-member city council (referred to as the city commission) governs the city, fusing both executive and legislative responsibilities (Figure 5.4). Each commission member also serves as the head of a city department. The commission selects one of its members to serve as mayor. The mayor, who represents the city at ceremonial gatherings and who presides over commission meetings, possesses no more authority than any other commissioner.

In theory, the commission system provides for quick action by eliminating the separation of powers: the city's legislators and executive department heads are one

Figure 5.4 **Commission Structure**

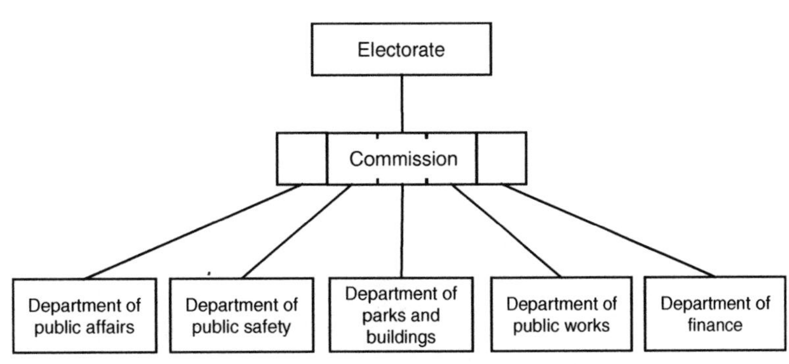

and the same. Yet, the disadvantages of the commission plan are fairly overwhelming. Each commissioner may represent the narrow view of his or her own department, with no one speaking out for the "public good" of the entire city. Commission members may also be reluctant to reduce the budget requests of other departments, fearing that such efforts will likely result in retaliation by other commissioners. Even more devastating, there is no guarantee that an elected commissioner possesses the administrative skills necessary to manage a large city department, especially as voters rarely take a candidate's administrative capabilities into account when casting their ballots.

THE COUNCIL-MANAGER (CITY MANAGER) SYSTEM

In 1908, Staunton, Virginia, established a new form of government, one that gave extensive administrative authority to a general city manager. The success of the Staunton innovation led Richard Childs, president of the good-government National Municipal League, to tout the virtues of the council-manager government, making the council-manager system a key part of the League's *Model City Charter*. Dayton, Ohio, became the first city of significant size to adopt the "good government" council-manager system. The plan soon spread like wildfire across the nation.

Under the **council-manager system**, the city council appoints a professionally trained manager who is given responsibility for running the daily affairs of the city. The council enacts new laws and sets overall policy, but administrative matters fall totally within the domain of the city manager. The manager—not the mayor—is placed in charge of departmental heads and supervises their performance and the operations of municipal agencies (see Figure 5.5).

Under the council-manager arrangement, the city council functions as the equivalent of a private corporation's board of directors. The city council sets overall policy direction for the city but leaves the details of day-to-day administration to a profes-

Figure 5.5 **Council-Manager Structure**

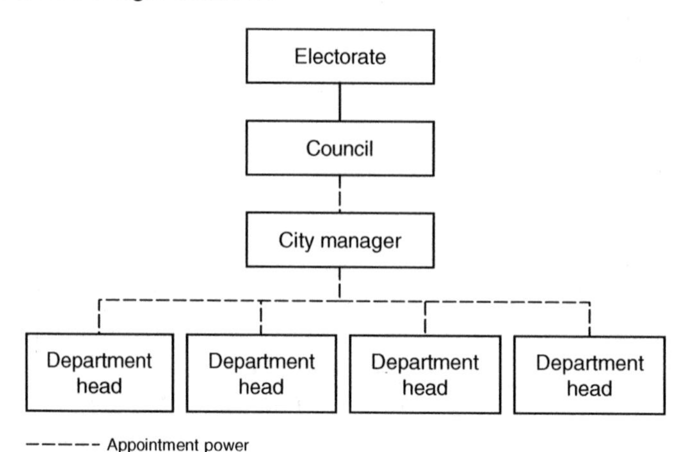

sional manager. The council retains the right to fire and replace a manager whose service proves disappointing.

Under the classic council-manager plan, the city council selects one of its own members to serve as mayor. The mayor presides over council meetings, signs federal aid agreements, and represents the city in ceremonial gatherings. The chosen mayor, however, possesses no meaningful administrative, appointive, or veto powers. Dallas has a slight variant of the system, with the mayor elected citywide. Popular election does give the mayor certain leadership prerogatives. Yet, even in Dallas, it is still quite clearly the professional manager, not the elected mayor, who controls city administration.

The council-manager system is commonly found in suburbs and in midsize cities. Communities in the South and the West also tend to employ the council-manager arrangement. Phoenix, San Diego, Dallas, San Antonio, San Jose, Sacramento, Long Beach, Santa Ana, Las Vegas, Tucson, Austin, Fort Worth, Oklahoma City, Jacksonville, Charlotte, Memphis, and Virginia Beach are all noteworthy council-manager cities. The council-manager system can also be found outside the Sunbelt in Kansas City and Wichita.

The council-manager system seeks to place the complex tasks of running a city in the hands of a well-trained professional. City managers possess expertise in such areas as accounting, budgeting, personnel management, and civil engineering. In contrast to an elected mayor, the decisions made by a manager are less influenced by short-term electoral and partisan considerations. City managers are also committed to high ethical standards. With its emphasis on expertise and professionalism, the council-manager system seeks to reduce the level of conflict in city and suburban decision making.[45]

Yet, conflict can emerge in a council-manager city as there is no clear line separating policy formulation (the job given to the city council and mayor) from administration (the job of the city manager). Managers cannot avoid policy-related activities. A city manager by necessity is involved in agenda setting, proposal development, and project advocacy.[46] The modern city manager understands that policy initiation and formulation are important parts of the job, and that he or she must devote considerable time to policy development and efforts to forge a consensus in a city.[47]

The most successful managers are initiators of policy who provide information and policy advice that inform council decision making. City council members, who often serve part-time and are poorly remunerated for their work, frequently lack the ability to study and review alternative plans in detail. Council members seldom have the assistance of a well-staffed legislative research office. As a result, council members are quite dependent on research, advice, and recommendations provided by the city manager.

Still, the most effective city managers are careful in how they lead and exercise influence. Many are reluctant to take the public stage. They prefer to handle matters quietly rather than engage in visible combat with members of the council. The city manager serves at the pleasure of the city council, and the wise manager knows that the council may fire a manager who bucks their policy direction or otherwise oversteps the boundaries of the office.[48]

Relatively few city managers play the role of the aggressive *political activist* who attempts to build a power base and push the city council in a particular policy direction. Most managers, by contrast, focus on their administrative responsibilities and conceive of their larger policy role as that of an *expert adviser* who provides information and recommendations to the city council.[49]

In a number of cities, the mayor and manager are competitors for influence. The public expects the mayor, as the most visible official in the city, to lead. A mayor may accuse a policy-oriented city manager of improperly straying beyond the sphere of administration. City managers, in turn, charge that the mayor and council members improperly intrude into administration.

The council-manager system operates most smoothly when all participants recognize their assigned roles. The city council establishes a city's overall *mission* or sense of direction, setting forth the city's general philosophy regarding taxing, spending, and growth. The council and city manager jointly decide specific questions of *policy*, for instance, determining exactly what services will be provided and which projects will be built. City managers, however, dominate program *management and administration*: matters dealing with personnel, budgeting, purchasing, contracting, data processing, and the daily workings of municipal programs. Council members, however, often intervene in administration in response to constituent complaints.[50]

Some city councils are reluctant to dismiss a manager who is not performing very well. A municipality that gains a reputation as being "hostile" to city managers will find it difficult to recruit a truly talented manager. In smaller communities, part-time council members may be reluctant to undertake the time-consuming tasks of screening and interviewing candidates for manager. Constant turnover in the manager's office can also be disruptive to municipal operations.

The nation's biggest cities have spurned the council-manager arrangements, as an appointed manager lacks an important tool of leadership, the legitimacy that derives from democratic election. A city manager is in a weaker position than an elected mayor in being able to command media attention and rally public support behind an issue.

In Cincinnati and Toledo, critics argued that the council-manager system impeded the ability of the local government to cope with long-term economic decline. The roots of these cities' economic problems lie well beyond the city's form of government. Still, both cities lacked a dynamic, visible official who could speak for the community when courting businesses. As a result, both cities acted to strengthen the mayor's office, while still maintaining aspects of managerial government. In Cincinnati, the mayor gained the right to appoint and replace the city manager and council committee chairs. The mayor also gained the ability to formulate and present a budget to the city council.[51] El Paso, however, moved in the opposite direction, getting rid of its strong-mayor system and selecting its first city manager in 2004.

San Diego has modified elements of its city-manager system in order to provide for strengthened mayoral leadership. During his eleven-year tenure (1971–1982) as mayor, Pete Wilson (who would later be elected governor and U.S. senator) virtually "created" a modern mayoral office, choosing to tackle difficult problems that the city manager was unwilling to resolve. Wilson tried to mediate between growth-oriented business groups (that had an ally in the city manager's office) and neighborhood activists and taxpayer groups critical of new growth projects. Wilson found that the city's council-manager form of government imposed a "structural straitjacket" on his leadership efforts.

Voters rejected a ballot measure to bring a strong-mayor system to San Diego. Still, Wilson won approval of other measures that strengthened the mayor's office. The mayor gained new rights to name the members and chairs of city council committees and various city boards and commissions. The mayor also gained the ability to determine what issues would be presented to the full city council.[52] Wilson's successors, however, confronted a city manager and city council intent on regaining their prerogatives.

Other California cities have similarly acted to strengthen the mayor's office. San Jose, Oakland, Sacramento, and Hayward all switched to the citywide election of mayors. In these and other cities, racial minorities and homeowner groups sought to create offices that would reduce the influence of city managers tied to the old business-oriented governing regimes.[53] San Jose also sought an elected executive who possessed the power to deal with the problems brought on by the city's rapid growth.

In Oakland, a black-liberal coalition succeeded in making the mayoral position full-time, a change that they hoped would provide the leadership to combat the city's economic and social problems. Former (and future!) California governor Jerry Brown, elected mayor in 1998, sought to further strengthen the office. Brown, however, lost a 2002 referendum to make the changes permanent. Nonetheless, Brown gained newfound mayoral authority that he used to dismiss Oakland's city manager.

In Sacramento, Mayor Kevin Johnson similarly pushed the city to amend its council-manager system, which, according to Johnson, undermined the mayor's ability to initiate strong programs necessary for the city's economic rebound. Johnson complained that the city's council-manager system forced the mayor to do "everything by committee." He argued that a mayor who is little more than just one vote on the city council lacks the "clout" to provide effective policy direction.[54]

ADAPTED CITIES: THE HYBRID STRUCTURES OF THE MODERN U.S. CITY

The formal structures of a city's government are not fixed but are actually quite "malleable."[55] Over time, cities have altered their initial charter arrangements, borrowing successful elements from other cities. There are few mayor-council and council-manager cities today that exactly fit the ideal models or types outlined in this chapter. Rather, most cities are hybrids, having adopted various features from alternative governmental structures. Even strong-mayor cities temper partisanship through merit-based hiring practices (see Chapter 6), requirements for competitive bidding when issuing city contracts, and strengthened accounting procedures and local ethics laws.

Mayor-council cities often have a **chief administrative officer (CAO)** to provide the mayor with the technical and policy assistance of a professional. In many cities, the CAO is a city-manager-like careerist who can serve as a source of continuity and institutional memory in city affairs. The CAO is an experienced city-hall hand who can offer policy advice and help tutor a mayor in the intricacies of budget preparation and other governmental processes. In New York and a number of other cities, however, the mayor nominates the CAO, an appointive process that increases the position's responsiveness to the mayor while decreasing its professional independence.[56]

Council-manager cities have likewise begun to adopt features associated with the strong-mayor system. As our brief review of San Diego, Oakland, and other California cities has already underscored, a number of council-manager cities have switched to citywide election of the mayor in order to strengthen the leadership potential inherent in the mayor's office. New procedures for citizen participation have also diminished some of the insulation of managerial government.

City Councils: Not Quite the Same Animal as the U.S. Congress

Unlike the United States Congress, the members of a city council generally serve part-time and are often rather poorly paid. While the council members of many big cities may receive good salaries, in other cities the annual compensation for council service is quite low. Dallas in 2010 paid council members only $37,500, Mobile (Alabama) $19,800 plus meeting expenses and a $325 per month expense account, Irvine (California) a paltry $10,560, and Fullerton (California) less than $9,000.[57]

City legislatures are also hampered by their infrequent sessions. Only half of the nation's cities with populations greater than 500,000 even hold weekly council meetings. In smaller communities, councils meet less frequently, usually every other week and, in some cases, once a month.[58]

Quite unlike the United States Congress and the nation's state legislatures, city councils are seldom organized along party lines, with the majority political party controlling the body's operations. In nonpartisan cities, members run for office with no avowed Democratic or Republican party affiliation (see Chapter 6).

Legislative committees, key components of the U.S. House and Senate legislative processes, play a much less significant role in local governments. Compared to the houses of Congress, city councils are generally too small in size to allow for the development of an effective committee system. Part-time and underpaid council members also lack a commitment to ongoing committee work. Compared to the Congress, city councils conduct relatively few public committee hearings on proposed legislation. City councils seldom use committees to oversee the actions of the executive branch. Rather than depend on the work of committees, city councils are reliant on the policy advice provided by the city manager, the mayor, and other support staff.[59]

City councils further suffer from frequent turnover. Unlike members of the U.S. Congress, few council members serve extended legislative careers. Council members typically leave office voluntarily, seeking to devote energy to private careers and home lives or to run for higher office. Only about half of a newly elected council class can still be found serving on a council five years later.[60]

The short duration of council careers diminishes a council's ability to develop the knowledge necessary for informed independent action. Amateur, part-time legislators are in a poor position to challenge the reports and recommendations of the city manager, municipal department heads, and professional consultants.

In a great many cities, **term limitations** prohibit a council member from serving more than two or three consecutive terms. The term limitations movement arose in protest against the U.S. Congress, where members serve long careers in office and seldom risk defeat at the ballot box. Yet, as we have seen, the situation at the local level is quite different, as city councils experience substantial turnover due to voluntary retirements. "Term limits" may actually be medicine for a disease that does not exist in a great many cities. City councils need members who have gained knowledge and experience on the job. Term limits force a council's few experienced members to leave office.

Can the operations of city councils be improved? Of course. First, city councils need greater staff support if council members are to act as informed and independent voices in local affairs. Second, legislators need to be paid adequate compensation if they are expected to devote the considerable time necessary to do the public's business. Third, cities that have two-year terms for council members might consider shifting to four-year terms. The burden of frequent election (especially with the fundraising that electoral campaigns require in big cities) can lead talented and capable council representatives to retire voluntarily from office. Finally, as a number have already begun to do, city councils need to make council committees a regular part of city-council operations.[61]

Women in Local Government

As of January 2011, only 8 of the largest 100 U.S. cities had women mayors, a number that was actually down from the 13 cities with women mayors in 2005. Annise D. Parker was mayor of Houston, the nation's fifth largest city. Other prominent women mayors included Stephanie Rawlings-Blake of Baltimore (number 22 in city size), Ashley Swearengin of Fresno (number 42), Jean Quan of Oakland, California (number 45), and Pam Iorio of Tampa (number 61). Only 11.7 percent of cities of over 100,000 people had women mayors, a figure that was slightly below the 15.6 percent level achieved in 2005.[62]

Women in the mid-1990s held over 20 percent of the council seats in medium and large cities, a figure that was a bit better than in the U.S. Congress, where female membership had risen to 17 percent.[63] In more recent years, the difference between women's representation in the national and local government has narrowed considerably. Not too long ago, women had a greater presence in city councils than in the U.S. Congress, where they were even more severely underrepresented. Service at the local level posed less interference with child care and the other family responsibilities borne by women. Where women had great difficulty raising the considerable sums of money necessary to run for Congress, women in local races were able to rely on the support that they had built as a result of their activism in community groups and civic associations.[64] Local politics also focuses on matters such as affordable housing, social welfare, and education, policy areas of special concern to women: "[T]he local level is where many of the problems that are of most concern to women are addressed, and consequently where many women are introduced to political gladiatorial combat."[65]

Houston mayor Annise Parker was inaugurated mayor of Houston in 2010. An openly lesbian candidate, Parker's victory points to the changing demography and the electoral importance of new groups in a city renowned for its conservative politics. Parker's success shows the importance of skillful coalition building. In her campaign, Parker stressed economic development issues, neighborhood responsiveness, and fiscal prudence. Courtesy of Zblume through Wikimedia Commons. http://commons.wikimedia.org/wiki/File:Annise_Parker.JPG.

Women's style in the local arena differs slightly from that of men. One study of city managers has revealed that, compared to men, female managers are more likely to emphasize leadership approaches based on communication and conciliation. Women try to bring city officials together in an effort to resolve a dispute. Men, by contrast, were more willing to rely on the formal authority of office and simply dismiss an agency head who has lost the council's confidence.[66] Other studies similarly point to the more collegial leadership styles of women.[67] Female city council members also devote more time to their legislative work than do their male counterparts and have longer careers of local legislative service.[68] The increased participation of women in local government has the potential to alter the prevailing style of politics in a city.

THE DIFFICULT TASK OF MAYORAL LEADERSHIP

An analysis of a city's charter and formal governing structure does not reveal everything about the possibilities of local leadership. Chicago, for instance, largely fits the weak-mayor model.[69] Yet, Mayor Richard J. Daley, the legendary "boss" of Chicago in the 1950s and 1960s, and his son Richard M. Daley, the longest-tenured mayor in the city's history, were able to wield considerable power, using their dominance in the local Democratic Party organization to gain effective control over the city council. Over the years, the mayor's office also secured new budgetary powers and, as we previously noted, expanded control over the city's school system.

In a great many cities, however, mayors are denied the resources for effective leadership. Only 15 percent of America's communities have a mayor who serves full time.[70] Part-time, poorly paid mayors who lack adequate staff assistance are in a weak position to impress their policy vision on a city, challenge the recommendations of a city manager, provide oversight of administration, lobby for state and federal grants, and deal with the heads of major corporations.

City problems are so voluminous and complex that the modern city is often said to be "ungovernable."[71] Yet, in recent years, a number of mayors have shown the "ungovernability" thesis to be a vast overgeneralization. Even in New York, the nation's biggest and allegedly most ungovernable city, Mayors Rudy Giuliani and Michael Bloomberg demonstrated ability to lead and govern.[72]

Leadership depends on a mayor's skill, orientation, and personality, not just the formal prerogatives of office. Even in the council-manager system, where a mayor is denied many of the resources for leadership, mayors with the will, skill, and proper orientation can still lead. In council-manager cities, the effective mayor often plays the role of coordinator or director, acting as a facilitator and cooperative team builder.[73]

MINORITY MAYORS AND THE DEBATE OVER DERACIALIZATION

African American and Latino mayors often face a difficult choice in governing. Should they attempt to build broad multiracial support for economic development projects and other programs of assistance to the city? Or should they focus their efforts on changing conditions in the city's poorest neighborhoods, even at the risk of alienating potential allies outside the mayor's core constituency?

First-generation minority mayors came out of the civil rights tradition and were ready to battle for change in cities that were polarized along racial lines. Carl Stokes won Cleveland's mayoralty in 1967 to become one of the nation's first big-city black mayors. Stokes had the support of a biracial coalition of black voters and white liberals. But once in office, his agenda stalled. Stokes found that he could not push for changes that would benefit inner-city neighborhoods while simultaneously catering to the concerns of white community leaders. Stokes eventually chose to pursue a redistribution agenda, a path of action that invited substantial criticism.[74] Detroit Mayor Coleman Young (1973–1993), a labor organizer who first entered the political arena during an age of overt racism and segregation, governed with an even more combative, polarizing "what goes around comes around" political style that irked whites and suburbanites.[75]

In contrast, San Antonio's Henry Cisneros (1981–1989), the first Mexican American mayor of a major U.S. city, toned down overt racial appeals and instead tried to build a governing coalition across racial lines. Cisneros sought to forge a consensus around local economic growth that would surmount the tensions dividing San Antonio's Anglo and Latino communities. Cisneros sought to bring new technology-related jobs to San Antonio, jobs that would benefit both the white population and the city's large Latino population. Activist groups like COPS (Communities Organized for Public Services), however, complained that the mayor was too concerned with the business district and new stadium construction and too often paid insufficient attention to changing conditions in the city's low-income residential neighborhoods.[76]

Tom Bradley, the five-term mayor of Los Angeles (1973–1993), made a similar choice and faced similar criticism. An African American, Bradley won the mayoralty by emphasizing his reputation for having been a "tough cop" in the Los Angeles Police Department. Bradley played down racial appeals. He was not a street radical or a poor-people's community leader who emphasized a redistribution agenda. Instead, Bradley built alliances with the business community and with white liberal groups, including organized labor and the city's Jewish community.

Critics charged that Bradley's *deracialized approach* was too deferential to the demands of developers and too focused on building a new downtown of glass skyscrapers to the neglect of poorer Los Angeles neighborhoods.[77] When a Korean storeowner shot a teenage black woman, Latasha Harlins, in the back of the head in a confrontation over a stolen bottle of orange juice, Mayor Bradley paid his respects in a visit to the store but did not express his sympathy to the Harlins family. The mayor also faced a chorus of boos and jeers when he spoke in the black community in the wake of the city's 1992 riots.[78]

Both Cisneros and Bradley were generally regarded as successful mayors. Yet critics charged that their agendas were too incremental, that the mayors could have done more to help racial minorities and the poor.

Cisneros, Bradley, Atlanta's Andrew Young, New York's David Dinkins, Philadelphia's Wilson Goode, Denver's Federico Peña, Seattle's Norman Rice, and Charlotte's Harvey Gantt are all noteworthy African American and Latino mayors who, in the later twentieth century, utilized a **deracialized approach to leadership**. These mayors toned down racial appeals and deemphasized redistribution. Instead, they emphasized good-government managerialism, economic development, and other measures that promised benefits across racial lines.[79] These mayors often walked a difficult line.

While much of the deracialization literature focuses on black politics, Latino candidates have similarly discovered the strategic value of deracialized appeals when running for office in electorates dominated by non-Hispanic whites.[80] In 2005, Antonio Villaraigosa won the Los Angeles mayoralty, having narrowly lost the race for mayor four years previous. Villaraigosa broadened his appeal to liberal whites, including Los Angeles' Jewish community. Villaraigosa did not play the "ethnic card" in various disputes: "He emphasized not ethnic assertion, but broad coalitions."[81]

Advocates argue that deracialization strategies represent a maturation of black and Latino politics. Deracialization enables racial minorities to win office in cities where they do not constitute a clear majority of the active electorate. Barack Obama's stunningly successful 2008 presidential campaign illustrates the electoral potential inherent in a deracialized political appeal.

Critics, however, counter that deracialization in the pursuit of office often leads to compromises in office after the election is won.[82] Moderate black mayors have pursued "policies of fiscal conservatism and downtown development,"[83] ignoring more far-reaching transformational change targeted on poorer neighborhoods: "Black politics is not maturing and may be degenerating."[84] It takes continuing pressure from community organizations, churches, labor unions, and civil rights groups to keep a minority mayor from caving in to the demands of business leaders and other influential elites.[85]

For a new generation of black mayors, however, the debate over deracialization just does not appear to be all that interesting. The first wave of big-city black mayors faced a particularly difficult situation: they were not always welcomed in city hall, and white politicians often sought to obstruct their policy agenda. In the 1960s and 1970s, the first wave of black mayors sought to continue the "struggle" of the civil rights movement, pursuing programs of racial equity.

Today, a new generation of African American mayors governs in much different circumstances. While racial equality has yet to be fully achieved, African Americans have gained entrance into, and increasing acceptance among, many sectors of American society. Many new-generation black mayors grew up in the post–civil rights era in racially integrated neighborhoods, attended largely white schools, and went to the best universities. These **postracial black mayors** are comfortable working across racial and ethnic lines. They are committed to change but also recognize the necessity of balancing a city's financial books and of working to win the support of the leaders of corporations and nonprofit organizations.[86] Newark's Cory Booker, Washington, DC's Adrian Fenty, Sacramento's Kevin Johnson, and Youngstown's Jay Williams all represent a new wave of young and dynamic postracial black mayors. (See Box 5.1, "A New Generation of Black Mayors: Newark's Cory Booker and Washington's Adrian Fenty.")

Booker, Fenty, and Johnson emphasized school reform.[87] They saw the importance of reenergizing schools where students were performing far below national standards. However, their efforts at school takeovers and the expansion of charter schools antagonized the traditional civil rights establishment and members of the black community who did not wish to put black positions in the school system at risk. In Los Angeles, Mayor Antonio Villaraigosa similarly backed charter schools and pushed to gain greater control over education in the Los Angeles Unified School District.[88]

Conclusion: The Limited Position of Cities and the Prospects for Local Leadership

The formal structure and powers of a local government are spelled out in a city's charter and vary from community to community. Charters grant a city only limited taxing, spending, and borrowing authority. In general, state laws reflect a distrust of local authority and a refusal to give local decision makers the taxing and land-use powers necessary to respond effectively to urban problems.

City charters tend to diffuse local governing authority, establishing independent boards and commissions that act as an impediment to strong, centralized

Box 5.1

A New Generation of Black Mayors: Newark's Cory Booker and Washington's Adrian Fenty

The shift to a new generation of black mayors is perhaps nowhere more evident than in Newark, New Jersey, where in 2006, Cory Booker, a Rhodes Scholar and graduate of Yale Law School, succeeded Sharpe James, a twenty-year veteran, as mayor. The change was all the more remarkable as Booker, running a deracialized campaign, had lost to James four years earlier. Booker had cast himself as a new-style black politician, promising to galvanize economic development and modernize the city's antiquated system of delivering public services. James, the old-style political street fighter, beat Booker by sharply attacking the newcomer as a privileged outsider who lacked "racial authenticity" in minority-majority Newark. James promoted himself as "The Real Deal," the authentic black man.

In 2006, James, with his administration under attack for various scandals, decided at the very last minute not to run yet one more time for mayor. Booker was now the front-runner. Despite having lost four years earlier, Booker did not jettison his new-black-politics style and suddenly offer himself to voters as a racialized candidate. Instead, Newark's voters "became more comfortable with the idea of his leadership." In the years since his initial electoral loss, Booker reached out to members of the city's black establishment, continuing his work in the community and taking up residence in Brick Towers, a public housing project in central Newark. Booker continued to emphasize his bridge-building policy views. But this time around he also ran as an anticrime candidate, as campaign research showed crime to be the most salient concern of inner-city residents. The Booker campaign also avoided minor mistakes that plagued the 2002 campaign; in 2006, Booker took special care to place blacks and Newarkers in visible campaign positions. Booker won over 70 percent of the vote, and his allies swept to control of the city council.[1] Four years later, Booker easily gained reelection.

Booker's deracialized appeal was a reflection of his education, his personal style, and his understanding of just what sort of alliances a mayor would have to build to begin to lift Newark out of its economic miseries. Newark would need the help of corporate leaders, nonprofit partners, and state and local officials. Booker reached out across racial lines.

Conditions of fiscal stringency led Booker to dismiss hundreds of city workers. He advocated vouchers as part of a strategy to shake up the city's failing school system. Members of the black establishment saw vouchers as a threat to inner-city schools and the job security of black teachers. Amiri Baraka, a black nationalist poet and sharp-tongued Booker critic, charged that the mayor was more concerned with developers and "rich white folks" than with local residents. According to Baraka, residents were beginning to refer to the city as "occupied Newark."[2]

In Washington, DC, Mayor Adrian Fenty largely reflected Booker's orientation. Fenty won the mayoralty at the young age of thirty-five. Fenty was the biracial son of a mixed marriage. He attended elite Oberlin College but later earned his law degree in the District from Howard University, the nation's leading historically black university. A lifelong resident of Washington, Fenty initially avoided some of the suspicions that had plagued Booker, who had grown up in an affluent white suburb and had to move to Newark in order to run his first mayoral race.

Fenty ran on his youthfulness, promising to bring much-needed managerial improvements and otherwise reinvigorate the District's government. He personally knocked on the doors of half of the homes in the District and promised to increase the responsiveness of the District to its citizens.

Fenty's deracialized campaign appealed to various constituencies in a city that was experiencing a surge in the number of white residents as result of gentrification. At the time of his 2006 election, the District's white population had grown to 38 percent. African Americans, 53 percent of the population, only barely held the majority.[3]

But Fenty's story has a quite different ending from Booker's. Fenty lost reelection in 2010, with black voters now rejecting the highly individualistic mayor whom they saw as too brash and irresponsive to traditional black constituencies. The city's crime rates had fallen, and Fenty had appointed a new school superintendent who brought numerous improvements to the District's schools, leading to gains in math and reading scores. Fenty's record earned him the endorsement of the *Washington Post* and should have earned him reelection. Yet, numerous African Americans criticized the mayor for failing to appoint African Americans to top city posts and for being too deferential to outside interests, especially to developers whose projects were displacing blacks from the inner city near the downtown.

Black voters who abandoned Fenty were especially rankled by his replacement of the District's school superintendent, an African American, with Korean American Michelle Rhee, the city's first nonblack schools' leader in four decades. Rhee, who came to the District from New York, dismissed hundreds of teachers and administrators for their poor performance, angering the teacher's union and a large number of African Americans. Vincent Gray, the soft-spoken moderate black council member, criticized Fenty for his "secrecy" and for "shutting out community voices" in the mayor's overreliance on experts, advisers, and contractors (including his old fraternity brothers!) from outside the community.[4]

Clearly, in DC, as in Newark, the times had changed—but not completely. The fiery black nationalism of former Washington mayor Marion Barry no longer played well in a city where the white population had increased and interactions across racial lines had become more the norm. In a city with a great many needs, Barry's race-based political appeals yielded to the managerial orientation of successors Anthony Williams, Adrian Fenty, and Vincent Gray. But as Fenty's 2010 defeat revealed, in cities with a large African American population, questions of racial authenticity do not disappear but remain submerged beneath the surface.

[1]Andra Gillespie, "Losing and Winning: Cory Booker's Ascent to Newark's Mayoralty," in *Whose Black Politics? Cases in Post-Racial Black Leadership*, ed. Gillespie (New York: Routledge, 2010), 67–84. The quotations describing Booker's campaigns can be found, respectively, on pp. 67, 72, and 71.

[2]Andrew Jacobs, "Newark Mayor Battles Old Guard and Rumors," *New York Times*, July 3, 2007.

[3]Rachel Yon, "The Declining Significance of Race: Adrian Fenty and the Smooth Electoral Transition," in Gillespie, *Whose Black Politics?,* 195–213.

[4]Nikita Stewart and Paul Schwartzman, "How Adrian Fenty Lost His Reelection Bid for D.C. Mayor," *Washington Post*, September 15, 2010; Robert McCartney, "Adrian Fenty, Vincent Gray and the Politics of Race and Class in D.C.," *Washington Post*, August 29, 2010; Mike DeBonis, "'Analysis' Polls Show Voters Like Fenty's Achievements, But Maybe Not His Style," *Washington Post,* August 30, 2010. The quotations are from a Vincent Gray television ad; see Mike DeBonis, "Gray, Fenty Debut New TV Ads," *Washington Post,* September 3, 2010, http://voices.washingtonpost.com/debonis/2010/09/gray_fenty_debut_new_tv_ads.html.

urban leadership. Municipal mayors seldom have the full range of appointive, budgetary, and veto powers comparable to that possessed by the president of the United States.

The strong-mayor system centralizes authority in the mayor's hand but suffers noteworthy shortcomings. An elected mayor may lack the managerial, planning, and budgeting skills essential to direct the affairs of a big city that is in many ways the equivalent of a major corporation. Once in office, an elected mayor may also be unduly influenced by political and partisan considerations.

The council-manager system offers the advantages of nonpartisan, trained, professional administration. Governance under the council-manager system emphasizes cooperation more than conflict. However, in numerous cities, councils and managers overstep their roles, which are not clearly demarcated, resulting in conflict. The council-manager system may also not be able to provide the strong leadership that big cities find in an elected executive who can command the attention of the media and claim to speak for the people.

Over the years, cities have modified and adapted their formal governing structures, borrowing structural elements that have worked well in other communities. As a result, there are few truly pure mayor-council and council-manager cities in the United States today. Instead, cities have hybrid forms of government. Mayors govern with the assistance of a professional CAO. A number of council-manager cities have increased the powers of the mayor so that the city can speak with one voice when courting potential new businesses. Requirements for citizen participation also diminish some of the insularity that used to characterize managerial government.

Mayors cannot rely on the formal powers of their office. Instead, effective leadership derives from an individual's skill and personal style, and is often reflected in a mayor's coalition-building abilities. Effective mayoral leadership remains quite elusive given both the intractable nature of many urban problems, the severe limitations of municipal authority, and, in many cases, the paucity of formal powers granted the mayor's office.

African American and Latino mayors face a particularly difficult dilemma in seeking to forge cross-racial political coalitions to promote new investment in the city without "selling out" the interests of poorer neighborhoods and citizens. A new generation of postracial mayors appears to have the comfort level, political skills, and willingness to cross racial lines and work with business and nonprofit leaders and suburban and state officials.

The manager-council plan was initially a Progressive Era reform designed to bring "good government" to the city. As we shall see in the next chapter, political reformers also introduced various other changes in their effort to improve governmental performance and to diminish the hold that political party "machines" and "bosses" had on city affairs. These "reforms" continue to shape access and power in the contemporary American city.

NOTES

1. *City of Clinton* v. *Cedar Rapids and Missouri Railroad Company*, 24 Iowa 455 (1868).

2. John F. Dillon, *Commentary on the Law of Municipal Corporations*, 5th ed. (Boston: Little, Brown, 1911), vol. 1, sec. 237.

3. *Atkins v. Kansas*, 191 U.S. 207 at 220–221 (1903); and *Trenton v. New Jersey*, 262 U.S. 182. 67LEd93j, 43 SCt 534 (1923).

4. Gerald E. Frug, *City Making: Building Communities without Building Walls* (Princeton, NJ: Princeton University Press, 2001), 50–51.

5. John Kromer, "Vacant-Property Policy and Practice: Baltimore and Philadelphia," discussion paper prepared for the Brookings Institution Center on Urban and Metropolitan Policy, Washington, DC, October 2002, www.brookings.edu/es/urban/publications/kromervacant.pdf.

6. John L. Mikesell, *Fiscal Administration: Analysis and Applications for the Public Sector*, 8th ed. (Boston: Wadsworth, 2010), 340.

7. David R. Berman, "State-Local Relations: Authority and Finances," *The Municipal Year Book 2010 [MYB 2010*] (Washington, DC: International City/County Management Association, 2010), 51.

8. David R. Berman, "State-Local Relations: Authority, Finance, and Regional Cooperation," *The Municipal Year Book 1998* [*MYB 1998*] (Washington, DC: International City/County Management Association, 1998), 66.

9. Berman, "State-Local Relations: Authority and Finances," *MYB 2010*, pp. 47–49; idem, "State-Local Relations: Authority and Finances," *The Municipal Year Book 2009* (Washington, DC: International City/County Management Association, 2009), 57–58.

10. For a detailed discussion of the variation in home-rule authority permitted in each of the fifty states, see Dale Krane, Platon N. Rigos, and Melvin B. Hill, eds., *Home Rule: A Fifty-State Handbook* (Washington, DC: Congressional Quarterly Press, 2000); and Berman, "State-Local Relations: Authority and Finances," *MYB 2010*, 47–57.

11. Marshal Pitchford, "The Fight over Residency Requirements: The Statehouse v. The Courthouse," *NEO (Northeast Ohio) Municipal Leader* (Spring 2006): 28–29, www.ralaw.com/resources/documents/MP_NEO_Mun_Leader_spring06.pdf; Henry J. Gomez, "Ohio Supreme Court Rules Against City Residency Requirements," *(Cleveland) Plain Dealer,* June 10, 2009.

12. Jesse J. Richardson Jr., Meghan Zimmerman Gough, and Robert Puentes, "Is Home Rule the Answer? The Influence of Dillon's Rule on Growth Management," discussion paper prepared for the Brookings Institution Center on Urban and Metropolitan Policy, Washington, DC, January 2003, www.brookings.edu/~/media/Files/rc/reports/2003/01metropolitanpolicy_jesse%20j%20%20richardson%20%20jr/dillonsrule.pdf.

13. Jon S. Vernick and Lisa M. Hepburn, "Twenty Thousand Gun-Control Laws?" research brief of the Brookings Institution Center on Metropolitan and Urban Policy, Washington, DC, December 2002, www.brookings.edu/es/urban/publications/gunbook4.pdf.

14. Miguel Bustillo, "Alimony Law Could Handicap a Fledgling Valley City," *Los Angeles Times,* January 10, 1999; Dean E. McHenry Jr., "The State's Role in Urban Secession: The Impact of Procedures on the Success of Urban Movements," paper presented at the annual meeting of the American Political Science Association, San Francisco, August 30–September 2, 2001; Raphael J. Sonenshein and Tom Hogen-Esch, "Bringing the (State) Government Back In: Home Rule and the Politics of Secession in Los Angeles and New York City," *Urban Affairs Review* 41, no. 4 (March 2006): 467–491.

15. Berman, "State-Local Relations: Authority and Finances," *MYB 2010*, 54. In response to the State of California's "hold up" of local sales tax revenues, a coalition of local governments succeeded in 2004 in gaining voter approval of a change in the state constitution that put severe limitations on the ability of the California legislature to borrow or take local property tax revenues.

16. Ibid.

17. Data for 1992 provided by the Bureau of the Census.

18. Berman, "State-Local Relations: Authority and Finances," *MYB 2010*, 54.

19. Ibid.

20. Michael A. Pagano, "City Fiscal Conditions in 2002," a report to the National League of Cities, Washington DC, 4.

21. Mark S. Rosentraub and Wasam al-Habil, "Why Metropolitan Governance Is Growing, as Is the Need for Elastic Governments," in *Governing Metropolitan Regions in the 21st Century,* ed. Don Phares (Armonk, NY: M.E. Sharpe, 2009), 42.

22. Various issues related to the property tax issues are discussed by Roy W. Bahl Jr., "Local Government Expenditures and Revenues," in *Management Policies in Local Government Finance*, 5th ed., ed. J. Richard Aronson and Eli Schwartz (Washington, DC: International City/County Management Association, 2004), 90–93; and Mikesell, *Fiscal Administration,* 490–492.

23. Berman, "State-Local Relations: Authority and Finances," *MYB 2010*, 54.

24. These and other issues concerning the local income tax are discussed by John L. Mikesell, "General Sales, Income, and Other Nonproperty Taxes," in Aronson and Schwartz, *Management Policies in Local Government Finance,* 305–309.

25. U.S. Census Bureau, *Public Education Finances 2008* (Washington, DC: June 2010), p. 11, Table 11, "States Ranked According to Per Pupil Elementary-Secondary Public School System Finance Amounts: 2007–2008."

26. Alvin D. Sokolow, "The Changing Property Tax and State-Local Relations," *Publius: Journal of Federalism* 28, no. 1 (Winter 1998): 165–187. For more details of how Proposition 13 and similar state ballot initiatives have served to "hollow out" or diminish local autonomy in California, see Peter Schrag, *The End of Paradise: California's Experience, America's Future* (New York: New Press, 1998), 163–167; David B. Magleby, "Ballot Initiatives and Intergovernmental Relations in the United States," *Publius: Journal of Federalism* 28, no. 1 (Winter 1998): 147–163.

27. Stephen P. Erie, Christopher W. Hoene, and Gregory D. Saxton, "Fiscal Constraints and the Loss of Home Rule: The Long-Term Impacts of California's Post-Proposition 13 Fiscal Regime," *American Review of Public Administration* 32, no. 4 (December 2002): 423–454.

28. Vladimir Kogan and Mathew D. McCubbins, "The Problem of Being Special: Special Assessment Districts and the Financing of Infrastructure in California," research paper of the University of Southern California Keston Institute for Public Finance and Infrastructure Policy, May 2008, www.usc.edu/schools/sppd/keston/research/documents/McCubinsProblemofBeingSpecial2008.pdf.

29. Steven Litt, "Cleveland Cuyahoga County Port Authority Approves $75 Million Bond Issue for Cleveland Museum of Art Expansion," *(Cleveland) Plain Dealer*, June 8, 2010; James F. McCarty, "Should the Port Authority Be Saved or Dismantled? Critics Say Other Public Entities Could Do the Job Better," *(Cleveland) Plain Dealer*, January 11, 2010.

30. Colin H. McCubbins and Mathew D. McCubbins, "Proposition 13 and The California Fiscal Shell Game," *California Journal of Politics and Policy* 2, no. 2 (2010), www.bepress.com/cjpp/vol2/iss2/6/; Theodore J. Stumm and Pamela Pearson Mann, "Special Assessments in Florida Cities and Counties: Dodging Amendment 10?" *Journal of Public Budgeting, Accounting, and Financial Management* 16, no. 2 (Summer 2004), www.allbusiness.com/legal/tax-law-property-tax/13481256-1.html.

31. Jack Citrin, "Proposition 13 and the Transformation of California Government," *California Journal of Politics and Policy* 1, no. 1 (2009), www.bepress.com/cjpp/vol1/iss1/16/.

32. Mark Baldassare, *When Government Fails: The Orange County Bankruptcy* (Berkeley: University of California Press, 1998).

33. Gretchen Morgenson, "Exotic Deals Put Denver Schools Deeper into Debt," *New York Times*, August 5, 2010; Amy Hetzner, "As the Value of Investments Plunge, 5 School Districts Pressured Over Loans," *Wall Street Journal*, January 3, 2010; idem, "Credit Ratings Lowered for 2 School Districts with Risky Investments," *Wall Street Journal*, April 19, 2010.

34. Kenneth K. Wong and Francis X. Shen, "City and State Takeover as a School Reform Strategy," *ERIC Digest* 174 (July 2000), www.ericfacility.net/databases/ERIC_Digests/ed467111.html.

35. Brian Gill, Ron Zimmer, Jolley Christman, and Suzanne Blanc, "State Takeover, School Restructuring, Private Management, and Student Achievement in Philadelphia," research paper published by the Rand Corporation, Santa Monica, CA, 2007, http://pdf.researchforaction.org/rfapdf/publication/pdf_file/262/Gill_B_State_Takeover.pdf.

36. The earlier stages in the state's fluctuating relations with Detroit schools are described by

Wilbur C. Rich, "Who's Afraid of a Mayoral Takeover of Detroit's Public Schools?" in *When Mayors Take Charge: School Governance in the City*, ed. Joseph P. Viteritti (Washington, DC: Brookings Institution Press, 2009), 148–167.

37. Jeffrey R. Henig, "Mayoral Control: What We Can and Cannot Learn from Other Cities," in Viteritti, *When Mayors Take Charge*, 19–45; Kenneth K. Wong. Francis X. Shen, Dorothea Agnostopoulos, and Stacey Routledge, *The Education Mayor: Improving America's Schools* (Washington, DC: Georgetown University Press, 2007).

38. Rene Sanchez, "Mayor Daley Takes Turn at the Board as Schools' Revolt Hits Chicago," *Washington Post*, July 13, 1995; Dorothy Shipps, "Updating Tradition: The Institutional Underpinnings of Modern Mayoral Control in Chicago's Public Schools," in Viteritti, *When Mayors Take Charge*, 117–147.

39. A 2001 ICMA survey of municipalities with a population over 2,500 showed that 53 percent had the council-manager plan, 38 percent the mayor-council form, and only 1 percent the commission arrangement. A number of smaller communities (5 percent of the respondents) reported that they were governed by a town meeting where all citizens are entitled to appear and participate in the making of local decisions. Also see Tari Renner and Victor S. DeSantis, "Municipal Form of Government: Issues and Trends," *The Municipal Year Book 1998* (Washington, DC: International City/County Management Association, 1998), 30–41.

40. David H. Folz and P. Edward French, *Managing America's Small Communities: People, Politics, and Performance* (Lanham, MD: Rowman & Littlefield, 2005), 15–21.

41. Renner and DeSantis, "Municipal Form of Government," 30–41.

42. John Gunyou, "'Weak Mayor' Model Is a Serious Handicap," *(Minneapolis-St. Paul) Star Tribune*, December 5, 2004.

43. Daniel Howes, "Bing Battles a Culture of Entitlement," *Detroit News*, October 8, 2009.

44. Edgar E. Ramirez de la Cruz, "County Form of Government: Trends in Structure and Composition," *The Municipal Year Book 2009* (Washington, DC: International City/County Management Association, 2009), 23.

45. Karl Nollenberger, "Cooperation and Conflict in Governmental Decision Making in Mid-Sized U.S. Cities," *The Municipal Year Book 2008* (Washington, DC: International City/County Management Association, 2008), 9–15.

46. Tari Renner, "Appointed Local Government Managers: Stability and Change," *The Municipal Year Book 1990* (Washington, DC: International City/County Management Association, 1990), 41 and 49–53; David N. Ammons and Charldean Newell, "'City Managers Don't Make Policy': A Lie; Let's Face It," *National Civic Review* 77 (March/April 1988): 124–132.

47. Jerri Killian and Enamul Choudhury, "Continuity and Change in the Role of City Managers," *The Municipal Year Book 2010* (Washington, DC: The International City/County Management Association, 2010), 10–18, esp. 13; Tansu Demir, "The Complementarity View: Exploring a Continuum in Political-Administrative Relations," *Public Administration Review* 69, no. 5 (September/October 2009): 876–888; John Nalbandian, *Professionalism in Local Government: Transformations in the Roles, Responsibilities, and Values of City Managers* (San Francisco: Jossey-Bass, 1991).

48. Siegrun Fox Freyss, "Matching City Power Structures and City Managers' Leadership Styles: A New Model of Fit," *The Municipal Year Book 2009* (Washington, DC: International City/County Management Association, 2009), 3–10. John Nalbandian, "The Manager as Political Leader," *National Civic Review* 90, no. 1 (Spring 2001): 63–73, describes the self-effacing style of Dennis Hays, the chief administrative officer of Wyandotte County, Kansas. Hays was an important part of the leadership team that brought NASCAR to Kansas City. Yet, he was reluctant to take the stage in public or engage in any activity that could be seen as political.

49. William F. Fannin and Don Hellriegel, "Policy Roles of City Managers: A Contingency Typology and Empirical Test," *Urban Affairs Quarterly* 13 (April 1985): 212–226. See also Poul Erik Mouritzen and James H. Svara, *Leadership at the Apex: Politicians and Administrators in Western Local Governments* (Pittsburgh, PA: University of Pittsburgh Press, 2002.

50. James H. Svara, *Official Leadership in the City: Patterns of Conflict and Cooperation* (New York: Oxford University Press, 1990); idem, "The Roles of the City Council and Implications for the Structure of City Government," *National Civic Review* 91, no. 1 (Spring 2002): 5–23.

51. John T. Spence, "Charting Progress of the Empowered Mayor: The 'Stronger Mayor' in Cincinnati, Ohio," in *The Facilitative Leader in City Hall*, ed. James H. Svara (Boca Raton, FL: CRC Press, 2009), 253–279.

52. Glen Sparrow, "The Emerging Chief Executive: The San Diego Experience," *National Civic Review* (December 1985): 538–547; Glen W. Sparrow, "The Emerging Chief Executive 1971–91: A San Diego Update" in *Facilitative Leadership in Local Government: Lessons from Successful Mayors and Chairpersons*, ed. James H. Svara (San Francisco: Jossey-Bass, 1994), 187–199.

53. Rufus P. Browning, Dale Rogers Marshall, and David H. Tabb, *Protest Is Not Enough: The Struggle of Blacks and Hispanics for Equality in Urban Politics* (Berkeley: University of California Press, 1984), 201–202.

54. Stu Woo, "'Weak' Mayor Seeks Assistance to Reshape Sacramento," *Wall Street Journal*, December 5, 2009.

55. The material presented here on the hybrid city borrows largely from H. George Frederickson, Gary A. Johnson, and Curtis H. Wood, *The Adapted City: Institutional Dynamics and Structural Change* (Armonk, NY: M.E. Sharpe, 2004).

56. Kimberly L. Nelson and James H. Svara, "Adaptation of Models versus Variations in Form: Classifying Structures of City Government," *Urban Affairs Review* 45, no. 4 (2010): 552–554.

57. Salary figures from official city government Web sites.

58. Tari Renner and Victor S. DeSantis, "Contemporary Patterns and Trends in Municipal Government Structures," *The Municipal Year Book 1993* (Washington, DC: The International City/County Management Association, 1993), 66.

59. John P. Pelissero and Timothy B. Krebs, "City Council Legislative Committees and Policymaking in Large United States Cities," *American Journal of Political Science* 41, no. 2 (April 1997): 499–518.

60. Timothy Bledsoe, *Careers in City Politics: The Case for Urban Democracy* (Pittsburgh: University of Pittsburgh Press, 1993), 113–119 and 126–128.

61. Ibid., 18–82; Susan MacManus, "The Resurgent City Councils," in *American State and Local Politics: Directions for the 21st Century*, ed. Ronald E. Weber and Paul Brace (New York: Chatham House, 1999), 166–172.

62. "Women in Elective Office 2005" and "Women in Elective Office 2011," fact sheets prepared by the Center for American Women in Politics, Eagleton Institute of Politics, Rutgers, The State University of New Jersey. The most recent fact sheet is available at www.cawp.rutgers.edu/fast_facts/levels_of_office/documents/elective.pdf.

63. Bledsoe, *Careers in City Politics*, 46, 122, and 177–178. Women's representation in legislative office has generally improved—but slowly—over time. By 2011, women held 16.4 percent of the seats in the U.S. House of Representatives, 17 percent of the seats in the U.S. Senate, and 23.4 percent of seats in state legislatures. See "Women in Elective Office 2011."

64. R. Darcy, Susan Welch, and Janet Clark, *Women, Elections, and Representation* (New York: Longman, 1987), 33–34.

65. M. Margaret Conway, Gertrude A. Steuernagel, and David W. Ahern, *Women and Political Participation* (Washington, DC: CQ Press, 1997), 113.

66. Robert A. Schumann and Richard L. Fox, "Women Chief Administrative Officers: Perceptions of Their Role in Government," *The Municipal Year Book 1998* (Washington, DC: International City/County Management Association, 1998), 116–122.

67. Susan Abrams Beck, "Acting as Women: The Effects and Limitations of Gender in Local Government," in *The Impact of Women in Public Office,* ed. Susan J. Carroll (Bloomington: University of Indiana Press, 2001), 49–67, looked at suburban legislatures and concluded that the difference between male and female legislative styles is subtle but significant.

68. Bledsoe, *Careers in City Politics*, 46, 122, and 177–178.

69. Melvin G. Holli, "Mayors," (Electronic) *Encyclopedia of Chicago*, Chicago Historical Society, 2005, http://encyclopedia.chicagohistory.org/pages/795.html.

70. Renner and DeSantis, "Municipal Form of Government," 35–37.

71. Written in the midst of the tumultuous 1970s, the thesis of Douglas Yates' *The Ungovernable City* (Cambridge, MA: MIT Press, 1977) now seems overly pessimistic and dated. The same period in New York City history was similarly portrayed in a more recent volume with the same title: Vincent Cannato, *The Ungovernable City: John Lindsay and His Struggle to Save New York* (New York: Basic Books, 2002).

72. Fred Siegel, *Prince of the City: Giuliani, New York, and the Genius of American Life* (San Francisco: Encounter Books, 2004); Richard M. Flanagan, *Mayors and the Challenge of Urban Leadership* (Lanham, MD: University Press of America, 2004). For a quite different view of Giuliani's tenure in office and leadership, see Wayne Barrett, *Rudy! An Investigative Biography of Rudy Giuliani* (New York: Basic Books, 2001); and Andrew Kirtzman, *Rudy Giuliani: Emperor of the City* (New York: HarperCollins, 2001).

73. Svara, *Official Leadership in the City*, 81–121; idem, *The Facilitative Leader in City Hall.*

74. Charles H. Levine, *Racial Conflict and the American Mayor* (Lexington, MA: Lexington Books, 1974).

75. The quotation is from Mayor Young. See also Wilbur C. Rich, *Coleman Young and Detroit Politics: From Social Activist to Power Broker* (Detroit: Wayne State University Press, 1999).

76. Carlos Muñoz Jr. and Charles P. Henry, "Coalition Politics in San Antonio and Denver: The Cisneros and Peña Mayoral Campaigns," in *Racial Politics in American Cities,* ed. Rufus P. Browning, Dale Rogers Marshall, and David H. Tabb (White Plains, NY: Longman, 1990), 179–190; Rodolfo Rosales, *The Illusion of Inclusion: The Untold Story of San Antonio* (Austin: University of Texas Press, 2000), esp. chap. 7.

77. Raphael J. Sonenshein, *Politics in Black and White: Race and Power in Los Angeles* (Princeton, NJ: Princeton University Press, 1993); James A. Regalado, "Organized Labor and Los Angeles City Politics: An Assessment in the Bradley Years, 1973–89," *Urban Affairs Quarterly* 27 (September 1991): 87–108.

78. J. Phillip Thompson III, *Double Trouble: Black Mayors, Black Communities, and the Call for a Deep Democracy* (New York: Oxford University Press, 2006), 136–139, esp. 138.

79. Huey L. Perry, ed., *Race, Politics, and Governance in the United States* (Gainesville: University Press of Florida, 1997); Richard A. Keiser, "Philadelphia's Evolving Biracial Coalition," in *Racial Politics in American Cities,* 3d ed., ed. Rufus P. Browning, Dale Rogers Marshall, and David H. Tabb (New York: Longman, 2003), 77–112; Rodney E. Hero and Susan E. Clarke, "Latinos, Blacks, and Multiethnic Politics in Denver: Realigning Power and Influence in the Struggle for Equality," in ibid., 309–330; and Richard A. Keiser, *Subordination or Empowerment? African-American Leadership and the Struggle for Urban Political Power* (New York: Oxford University Press, 1997), 90–131.

80. Eric Gonzalez Juenke and Anna Christina Sampaio, "Deracialization and Latino Politics: The Case of the Salazar Brothers in Colorado," *Political Research Quarterly* 63, no. 1 (March 2010): 43–54.

81. Raphael J. Sonenshein and Susan H. Pinkus, "Latino Incorporation Reaches the Urban Summit: How Antonio Villaraigosa Won the 2005 Los Angeles Mayor's Race," *PS: Political Science and Politics* 38, no. 4 (2005): 713–721; the quotations appear, respectively, on pp. 715 and 725.

82. Huey L. Perry, "Deracialization as an Analytical Construct in American Urban Politics," *Urban Affairs Quarterly* 27, no. 2 (1991): 181–191.

83. David C. Smith, "Recent Elections and Black Politics: The Maturation or Death of Black Politics?" *PS: Political Science and Politics* 23 (June 1990): 161. See also Robert T. Starks, "A Commentary and Response to 'Exploring the Meaning and Implications of Deracialization in African-American Urban Politics,'" *Urban Affairs Quarterly* 27 (December 1991): 221.

84. Smith, "Recent Elections and Black Politics," 160.

85. Thompson, *Double Trouble*, esp. 15–16, 156, and 265–267.

86. This paragraph is largely based on Andra Gillespie, "Meet the New Class: Theorizing Young Black Leadership in a 'Postracial' Era," in *Whose Black Politics? Cases in Post-Racial Black Leadership,* ed. Andra Gillespie (New York: Routledge, 2010), 9–42.

87. Nikita Stewart, "Young Black Mayors Combine to Remodel the Political Arena," *Washington Post,* March 8, 2009; "Education that Works: Ideas for Sacramento," (working paper from the March 2009 Education Summit, presented by Sacramento Mayor Kevin Johnson, September 1, 2009), www.cityofsacramento.org/mayor/documents/educationThatWorks_ideasForSacramento.pdf.

88. Howard Blume, "Villaraigosa Backs Charter Schools Bids, Rips Cortines," *Los Angeles Times*, June 25, 2010.

6 The Machine, Reform, and Postreform City

For much of the nineteenth and the twentieth centuries, strong political party organizations or **political machines** dominated big cities, especially in the Northeast and the Midwest. New York, Boston, Philadelphia, Pittsburgh, Jersey City, New Haven, Albany, Chicago, Cincinnati, and Kansas City all had political machines at major points of their development. While strong local party organizations were less prevalent in the South and West, party "boss rule" also emerged in Memphis, New Orleans, San Antonio, Tampa, and San Francisco.

At its peak power, the urban machine was a top-down organization characterized by **centralized control**. The leaders of the local party organizations—the **political bosses**—gave marching orders to city council members and to ward, precinct, and block captains. The Hague organization, which ruled Jersey City well into the late 1940s, typifies the machine's command structure: "Complete obedience is necessary from the bottom to the top; officials are not supposed to have ideas on public policies, but to take orders."[1] In boss-ruled Chicago, the city council functioned less as an independent legislature and more as a "rubber stamp" of the decisions made by the city's Democratic Party bosses.[2] In many cities, the political boss was not always the mayor or even a top elected official. The fabled bosses of **Tammany Hall**, New York's Democratic Party machine—William Marcy Tweed, Richard Croker, John Kelly, and Charles F. Murphy—operated from offstage.

Political reformers criticized the machine's parochialism and corruption. (See Box 6.1, "Is There Such a Thing as 'Honest Graft'? Corruption and Machine Politics.") The reform movement sought rule changes that would introduce "good government" by undercutting the power of the party organizations. The reformers wanted to free city officials to pursue the "public interest," not the machine's narrow partisan interests. The reformers sought to reduce the power of politically beholden elected officials by placing decision-making authority in the hands of competently trained, expert administrators.

The wars fought between the urban machine and the political reformers wound up reshaping the structures and rules of municipal government. The reformers introduced

Box 6.1

Is There Such a Thing as "Honest Graft"? Corruption and Machine Politics

At their worst, machine politicians were notoriously corrupt, taking **graft** or payoffs in exchange for political favors. The corruption of New York's Tweed Ring, which in the late 1800s drained millions of dollars from the municipal treasury, took the city to the brink of bankruptcy.

Tammany district leader George Washington Plunkitt, who made a fortune in politics, defended the seemingly indefensible practice of taking graft. Plunkitt disingenuously claimed that there was a difference between honest and dishonest graft, and that no Tammany official ever made a penny through "dishonest graft," by blackmailing saloon keepers or stealing from the public treasury. Instead, Plunkitt argued that Tammany politicians displayed good business foresight, taking advantage of what he called "honest graft":

> There's an honest graft, and I'm an example of how it works. . . . My party's in power in the city, and it's goin' to undertake a lot of public improvements. Well, I'm tipped off, say, that they're going to layout a new park at a certain place.
>
> I see my opportunity and I take it. I go to that place and I buy up all the land I can in the neighborhood. Then the board of this or that makes its plan public, and there is a rush to get my land, which nobody cared particular for before.
>
> Ain't it perfectly honest to charge a good price and make a profit on my investment and foresight? Of course, it is. Well, that's honest graft.[1]

Plunkitt was an outrageous character who requested that the epitaph on his headstone read: "He Seen His Opportunities and He Took 'Em." Of course, despite his protestations, "honest graft" is not at all honest. Today, public officials are prosecuted for using their insider knowledge to gain personal enrichment.

Unfortunately, modern era political party organizations continue to exhibit the machine's tendency toward political corruption. In Atlantic City, New Jersey, the mayor and other elected officials were convicted of having taken bribes from criminal elements associated with the casino industry. In 2003, Bridgeport, Connecticut, Mayor Joseph Ganim, the leader of the Democratic organization, was convicted on charges of bribery, extortion, and racketeering.[2] In Chicago, Mayor Richard M. Daley's long term of service was marred by a stream of revelations that members of his administration had taken bribes and shaken down companies for political contributions in exchange for the award of city contracts. Officials in Chicago also falsified test scores in order to steer jobs to their political friends.

[1]William L. Riordan, *Plunkitt of Tammany Hall*, ed. Terrence J. McDonald (Boston: Bedford Books of St. Martin's Press, 1994), 49.

[2]Peter F. Burns, *Electoral Politics Is Not Enough: Racial and Ethnic Minorities and Urban Politics* (Albany: State University of New York Press, 2006), 15–16.

a number of political reforms, including **civil service systems** (where municipal officials are hired according to test scores and merit, not because of the work they did for a political party in the past election campaign), nonpartisan and at-large elections, and the voter initiative and referendum processes that are now commonplace features of local government across the United States.

The reforms, however, proved to be imperfect. The reformers "cleaned up" city politics, increasing professional standards and reducing partisan parochialism. But the reforms came at a cost: they created a city where civil service–protected bureaucracies became the new power centers, power centers that were not always responsive to the concerns of citizens. In the **postreform city**, a new generation of reformers introduced still further changes in an effort to debureaucratize procedures and increase citizen influence in government.

WHY URBAN MACHINES LASTED FOR SO LONG

A POLITICAL TRADING ORGANIZATION

Machine politics was an **exchange process**. The political machine traded favors for votes. The machine rewarded its friends and punished its enemies; it dispensed specific **benefits** (such as jobs and building permits) that were denied to people and businesses who failed to support the machine. Under the **patronage** or **spoils system**, the winning party distributed government jobs and lucrative contracts to its supporters, following the old adage: "To the victors belong the spoils of war."

IMMIGRANTS AND THE BIG-CITY POLITICAL MACHINE

During the 1800s and early 1900s, large numbers of immigrants came from Europe at a time when there was no national welfare system to aid people in need. Machine captains offered shelter and emergency assistance, help in finding jobs, and even help with gaining citizenship—all in exchange for immigrant votes. (See Box 6.2, "Film Images of the City: The Tammany Machine and *The Gangs of New York*.") During the severe winter of 1870–1871, New York boss William M. Tweed "spent $50,000 of his personal funds in his own ward and gave each of the city's aldermen $1,000 out of his own pocket to buy coal for the poor."[3] Between 1869 and 1871 the Tammany-controlled city treasury gave well over a million dollars to the Roman Catholic Church and other religious charities, helping to solidify the machine's hold among New York's immigrants.[4]

The machine sought to build its personal bond with the immigrants. George Washington Plunkitt, a district leader in New York's early twentieth-century Tammany Hall, bragged: "I know every man, woman, and child in the Fifteenth District, except them that's been born this summer—and I know some of them, too."[5] Machine captains attended weddings, funerals, Irish wakes, and Jewish bar mitzvahs. They even gained gratitude by paying for funerals, saving "indigent families from the unimaginable horror of having one of their own buried by the county."[6]

Box 6.2
Film Images of the City:
The Tammany Machine and The Gangs of New York

Martin Scorsese's *The Gangs of New York* (starring Leonardo DiCaprio, Cameron Diaz, and Daniel Day-Lewis) presents pre–Civil War New York at a time when "Boss" William Marcy Tweed was just beginning his rise to power as Tammany leader. In an era when there was no municipal fire department, both Tweed and his political rivals organized voluntary fire companies that rushed to the scene of a fire in an effort to earn the gratitude of voters. Tammany assistants also "worked the docks," greeting the Irish immigrants upon their arrival in America on the so-called coffin ships, a reference to the large number of passengers who died during the perilous trans-Atlantic voyage.

The film documents the extreme poverty of the new arrivals and their need for assistance. Scorsese does not portray the machine leaders as benevolent or caring; indeed, the machine's henchmen could be brutal and corrupt. Their sole concern was to win votes and claim power. Gangs and saloons served as the machine's recruiting grounds.

As *The Gangs of New York* further reveals, Tammany Hall initially started out as a sort of social club, an organization of nativist Protestants who detested the incoming Irish-Catholic immigrants. But Tammany's ambitious leaders soon recognized the importance of appealing to the city's burgeoning number of Irish voters, who could provide the key to electoral victory. The political machines operated during a time of fierce interethnic prejudices and rivalries. Upper-class Protestant "high society" resented the growing numbers of Irish Catholics and the waves of immigration that would soon follow. By comparison, the big-city political machine, whatever its shortcomings, was more responsive to the needs of the immigrants.

Yet, the political machine was not always a friend of immigrants and the working class. Machine leaders often had the financial backing of slumlords and powerful factory owners. As a consequence, machine politicians did not attempt to improve housing conditions in slum tenement districts, nor did they lead the fight to change the dangerous working conditions that the immigrants faced in urban sweatshops.

The machine provided America's new arrivals with a highly symbolic **channel of social mobility**. At a time when immigrants were excluded from the upper rungs of society and the business world, their voting numbers assured them of a place in the electoral arena and the ability of group members to advance up the ladder of political power.

Some analysts have celebrated the urban machine as a **rainbow coalition**, a pastiche of different immigrant groups with machine leaders skillfully dispensing jobs and other benefits to the various ethnic groups in the immigrant city. Yet, such an assessment overly glorifies the machine: "[T]o view the old urban machine as vehicles for inclusion and massive upward mobility is a romantic misreading of the past."[7] The leaders of the urban machine did not willingly share benefits with each enter-

Contemporary Ethnic Politics: Antonio Villaraigosa, the first Latino to be elected Mayor of Los Angeles, extends his appeal to a different ethnic constituency by attending the city's Chinatown parade (2006). Courtesy of Wikimedia Commons through Flickr and Jim Winstead. http://commons.wikimedia.org/wiki/File:Antonio_Villaraigosa_(Chinatown_parade).jpg.

ing group of arrivals. Machine politicians commanded only a fairly limited supply of patronage. Irish machine leaders like Boston's legendary Michael J. Curley kept most jobs for the members of their own ethnic group, giving relatively few jobs to others. In Chicago, the Irish-led Democratic machine similarly preserved the lion's share of jobs for its own ethnic group, dispensing lesser benefits to Polish, Italian, and African Americans.[8]

THE MACHINE AND AFRICAN AMERICAN VOTERS

Even where black voters were crucial to the machine's electoral success, machine leaders seldom, if ever, dispensed a commensurate share of benefits to African Americans. In Memphis in the early and mid–twentieth century, "Boss" E.H. Crump accorded African Americans a subordinate position in his political organization. As Memphis had few immigrants, Crump astutely recognized that black votes could provide his margin of victory. He appointed African Americans to positions in the municipal bureaucracy and even named monuments after prominent local black citizens—rarities in the Old South. Crump's political lieutenants encouraged African American voter registration, even paying the poll tax so that a selected number of blacks would be able to vote. Yet, once Crump cemented his power in office, he had less need to cater to black voters. Fewer African Americans were permitted to register to vote, and the machine drew back on the benefits it dispensed to the black community.[9]

The Chicago Democratic organization, led in the 1950s and 1960s by the first Mayor Daley, the legendary Richard J. Daley, dispensed jobs and welfare-style benefits to its African American supporters but would not push for housing and school desegregation.[10] Chicago built a **second ghetto**, a virtual "wall" of high-rise public housing to keep the city's black population from spilling over into white ethnic neighborhoods.[11] The Dan Ryan Expressway "was shifted several blocks during the planning stage to make one of the ghetto walls."[12] Irish machine captains even continued to represent wards or districts that had gained an African American majority. In Chicago, "The Daley political machine functioned not as a ladder of political empowerment but as a lid blocking African American political empowerment."[13]

The Political Machine and the Business Community

The political machine rewarded its business friends with building permits, city licenses, and lucrative franchises and construction contracts. A behind-the-scenes agreement between a business owner and a political boss served to assure that various city agencies would award all of the necessary licenses, zoning variances, inspection permissions, and approvals that a business required. In return, business owners gave machine leaders either a cash kickback or control over a number of jobs that the machine could dispense to its supporters in return for their votes.

The machine's ties to its business constituency meant that the party organization did not always act in the interests of its mass base of voters. In industrial-age New York City, party officials received payoffs and overlooked the unsafe conditions of industrial sweatshops and overcrowded tenement buildings. In Chicago, mayors Richard J. Daley and Richard M. Daley pursued a downtown growth agenda that won the support of prominent business and civic leaders, but, according to critics, slighted the needs of poorer neighborhoods.[14]

Why Political Machines Declined

A growing **national prosperity** and **gains in education** undermined the machine. As voters became more affluent, they no longer needed the benefits the machine offered. Better-educated voters were less willing to trade their votes for the machine's favors.

The expanded **provision of government social welfare and housing services**, beginning with Franklin Roosevelt's New Deal, meant that citizens no longer had to work for the machine on election day and vote for the machine's slate of candidates in order to obtain public services. Machine captains just could not compete with the growing welfare state when it came to dispensing cash relief, housing, and food assistance.

For a long time, f**ederal laws restricting immigration**, especially those enacted in the 1920s, denied the political machine an important pool of potential supporters. With the spigot tightened on immigration from Europe, political machines had to look elsewhere for support. African Americans and Hispanics still needed the jobs and limited benefits the machine could provide.

Racial polarizations also eventually took their toll. Over time, black voters withdrew their support from ethnic-white-dominated political organizations that refused to challenge segregated housing and school segregation and that accepted as normal the underprovision of services in minority areas of the city. In 1983, Congressman Harold Washington became Chicago's first elected African American mayor, having run against the political machine and its "plantation politics" mentality of giving jobs and favors to those members who accepted the machine's biases and the segregated, second-class status of African Americans in Chicago. Harold Washington promised a fairer distribution of city services and a greater focus on the city's neighborhoods.[15] Since Harold Washington's death in office due to a heart attack, no black candidate in Chicago has been able to replicate Washington's difficult balancing act of mobilizing black voters while also winning support from the Hispanic community and the city's Lakefront liberals.[16] Richard M. Daley adapted machine practices to a new era to become Chicago's longest-serving mayor. (See Box 6.3, "Chicago's New Daley: The Machine Adapts to Changed Times.") He attracted support from key African American constituencies, especially black middle-class voters, and the pivotal Latino community. His campaign organization gave contributions to those African-American churches whose leaders were willing to work within the confines of the machine's patronage tradition.[17] He distributed aid to neighborhood organizations that supported the mayor's agenda of growth, tourism, and gentrification.[18] In his later reelection campaigns, Daley won more than 80 percent of the Latino vote. As one leading political analyst concluded in his observations of Richard M. Daley's long tenure: "A White-Latino coalition now governs Chicago."[19]

Big-city machines were already suffering advanced decline when **changes in the mass media** further impaired the ability of machine captains to effectively reach voters. In an age of television and the automobile, city residents no longer looked to political clubhouse dances and machine-sponsored picnics for entertainment. Television and computers also changed the conduct of elections. Even in Chicago, in "the last bastion of party machine politics, the era of cash-based, candidate-centered electoral politics has arrived."[20] Richard M. Daley created a new-style political machine where "old-style patronage and corruption now coexist with multimillion dollar campaign contributions from global corporations, high-tech public opinion polling, and media manipulation. . . . [R]ich individuals and global businesses, law firms, and financial institutions contribute the millions of dollars necessary to hire national political consultants like David Axelrod to do public opinion polling, direct mail, and slick TV ads."[21] Axelrod would achieve fame in the national arena as the top political strategist in the 2008 campaign that took Barack Obama from Chicago to the White House.

The various rule changes enacted by the political **reform movement** also helped undercut the power of the big-city political machine. The **direct primary** undermined boss control of party nominations. In a direct primary, the people themselves—not

Box 6.3
**Chicago's New Daley:
The Machine Adapts to Changed Times**

Like his father, the legendary "Boss" Richard J. Daley, Mayor Richard M. Daley sought to centralize power in city hall. But Richard M. Daley governed in an age when the courts had sharply limited job patronage. He could not amass the patronage armies of his father, even though his administration often skirted civil service and competitive bidding rules in order to steer jobs to supporters.

Richard M. Daley did not seek to project the image of an old-style political boss. Instead, he cast himself in the role of a good-government reformer, a capable city executive who can effectively manage a large city's affairs. Richard M. sought to win the location of global firms for Chicago. He promoted Chicago's downtown as a center of global business. He built Millennium Park, with its dramatic public and event spaces, as testimony to the city's pride. He appealed to tax-conscious middle-class voters, leasing parking garages and Midway Airport and privatizing parking meter collections in order to gain new service efficiencies.

Yet the mayor did not totally reject his machine-politics heritage. The privatization of services provided Daley with a source of **pin-stripe** or **contract patronage**; the mayor rewarded political supporters with no-bid consulting contracts, legal work, and other city favors. The mayor received millions of dollars in campaign donations from the financial services industry, construction firms, and labor unions, all members of the city's growth coalition.

Daley also made substantial efforts to appeal to Chicago's black citizens. Upon taking office, he appointed a black woman, Avis LaVelle, as his press secretary. He also appealed to the city's Hispanic community, winning the key endorsement of 26th Ward Alderman Luis Gutierrez, whom Daley would later endorse for Congress. Daley's coalition-building efforts made it difficult for the city's minorities to unify behind a possible opponent.

Daley's pragmatic approach to governance won him repeated reelection. His tenure in office was no simple return to the machine politics of his father. Rather, Richard M. Daley's governing approach was "part machine/part reform." It was "machine politics reform style."

In 2010, Richard M. Daley finally retired, having served twenty-two years as mayor and having led Chicago's economic rebirth as a global center. He was succeeded in office by Rahm Emanuel, who left his job as chief of staff to President Barack Obama in order to assume the burdens of Chicago's mayoralty.

Sources: Timothy W. Martin, "Chicago Banks on Private Parking," *Wall Street Journal,* December 3, 2008; Rudolph Bush and Dan Mihalopoulos, "Daley Jobs Chief Guilty: Jury Convicts 4 in City Hiring Fraud; Feds Say, 'Stay tuned,'" *Chicago Tribune,* July 7, 2006; Dick Simpson, *Rogues, Rebels, and Rubber Stamps: The Politics of the Chicago City Council from 1863 to the Present* (Boulder, CO: Westview Press, 2001), 253–262, 269–272, 278–281, and 287–290; William J. Grimshaw, *Bitter Fruit: Black Politics and the Chicago Machine* (Chicago: University of Chicago Press, 1992), 206–224; and Larry Bennett, "Chicago's New Politics of Growth," in *The New Chicago: A Social and Cultural Analysis*, ed. John P. Koval et al. (Philadelphia: Temple University Press, 2006), 44–55. The quotations in the last paragraphs are from Grimshaw, *Bitter Fruit*, 206.

Political party machine leaders often took financial kickbacks and other favors from industrialists and landlords. As a result, the political machine did little to combat the unhealthy conditions of the slum tenements and sweatshops of the immigrant city. By contrast, social reformers such as Jacob Riis sought improved housing, sanitation, and schools and an end to child labor.

Cigar Makers and Children at Work in a Tenement Home Workshop, New York City, 1890. Taken by Jacob Riis. http://commons.wikimedia.org/wiki/File:Bohemian_Cigarmakers.jpg.

Young girls at work in a Chicago sweatshop, 1903. http://commons.wikimedia.org/wiki/File:1903sweatshopchicago.jpg.

party leaders—select the party's nominees who run for office in the ensuing general election. **Voter registration requirements** eliminated fraudulent voting and also served to reduce the voter turnout of lower-class citizens, a constituency that often voted for the machine's slate of candidates. **At-large voting rules** sought to limit the ability of machine politicians to win office by delivering projects and specific favors to small geographic constituencies. **Nonpartisan systems** kept party labels off the ballot, forcing voters to give their attention to individual candidates rather than blindly voting for the party slate as urged by machine captains.

The institutionalization of local **merit employment systems** (also called **civil service systems**) was the political reform that most hurt the machine. Civil service required municipal hiring based on merit, that is, based on test scores and job qualifications. Civil service took away from the machine the most important asset—jobs—that it could trade to recruit its army of canvassers and voters. A century ago, Tammany captain George Washington Plunkitt had complained bitterly of "the curse of civil service reform,"[22] foreseeing the ruin that merit hiring rules would bring to the political machine.

Today, almost every city in the country uses a system of merit hiring. U.S. Supreme Court decisions also placed sharp limitations on partisan-based hiring, firing, and promotion. In its 1990 *Rutan* decision, the Court ruled that politically based hiring and promotion was an unconstitutional denial of an individual's First Amendment rights of freedom of speech, belief, and association.[23]

A Look at the Reform Movement: Who Were the Reformers?

The reformers sought to transform local government. They argued that a modern big city could not afford patronage, payoffs, and political favoritism. The reformers sought to have the city run more "like a business" with decision making placed in the hands of highly skilled managers who possessed competencies in technical areas such as planning, budgeting, accounting, personnel, and civil engineering.

The reformers emphasized **neutral expertise**: expert administrators should be able to do their jobs free from political pressures. The reformers argued that political parties were irrelevant to the essential tasks of local government—that there was no Democratic or Republican way to pick up the trash, pave streets, or control the flow of traffic.

Yet, it is too simplistic to view the reformers solely as believers in "good government" who fought against the parochialism and excesses of the political machine. The reformers had a variety of motivations. While many reformers were committed to the ideals of good government, others sought to reshape the rules of city politics in order to preserve their own power.[24] They sought to keep the control of city hall out of the hands of the growing urban immigrant population. The battle between the political machine and the reformers took place in an era of deep-seated class and ethnic antagonisms. America's more established social groups were reluctant to cede power to the big-city machine and its immigrant base.

Upper-class citizens and business owners often dominated municipal reform.[25] They did not want the city to levy taxes in order to provide benefits to the immi-

"The American River Ganges: The Priests and the Children." This savage anti-Irish editorial cartoon, from *Harper's Weekly*, 1871, illustrates the degree to which ethnic tensions and hatreds helped to shape the battle between the urban political machine and the political reformers. This Reform cartoon presents Irish priests as crocodiles ready to devour American schoolchildren. New York's Boss Tweed sits above and idly watches the alleged Irish threat to America's schools and its children. From Library of Congress, Prints and Photographs Division, Washington, DC 20540 USA. http://www.loc.gov/pictures/resource/cph.3a00747/.

grants and the poor. In Sunbelt cities, business-led reform groups headed efforts to keep taxes low by limiting public service provision in African American, Latino, and working-class communities.[26] The rule changes they proposed were not simply the embodiment of good-government principles, they were also weapons used by the established groups to undercut the growing power of more recently arrived groups.

A brief look at San Francisco and Miami underscores how reformed voting rules diminished minority power. For many decades, San Francisco had a reformed system of at-large elections. Minorities won no seats on the city's Board of Supervisors: with their population concentrated in only a portion of the city, they were outvoted in races that were run citywide. In 1977, the city changed the rules and switched the "unreformed" system of district elections: the composition of the Board of Supervisors immediately changed. For the first time, a black woman, a Chinese American, and an avowedly gay activist—Harvey Milk—all won seats in the city's legislature. Each was elected by a district constituency. Harvey Milk won easily in a district that encompassed the gay population of San Francisco's Castro district. He had lost earlier races that were conducted at large.

Metropolitan Miami-Dade County's reformed system of nonpartisan and at-large elections similarly served to dissuade "candidates from running as strong advocates of minority political interests."[27] Community activists and racial minorities lacked the support of suburban voters and the extensive funding base necessary to win a countywide race. A switch to "unreformed" voting rules, however, changed all that. Judicial action forced the county in 1993 to institute a system of district elections. The new voting system immediately resulted in the election of an increased number of Hispanics and African Americans to the Metro Commission.

There were at least two branches of the reform movement, each motivated by different reasons. The **structural reform movement** was dominated by business owners, elite social groups, and others antagonistic to the immigrant newcomers. The structural reformers pressed for the adoption of civil service systems, nonpartisan and at-large elections, and other rule changes that would diminish the influence of lower-class voters. The structural reformers sought rules that would "bias the electoral arena in their favor." By "narrowing the electorate," the structural reformers sought "to maintain power and reduce electoral competition."[28]

The **social reform movement** was quite different: social reformers actually sought to aid the immigrants and the disadvantaged. Social reformers sought to replace the corrupt political machine with a government that would be more committed to better schools and housing and improved health and workplace safety for factory workers.[29] Social reformers were not always the allies of the business-led structural reformers. Many business leaders opposed the social reforms because they did not wish to pay additional taxes to support expanded programs in service to disadvantaged groups.

Women played prominent roles in many social reform organizations. At a time when women were confined to the traditional domestic roles of housewife and mother, women found socially acceptable outlets for public activity in their work with **settlement houses** (social work-style institutions that provided care for poor and immigrant women), charitable societies, and other religious and social reform associations devoted to improving the lives of women and children.[30]

THE REFORMS AND THEIR IMPACT

In Chapter 5, we examined two important structural reforms: the council-manager and commission systems of government. We now examine other structural reforms that have had a lasting influence on city politics.

AT-LARGE ELECTIONS

In a system of **at-large elections**, citizens vote for council members citywide, not by district. At-large election systems are popular. Nearly half of local governments in the United States employ at-large voting systems. Another 25 percent of cities rely on a **combination** or **mixed electoral system**. Under a mixed electoral system, some council members are elected citywide while the rest of the council run in smaller voting districts.[31]

Officials elected at large have the whole city as their constituency. They tend to pay greater attention to citywide concerns, as opposed to officials elected from wards who may cater to the more parochial concerns of smaller geographical districts. The reformers further argued that an at-large system would enable high-quality candidates to serve on the city council, as the best-qualified candidates are not scattered, one per district, throughout the city.

But as the San Francisco and Miami Metro cases serve to indicate, at-large voting systems can have a discriminatory impact: they make it difficult for a geographically concentrated or ghettoized minority group to elect members to office.[32] When elections are conducted by district, a minority group that dominates a geographical area can easily elect "one of their own" to the city council. When races are run city- or countywide, such a minority is likely to be easily outvoted.

For decades, at-large voting rules worked against Africa American representation on the Boston city council. Until the 1980s, only a single black Bostonian, Thomas Atkins, was able to win election to the city council; white voters in the city dominated all at-large matchups. Boston eventually abandoned its at-large system in favor of a mixed electoral system where nine members are elected from districts and four are elected citywide. African Americans were able to win contests in minority-dominated areas of the city. But the plan's inclusion of four at-large council seats, almost certain to be won by white candidates, helps to assure the continuing dominance of more conservative white voices.[33]

Minority activists, especially poor people's advocates, often find it difficult to raise the vast sums of money required for a citywide campaign with its reliance on paid media advertising. At-large and district elections favor different types of candidates. At-large systems reward those office seekers who are visible citywide or who are acceptable to big donors and a broad base of voters across the city. A system of district elections, by contrast, puts a lesser premium on money and political moderation. Instead, election by district provides a route to office for grassroots activists who have strong neighborhood backing, even if they are not well known outside the district.

History reveals that at-large voting systems have often been used as a weapon of discrimination, a tool to undermine minority voting rights. Cities in the South enacted at-large voting systems in an attempt to keep newly enfranchised blacks from winning municipal office.[34] In the 1960s, at a time when African Americans in the South were finally gaining the right to vote, twenty county governments and boards of education in Georgia suddenly switched from district to at-large voting rules, an effort to limit the electoral chances of black candidates. The State of Mississippi even passed legislation requiring that all county boards of supervisors and county school boards be elected at large.[35] In both the North and the South, city leaders who did not wish to see African Americans gain control of the city council turned to a strategy of annexing white suburbs, knowing that the former suburbanites would help to outvote African Americans in municipal electoral contests conducted at large.

The national government responded to such abuses by passing the **Voting Rights Act (VRA) of 1965**. One section of the act prohibits cities with a history of discrimination from manipulating voting rules in order to diminish the possibilities of electing minority candidates. Civil rights groups went to court and began to challenge at-large voting systems. Dallas in 1991, responding to pressures from the judiciary, replaced its system of at-large elections with a new "14–1 plan": fourteen council members were elected by district, with only the mayor elected citywide. The initial elections held under the 14–1 plan showed the potential inherent in district elections. Four African Americans and two Hispanics immediately gained election to the Dallas city council. By 2008, racial minority members (four blacks and three Hispanics) made up nearly half of the city council. Critics charge, however, that the increased use of district elections has also resulted in heightened parochialism and corruption.[36]

In cities where the Latino population is geographically concentrated, district systems generally help to promote the election of Latino council candidates.[37] Yet, when compared to blacks, the Hispanic population is less segregated or ghettoized. As a result, a switch to district elections does not generally produce the same extensive political gains for Latinos as it does for African Americans.[38]

Election by district raises important questions as to how a district's boundaries should be drawn. Throughout U.S. political history, political parties in power have resorted to **gerrymandering**—the creation of strangely drawn voting districts—in an effort to increase their own chances of election while diminishing the ability of the opposing party to gain office. But in more recent years, gerrymandering has been used with a more positive end in mind. Under a process that can be called **racial gerrymandering**, legislators have drawn weirdly shaped district lines in order to create **minority-majority districts** and increase the election of underrepresented racial minorities. In Chicago, the city's Latino minority is somewhat geographically spread, a situation that makes it difficult for a Latino to win office when geographically compact districts are created. The first Latino was elected to the U.S. House of Representatives from Chicago only after a new congressional district was drawn in the shape of a "C": two separate Latino sections of the city were connected by a very narrow strip of land that ran along an interstate highway (see Figure 6.1).

The Supreme Court has issued a complex set of rulings as to when a state or city may and may not take race into account in an attempt to create minority dominated voting districts. At times, the Court has thrown out districts with overly "bizarre"[39] shapes, especially in cases where race appeared to have been "the overriding or predominant factor" in drawing district lines.[40] Yet, the Court rulings allow state and local officials to consider minority representation as *one* of a number of goals when drawing legislative districts.[41] Hence, the states and localities continue to shape districts to aid the election of underrepresented African Americans and Latinos, but their efforts to do so must remain within the parameters set forth by the federal courts.

Do at-large voting rules discriminate against all underrepresented groups? It appears that at-large systems do *not* negatively affect the election of women. Various studies have found that at-large voting rules have no overwhelming effect on the representation of women: in some instances, women actually fare slightly better in races conducted citywide.[42] Why do at-large elections work against racial minorities but not women? The reason is simple: at-large election systems hurt spatially concentrated minorities, and women are neither a spatially segregated group nor a minority.[43]

Figure 6.1 **Chicago's Hispanic Congressional District, the Fourth Congressional District, Mid-1990s**

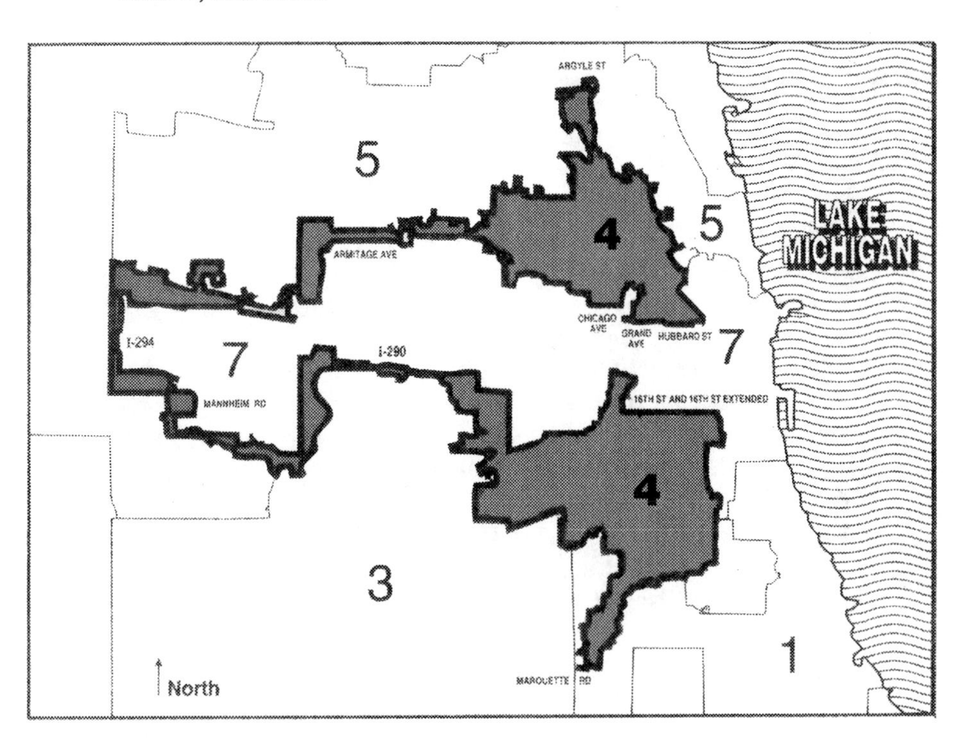

Do at-large elections discriminate against the election of gays and lesbians to local legislative office? Where lesbians and gays reside in a "gay ghetto," a system of district election acts much as it does for African Americans and can aid chances of electoral success.[44] But in cities where the gay and lesbian population is more geographically dispersed, the situation is more analogous to that of women, with district elections providing no clear and consistent advantage.[45] As we have already seen, San Francisco's switch to district elections led to the election of gay activist Harvey Milk in 1977. Today, however, San Francisco's gay and lesbian population is so large, politically active, and geographically spread throughout the city that avowedly homosexual candidates can win local office even in races that are conducted citywide.[46]

The 2009 election of openly lesbian candidate Annise Parker as mayor of Houston further indicates the electability of a gay or lesbian candidate in a citywide race. Parker won by emphasizing her fiscal moderation and experience as controller, qualifications that, at a time when the city was suffering economic difficulties, won her support from moderate conservatives and the endorsement of the *Houston Chronicle*.[47]

In sum, at-large elections do not necessarily constitute "good government," if by "good government" we mean responsiveness to neighborhood concerns and the fair representation of minorities. As Amy Bridges reports in her review of southwestern cities, the introduction of district elections can actually have a number of salutatory benefits for a city:

> Dramatic political changes appeared in the immediate aftermath of changes to district elections. More candidates ran for open seats; issues were more prominent in campaigns; portraits of districts, neighborhoods, and the concerns of their residents appeared in the news; candidates boasted their familiarity with neighborhoods they hoped to represent. Newly elected city councils were more racially diverse than the councils of big-city reform.[48]

NONPARTISAN ELECTIONS

In **nonpartisan elections** candidates run for office without party designations next to their names on the ballot. Nonpartisan ballots force voters to focus on the quality of the individual candidates and on local issues, not on a candidate's party affiliation or stance on national issues.

Nonpartisan election is one of the lasting legacies of the reform movement. Over three-fourths of the local governments in the United States use the nonpartisan ballot.[49] In the West, virtually all local contests for office are nonpartisan. In Arizona since 2010, state legislation requires that all cities and towns have nonpartisan electoral systems. The Republican-controlled state legislature pushed the measure in order to force Democrat-dominated Tucson to remove party labels from the local ballot. Even in Chicago, the legendary political machine city, city council elections are formally nonpartisan. The city also changed its laws to make the election for mayor nonpartisan as well.

The fact that elections in machine-dominated Chicago are technically nonpartisan underscores the fact that nonpartisan systems do not work the exact same way in every city across the country. In communities with a strong nonpartisan tradition, political party organizations play little or no role in the election process. In cities like Chicago, however, partisan activity lurks just below the surface, and party leaders continue to play important roles in slating candidates, raising funds, and turning out the vote.

Houston is another city where political party activity continues despite the city's nonpartisan electoral system. In 2001, Orlando Sanchez, a registered Republican, ran campaign commercials that featured former president George Herbert Walker Bush (a Houston resident) and post-9/11 hero Rudy Giuliani, the Republican mayor of New York. Incumbent Lee P. Brown, a registered Democrat, was aided by local Democratic organizations.[50] In 2009, however, partisan activity receded, and two Democrats, Annise Parker and Gene Locke, squared off in the second round or "runoff" election.

There are shortcomings of nonpartisan systems. The absence of party labels confuses voters: in races for lower offices, party labels provide cues or shortcuts that help voters to choose among candidates about whom they know little.[51] In low-visibility city council and county board races, a party label provides a helpful hint as to the basic policy orientations of a candidate.

Nonpartisan systems encourage ethnic voting, as evident in the historic success in Boston of candidates with obviously Irish or Italian names. When party labels are not on the ballot, voters turn to whatever cue or hint is readily available, including the ethnicity of a candidate's name.

Nonpartisan electoral systems aggravate the **class bias in voting turnout**. Better-educated middle- and upper-class citizens are political self-starters who sort through the candidates' promises and then go out to vote. In contrast, without the hints provided by party labels, less-educated lower-class people are more likely to be confused and stay home. In cities where elections are truly nonpartisan, there is also no organization of local party workers to telephone and drive lower-class citizens to the polls on election day.

Nonpartisan school board elections produce extremely low voter turnout, especially when school contests are held on a date when there are no races for other office. Reformers argued for the virtue of **off-year** or **off-time scheduling of school board elections and elections for local office**. Such a calendar allows voters to focus on the issues unique to the race at hand. Candidates for offices such as a school board should not have to answer questions that arise from other contests. Yet, when local elections are held on dates when no major electoral contests are scheduled, turnout can run as low as 10–15 percent—at times even lower! Such poor voter turnout undermines the democratic nature of elections. When voter turnout is so poor, organized interest groups with a material stake in an issue can dominate an election. Low-turnout school elections and bond referenda give inordinate power to teachers and other employees of the school system and their immediate families. Moving local elections to the same date as national or even state elections would greatly expand voter turnout in local races.[52]

Initiative, Referendum, and Recall: Reforms for Direct Democracy

The Progressive Era reformers used **three institutions of direct democracy**—the *initiative, referendum*, and *recall*—to weaken the grip of political parties and powerful private interests on the political process. Today, provisions for referenda and recall elections can be found in states and communities across the United States. But there are important regional variations. The three institutions of direct democracy are a commonplace part of government in the Southwest and the West. Yet, while 90 percent of western cities allow for the initiative and recall, only a third of mid-Atlantic states permit such ballot alternatives.[53]

Citizens have used the initiative, referendum, and recall to force an otherwise irresponsive government to respond to their needs. But each of these tools is also subject to criticism. In more recent years, powerful groups have used the devices of direct democracy to advance more narrow and self-serving interests, not the public's interest.

The Initiative and Referendum

Under the **initiative process**, the voters themselves write and then cast ballots on a proposed piece of legislation, bypassing a legislature that may have lost touch with the people. Where the initiative is permitted, the laws of each state and locality specify the number of signatures needed to put a proposed piece of legislation or a charter amendment before the voters.

Critics argue that the initiative process is fundamentally flawed. Initiatives are often poorly drafted and subject to legal challenge. More important, the initiative bypasses the processes of **representative government** that allow elected officials to balance the competing perspectives of different groups of voters. Legislation by initiative does not allow for fine-tuning and compromise; voters simply cast their ballots "Yes" or "No" on the measure appearing on the ballot. A proposal's backers are likely to exaggerate the measure's benefits. Opponents, in their media advertising, similarly exaggerate the predicted ills that may result from the passage of a ballot measure. Amid a flurry of specious claims, passions may overtake reason.

California's **Proposition 13**, the very important 1978 measure that limited property taxes in the state, illustrates both the virtues and major shortcomings of the initiative process. Voters took the steps to enact Proposition 13 into law because the state legislature was irresponsive in giving Californians much-needed relief from soaring property taxes. But California's voters did not foresee that the measure would give the lion's share of the tax reductions to big corporations and other large property holders, with the resulting revenue losses forcing sharp cutbacks in municipal services and the public schools.[54] In an effort to find new ways to fund basic services, local governments raised user charges and fees, a move that further hurt lower- and middle-income residents and schoolchildren.[55] Proposition 13 ultimately also wound up diminishing local control of education; caught in a fiscal bind, school districts accepted additional fiscal assistance from the state of California, increasing their dependence on decisions made in the state capital.[56]

Modern-day initiative campaigns can be quite expensive. More privileged interest groups hire professional firms to garner the necessary signatures to place a measure on the ballot. The prominence of **paid petition circulators** diminishes the democratic nature of the initiative process, as signature gathering no longer serves as a proxy indicator for the public's genuine interest in a proposed measure.[57]

Big-money groups spend lavishly on media campaigns to win support for their side of a ballot issue. The gambling industry effectively financed the campaigns to bring casino gambling to Atlantic City (New Jersey) and Ohio and a state lottery to California. In the state of Washington, Microsoft cofounder and billionaire Paul Allen, owner of the Seattle Seahawks, spent over $10 million on an initiative drive to have state taxpayers fund a new football stadium. Allen's spending may have provided the margin of victory: the measure passed with 51 percent voter approval.[58] However, money does not always guarantee success at the ballot box.

The **referendum** is similar to the initiative, except that the process typically starts not with voter signatures but by a decision of the legislature to put an item before the citizens for their approval or disapproval. In some cities, citizens can petition for a referendum or public vote on a bill that has previously been passed by the council. In Ohio and Wisconsin, aggrieved public workers gathered signatures to put on the ballot a referendum to repeal controversial newly 2011 state laws that restricted the collective bargaining rights and health benefits of local schoolteachers and other public servants, including, in Ohio, police officers and firefighters.

In Cape Cod (Massachusetts), Minneapolis, and numerous Sunbelt cities, neighborhood, taxpayer, and environmental groups have at times used the initiative and referendum processes to counter the power of local growth coalitions. In a process that has been called **ballot-box planning** or **electoral land-use planning**, voters angered by classroom overcrowding, increased pollution, traffic congestion, and the prospects of additional taxation have resorted to the initiative and referendum processes to stop new development projects. Antigrowth measures adopted at the ballot box tend to be more extreme than the growth control measures adopted by city councils.[59]

In Seattle, grassroots activists pushed for the enactment of Initiative 31, the Citizens' Alternative Plan, to slow the pace of downtown skyscraper and office development. Seattle activists also used the initiative and referendum routes to commit the city to the construction of a monorail, financed largely by a new tax levied on automobiles.[60] In 1997, Minneapolis citizens voted to limit city financial assistance for any new professional sports facility.[61]

In San Francisco, voters approved Proposition M, which placed a cap on annual new construction and required developers to pay various **linkage fees** to support affordable housing and other public services. Proposition M is one of the toughest antigrowth measures in the United States. Yet, in San Francisco, as in San Diego and other California cities, such measures have not brought a halt to new development. In the face of voter-imposed growth limitations, developers offer new public amenities and make whatever other compromises are necessary to win endorsement of their plans.[62]

The Recall

Under the **recall process**, citizens sign petitions in order to hold a special vote to decide whether an official should be removed from office before the normal end of the official's term. The threat of a recall election can lead elected office holders to pay greater heed to the wishes of the people.

In a number of smaller cities and suburbs, recall efforts have become a regular part of local politics. In 2008, the citizens of tiny Arlington, Oregon, decided by a narrow vote to remove Mayor Carmen Kontur-Gronquist from office after pictures posted on MySpace showed the scantily clad single mother posing on a fire truck.

In states that permit local recall elections, big-city mayors have to deal with a recall threat. Cleveland's Dennis Kucinich and San Francisco's Dianne Feinstein were two big-city mayors who successfully won recall elections and were able to complete their terms in office. In 2008 anti-immigrant forces attempted to oust Phoenix Mayor Phil Gordon for failing to take aggressive steps against illegal immigrants. But the Phoenix recall movement fizzled when organizers failed to submit the necessary signed petitions.[63] In 2010, billionaire Norman Braman announced that he was launching an effort to recall Miami-Dade Mayor Carlos Alvarez as a result of the county's decision to raise property taxes by 14 percent in an effort to reduce its budgetary shortfall. In Omaha, mayoral recall elections are so frequent that they are considered a routine feature of the local political landscape.[64]

Critics argue that recall efforts intrude on responsible, representative government. Under the threat of a recall, an elected official may be more responsive to the demands of recall organizers than to the needs of the general public. Recall efforts can also be overused. In some communities, antitax activists begin a recall campaign any time a local official considers raising taxes, even when a revenue increase is needed to keep schools open or to get a community out of a tight fiscal squeeze. In San Jose, a special 2009 local recall election was scheduled when Councilwoman Madison Nguyen voted to refer to the local commercial strip as "the Saigon business district" instead of "Little Saigon,"[65] the name preferred by many of the city's Vietnamese refugees who had fled communism.

Recall elections can also be used to reinforce local exclusion. In wealthy suburban Westport, Connecticut, a recall attempt was launched when school board members voted to admit twenty-five inner-city students to Westport schools. In affluent Birmingham, Michigan, city commissioners who voted to provide subsidized housing to the poor and the elderly were recalled from office.[66]

In 2003, Californians removed Gray Davis from the state governorship, only a year after he had won reelection, replacing him with Arnold Schwarzenegger. Recall advocates argued that the vote was justified, that Davis had hid the extent of the state's fiscal difficulties and had failed to initiate the necessary steps to alleviate the state's fiscal crisis.[67]

Civil Service and Merit Personnel Systems

As we mentioned earlier, **civil service personnel systems** provide for the recruitment and advancement of government workers on the basis of merit. Merit-system hiring rules reduced political patronage and helped bring better-qualified workers into city government. Civil service protections also make it difficult for elected officials to fire municipal workers, thereby giving career public servants the protection necessary for them to do their jobs free from improper political intrusion.

Despite its record of success, the civil service system also compounds problems of governmental performance and accountability. The elaborate hiring procedures, detailed pay schedules, and protections of civil service personnel set forth by civil service rules wind up diminishing the flexibility that a municipality has when attempting to recruit and keep top-quality personnel. Civil service rules also make it difficult for a city to dismiss underperforming workers. Critics charge that civil servants enjoy virtual lifelong tenure protection and, as a result, do not work especially hard. With little fear of being fired, some civil servants do not readily follow the policy directives of elected officials.

Management experts often recommend that the rigidities of civil service be reduced in order to improve the performance and efficiency of government operations. Cities with a strong good-government ethos and an active investigatory media may find that they can safely relax some civil service restrictions. However, in Rhode Island, Delaware, Illinois, Maryland, New Jersey, and West Virginia—states where there is still a relatively current history of political corruption and cronyism—any relaxation of civil service rules could open the door to machine-style abuses.[68]

The Growth of Bureaucratic Power

Merit personnel systems and other reforms have had the unfortunate consequence of bureaucratizing city government. Mayors and city managers found that they could not even easily dismiss officials who refused to follow their policy leads. (See Box 6.4, "Los Angeles: Can Anyone Fire Chief Gates?") The political reform movement had produced a city that is "well-run but ungoverned." Municipal bureaucracies are "'islands of functional power' before which the modern mayor stands denuded of authority."[69]

Their power in running the city is so great that Theodore Lowi refers to the municipal agencies as the **New Machines**.[70] Citizens soon began to seek new changes to debureaucratize the city, to make municipal administration more flexible and responsive to neighborhood needs.

A NEW GENERATION OF REFORM MEASURES: THE POSTREFORM CITY

Racial minorities, middle-class taxpayers, grassroots activists, and environmentalists all complained about the lack of responsiveness of city officials. In contrast to the earlier Progressive Era reform movement, the new reformers did not emphasize only the importance of cost-cutting efficiency; instead, the new reformers sought to increase governmental responsiveness, fairness, and equity.

The new reformers argued for measures that would allow for increased citizen participation in government. City after city also began to return to district elections (or a mixed system of elections) in an effort to increase the responsiveness of government to neighborhood concerns. New ethics laws and campaign finance regulations sought to reduce the influence that money enjoyed in the local political arena. In some cities, the new reformers also sought to strengthen the leadership power inherent in the mayor's office so that the city could act quickly and speak with one voice in the pursuit of jobs and economic development.

Over the past third of a century, city after city modified various elements of its reformed structures. San Jose, Long Beach, Sacramento, Stockton, Oakland, Watsonville, Tacoma, San Antonio, Dallas, Fort Worth, El Paso, Albuquerque, Richmond, Montgomery, Charlotte, and Raleigh all reinstituted district elections (in some cases creating a hybrid or mixed electoral system) in an effort to increase the city's responsiveness to its African American and Hispanic neighborhoods.

In Seattle a grassroots group has called for a charter amendment to allow for the election of half of the city council by district, rather than continuing to elect all nine council members at large. San Diego, Oakland, San Jose, Sacramento, Stockton, and Cincinnati all increased the power of the elected mayor, diminishing the authority of the city manager.[71]

Kansas City Mayor Emanuel Cleaver urged changes that would strengthen the mayor's office, arguing that Kansas City could no longer afford a mayor who was little more than a prominent member of the city council:

> Kansas City is now a big-league city and when the mayor of the city sits around with the president and CEO of a major corporation trying to get them to relocate here, the mayor is at a disadvantage, because other mayors can cut the deal at the table. We are at a disadvantage in many instances when we are out competing.[72]

Box 6.4

Los Angeles: Can Anyone Fire Chief Gates?

In 1992, a tense Los Angeles awaited the verdict in the trial of the four officers accused of beating a black motorist, Rodney King. The beating had been caught on videotape and was aired repeatedly on television. But there was always the chance that, with the trial having been moved to white suburban Simi Valley, a jury would fail to convict the officers, despite the video evidence that seemed so unambiguous.

Los Angeles police chief Daryl Gates did not take direct charge of a potential riot situation, deciding, instead, to attend a political fund raiser. When the jury announced its "not guilty" verdict, inner-city areas of Los Angeles became witness to spasms of violence. The police quickly withdrew from the South Central riot area, for fear that their continued presence would only serve to precipitate new incidents of violence.

The withdrawal, however, proved counterproductive, as it allowed the violence to escalate. One particularly dramatic piece of televised news footage showed a gang of violent thugs pulling a driver, Reginald Denny, from his truck, kicking him, and dropping a cement block on his head. There were no police officers in sight.

Mayor Tom Bradley and other critics sought to remove the police chief from office. But the mayor lacked the formal authority to fire the city's "top cop," who was also the mayor's political adversary. Mayor Bradley and Chief Gates just did not get along. The chief had even refused to meet with the mayor to discuss preparations as a combustible city awaited the Rodney King jury verdict. As Gates later revealed in his memoir, he and the mayor "were scarcely on speaking terms"; they had learned over time "to tolerate each other, barely speaking only when we had to, mainly by telephone." The mayor recalled that he had not spoken to the police chief in thirteen months![1]

Los Angeles is known as America's most reformed big city. The political reform movement was so strong in Los Angeles that professional department heads were given virtual independence from elected leaders. Chief Gates' successor, Willie Williams, observed that the city's top cop was under no legal obligation to meet with the mayor: "I don't have one operating superior. . . . The first six months I thought I was mayor!"[2]

Gates' mishandling of the South Central disturbances coupled with the revelation of scandals in the Los Angeles Police Department soon led voters to change the city charter, giving the mayor greater authority over the department by subjecting the position of the police chief to reappointment every five years. In 2002, Mayor James Hahn refused to renew the appointment of Police Chief Bernard Parks, underscoring the dramatic break that had been made with LA's reform-model heritage of insulating professionals against elected officials.

[1]Daryl F. Gates, *Chief: My Life in the LAPD* (New York: Bantam Books, 1992); see also: Raphael J. Sonenshein, *Politics in Black and White: Race and Power in Los Angeles* (Princeton, NJ: Princeton University Press, 1993), 210–226; and Lou Cannon, *Official Negligence: How Rodney King and the Riots Changed the LAPD* (New York: Books/Random House, 1997), 121–122; Raphael J. Sonenshein, "Memo to the Police Commission: Govern Now and Spin Later," *Los Angeles Times*, December 10, 2001.

[2]Los Angeles police chief Willie Williams, comments to the annual meeting of the National Civic League, Los Angeles, November 13, 1992.

Sacramento Mayor Kevin Johnson similarly argued for charter changes to give the mayor's office additional powers over budgeting and personnel.[73]

ETHICS LAWS AND CAMPAIGN FINANCE REFORM

Conflict-of-interest laws and **requirements for financial disclosure** seek to bring to light situations where public officials may have business and other ties that raise questions of impropriety. **Open-meeting** or **sunshine laws** prohibit government officials from conducting public business in unofficial gatherings outside of public scrutiny. Yet, in numerous cities, officials evade the mandate for transparency. California state law bars public officials from doing business in closed forums. Yet, the Los Angeles County Board of Supervisors has met in informal sessions where it has reached a consensus on 90 percent of the board's business to be later voted on in public.[74]

Local **campaign finance reform** measures seek to limit the influence of private money in politics. Albuquerque, New Mexico, imposed a **limit on campaign spending**, setting a ceiling on the total amount that a candidate can spend in an electoral race. New York, San Francisco, and Austin (Texas) are among the cities that have imposed a limit or **ceiling on political contributions**. New York City for 2009 set a limit of $2,750 for an individual's contributions to a city council candidate and $4,950 to a candidate for mayor or other citywide office. Donations by contractors and people "doing business" with the city were subject to even more stringent restrictions, a maximum of only $250 to a city council candidate and $400 to a mayoral hopeful. Pasadena, Claremont, and Santa Monica have similarly tough rules on political donations, accompanied by stringent **limits on gift giving**: a person who does business with the city cannot give a public official a gift valued in excess of $25.[75]

Ceilings on individual political contributions force a candidate to search for a broad funding base; office seekers are not able to rely on the financial support of a few wealthy donors. Beyond that, however, the reform measures have not had a very great influence on local politics. Contribution limits have not stimulated new electoral competition. Limits on campaign spending may even lessen the ability of a campaign to engage and educate the electorate.[76] Contribution limits that are set unreasonably low can impede a candidate's ability to reach voters. Austin law limits to only $300 the amount that an individual or political action committee can contribute to a candidate for municipal office. In San Francisco, a judicial ruling struck down similar provisions of the city's campaign finance statutes as they restricted the ability of candidates to communicate with voters.[77]

Portland (Oregon) and Albuquerque have taken even stronger steps in the effort to minimize the influence of private money. These cities provide for the **full public funding** of citywide campaigns: the city's taxpayers pay for the candidates' campaign bills. A small but somewhat larger number of communities (including Austin, Boulder, Long Beach, Los Angeles, Miami-Dade County, New York, Oakland, Petaluma, San Francisco, and Tucson) provide for the **partial public funding** of elections, where taxpayer funds help to reduce candidates' reliance on special interest money. Candidates who choose to accept public money voluntarily agree to limit their overall campaign spending and abide various accompanying campaign rules. New York City requires recipients of public funding to engage in series of public campaign debates. The city offers a generous 6 : 1 match of public to private dollars in an attempt to get candidates to participate in the public funding system.

U.S. Supreme Court rulings have severely undermined national and local efforts to reduce the influence of money in political campaigns. The Court's decision in its very important 1976 ***Buckley v. Valeo*** decision created an **independent expenditures** loophole in campaign finance laws. Candidates and citizens have a First Amendment right to free speech that they cannot be forced to surrender. Candidates and independent groups (and even political parties, as the Court later added) have a right to spend unlimited amounts of money in political races unless they voluntarily surrender that right. In 2010, the Supreme Court went even further, overturning federal laws that barred corporations and labor unions from making campaign contributions.[78] The Court's logic in *Arizona Free Enterprise v. Bennett* (2011) casts doubts as to the constitutionality of state and local public funding provisions that dispense additional funds to a candidate who faces a well-financed opponent who refuses to abide by voluntary spending limits.

The judicial rulings helped lead to a virtual explosion of spending in local elections. In Los Angeles, independent expenditures grew to "unprecedented levels" as spending by businesses, political parties, and labor unions reentered the local arena.[79] In 1993, the New York State Democratic Party spent a half million dollars on radio and direct mail advertising in support of incumbent Mayor David Dinkins, money that was not counted against Dinkins's allowable spending ceiling under New York law.[80]

The Supreme Court's ruling effectively meant that billionaire New York Mayor Michael Bloomberg had a free-speech right to spend vast sums of his own money on his election campaigns, making a mockery of the city's attempts to rein in campaign spending. In 2001, Bloomberg spent $75 million of his own money in his mayoral race, over $50 million more than the amount spent by his opponent. As his opponent's campaign manager observed, Bloomberg "bought it [the mayoralty] fair and square, and by spending a historic amount on television ads he controlled the airwaves and altered people's perception of reality." Bloomberg aired 6,500 television ads, as compared to the 2,500 aired by his opponent. Bloomberg spent $90 for each vote he received.[81]

In his reelection campaigns, the advantages enjoyed by the billionaire candidate were even more apparent. In 2005, Bloomberg's spending rose to $85 million, four times the total spent by his opponent.[82] In 2009, Bloomberg won reelection by spending over $100 million of his own money—$174 for every vote he won.[83]

Judicial rulings have allowed "interested money" to find various ways around various campaign finance regulations. In a process known as **bundling**, intermediaries collect contributions from numerous interest group members and present them to a campaign in one large lump sum; the candidate knows which interest group raised the funds. Billionaire real estate tycoon and developer Donald J. Trump testified about his ability to circumvent a New York State law that limited a corporation's contributions to $5,000; he simply made the campaign contributions through eighteen subsidiary corporations.[84]

TERM LIMITS

In the 1990s, an anti-incumbency mood led voters across the nation to restrict the number of terms that elected officials could serve. Anti-incumbency sentiment was initially directed against members of Congress who enjoyed long careers in office. But quite soon, term limitation activists turned to the state and local arenas, imposing ceilings on the length of service of subnational legislators and elected executives.

Local term limits spread like wildfire. In 1992, fewer than 300 municipalities had term limits. By 1998, a mere half dozen years later, the number swelled to nearly 3,000.[85] Cincinnati, Houston, Jacksonville, Kansas City, Los Angeles, New Orleans, New York, San Antonio, San Francisco, San Jose, and Washington, DC, are among the nation's more populous cities with term limitations. Typically, **term limitation measures** allow city and county legislators to serve only two or three consecutive terms in office. About 10 percent of cities also limit the service of their elected chief executive, allowing, for instance, a mayor only two four-year terms in office.[86]

Advocates of term limitations point to the virtues of having citizen-legislators in government. They scorn the long tenure typically enjoyed by members of Congress, a length of service that can put some distance between the elected representative and the people.

The attack on electoral careerism, however, makes less sense in most cities, where substantial legislative turnover is the norm. In small- and medium-size cities, city council positions tend to be poorly paid and understaffed. Each election season sees numerous council members leaving office—from frustration or for the opportunity to run for higher office—bringing substantial "new blood" to the city legislature.[87] Some smaller communities even have great difficulty in finding people willing to serve for such little compensation. A shortage of candidates led more than sixty Colorado communities to repeal or modify their term limitations statutes.[88]

Critics point to the loss of **institutional memory** when term limitations force the few experienced legislators with deep knowledge of local affairs to leave office. Term limitations can produce a legislature of novices who are dependent on the information and advice provided by the city manager, the municipal bureaucracy, legislative staff, and special-interest groups. Yet, there is no solid evidence to show that a system of term limits actually results in a shift of power to the city manager and local administrators.[89]

Nor do term limitations pose an insurmountable obstacle to the ambitions of "career" politicians. Term limitations can result in a game of "musical chairs" when officials facing the end of their allowed period of tenure in one public office simply announce their candidacy for another office.[90]

In more recent years, the local term limitations movement has slowed. Los Angeles voters in 2006 eased restrictions, permitting council members to serve a third four-year term. In 2008, New York's city council likewise relaxed its rules so that its own members and popular mayor Michael Bloomberg could run for a third term in office.[91] San Antonio raised the limits on local legislative service from four to eight years. Facing tough economic times, cities began to look at ways to strengthen—not to limit—local leadership.

CONCLUSION: THE POSTREFORM CITY

The reform movement reshaped local politics, reducing corruption, patronage, and partisan favoritism in favor of increasing technical competence and professionalism in government. The reform movement was so successful and all-pervasive that even cities normally regarded as "unreformed" have numerous reform-style innovations and procedures to improve managerial competency and increase public accountability: civil service personnel systems; sunshine laws; ethics rules for auditing, budgeting, purchasing, and competitive bidding; and the creation of a city-manager-like chief administrative officer (CAO) position to assist the mayor.[92]

A number of the first-generation reforms created new problems for the city, diluting the power of lower-class and minority voting groups while vesting new power in highly insulated municipal agencies. City residents became increasingly dissatisfied with depersonalized program administration by municipal agencies that were not responsive to neighborhood needs.

A newer generation of reformers is no longer concerned solely with managerial efficiency, although, certainly, everyone recognizes the need for cities to find new ways to lower the costs of public services. Contemporary reform efforts do no suffer the same class and ethnic biases that plagued the earlier generation of structural reforms. The new reformers emphasize the importance of citizen participation[93] and the democratic representation of diverse populations. The new reform movement has sought to strengthen urban leadership and enhance regional cooperation.[94]

In a global age, localist patronage-based organizations have given way to a "new political culture" as cities emphasize quality-of-life improvements, effective leadership, and a high-amenity approach to economic development.[95] Even the Chicago machine has adjusted to globalization, with city leaders relying less on classic job patronage and more on attracting global firms, creating new employment opportunities, and winning the votes of new immigrant groups in the city.[96]

NOTES

1. Dayton David McKean, *The Boss: The Hague Machine in Action* (Boston: Houghton Mifflin, 1940), 271.

2. Dick Simpson, *Rogues, Rebels, and Rubber Stamps: The Politics of the Chicago City Council from 1863 to the Present* (Boulder, CO: Westview Press, 2001).

3. Martin Shefter, "The Emergence of the Political Machine: An Alternative View," in *Theoretical Perspectives on Urban Politics*, ed. Willis D. Hawley and Michael Lipsky (Englewood Cliffs, NJ: Prentice Hall, 1976), 22.

4. John M. Allswang, *Bosses, Machines, and Urban Voters* (Port Washington, NY: Kennikat Press, 1977), 52.

5. William L. Riordan, *Plunkitt of Tammany Hall*, ed. Terrence J. McDonald (Boston: Bedford Books of St. Martin's Press, 1994), 62.

6. Donald L. Miller, *City of the Century: The Epic of Chicago and the Making of America* (New York: Touchstone, 1996), 454.

7. Clarence N. Stone, "Urban Political Machines: Taking Stock," *PS: Political Science and Politics* 29 (September 1996): 446–450.

8. Steven P. Erie, *Rainbow's End: Irish Americans and the Dilemmas of Urban Machine Politics, 1840–1985* (Berkeley: University of California Press, 1988); Tomasz Inglot and John P. Pelissero, "Ethnic Political Power in a Machine City: Chicago's Poles at Rainbow's End," *Urban Affairs Quarterly* 28, no. 4 (June 1993): 526–543.

9. Marcus D. Pohlmann and Michael P. Kirby, *Racial Politics at the Crossroads: Memphis Elects*

Dr. W.W. Herenton (Knoxville: University of Tennessee Press, 1996), 62–63, and 100–104; G. Wayne Dowdy, *Mayor Crump Don't Like It: Machine Politics in Memphis* (Jackson: University Press of Mississippi, 2006).

10. Richard A. Keiser, *Subordination or Empowerment? African-American Leadership and the Struggle for Urban Political Power* (New York: Oxford University Press, 1997), 34–35; William J. Grimshaw, *Bitter Fruit: Black Politics and the Chicago Machine, 1931–1991* (Chicago: University of Chicago Press, 1992); Peter Skerry, "Political Institutions and Minority Mobility in the USA," in *Ethnicity, Social Mobility, and Public Policy: Comparing the US and UK,* ed. Glenn C. Loury, Tariq Modood, and Steven M. Teles (Cambridge: Cambridge University Press, 2005), 479–481.

11. Arnold R. Hirsch, *Making the Second Ghetto: Race and Housing in Chicago Politics, 1940–1960,* rev. ed. (Chicago: University of Chicago Press, 1998) describes the complicity of the Chicago machine in public housing segregation.

12. Mike Royko, *Boss: Richard J. Daley of Chicago* (New York: Signet, 1977), 137.

13. Richard A. Keiser, "Explaining African-American Political Empowerment: Windy City Politics from 1900 to 1983," *Urban Affairs Quarterly* 29 (September 1993): 112.

14. Keiser, *Subordination or Empowerment?* 35–38.

15. Pierre Clavel and Wim Wiewel, eds., *Harold Washington and the Neighborhoods* (New Brunswick, NJ: Rutgers University Press, 1991); Joel Rast, *Remaking Chicago: The Political Origins of Urban Industrial Change* (DeKalb: Northern Illinois University Press, 1999), esp. 103–104.

16. Michael B. Preston, "The Resurgence of Black Voting in Chicago: 1955–1983," in *The Making of the Mayor: Chicago 1983,* ed. Melvin G. Holli and Paul M. Green (Grand Rapids, MI: Wm. B. Eerdmans, 1984), 48.

17. Frederick C. Harris, "Black Churches and Machine Politics in Chicago," in *Black Churches and Local Politics: Clergy Influence, Organizational Partnerships, and Civic Empowerment,* ed. R. Drew Smith and Fredrick C. Harris (Lanham, MD: Rowman and Littlefield, 2005), 131.

18. John J. Betancur and Douglas Gills, "Community Development in Chicago: From Harold Washington to Richard M. Daley," *Annals of the American Academy of Political and Social Science* 594, no. 1 (2004): 92–108.

19. Dick Simpson and Tom M. Kelly, "The New Chicago School of Urbanism and the New Daley Machine," *Urban Affairs Review* 44, no. 2 (November 2008): 228; see also p. 234.

20. Anthony Gierzynski, Paul Kleppner, and James Lewis, "Money or the Machine? Money and Votes in Chicago Aldermanic Elections," *American Politics Quarterly* 26, no. 2 (April 1998): 171.

21. Simpson and Kelly, "The New Chicago School of Urbanism and the New Daley Machine," 229–231. J. Cherie Strachan, *High-Tech Grass Roots: The Professionalization of Local Elections* (Lanham, MD: Rowman and Littlefield, 2003) observes the rise of "new-style campaigns" in cities across the United States. Local races are no longer dominated by volunteers and party organization. Instead, candidates for local office need to raise substantial sums of money in order to pay for media and the assistance of professional campaign consultants.

22. Riordan, *Plunkitt of Tammany Hall*, 54.

23. Anne Freedman, *Patronage: An American Tradition* (Chicago: Nelson-Hall, 1994), 1–8 and 109–111 reviews the Court's *Rutan* decision and Justice Antonin Scalia's dissent defending patronage as an American political tradition.

24. Jessica Trounstine, *Political Monopolies in American Cities: The Rise and Fall of Bosses and Reformers* (Chicago: University of Chicago Press, 2008).

25. Samuel P. Hays, "The Politics of Reform in Municipal Government in the Progressive Era," *Pacific Northwest Quarterly* 55 (1964): 157–169, repr. in *Readings in Urban Politics: Past, Present, and Future,* ed. Charles H. Levine and Harlan Hahn (White Plains, NY: Longman, 1984), 54–73. See also Amy Bridges and Richard Kronick, "Writing the Rules to Win the Game: The Middle-Class Regimes of Municipal Reformers," *Urban Affairs Review* 34, no. 5 (May 1999): 691–706; and Glenda Elizabeth Gilmore, ed., *Who Were the Progressives?* (Boston: Bedford/St. Martin's, 2002).

26. Amy Bridges, *Morning Glories: Municipal Reform in the Southwest* (Princeton, NJ: Princeton University Press, 1997), esp. 151–174.

27. Christopher L. Warren, John G. Corbett, and John F. Stack Jr., "Hispanic Ascendancy and Tripartite Politics in Miami," in *Racial Politics in American Cities*, 2d ed., ed. Rufus P. Browning, Dale Rogers Marshall, and David H. Tabb (New York: Longman, 1990), 158.

28. Jessica L. Trounstine, "Monopoly Government in American Cities," paper presented at the Center for the Study of Democratic Politics, Princeton University, Princeton, New Jersey, February 23, 2006, www.princeton.edu/~csdp/events/pdfs/seminars/Trounstine022306.pdf.

29. Melvin G. Holli, *Reform in Detroit: Hazen S. Pingree and Urban Politics* (New York: Oxford University Press, 1969) delineates the difference between social reformers and structural reformers. For other descriptions of the more progressive branches of reform politics, see Todd Swanstrom, *The Crisis of Growth Politics: Cleveland, Kucinich, and the Challenge of Urban Populism* (Philadelphia: Temple University Press, 1985) and Kenneth Finegold, *Experts and Politicians: Reform Challenges to Machine Politics in New York, Cleveland and Chicago* (Princeton, NJ: Princeton University Press, 1995).

30. Sarah Deutsch, *Women and the City: Gender, Space, and Power in Boston, 1870–1940* (New York: Oxford University Press, 2000).

31. National League of Cities, "At-Large, District, and Mixed-System Elections," n.d., www.nlc.org/about_cities/cities_101/168.aspx.

32. See, for instance, Albert K. Karnig, "Black Representation on City Councils: The Impact of District Elections and Socioeconomic Factors," *Urban Affairs Quarterly* 12 (December 1976), esp. 229. A system of district voting aids the election of a racial minority only when a group's population is highly concentrated and voting patterns are highly polarized by race. See Jessica Trounstine and Melody E. Valdini, "The Context Matters: The Effects of Single-Member versus At-Large Districts on City Council Diversity," *American Journal of Political Science* 57 (July 2008): 554–569.

33. William E. Nelson Jr., *Black Atlantic Politics: Dilemmas of Political Empowerment in Boston and Liverpool* (Albany: State University of New York Press, 2000), 63 and 78–84.

34. J. Morgan Kousser, "The Undermining of the First Reconstruction: Lessons for the Second," in *Minority Vote Dilution*, ed. Chandler Davidson (Washington, DC: Howard University Press, 1989), 32–33.

35. Chandler Davidson, "Minority Vote Dilution: An Overview," in Davidson, *Minority Vote Dilution*, 11.

36. Gromer Jeffers Jr., "20 Years After Lawsuit, Debate over Dallas City Council's 14–1 System Persists," *Dallas Morning News*, May 16, 2008.

37. Timothy B. Krebs and John P. Pelissero, "City Councils" in *Cities, Politics, and Policy*, ed. John P. Pelissero (Washington, DC: CQ Press, 2003), 174; David L. Leal, Valerie Martinez-Ebers, and Kenneth J. Meier, "The Politics of Latino Education: The Biases of At-Large Elections," *Journal of Politics* 66 (November 2004): 1224–1244.

38. Trounstine and Valdini, "The Context Matters," 563–565. Rodney E. Hero, *Latinos and the U.S. Political System: Two-tiered Pluralism* (Philadelphia: Temple University Press, 1992), 141–142, summarizes the conflicting results of the studies attempting to research the impact of at-large systems on Latino representation.

39. *Shaw v. Reno* 509 U.S. 630 (1993).

40. *Miller v. Johnson* 515 U.S. 900 (1995). See also *Shaw v. Hunt* 517 U.S. 899 (1996).

41. Gerard R. Webster, "The Potential Impact of Recent Supreme Court Decisions on the Use of Race and Ethnicity in the Redistricting Process," *Cities* 14, no. 1 (1997): 13–19; Christina Rivers, "'Conquered Provinces'? The Voting Rights Act and State Power," *Publius: Journal of Federalism* 36, no. 3 (2006): 421–442.

42. Susan A. MacManus, "How to Get More Women in Office: The Perspectives of Local Elected Officials (Mayors and City Councilors)," *Urban Affairs Quarterly* 28 (September 1992), 164–165 and 167n2; Susan A. MacManus and Charles S. Bullock III, "Women and Racial/Ethnic Minorities in Mayoral and Council Positions," *Municipal Year Book 1993* (Washington, DC: International City/County Management Association, 1993), 78; Trounstine and Valdini, "The Context Matters," 563–565.

43. District election systems are less crucial to the election of black women and Latinas than to the election of African American and Latino men to a city council. See Trounstine and Valdini, "The Context Matters," 554–569.

44. James W. Button, Kenneth D. Wald, and Barbara A. Rienzo, "The Election of Openly Gay Public Officials in American Communities," *Urban Affairs Review* 35, no. 2 (November 1999): 188–209, esp. 199–203.

45. Gary M. Segura, "Institutions Matter: Local Electoral Laws, Gay and Lesbian Representation, and Coalition Building Across Minority Communities," in *Gays and Lesbians in the Democratic Process,* ed. Ellen D.B. Riggle and Barry L. Tadlock (New York: Columbia University Press, 1999), 225.

46. Ibid., 230.

47. Bradley Olson, "Annise Parker Elected Houston's Next Mayor: Nation Watches as City Becomes the Largest in U.S. to Choose an Openly Gay Leader," *Houston Chronicle,* December 15, 2009.

48. Bridges, *Morning Glories*, 200.

49. National League of Cities, "Partisan vs. Nonpartisan Elections," n.d., www.nlc.org/about_cities/cities_101/169.aspx.

50. Jim Yardley, "In Houston, a 'Nonpartisan' Race Is Anything But," *New York Times*, November 30, 2001.

51. Anthony Downs, *An Economic Theory of Democracy* (New York: Harper and Row, 1957), 234. See pp. 207–238 for Downs's discussion as to the "costs" to citizens of becoming informed and why citizens rely on party labels and other shortcuts.

52. Zoltan L. Hajnal and Paul G. Lewis, "Municipal Institutions and Voter Turnout in Local Elections," *Urban Affairs Review* 38, no. 5 (May 2003): 645–668; Neal Caren, "Big City, Big Turnout? Electoral Participation in American Cities," *Journal of Urban Affairs* 29, no. 1 (2007): 31–46. Interestingly, Caren finds that council-manager cities also suffer depressed turnouts as voters apparently see less at stake in municipal elections when a manager is given substantial authority in a city's affairs.

53. Tari Renner and Victor S. DeSantis, "Contemporary Patterns and Trends in Municipal Government Structures," *The Municipal Year Book 1993* (Washington, DC: International City/County Management Association, 1993), 68–69.

54. David O. Sears and Jack Citrin, *Tax Revolt: Something for Nothing in California* (Cambridge, MA: Harvard University Press, 1982); Peter Schrag, *Paradise Lost: California's Experience, America's Future* (New York: Norton, 1998), 188–256; James Sterngold, "Hard Times Fuel Debate on the Initiative Process," *San Francisco Chronicle,* August 18, 2003.

55. Christopher Hoene, "Fiscal Structure and the Post-Proposition 13 Fiscal Regime in California's Cities," *Public Budgeting and Finance* 24, no. 4 (December 2004): 51–72.

56. Ibid., 70–72.

57. Richard J. Ellis, *The Democratic Delusion: The Initiative Process in America* (Lawrence: University Press of Kansas, 2002), 49–61; Dennis F. Thompson, *Just Elections: Creating a Fair Electoral Process in the United States* (Chicago: University of Chicago Press, 2002), 139.

58. Galen Nelson, "Putting Democracy Back Into the Initiative and Referendum," in *Democracy's Moment: Reforming America's Political System for the 21st Century*, ed. Ronald Hayduk and Kevin Mattson (Lanham, MD: Rowman and Littlefield, 2002), 159. A reasonably balanced assessment of the initiative process is presented by Larry J. Sabato, Howard R. Ernst, and Bruce R. Larson, eds., *Dangerous Democracy? The Battle Over Ballot Initiatives in America* (Lanham, MD: Rowman and Littlefield, 2001).

59. Elisabeth R. Gerber and Justin H. Phillips, "Evaluating the Effects of Direct Democracy on Public Policy: California's Urban Growth Boundaries," *American Politics Research* 33, no. 2 (2005): 310–330.

60. Anne F. Peterson, Barbara S. Kinsey, Hugh Bartling, and Brady Baybeck, "Bringing the Spatial In: The Case of the 2002 Seattle Monorail Referendum," *Urban Affairs Review* 43, no. 3 (January 2008): 403–429.

61. Roger W. Caves, *Land Use Planning: The Ballot Box Revolution*, Sage Library of Social Research, vol. 187 (Newbury Park, CA: Sage, 1992), and Patrick Sweeney, "Minneapolis Residents Cap

Stadium Spending" *(St. Paul) Pioneer Press*, November 5, 1997). For a review of the various ballot measures limiting growth in San Francisco, see Richard Edward DeLeon, *Left Coast City: Progressive Politics in San Francisco, 1975–1991* (Lawrence: University of Kansas Press, 1992).

62. Elisabeth R. Gerber and Justin H. Phillips, "Direct Democracy and Land Use Policy: Exchanging Public Goods for Development Rights," *Urban Studies* 41, no. 2 (2004): 463–479.

63. Casey Newton, "Group Organizes Recall Against Gordon," *Arizona Republic*, April 30, 2008,

64. A. G. Sulzberger, "For Omaha Mayors, Recall Elections Are Almost Routine," *New York Times* January 26, 2011.

65. John Woolfolk, "Both Sides in San Jose's 'Little Saigon' Furor Plotting Next Moves," *San Jose Mercury News*, October 10, 2008.

66. See Joseph F. Zimmerman, *The Recall: Tribunal of the People* (Westport, CT: Praeger, 1997), 97–130 for the details of this and other local recall efforts.

67. Daniel Weintraub, "The Recall's a Democratic Revolt Against Ruling Elites," *Sacramento Bee*, July 6, 2003; Larry N. Gerston and Terry Christensen, *Recall! California's Political Earthquake* (Armonk, NY: M.E. Sharpe, 2004); Mark Baldassare and Cheryl Katz, *The Coming Age of Direct Democracy: California's Recall and Beyond* (Lanham, MD: Rowman and Littlefield, 2008).

68. Robert Maranto and Jeremy Johnson, "Bringing Back Boss Tweed: Could At-Will Employment Work in State and Local Government and, If So, Where?" in *American Public Service: Radical Reform and the Merit System*, ed. James S. Bowman and Jonathan P. West (Boca Raton, FL: CRC Press, 2007), 77–100.

69. The quotations are from Theodore Lowi, "Machine Politics-Old and New," *Public Interest* 9 (Fall 1967): 86–87.

70. Ibid.

71. Browning, Marshall, and Tabb, *Protest Is Not Enough*, 201–202, in their study of ten communities in northern California, similarly found that "minority incorporation" was strengthened in cities that modified their old reformed structures of government. For a description of the changes that Cincinnati made in an effort to increase the leadership potential of the mayor's office, see John T. Spence, "Looking for Accountability and Efficiency in Council-Manager Government: The Case of Cincinnati," *National Civic Review* 95, no. 4 (Winter 2006): 42–47.

72. Rob Gurwitt, "Nobody in Charge," *Governing* (September 1997), 20-24.

73. Ryan Lillis, "Johnson Starts Push for Strong Mayor," *Sacramento Bee*, December 12, 2008; Loretta Kalb, "Sacramento Judge Intends to Bar Strong-Mayor Proposal from Ballot," *Sacramento Bee*, January 15, 2010.

74. Evelyn Larrubia, "Supervisors' Decisions Made Mostly Behind Closed Doors," *Los Angeles Times*, March 26, 2002.

75. Jia-Rui Chon, "Court Gives Campaign Finance Laws a Green Light," *Los Angeles Times*, May 21, 2005.

76. Jeffrey Kraus, "Campaign Finance Reform Reconsidered: New York City's Public Finance Program after 15 Years," paper presented at the annual meeting of the Midwest Political Science Association, Chicago, April 7, 2005, www.allacademic.com/meta/p86293_index.html.

77. Carl Castillo and Mike McGrath, "Localism and Reform: The Benefits of Political Diversity," *National Civic Review* 90 (Summer 2001): 140–142.

78. *Citizens United v. Federal Election Commission*, 558 U.S. 876 (2010).

79. Los Angeles City Ethics Commission, *Campaign Finance Reform in Los Angeles: Lessons from the 2001 City Elections, Executive Summary*, October 2001, 3, http://ethics.lacity.org/news.cfm.

80. "Campaign Finance Chicanery" (editorial), *New York Times*, October 13, 1993.

81. Michael Cooper, "At $92.60 a Vote, Bloomberg Shatters an Election Record," *New York Times*, December 4, 2001; Michael Cooper, "Final Tally: Bloomberg Spent $75.5 Million to Become Mayor," *New York Times*, March 30, 2002. For a more detailed analysis, see New York City Campaign Finance Board, *An Election Interrupted . . . The Campaign Finance Program and the 2001 New York City Elections, Part I* (New York, 2002).

82. Michael D. Shear, "N.Y. Mayor Bloomberg Leaves GOP," *Washington Post*, June 20, 2007.

83. Michael Barbaro, "Bloomberg Spends $102 Million to Win 3rd Term," *New York Times*, November 27, 2009.

84. Joyce Purnick, "Koch to Limit Contributions in Race," *New York Times*, June 21, 1988.

85. U.S. Term Limits Organization, "U.S. Term Limits," Washington, DC, 1998, www.free-market.net/partners/u/ustl.html.

86. National League of Cities, "Term Lengths and Term Limits," n.d., www.nlc.org/about_cities/cities_101/172.aspx (accessed January 4, 2009).

87. Victor S. DeSantis and Tari Renner, "Term Limits and Turnover Among Local Officials," in *Municipal Year Book 1994* (Washington, DC: International City/County Management Association, 1994), 36–42.

88. Peggy Lowe and Ellen Miller, "Term Limits Hurt Small Towns," *Rocky Mountain News,* December 2, 2002, www.msnbc.com/local/rmn/DRMN_1581934.asp?cp1=1.

89. Mark P. Petracca and Karen Moore O'Brien, "Municipal Term Limits in Orange County, California," *National Civic Review* (Spring-Summer 1994): 192–193.

90. Courtney Gross, "Musical Chairs: Shuffling Seats in City Government," *Gotham Gazette*, March 29, 2008, www.gothamgazette.com/article/issueoftheweek/20080329/200/2479.

91. Sewell Chan, "Council Votes, 29 to 22, to Extend Term Limits," *New York Times*, October 23, 2008.

92. H. George Frederickson, Gary A. Johnson, and Curtis Wood, *The Adapted City: Institutional Dynamics and Structural Change* (Armonk, NY: M.E. Sharpe, 2004), 52–67.

93. Pradeep Chandra Kathi and Terry L. Cooper, "Democratizing the Administrative State: Connecting Neighborhood Councils and City Agencies," *Public Administration Review* 65, no. 5 (September 2005): 559–567.

94. Alan L. Saltzstein, Colin Copus, Raphael J. Sonenshein, and Chris Skelcher, "Visions of Urban Reform: Comparing English and U.S. Strategies for Improving City Government," *Urban Affairs Review* 44, no. 2 (November 2008): 155–181. Megan Mullin, Gillian Peele, and Bruce E. Cain, "City Caesars? Institutional Structure and Mayoral Success in Three California Cities," *Urban Affairs Review* 40, no. 1 (September 2004): 19–43, describes the structural reforms instituted in San Francisco, Oakland, and San Jose in an effort to strengthen city leadership.

95. Terry Nichols Clark, "Old and New Paradigms for Urban Research: Globalization and the Fiscal Austerity and Urban Innovation Project," *Urban Affairs Review* 36, no. 1 (September 2000): 3–45.

96. Simpson and Kelly, "The New Chicago School of Urbanism and the New Daley Machine," 213–238.

7 Citizen Participation

In the immediate aftermath of Hurricane Katrina in 2005, state officials in Louisiana gave strong consideration to innovative ideas for rebuilding an area that had lost thousands of families to outmigration. Prominent members of the national planning community presented state officials with visionary recommendations to shrink the physical "footprint" of New Orleans. The planners argued that rebuilding the shrunken city should reflect "smart growth" principles: the most devastated, low-lying areas would be returned to green space, providing a natural buffer to help protect the city against future floods. The planners proposed that new housing in poorer neighborhoods be built according to the principles of New Urbanism (a school of thought that we discuss further in Chapter 9) in order to establish a sense of community among poor New Orleanians. The planners proposed that small housing units be built close to one another and neighborhood stores, promoting both walkability and a sense of neighborliness. Targeting reconstruction efforts, instead of attempting to rebuild every devastated neighborhood, would also save the state considerable money.

State leaders were initially quite receptive to the visionary reconstruction plans. However, the residents of New Orleans' poorer low-lying neighborhoods, the areas hardest hit by the flooding, were outraged that there would be no effort to restore their communities. Defenders of traditional New Orleans further objected that the New Urbanism housing was too modern it its design and was contrary to the aesthetics and the unique architectural heritage of New Orleans. ACORN (the Association for Community Organizations for Reform Now) and other grassroots groups mobilized against the rebuilding plans, arguing that the plans would constitute a second catastrophe inflicted on poor African American neighborhoods in the Crescent City.

Faced with the intense opposition of community groups, state and municipal leaders retreated and turned away from the more visionary rebuilding strategies. New plans were drawn up with a strengthened emphasis on transparency and citizen participation. Reconstruction wound up being an excruciatingly slow and frustrating process, but the rebuilding effort no longer shut out the concerns of the city's poorer residents.[1]

The tale of post-Katrina New Orleans testifies to the importance of bringing everyday residents of a city into the decision-making process. Municipal bureaucrats, professional planners, elected officials, and expert advisers do not always know best; their views do not always reflect those of the people they serve. **Citizen participation** refers to the variety of mechanisms that a city can use in order to allow local residents the ability to influence the making of municipal decisions that have important effects on their daily lives.

Too often, citizen participation is portrayed solely as an effort to empower the poor. Yet, as we shall see, middle-class citizens are often the primary beneficiaries of citizen participation efforts. Middle-class citizens have the education, skills, and initiative to take advantage of the new channels created to enhance citizen influence. (See Box 7.1, "Who Participates in Citizen Participation?") Suburbanites have used participatory processes to gain greater parental control over the local school curriculum, to limit school busing, to stop the construction of costly new sports stadiums, to reject proposals to consolidate local governments, and to veto growth projects that would require higher levels of taxation while adding to traffic congestion, urban sprawl, and school overcrowding.

THE ROOTS OF URBAN PARTICIPATION

In the 1950s and 1960s, urban renewal and highway construction programs tore down vast areas of housing in the city, displacing core-city residents. Municipal and state planners gave little respect to the concerns of the residents whose homes and communities lay in the path of progress.

The ills of such top-down decision making were all too apparent. Urban renewal programs tore down habitable dwelling units, not just slum structures. Urban highways divided and destroyed city neighborhoods. Lower- and middle-class families were pushed out of their homes to make way for new highways, university campuses, hospitals, and expanded central business districts. Initially, redevelopment and highway officials did not even re-house displaced residents, as this responsibility was left to other agencies that lacked the resources and the interest to help displacees.[2]

The highway and renewal programs destroyed the **social fabric** that existed in poor neighborhoods, places where friends and family members helped to care for one another's children and where neighbors watched over life on the streets from their windows. The sense of neighborhood found in old low-rise areas of the city was not reestablished in newly built high-rise public-housing towers, where tenants, fearful of crime, lived behind locked doors. The social conditions of the high-rises deteriorated and in many ways became worse than the low-rise neighborhoods they had replaced.

In New York, San Francisco, Boston, Baltimore, Miami, Portland (Oregon), and numerous other cities, poor and working-class residents rebelled against highway and urban renewal projects that promised to destroy and transform their neighborhoods.[3] Local residents demanded to have a voice in the making of decisions that affected their lives so significantly. Eventually, regulations governing the programs were altered to allow for greater citizen participation.

By the1960s, the federal government began to change the rules governing urban aid programs in order to promote citizen participation.[4] President Lyndon Johnson's

Box 7.1

Who Participates in Citizen Participation?

Do requirements for citizen participation help to empower racial minorities and the urban poor? Or do middle-class citizens take maximum advantage of the opportunities created by participatory processes?

Evidence from the operation of New York City's community board system helps provide an answer these questions. New York created fifty-nine community boards in an effort to enhance citizen influence in decisions concerning neighborhood land use, budgeting, and service delivery.

The boards are only advisory, and final decision-making authority rests with municipal agencies. Still, activist community boards have been able to force developers to scale back the size of a development or add off-street parking and other community amenities in return for a favorable board recommendation. In the Red Hook section of Brooklyn, the giant Swedish retailer IKEA gained board support for a big-box superstore only after agreeing to offer job training for local residents and to set up a shuttle bus to run from a nearby subway station in an effort to minimize traffic congestion.[1]

Developers complain that the community board system gives too much power to the self-anointed citizen activists. But the record shows that the boards tend to seek minor adjustments in development plans and seldom pose a serious impediment to major growth projects.[2]

Evidence from Minnesota as well as New York points to the potential class bias of such participatory systems. Middle-class homeowners, especially in predominantly white communities, used participatory processes to secure their budget priorities.[3] Lower-class residents were less effective.

In Los Angeles, homeowners dominated the system of eighty-six neighborhood boards created to decentralize city government. The boards did not adequately reflect the region's ethnic diversity and the concerns of the poor. As one study found, "Latinos are underrepresented, and boards are disproportionately wealthy, white, and highly educated."[4]

Certainly, citizen participation mechanisms can be an important vehicle to help empower the poor. Yet, it appears that they help the urban middle class even more.

[1]Bruce F. Berg, *New York City Politics: Governing Gotham* (New Brunswick, NJ: Rutgers University Press, 2007), 24–31.

[2]Mark Berkey-Gerard, "Community Board Reform," *Gotham Gazette,* March 6, 2006, www.gothamgazette.com/article/issueoftheweek/20060306/200/1779; Tom Angotti, *New York for Sale: Community Planning Confronts Global Real Estate* (Cambridge, MA: MIT Press, 2008).

[3]Robert F. Pecorella, "Community Input and the City Budget: Geographically Based Budgeting in New York City," *Journal of Urban Affairs* 8 (Winter 1986): 58–59; Susan S. Fainstein and Clifford Hirst, "Neighborhood Organizations and Community Planning: The Minneapolis Neighborhood Revitalization Program," in *Revitalizing Urban Neighborhoods,* ed. W. Dennis Keating, Norman Krumholz, and Philip Star (Lawrence: University Press of Kansas, 1996), 86–111.

[4]Juliet Musso, Christopher Weare, Mark Elliot, Alicia Kitsuse, and Ellen Shiau, "Toward Community Engagement in City Governance: Evaluating Neighborhood Council Reform in Los Angeles," an Urban Policy Brief of the USC Civic Engagement Initiative and USC Neighborhood Participation Project, 2007, p. 1, www.usc-cei.org/userfiles/file/Toward%20Community.pdf.

In the 1950s and the 1960s, Jane Jacobs led the fight against various urban renewal projects, including a proposed new highway that would cut through her Lower Manhattan East Village neighborhood. Jacobs argued for the importance of bringing citizen voices into the decision-making process. She argued that redevelopment projects conceived by outsiders often destroyed the sense of community that existed in poor and working-class neighborhoods. From the Library of Congress, Prints and Photographs Division, Washington, DC 20540 USA, http://www.loc.gov/pictures/resource/cph.3c37838/.

Community Action Program (CAP), a central element in his "War on Poverty," required the "**maximum feasible participation**" of the poor. The results, however, were often quite disappointing. Turnout in the initial elections for community action boards, for instance, often hovered at 5 percent or less.[5]

In the decades that followed, federal requirements for citizen participation expanded to more than 150 programs, including coastal zone management, water pollution control, and regional development, to cite only a few. In program area after program area, federal law required state and local agencies to "hold hearings," "involve citizens," establish "community advisory boards," and "seek consultation with affected parties" as a condition of receiving federal aid. The Community Development Block Grant (CDBG) program, the nation's largest urban aid program, requires cities to specify how the residents of low- and moderate-income neighborhoods have been made a part of the process in deciding how CDBG funds are spent.

Republican administrations in Washington have been less enthusiastic than the Democrats about federal requirements for citizen participation. Republican leaders argued that such participatory processes were unnecessary, as municipal elections already provided for the legitimate expression of the people's will. The Republicans did not wish to establish new channels of participation that would enable local activists to challenge the program choices made by a city's duly elected leaders.

Yet, despite the criticisms, the concept of citizen engagement has proved to be quite popular. There is something inherently democratic about allowing people who are directly affected by a decision to have a say in the making of that decision. Consequently, Republican administrations in Washington have been able only to temper—not roll back—the participatory requirements of federal aid programs.

State ordinances similarly seek to facilitate citizen participation but are generally less extensive than federal requirements. Only half the states, for instance, require local governments to publish proposed local budgets or otherwise make such documents available for public inspection.[6]

LEVELS OF CITIZEN PARTICIPATION

The past half century has seen a virtual revolution in citizen participation as governmental agencies across the United States made requirements for citizen engagement a commonplace feature of public programs. Too often, however, the participatory processes yield a level of citizen influence that is more illusory than real.

Sherry Arnstein's eight-rung **ladder of citizen participation** (see Figure 7.1) helps to sort through the vast maze of participatory mechanisms.[7] On the bottom of the ladder are participatory devices that she labels *manipulation* and *therapy*, participatory vehicles that are so rudimentary that they can even be viewed as *nonparticipation*.

1. *MANIPULATION*

Manipulation occurs when agency officials are not concerned with learning about what citizens think. Instead, the agency establishes a participatory process as a strategy for making citizens more willing to accept a course of action that an agency has largely already adopted. The process can be labeled **co-optation**: citizens are brought into the decision-making process and given the illusion of power but are denied any real ability to influence important outcomes.

2. *THERAPY*

Sometimes, public officials use participatory processes in an attempt to control or even "improve" citizen behavior. Tenant meetings in public housing, for instance, can focus on changing the behavior of unruly residents, not on changing the conditions of public housing. Sometimes, social workers even regard citizen engagement as "healthy" or therapeutic, a means of helping poor people to overcome their "pathologies" and social disorganization.

Figure 7.1 **Eight Rungs on a Ladder of Citizen Participation**

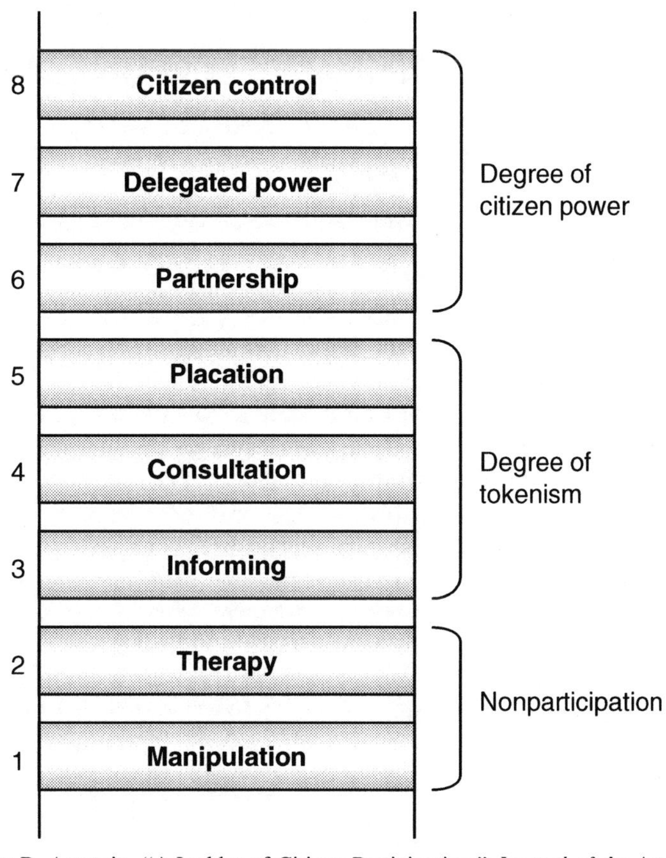

Source: Sherry R. Arnstein, "A Ladder of Citizen Participation," *Journal of the American Institute of Planners* 35 (July 1969): 217. Reprinted with permission from the *Journal of the American Planning Association*. Copyright © July 1969 by the American Planning Association.

3. *INFORMING*

In a one-way flow of information, a public official may speak at a neighborhood meeting, offering an elaborate presentation (even a PowerPoint show!) that reviews an agency's plans. The official presentation can be used to shape the agenda and ensuing discussion, leaving little time for members of the audience to bring up concerns of their own. One-way informational sessions held late in the policymaking process offer citizens only the most limited opportunity to affect a course of action that, for all intents and purposes, has already been set.

On the middle rungs of the ladder are the participatory devices that fall under the categories of *consultation* and *placation*. These devices offer **tokenism**, as citizens are given minor representation on a decision-making board or are allowed the ability to alter only small parts of an agency's plans. A good example of tokenism is provided by the effort of Cincinnati to redesign Washington Park, the green area lying in front of the city's historic Music Hall in the midst of the troubled Over-the-Rhine section of the city, just immediately to the north of its central business district. The parks department structured meetings to allow neighborhood residents a voice in choosing the designs of park benches, playground equipment, and a water-spray play feature. But the meetings did not offer residents an opportunity to challenge the park's upgrading, part of the larger efforts by planners to promote the gentrification and transformation of the area surrounding the park.

4. *Consultation*

Consultation occurs when municipal officials actively solicit and listen to community voices. Municipal officials may survey the residents of a neighborhood, distribute a questionnaire to the users of a municipal service, or hold public forums and neighborhood meetings.

Truly effective consultation, however, requires more than a one-time-only meeting or the administration of a survey.[8] A series of meetings—better yet, the formation of a residents' steering committee or task force that meets on a regular basis with city officials—is necessary for mutual education, understanding, and compromise.[9] A series of scheduled joint working sessions allows residents and public officials to learn about each other's concerns and to jointly fashion a collaborative solution.

The law enforcement approach known as **community policing** entails consultation through "beat meetings" and through citizen councils that bring neighborhood concerns to the attention of local law enforcement officials. More traditional officers, however, often are hesitant to allow community members to help shape police priorities. "Old school" officers often reduce such beat meetings to mere one-way informing sessions. In Chicago, the mayor's office and central police administration had to keep the pressure on officers to be more involved with the neighborhoods they policed.[10] By 2010, however, as the economic recession forced Chicago to make service cutbacks, the mayor reduced community policing efforts in order to put more patrol officers on the street.[11]

5. *Placation*

Even where participatory policing, schools, housing, health, and planning boards are created with the purpose of muting citizen discontent, the procedures can still provide real opportunities for influence. Local representatives can fight for program changes that reflect neighborhood need. Such opportunities for genuine influence are limited, however, in cases when community voices are easily outvoted by other board members.

Highest on the ladder are those forms of participation—*partnership, delegated power*, and *citizen control*—that denote power sharing, a real opportunity for local residents to join city officials in making important decisions.

6. *PARTNERSHIP*

Partnership denotes mutual power, where citizens and municipal officials share in decision making. One form of partnership allows neighborhood residents and the city a mutual veto; neither can do anything as a solo actor but must seek the consent of the other. An illustrative example of power sharing occurs when a city superintendent of schools must select a local school principal only from a list of qualified candidates screened by a local community board; neither the superintendent nor the community board can act without the other.

As we will discuss in greater detail later in this chapter, *community development corporations* (CDCs) embody the ideal of partnership. These neighborhood organizations form cooperative relationships, working with municipal, nonprofit, and private-sector actors in order to build new housing, health clinics, and even new commercial facilities in underserved neighborhoods.

7. *DELEGATED POWER*

Under delegated power, municipal officials give a community organization the authority to make significant decisions. Chicago in the 1980s and 1990s experimented with school decentralization, giving citizen-community boards specified budgetary and personnel powers. Dayton, Ohio, similarly gave neighborhood Priority Boards a limited ability to fund local projects.

This delegation of authority can be controversial. In Chicago, many school reformers had only limited faith in the wisdom of local parents and grassroots organizations. When the local boards failed to produce results, school reformers changed the law, abridging decentralization in order to give greater authority to Chicago's mayor.[12]

8. *CITIZEN CONTROL*

Citizen control (or **community control**) exists when residents possess final authority over a program. A neighborhood board—not city officials—operates a facility or otherwise retains final authority in deciding how a program is run.

The bitter controversy over school decentralization that occurred in New York City in 1968 still serves as a potent reminder of the explosive potential of community control. The New York Board of Education set up a system of community control in the Ocean Hill-Brownsville section of Brooklyn, a predominantly poor and African American neighborhood. The community board took dramatic steps to reshape the school's workforce, which they saw as unresponsive to the needs of neighborhood children. The local board dismissed a number of white teachers (most of whom were Jewish) and hired classroom instructors who were not members of the United Federation of Teachers. The board sought to transfer teachers it did not want to other schools. The New York teachers' union objected, the community board refused to yield, and teachers across the city walked out in a series of strikes that closed the city's schools and raised racial and ethnic tensions to the boiling point.[13]

Not surprisingly, public officials are quite willing to utilize participatory mechanisms that lie at the bottom rungs of Arnstein's ladder. Public officials fear that more extensive power-sharing arrangements will exacerbate the debate over municipal priorities, adding to the difficulty of their jobs and slowing project execution.

KEYS TO MAKING CITIZEN ENGAGEMENT WORK

Why do participatory processes work well in certain cities and not in others? The experience of Indianapolis, Birmingham (Alabama), Portland (Oregon), and St. Paul—cities recognized for their records of citizen empowerment—provides a number of hints.[14]

First, neighborhood residents are more willing to participate when a city turns over real authority to the citizen bodies. Residents will commit time only to meetings and processes that have the power to make real policy and spending decisions, rather than to issue advisory reports that city officials can ignore. Los Angeles' eighty-six elected neighborhood councils are structurally weak as they possess only advisory power. The neighborhood bodies lack clearly established channels for interaction with the mayor, city council, and municipal departments.[15]

Second, participation works best in cities where the municipal government establishes a civic "culture" and a demonstrated record of working in partnership with neighborhood groups. A city's leaders must be committed to building a culture of participation, dispensing rewards and sanctions that will persuade municipal bureaucrats to commit to power sharing.

Third, participatory processes are best instituted throughout the city as opposed to being introduced in only a few troubled neighborhoods. Participatory arrangements that are implemented only in selected neighborhoods fail to signify city hall's full commitment to participation.

Finally, outside assistance is often critical to the success of participatory efforts.[16] (See Box 7.2, "Learning from the Pacific Northwest: Supporting Neighborhood Engagement.") Governmental grants, corporate philanthropy, and nonprofit sponsorship provide community groups with the financial resources for newsletters and surveys, the maintenance of community headquarters, and the rental of space for larger community meetings and events. Without outside financial support, neighborhood organizations often are unable to communicate effectively with residents on an ongoing basis.

The City of Indianapolis created a Neighborhood Resource Center to foster grassroots activism. Nonprofit institutions played a critical role, with the Lilly Endowment, the Ford Foundation, and the Annie Casey Foundation all helping to fund a Neighborhood Power Initiative that provided staff and training assistance to community groups.[17]

Effective citizen participation requires that a city do more than merely announce a **public hearing**. The typical public hearing or open forum is a very crude tool of engagement that fails to offer citizens the depth of information and continuing dialogue with city officials required for a true partnership. Cities have a variety of participatory mechanisms that go beyond public hearings. **Planning charrettes** allow citizens to help work on a project's design. Joint steering committees and task

Box 7.2
Learning from the Pacific Northwest: Supporting Neighborhood Engagement

In Portland, Seattle, and other Pacific Northwest cities, grassroots activism is a prominent feature of local politics. Citizen groups in the Northwest are particularly active in fighting to preserve the region's natural environment and fabled quality of life, opposing the threats posed by unbridled growth.

Citizen engagement in the Pacific Northwest is ingrained in the local culture and is an expected part of local decision making. King County (greater Seattle) routinely conducts a series of small-group forums across the county, using volunteers to solicit public feedback on various policy issues. The participants share their opinions and insights on an issue, after having viewed a video and read a summary of the key facts and competing perspectives. Municipal bureaucrats are careful not to manipulate the forums. A citizens' steering committee, not a municipal agency, selects the topics for group discussion.[1]

The City of Seattle offers extensive assistance to help neighborhood groups to develop their own plans while respecting the needs of the larger city. A Neighborhood Planning Office and a Neighborhood Matching Fund provide community groups with the staff and financial assistance and technological support in areas such as geographic information system (GIS) mapping "to help neighborhood groups do good planning work." The city encourages mutual education and the building of a long-term collaborative relationship between the city and neighborhood groups. Seattle has thirteen district councils. The decentralization of departments further encourages municipal administrators to work with neighborhood groups. By supporting collaborative action, the city seeks to offer citizens a more constructive alternative to grassroots militancy and oppositional politics.[2]

The Seattle/Portland model represents the working of grassroots democracy at its finest. Critics, however, note that such neighborhood planning may give excessive voice to NIMBY ("not in my backyard") activists opposed to growth. The fervent opposition of neighborhood and environmentalist groups served to thwart a number of economic development projects, including efforts to bring new office growth to Seattle's old downtown.

[1]"King County, WA Initiates Community Forums Program," *PA Times* (ASPA Newsletter April 2008): 8.

[2]Carmen Sirianni, "Neighborhood Planning as Collaborative Democratic Design: The Case of Seattle," *Journal of the American Planning Association* 73, no. 4 (Autumn 2007): 373–387. The quotation appears on p. 374. See also Seattle Planning Commission, *Citizen Participation Evaluation: Executive Summary*, March 2000, www.seattle.gov/planningcommission/docs/part_EXECSM.pdf.

forces allow a small group of residents and public officials to discuss and negotiate a project's details. Citizen review panels, neighborhood surveys and focus groups, and interactive Web sites all allow for informed participation.[18]

The use of **citizen juries** is an innovative process, where a group of ordinary citizens is given detailed information regarding policy choices. The group then discusses its preferences and possible trade-offs in an attempt to come up with the best, and maybe even the most creative, solution to a difficult problem. **Deliberative polling** has a similar intent. A deliberative poll does not seek to uncover the present state of public opinion. Instead, the pollster seeks informed opinion. The deliberative pollster asks for the respondent's opinion only after the respondent is given detailed and balanced information on a set of policy issues.[19]

THE EVOLUTION OF COMMUNITY ORGANIZATIONS: FROM PROTEST TO PARTNERSHIP AND SERVICE PROVISION

Up to this point, this chapter has reviewed formal mechanisms to allow greater engagement in municipal decision making. But urban participation is not confined solely to formal participatory venues. Neighborhood mobilization and organizing efforts—including street protests—are also important vehicles of grassroots involvement.

The presidential election campaign of Barack Obama brought renewed attention to the important role of community organizing in the American city. After finishing college, Obama moved to the South Side of Chicago, where he worked as an organizer for the Calumet Community Religious Conference and its Developing Communities Project. Obama "helped build and guide a small network of grassroots groups that agitated for better playgrounds, improvements in trash pickup and the removal of asbestos from public housing."[20] After finishing law school, Obama returned to Chicago and taught classes on the community organizing techniques publicized by social activist Saul Alinsky.[21]

Alinsky was a renowned and often feared community organizer who worked for the Industrial Areas Foundation (IAF). Alinsky and IAF-style organizing provided insights as to how the "have-nots" and "have-little-want-mores"[22] can uncover their own power resources in order to pressure city officials to respond to the needs of often-ignored communities.

What are the steps that community organizing entails? Under the **Alinsky/IAF method of community organizing**, the organizer works in tandem with individuals, including church and religious leaders, who command great respect in a neighborhood.[23] Together, they seek to uncover residents' most salient grievances. Identifying the injustices, the organizer **rubs wounds raw** in order to spur the community to action. The organizer **freezes the target** of the protest action, refusing to allow the target to shift blame or responsibility to others.

The organizer does not always choose to fight the biggest problems facing a community. At least initially, the organizer must choose small, winnable targets that allow for a **quick victory** that will build the community's spirit and mobilize followers for future battles.

The IAF organizing approach has won important victories in Los Angeles, cities in Texas, and in communities throughout the Southwest, especially where Latino organizations have been able to build on their community's roots in the Catholic church.[24] In El Paso, a city with a population that is two-thirds Hispanic, EPISO (the El Paso Interreligious Sponsoring Organization) conducted its grassroots campaigns with the assistance of local churches.[25] In San Antonio, Communities Organized for Public Services (COPS), a federation of more than twenty neighborhood groups, fought to correct the underprovision of infrastructure and other services in the Mexican sections of the city. Like other IAF organization, COPS used **mass accountability meetings** to pressure invited public officials to make promises to act.[26] In meetings crowded with large numbers of neighborhood residents, public officials were often asked to make policy commitments, promises that community leaders would later demand that the officials fulfill.

Beginning in 1970s and 1980s, community groups began to change their style of action, no longer giving the same emphasis to conflict and public combat that Alinsky did in an earlier period. Instead of fighting public officials, neighborhood organizations sought to build more enduring and cooperative relationships with governmental organizations, important financial institutions, major corporations, and nonprofit associations. A newer generation of community organizers came to recognize the importance of establishing good relations with groups that held the resources critical to neighborhood housing, job training, economic development, health care, and school programs.[27] Community organizations still resort to protest actions when a situation requires it. Yet, in more recent years, IAF organizations have turned away from confrontation in favor of "values-based organizing" that seeks to build "collaborative leadership."[28] (See Box 7.3, "What Went Wrong with ACORN?")

In San Antonio, Communities Organized for Public Services typifies the evolving approach of community organizations. COPS has gone beyond protest actions to emphasize a sustained voter registration drive that added to the organization's electoral power and gained COPS a regular seat at the local bargaining table when important decisions are made. Once dismissed by municipal leaders as a rabble-rousing group, COPS in more recent years was awarded numerous honors by the city for its record of public service.[29] Once an outsider, COPS has come to enjoy the leverage that derives from building long-term, collaborative relationships with government and private-sector leaders.[30]

Community organizations have become increasingly involved with the provision of housing, education, and health-care services, all activities in the "domestic" sphere traditionally left to women. As a result, women have assumed leadership roles in many community groups. Women have usually provided much of the back-office work, including the clerical assistance and many mundane tasks necessary to sustain such organizations. Women often occupy leadership positions in community groups that deal with housing, health, and social policy matters, issues of concern to women and their families.

The rise of women to leadership positions has altered the style of neighborhood action. With women determining strategy, community organizing lost some of the "conflict orientation"[31] and the tough "macho" posturing that characterized Saul Alinsky and an earlier generation of community organizers (See Box 7.4, "Women and Community Organizing.")

The change in focus of community groups is clearly reflected in the slogan adopted by The Woodlawn Organization (TWO) on Chicago's poor and black South Side: "From Protest to Programs." In the 1960s and 1970s, The Woodlawn Organization, rooted in the Alinsky tradition, organized boycotts of local stores that shortchanged residents (i.e., merchants who "short-weighed" the meat and other products they sold).

Box 7.3

What Went Wrong with ACORN?

Strong neighborhood organizations can be seen as an expression of democracy. Yet, more conservative political groups and Republicans often argue that government should not support the work of activist community organizations that push for the expansion of social programs and whose members support the election of Democratic candidates. The critics further charge that neighborhood organizations are too often dominated by unethical and corrupt poverty "hustlers" who are more interested in profiting from publicly funded programs than in building programs that effectively serve a community. Conservatives focused their guns on ACORN (the Association of Community Organizations for Reform Now), a nationwide organization of 174 local poor-people's groups.

Over the years, ACORN had built a record of accomplishment: fighting the redlining of communities by banks, documenting predatory lending practices that led to the rash of home foreclosures in poor neighborhoods, fighting for the working poor to be paid a "living wage," assisting home reconstruction in the poorest sections of New Orleans after Hurricane Katrina, and registering poorer Americans to vote.[1] Like other community groups, ACORN over the years moderated its actions, becoming increasingly involved with running job training programs and other programs that expanded service provision in poor neighborhoods. Yet, in important ways, ACORN was also a throwback to the organizing model of the 1960s. ACORN chose to emphasize high-profile protests and political actions as opposed to building stable working partnerships with more established groups.

Conservatives scorned ACORN for corruption, the embezzlement of funds,[2] and blatant politicization. Republicans accused ACORN of voter registration fraud, of having misused public monies in helping noncitizens and other unqualified voters to register and vote for Barack Obama and other Democratic candidates.

A 2009 undercover "sting" operation, arranged and video-recorded by a couple of conservative activists, seemed to confirm some of the worst suspicions about ACORN. The conservative activists, pretending to be a prostitute and a pimp, went to the Brooklyn, New York, ACORN office and asked for advice as to how to receive federal assistance. The local ACORN official counseled the pair, apparently even encouraging them to lie in filling out aid applications.

Embarrassed by the revelations, members of Congress began to retreat from their support of ACORN. New laws restricted ACORN's participation in government-funded programs. The Census Bureau dropped ACORN as a partner in aiding the decennial count in poorer neighborhoods. Cut off from funding, ACORN shut the doors of regional and local offices and faced the prospect of bankruptcy. ACORN's misbehavior put the organization at political risk; its excesses had weakened one of the most important advocacy groups for the urban poor.

How did ACORN go wrong? Why did it become the focus of the attacks of conservatives? ACORN's continued involvement in electoral politics and aggressive protest politics raised its national profile and made the group a convenient target of the political Right. ACORN did not root out misbehavior and "trim its sails" in an era when heightened political polarizations should have dictated caution.

A media with a penchant for seizing on scandals quickly latched onto the ACORN pimp-and-prostitute story.

Nonprofit and community groups that do the public's work and rely on outside funders must show a concern for ethical behavior and maintaining the public's trust. ACORN failed to institute the appropriate controls to assure the financial and program probity of its members. Nonprofit and community organizations must take special care to safeguard their public image and their reputation for integrity. ACORN was insensitive to such needs and was unwilling to implement such reforms.

Community activist and theorist Harry Boyte offers one additional insight as to why ACORN ran off course. According to Boyte, ACORN spurned the traditional IAF organizational approach of working with the more established neighborhood organizations such as churches and labor unions.[3] ACORN chose to go it alone and not be tied to the more conservative ways of older neighborhood groups. As a result, ACORN was not anchored in the values of faith-based service and the democratic dialogue of labor unions at their best. Nor did ACORN have friends that could strongly caution the organization of the dangers posed by the organization's excesses.

[1]Robert Fisher, ed., *The People Shall Rule: ACORN, Community Organizing, and the Struggle for Economic Justice* (Nashville, TN: Vanderbilt University Press, 2009); John Atlas, *Seeds of Change: The Story of ACORN, America's Most Controversial Antipoverty Community Organizing Group* (Nashville, TN: Vanderbilt University Press, 2010); Maude Hurd and Steven Kest, "Fighting Predatory Lending from the Ground Up: An Issue of Economic Justice," in *Organizing Access to Capital: Advocacy and the Democratization of Financial Institutions,* ed. Gregory D. Squires (Philadelphia: Temple University Press, 2003), 119–134; Pablo Eisenberg, "Dropping Acorn: What About the Other Side of the Story?" *Journal of Philanthropy,* September 18, 2009; John Atlas and Peter Dreier, "The Acorn Scandal Offers Key Lessons to All Charities," *Journal of Philanthropy*, December 10, 2009.

[2]Stephanie Strom, "Funds Misappropriated at 2 Nonprofit Groups," *New York Times,* July 9, 2008.

[3]Harry C. Boyte, *Everyday Politics: Reconnecting Citizens and Public Life* (Philadelphia: University of Pennsylvania Press, 2004), 49.

TWO also threatened to transport ghetto residents to downtown department stores to mill around and maybe scare away middle-class customers, unless store managers agreed to more inclusive hiring practices. TWO carried on notable battles with the University of Chicago over plans for campus expansion that threatened to displace community residents.

Over the years, however, TWO became less focused on protest actions and more concerned with using the organization to run housing programs and deliver vital services to community residents. The organization turned its attention to rehabilitating low-income housing, operating day-care centers, and bringing dental services to families in this very poor section of Chicago. Instead of organizing protests critical of government and private business, TWO established working relationships with public, private, and nonprofit organizations in order to expand its community-based programs.[32]

In Baltimore, Baltimoreans United in Leadership Development (BUILD) provides another example of a community organization that seeks to balance political and protest actions with the daily effort required to manage and deliver essential com-

Box 7.4
Women and Community Organizing

As Larry Bennett observed in his study of Chicago, "women are important participants in virtually every neighborhood organization. . . . [P]olitical work directed at neighborhood-, housing-, and school-related issues represents a field where women, for generations, have had a conspicuous impact."[1]

Why do women play a prominent role in tenant organizing in low- and moderate-income neighborhoods? The answer is simple. Subsidized housing is, to a great extent, a women's issue. Poverty in the United States is linked to female-headed families, a condition that is known as the **feminization of poverty**. Female-headed households make up a large portion of the population in need of subsidized housing.

Cynthia Reed, the president of the Sheridan-Gunnison Tenants' Association in Chicago's Uptown neighborhood, explained her involvement as a matter of self-interest: Low-income, single mothers raising children have little real alternative in their search for quality housing. They must battle to preserve their subsidized homes, even if it means that they have less time for work and their children.[2]

In the new community action, leaders often come from "the more invisible tier of community leaders, most frequently women who worked behind the scenes." Women build their political skills through activity in PTA groups, church groups, and other neighborhood associations. As one member of San Antonio's Communities Organized for Public Services (COPS) related, women are "community sustainers" who focus not on theatrical political combat but on doing whatever it takes to provide improved schools and family services.[3]

Yet, the roles that women play seem to vary greatly according to nationality and a community's customs. In the fight to maintain affordable housing in Chicago, African American women played dominant leadership roles. In the Nigerian, Ethiopian, and South Asian communities, in contrast, men were more likely than women to get involved. Women from the Middle East were most restrained when it came to the fight to preserve affordable housing.

[1]Larry Bennett, *Neighborhood Politics: Chicago and Sheffield* (New York: Garland, 1997), 246.

[2]The Reed interview is related by Philip Nyden and Joan Adams, "Saving Our Homes: The Lessons of Community Struggles to Preserve Affordable Housing in Chicago's Uptown," a report completed by researchers at Loyola University of Chicago in collaboration with Organization of the Northeast, Chicago, April 1996.

[3]The quotations in this paragraph are from Harry C. Boyte, *Everyday Politics: Reconnecting Citizens and Public Life* (Philadelphia: University of Pennsylvania Press, 2004), 52.

munity services. Working from a membership base of forty-five to fifty churches in the city's African American community, BUILD fought bank redlining and unfair auto insurance rates. BUILD used mass-membership meetings to pressure mayoral and council candidates into making important policy commitments. The organization also campaigned for legislation that would require a "living wage" be paid to workers in Baltimore.

But beyond these high-visibility political actions, BUILD assumed daily management responsibilities in running education and human resource programs in Baltimore's poorer neighborhoods. It sought out partners with businesses in order to offer jobs and job training opportunities as rewards to students who stay in school and who graduate with good grades and good attendance records. BUILD raised public and private monies to establish a Child First Authority to provide extended-day programs, homework assistance, and a safe after-school environment.[33]

COMMUNITY DEVELOPMENT CORPORATIONS

The work of community development corporations has provided some of the "good news" in cities over the past few decades. A **community development corporation (CDC)** is a neighborhood-based organization that works in partnership with public and private actors in order to increase investment in low-income communities.[34] CDCs tend to focus on building and providing affordable housing and neighborhood economic development. In 2005, an estimated 4,600 CDCs were operating in the 50 states.[35]

CDCs have had their greatest success in the rehabilitation and construction of affordable housing. Over 90 percent of all CDCs are engaged in housing activities, working with government agencies, mortgage lenders, and corporate officials in order to piece together the financing for housing at low and moderate prices.

The Nehemiah Project is the work of a faith-based CDC that was established under the leadership of the Reverend Johnny Ray Youngblood in the East Brooklyn section of New York City. More than fifty religious congregations of the United Congregations of East Brooklyn joined together to build 5,000 affordable, owner-occupied single-family homes, providing stability to a neighborhood that had once been plagued by vacant lots. United Congregations of East Brooklyn also established a health clinic in the neighborhood and a job-mentoring program that encouraged students to stay in school.[36]

As the East Brooklyn story demonstrates, CDCs can be quite active in areas beyond housing construction and rehabilitation. CDCs run health clinics, day-care centers, and job training programs. CDCs offer youth activities and after-school programs. CDCs organize food pantries and neighborhood cleanups. CDCs essentially are **gap fillers**. These organizations seek to promote new investment and provide a multitude of community services, attempting to correct the problems that were created when financial institutions, private developers, and other institutions abandoned declining neighborhoods.[37]

CDCs emphasize self-help and consensus building rather than confrontation. They pursue **bridge-building strategies**,[38] that is, the formation of partnerships with organizations and institutions outside the neighborhood. CDCs ask banks, private investors, corporate managers, nonprofit organizations, and government agencies each to pick up a piece in helping to finance a neighborhood project. Private and institutional investors are more willing to invest in such projects when they see that CDC coordination and know-how will reduce the risk of failure.[39]

CDCs have had to pay a price for their success. Despite their roots in a community, a CDC cannot serve as a strong political voice for a poor neighborhood. CDCs have for the most part spurned political mobilization for "consensus organizing"[40] and a "conflict-free"[41] approach to finding partners for community investment. CDC officials are reluctant to criticize people and organizations whose financial support may be crucial to future neighborhood projects. The more politicized neighborhood activists charge that community development corporations exhibit a "disdain"[42] for political advocacy and protest actions. CDCs, according to their critics, "have lost their grassroots mentality."[43] Local activists further question the degree to which CDCs can be regarded as representatives of a neighborhood when nonresidents with critical financing and legal skills often occupy key positions on CDC boards.

Whatever their imperfections, CDCs have enjoyed great success in bringing new units of affordable housing and improved community services to inner-city areas.[44] But the work of CDCs is highly dependent on continued outside support and funding, including the **Low Income Housing Tax Credit (LIHTC)**, which increases the willingness of private institutions to invest in CDC projects. Should the LIHTC be cut or abandoned, CDCs would no longer be able to find investment partners for much of their work.

E-Government and E-Participation

E-government (or "electronic government") provides a number of tools that can bring government closer to the people. Municipal agencies use e-mail, Web sites, Webcasts of public meetings, technology-assisted "virtual participation,"[45] and even blogs and social networking sites (such as Facebook and MySpace) to inform citizens of local events and municipal regulations. The new technology also affords citizens a vehicle to register service requests and complaints without having to visit city hall.

Cities are just beginning to tap the interactive and two-way communications capacity of the Web.[46] As a survey of New Jersey municipalities revealed, governments use the Web for a variety of purposes, but "e-democracy" is the "least practiced" form of e-government.[47] Municipal agencies primarily create Web sites to make announcements and communicate with citizens, efforts that improve service responsiveness. As a national survey discovered, few cities use the Web to offer new opportunities for democratic participation.[48] The presence of a separate information technology (IT) department spurs other departments to pursue more advanced e-government practices.[49]

What does e-democracy look like? West Hartford, Connecticut, employed an interactive, real-time citizen survey that gave respondents policy-related information and then asked them to choose their desired levels of municipal service provision and taxation. As each respondent made the choice to increase or decrease the level of a specified service, the computerized program revealed the effect that the change would have on the respondent's tax bill.[50] Only a relatively small handful of cities, however, have sought to use the new technology for online dialogue and interactive planning.[51]

Seattle is the rare exception, a city that has exhibited strong leadership in promoting the interactive use of the Web. Seattle established a municipal department, the Office of Electronic Communications, to deepen e-democracy. The city also set up a Web site for e-participation (www.seattlechannel.org) that is separate and distinct from the city's main Web site. The "Democracy Portal" (as the city government refers to the e-participation Web site) presents a review of municipal-related news and organizes information by issues in an effort to provide citizens with the information necessary for effective participation. The site also has links that connect viewers to various municipal meetings televised by the city's cable channel. In Seattle, city council meetings are televised, with citizens invited to submit their opinions to public hearings via e-mail.[52]

A municipality's use of Web-based communications poses important questions concerning democracy and representativeness, especially as "online discussions pose a risk of being 'hijacked' by narrow interests."[53] Municipal administrators are often reluctant to offer citizens the opportunity of e-engagement. Administrators fear that online discussion boards and other forms of e-participation may serve to amplify the most critical and antigovernment voices in a community and may ultimately wind up interfering with an agency's ability to perform its job.

CONCLUSION: THE IMPORTANCE OF BOTTOM-UP PARTICIPATION AND THE ROLE OF GOVERNMENT

Over the past half century, communities across the United States have experienced a virtual revolution in citizen participation. Citizens expect their voices to be heard when a city makes decisions that directly affect their lives. Public agencies have responded with a vast array of participatory programs. The federal and state governments have promoted—even required—participation. To a great degree, citizen engagement has become a routine component of urban governance.

While many public agencies are still hesitant to enter into the more far-reaching partnership arrangements, a new generation of municipal officials has been schooled in the importance of being responsive to citizen-customers. These new professionals conceive of their roles as citizen-educators and advisers; they are public servants who seek to work in partnership with neighborhood groups.[54] Simply put, efficiency and effectiveness in public service delivery require that public officials gain the support and cooperation of the people being served.

Government cannot by itself solve complex urban problems. Cities lack the money necessary to tackle the difficult problems they face. The citizens' tax revolt and a wildly fluctuating economy have only served to reinforce the sense of limits in local government. Municipal officials have had to learn to do more with less. Municipal officials have come to recognize that working with community groups can extend the reach and effectiveness of public services.

Community organizations, too, have evolved over the years. While protest will always provide an important political resource for relatively powerless groups, neighborhood groups are less interested in fighting city hall than in identifying ways that their organizations can play an active role in running vital neighborhood programs.

Community-based organizations seek to build partnerships for better schools, housing, job training, and community health care. They have come to understand that power lies less in protest and more in their ability to get things done. While conflict strategies are sometimes unavoidable, community leaders recognize that excessive conflict can impede problem solving by disrupting the process of building coalitions across racial, class, and geographical lines.[55] Community development corporations, in particular, have helped to fill "the vacuum in U.S. housing policy" left by federal withdrawal.[56]

Yet, bottom-up action cannot by itself solve the urban crisis. Even CDCs, despite their impressive successes, lack the capacity to rebuild core-city neighborhoods.[57] CDCs, faith-based organizations, neighborhood planning commissions, and other community-based organizations all require government and corporate support and the assistance of nonprofit philanthropy to extend their problem-solving reach.

NOTES

1. Various authors describe how citizen action wound up altering the reconstruction plans for post-Katrina New Orleans. See: Carolyn J. Lukensmeyer, "Large-Scale Citizen Engagement and the Rebuilding of New Orleans: A Case Study," *National Civic Review* 96, no. 3 (Fall 2007): 3–15; Mtangulizi Sanyika, "Katrina and the Condition of Black New Orleans: The Struggle for Justice, Equity, and Democracy," in *Race, Place, and Environmental Justice After Hurricane Katrina: Struggles to Reclaim, Rebuild, and Revitalize New Orleans and the Gulf Coast*, ed. Robert D. Bullard and Beverly Wright (Boulder, CO: Westview Press, 2009), 87–111; Robert K. Whalen and Denise Strong, "Rebuilding Lives Post-Katrina: Choices and Challenges in New Orleans' Economic Development," in Bullard and Wright, *Race, Place, and Environmental Justice After Hurricane Katrina,* 183–203 (esp. 198–199); and Eugenie L. Birch and Susan M. Wachter, eds., *Rebuilding Urban Places After Disaster: Learning from Hurricane Katrina* (Philadelphia: University of Pennsylvania Press, 2006). For a discussion of how communities in neighboring Mississippi responded to rebuilding proposals that embodied New Urbanism principles, see Jennifer S. Evans-Cowley and Meghan Zimmerman Gough, "Evaluating New Urbanist Plans in Post-Katrina Mississippi," *Journal of Urban Design* 14, no. 4 (2009): 439–461.

2. Raymond A. Mohl, "Planned Destruction: The Interstates and Central City Housing," in *From Tenements to the Taylor Homes: In Search of an Urban Housing Policy in Twentieth Century America*, ed. John F. Bauman, Roger Biles, and Kristin M. Szylvian (University Park: Pennsylvania State University Press, 2000), 227.

3. Raymond A. Mohl, "Stop the Road: Freeway Revolts in American Cities," *Journal of Urban History* 30, no. 5 (2004): 674–706.

4. Alice O'Connor, "Swimming Against the Tide: A Brief History of Federal Policy in Poor Communities," in *The Community Development Reader*, ed. James DeFilippis and Susan Saegert (New York: Routledge, 2008), 9–27.

5. Renée A. Irvin and John Stansbury, "Citizen Participation in Decision Making: Is It Worth the Effort?" *Public Administration Review* 64, no. 1 (February 2004): 58–60.

6. Maureen Bernier and Sonya Smith, "The State of the States: A Review of State Requirements for Citizen Participation in the Local Government Budget Process," *State and Local Government Review* 36, no. 2 (Spring 2004): 140–150.

7. Sherry R. Arnstein, "A Ladder of Citizen Participation," *Journal of the American Institute of Planners* 35 (July 1969): 216–224. For an alternative ranking of public participation methods that emphasizes collaboration and delegated power, see Paul D. Epstein, Paul M. Coates, and Lyle D. Wray, with David Swain, *Results That Matter: Improving Communities by Engaging Citizens, Measuring Performance, and Getting Things Done* (San Francisco: Jossey-Bass, 2006), 198–201.

8. Brian Adams, "Public Meetings and the Democratic Process," *Public Administration Review* 64, no. 1 (February 2004): 43–54, argues that public hearings and meetings provide community groups with useful opportunities for influence despite the often-noted limitations of public hearings.

9. Barbara Faga, *Designing Public Consensus: The Civic Theater of Community Participation for Architects, Landscape Architects, Planners, and Urban Designers* (Hoboken, NJ: Wiley, 2006), 107–114.

10. Wesley G. Skogan, *Police and Community in Chicago: A Tale of Three Cities* (New York: Oxford University Press, 2006).

11. Fran Spielman and Frank Main, "Cops to Be Reassigned from Community Policing," *Chicago Sun-Times,* September 16, 2010.

12. Dorothy Shipps, *School Reform, Corporate Style: Chicago, 1880–2000* (Lawrence: University Press of Kansas, 2006).

13. Jerald E. Podair, *The Strike That Changed New York: Blacks, Whites, and the Ocean Hill-Brownsville Crisis* (New Haven, CT: Yale University Press, 2002).

14. Jeffrey Berry, Kent Portney, and Ken Thomson, *The Rebirth of Urban Democracy* (Washington, DC: Brookings Institution Press, 1993), esp. 34–39, 47–51, 61–63, and 295–299.

15. Juliet Musso, Christopher Weare, Mark Elliot, Alicia Kitsuse, and Ellen Shiau, "Toward Community Engagement in City Governance: Evaluating Neighborhood Council Reform in Los Angeles," an Urban Policy Brief of the USC Civic Engagement Initiative and USC Neighborhood Participation Project, 2007, 2–8, www.usc-cei.org/userfiles/file/Toward%20Community.pdf.

16. Carmine Sirianni, *Investing in Democracy: Engaging Citizens in Collaborative Governance* (Washington, DC: Brookings Institution Press, 2009), esp. chap. 3, which describes the extensive support provided for neighborhood engagement in Seattle.

17. Stephen Goldsmith, *The Twenty-First Century City: Restructuring Urban America* (Lanham, MD: Rowman and Littlefield, 1999), 159–163.

18. Barbara Faga, *Developing Public Consensus: The Civic Theater of Community Participation for Architects, Landscape Architects, Planners, and Urban Designers* (Hoboken, NJ: Wiley, 2006), 107–114.

19. For a description of how "deliberative polling" gives citizens information before seeking their responses, see James S. Fishkin, "Consulting the Public Through Deliberative Polling," *Journal of Policy Analysis and Management* 22, no. 1 (2003): 128–133.

20. Peter Slevin, "For Clinton and Obama, a Common Ideological Touchstone," *Washington Post,* March 25, 2007.

21. Ryan Lizza, "The Agitator: Barack Obama's Unlikely Political Education," *New Republic,* March 9, 2007.

22. Saul D. Alinsky gave the clearest description of his principles for organizing in his *Rules for Radicals* (New York: Vintage Books, 1971). Charles Silberman, *Crisis in Black and White* (New York: Vintage Books, 1964), 308–355, provides a briefer overview of Alinsky's organizing strategy, especially as applied by The Woodlawn Organization (TWO) in Chicago.

23. Alinsky sought to work with local churches. Still, some advocates of faith-based organizing argued that Alinsky's approach placed too much power in the hands of lay organizers and did not fully exploit the power inherent in religious language, prayer, biblical imagery, and local church leaders in multiracial organizing. See Richard L. Wood, *Faith in Action: Religion, Race, and Democratic Organizing in America* (Chicago: University of Chicago Press, 2002).

24. Mark R. Warren, *Dry Bones Rattling: Community Building to Revitalize America* (Princeton, NJ: Princeton University Press, 2001), esp. 20–22, 191–210, and 239–247.

25. Donald C. Reitzes and Dietrich C. Reitzes, *The Alinsky Legacy: Alive and Kicking* (Greenwich, CT: JAI Press, 1987), 129–131; Robert H. Wilson and Peter Menzies, "The Colonias Water Bill: Communities Demanding Change," in *Public Policy and Community: Activism and Governance in Texas,* ed. Robert H. Wilson (Austin: University of Texas Press, 1997), 241–242 and 245–248.

26. Reitzes and Reitzes, *The Alinsky Legacy,* 117–126.

27. Mike Eichler, *Consensus Organizing: Building Communities of Mutual Self Interest* (Thousand Oaks, CA: Sage, 2007).

28. Harry C. Boyte, *Everyday Politics: Reconnecting Citizens and Public Life* (Philadelphia: Univer-

sity of Pennsylvania Press, 2004), 51 and 122. See also Robert Fisher, "Neighborhood Organizing: The Importance of Historical Context," in DeFilippis and Saegert, *Community Development Reader,* 191; and Mark Warren, "A Theory of Organizing: From Alinsky to the Modern IAF," in ibid., 194–203.

29. Heywood T. Sanders, "Communities Organized for Public Service and Neighborhood Revitalization in San Antonio," in Wilson, *Public Policy and Community: Activism and Governance in Texas*, 36–68; Warren, *Dry Bones Rattling*, 56–57.

30. J. Rick Altemose and Dawn A. McCarty, "Organizing for Democracy Through Faith-Based Institutions: The Industrial Areas Foundation in Action," in *Alliances Across Difference: Coalition Politics for the New Millennium*, ed. Jill M. Bystydzienski and Steven P. Schacht (Lanham, MD: Rowman and Littlefield, 2001), 133–145.

31. Susan Stall and Randy Stoecker, "Community Organizing or Organizing Community: Gender and the Crafts of Empowerment," in DeFilippis and Saegert, *The Community Development Reader*, 245.

32. Richard C. Hula and Cynthia Jackson-Elmoore, "Nonprofit Organizations, Minority Political Incorporation, and Local Governance," in *Nonprofits in Urban America*, ed. Hula and Jackson-Elmoore (Westport, CT: Quorum Books, 2000), 121–150.

33. Marion Orr, "Urban Regimes and Human Capital Policies: A Study of Baltimore," *Journal of Urban Affairs* 14, no. 2 (1992): 173–187; idem, "BUILD: Governing Nonprofits and Relational Power," *Policy Studies Review* 18, no. 4 (Winter 2001): 71–90; idem, "Baltimoreans United in Leadership Development: Exploring the Role of Governing Nonprofits," in Hula and Jackson-Elmoore, *Nonprofits in Urban America*, 151–167; and J. Phillip Thompson III, *Double Trouble: Black Mayors, Black Communities, and the Call for a Deep Democracy* (New York: Oxford University Press, 2006).

34. Ross Gittell and Avis Vidal, *Community Organizing: Building Social Capital as a Development Strategy* (Thousand Oaks, CA: Sage, 1998); Paul S. Grogan and Tony Proscio, *Comeback Cities: A Blueprint for Urban Neighborhood Revival* (Boulder, CO: Westview Press, 2000), 63–101; Robert J. Chaskin et al., *Building Community Capacity* (New York: Aldine de Gruyter, 2001); Avis C. Vidal, "CDCs as Agents of Neighborhood Change: The State of the Art," in *Revitalizing Urban Neighborhoods*, ed. W. Dennis Keating, Norman Krumholz, and Philip Star (Lawrence: University Press of Kansas, 1996), 149–163.

35. 2005 Census of Industry figures, cited by "Community Development Corporations (CDCs)," Community-Wealth.org, www.community-wealth.org/strategies/panel/cdcs/index.html.

36. Andrew Billingsley, *Mighty Like a River: The Black Church and Social Reform* (Oxford University Press, 2002), 145–146; Alexander Von Hoffman, *House by House, Block by Block: The Rebirth of America's Urban Neighborhoods* (New York: Oxford University Press, 2003), 66–69.

37. Gittell and Vidal, *Community Organizing*, 14–15 and 34–36; Sara E. Stoutland, "Community Development Corporations: Mission, Strategy, and Accomplishments," in *Urban Problems and Community Development*, ed. Ronald F. Ferguson and William T. Dickens (Washington, DC: Brookings Institution Press, 1999), 193–240.

38. Barbara Ferman and Patrick Kaylor, "The Role of Institutions in Community Building: The Case of West Mt. Airy, Philadelphia," in Hula and Jackson-Elmoore, *Nonprofits in Urban America*, 93–120. Also see Warren, *Dry Bones Rattling*, 98–123. Myung-Ji Bang, "Understanding Gentrification: The Role and Abilities of Community-Based Organizations in Changing Neighborhoods" (paper presented at the annual meeting of the Urban Affairs Association, New Orleans, March 16–19, 2011) details how CDCs in low-income neighborhoods of post–Hurricane Katrina New Orleans formed links with partnering organizations in order to provide affordable housing and limit gentrification.

39. Sean Zielenbach, *The Art of Revitalization: Improving Conditions in Distressed Inner-City Neighborhoods,* vol. 12, *Contemporary Urban Affairs* (New York: Garland, 2000), 230–234. Herbert J. Rubin, *Renewing Hope Within Neighborhoods of Despair* (Albany: State University of New York Press, 2000), 98–132 and 163–188, points to the key role played by community-based development organizations in piecing together the funds for new community investment. CDCs serve as a community's intermediaries with government agencies, private corporations, banks and other credit institutions, and nonprofit foundations.

40. Gittell and Vidal, *Community Organizing*, 51–54; Michael Eichler, "Consensus Organizing: Sharing Power to Gain Power," *National Civic Review* (Summer–Fall 1995): 256–261. For an assessment of the accomplishments and weaknesses of CDCs, see William M. Rohe, "Do Community Development Corporations Live Up to Their Billing? A Review and Critique of the Research Findings," in *Shelter and Society: Theory, Research, and Policy for Nonprofit Housing*, ed. C. Theodore Koebel (Albany: State University of New York Press, 1998), 177–199. Thad Williamson, David Imbroscio, and Gar Alperovitz, *Making a Place for Community: Local Democracy in a Global Era* (New York: Routledge, 2003), 212–222 and 226–235, provide a sober yet positive overall assessment of the potential inherent in CDCs.

41. James DeFilippis, "Community Control and Development: The Long View," in DeFilippis and Saegert, *The Community Development Reader*, 34.

42. Larry Lamar Yates, "Housing Organizing for the Long Haul: Building on Experience," in *A Right to Housing: Foundation for a New Social Agenda*, ed. Rachel G. Bratt, Michael E. Stone, and Chester Hartman (Philadelphia: Temple University Press, 2006), 222.

43. Randy Stoecker, "The CDC Model of Urban Development: A Critique and an Alternative," in DeFilippis and Saegert, *The Community Development Reader*, 303. See also Robert Mark Silverman, "Caught in the Middle: Community Development Corporations (CDCs) and the Conflict between Grassroots and Instrumental Forms of Citizen Participation," *Community Development* 36, no. 3 (2005): 35–51; and Silverman, "CBOs and Affordable Housing," *National Civic Review* 97, no. 3 (Fall 2008): 26–31.

44. Chaskin et al., *Building Community Capacity*; Rachel G. Bratt, "Community Development Corporations: Challenges in Supporting a Right to Housing," in Bratt, Stone, and Hartman, *A Right to Housing,* 340–359; Norman Krumholz, W. Dennis Keating, Philip D. Star, and Mark C. Chupp, "The Long-Term Impact of CDCs on Urban Neighborhoods: Case Studies of Cleveland's Broadway-Slavic Village and Tremont Neighborhoods," *Community Development* 37, no. 4 (2006): 3–52.

45. Faga, *Designing Public Consensus*, 193–197.

46. Darrell M. West, "E-Government and the Transformation of Service Delivery and Citizen Attitudes," *Public Administration Review* 64, no. 1 (February 2004): 15–27; Sharon S. Dawes, "The Evolution and Continuing Challenges of E-Governance," *Public Administration Review* 68, S1 (December 2008): S86–S102.

47. Tony Carrizales, "Functions of E-Government: A Study of Municipal Practices," *State and Local Government Review* 40, no. 1 (2008): 15.

48. James K. Scott, "'E' the People: Do U.S. Municipal Government Web Sites Support Public Involvement?" *Public Administration Review* 66, no. 3 (May/June 2006): 341–353.

49. Carrizales, "Functions of E-Government," 20.

50. Mark D. Robbins, Bill Simonsen, and Barry Feldman, "Citizens and Resource Allocation: Improving Decision Making with Interactive Web-Based Citizen Participation," *Public Administration Review* 68, no. 3 (May/June 2008): 564–575.

51. Dawes, "The Evolution and Continuing Challenges of E-Governance," S96–S97.

52. Rona Zevin, "The Interface of PEG and the Internet," *Journal of Municipal Telecommunications Policy* (Summer 2005). A draft copy available at www.cityofseattle.net/html/citizen/edemocracy.htm.

53. Epstein et al., *Results That Matter*, 205.

54. Thomas A. Bryer, "Explaining Responsiveness in Collaboration: Administrator and Citizen Role Perceptions," *Public Administration Review* 69, no. 2 (March/April 2009): 271–283.

55. Clarence N. Stone, Jeffrey Henig, Bryan Jones, and Carol Pierannunzi, *Building Civic Capacity: The Politics of Reforming Urban Schools* (Lawrence: University Press of Kansas, 2001), 154.

56. Edward G. Goetz, "The Community-Based Housing Movement and Progressive Local Politics," in Keating, Krumholz, and Star, *Revitalizing Urban Neighborhoods*, 177.

57. W. Dennis Keating and Norman Krumholz, "Future Prospects for Distressed Urban Neighborhoods," in *Rebuilding Urban Neighborhoods: Achievements, Opportunities, and Limits*, ed. Keating and Krumholz (Thousand Oaks, CA: Sage, 1999), 193.

8 Improving Urban Services

THE BUREAUCRATIC CITY-STATE

The reform movement attacked the political machines by building the authority of municipal agencies and shielding them from political intrusion. The civil-service–protected bureaucracies became the new power centers of local government. As Theodore Lowi observed, "The legacy of reform is the bureaucratic city-state." Lowi labeled the urban service bureaucracies the "new machines" to underscore the power that their officials possess in the modern city.[1]

Citizens often find their dealings with the urban bureaucracy quite frustrating. Protected by civil service regulations and not easily removed from their jobs, local program administrators are not always responsive to the concerns of citizens.

Administrative agencies make the determinations that decide how a law's general provisions are applied to specific situations. Municipal bureaucrats possess considerable **administrative discretion**; they often have great leeway in deciding how a law will be implemented, for instance, when a traffic citation or building violation notice will be issued.

Writing a hundred years ago, the German sociologist Max Weber observed that the **specialization of tasks** is one of the defining characteristics of a bureaucratic organization; each member of the organization is trained to become an expert—a specialist—at the tasks he or she is assigned.[2] Yet, such specialization also leads to parochialism, as each work unit and administrator may see a problem only from a narrow vantage point. Police officers, for instance, have tended to approach problems of domestic violence from a law enforcement perspective. It took the passage of the Violence Against Women Act and continued pressures from women's groups to get police officers to work more closely with health-care providers, child-welfare workers, substance-abuse counselors, and members of the clergy when intervening on behalf of a battered woman.[3]

The more radical critics of government argue that the bureaucracy problem is so endemic that it cannot be cured, only bypassed. These critics seek to *privatize* city services—to contract out and have private businesses do the jobs once performed by municipal workers. The critics of government agencies also seek to offer citizens increased *choice*, ending their reliance on the public schools and other underperforming municipal agencies.

THE IMPORTANCE OF STREET-LEVEL BUREAUCRACY

The term **street-level bureaucrat** refers to "those men and women who in their face-to-face encounters with citizens, 'represent' government to the people."[4] Street-level bureaucrats are the "foot soldiers" of city government—the police officers, teachers, building inspectors, nurses, social-welfare caseworkers, and lower-court judges—who have regular contact with the public. These seemingly low-level public servants make important determinations that affect people's lives. A law enforcement officer who responds to a domestic violence call must decide if a woman's complaint is serious enough to merit further attention from law enforcement officers and the support of services provided by domestic abuse counselors and health-care and social-service professionals.[5] A teacher determines just how a classroom is run on a daily basis and just which students' needs are met. The success and failure of urban service delivery often rest with the bureaucrats who implement the program.

For a long while, city leaders gave little attention to the immense power possessed by lower-level officialdom. Instead, municipal leaders focused on policymaking at the top. After all, bureaucracies are structured according to the principle of **organizational hierarchy**, where subordinates are expected to follow orders from above and do what they are told in robot-like fashion. The street-level view of bureaucracy, in contrast, recognizes that lower-level officials often possess considerable leeway in deciding just how to respond to client needs. Police officers, housing inspectors, public-health nurses, social-service outreach workers, schoolteachers, and other public servants who work "in the field" possess a high degree of administrative **discretion** or autonomy, as their actions are not easily reviewed by superiors.[6]

Often, street-level public servants lack sufficient resources to do their job well. Overworked police officers and public school teachers are not always able to establish close relationships with the people they serve

To cope with such difficult work conditions, street-level bureaucrats often develop helpful **shortcuts and stereotypes**, looking for cues to client behavior and categorizing clients in a way that allows the administrator to work more effectively. Police officers, for instance, look for the "wrong" type of person walking down a residential street late at night. A teacher may give greater time to "deserving" students while ignoring others.

Street-level bureaucrats see such shortcuts as the necessary judgments made by an expert administrator. To an African American or Hispanic youth pulled over for being in the wrong neighborhood at the wrong time of day, however, such categorizations and stereotyping are seen as blatant discrimination. While most municipalities reject the official use of **racial profiling**, in Highland Park, a suburb of Chicago, police officers reported that superiors encouraged them to pull over minority drivers and use race as one of a number of cues in the fight against crime. In the face of public criticism, Highland Park modified its practices.[7]

It is too easy to focus on the problems posed by street-level discretion. It must also be noted that a great many street-level personnel are urban "heroes." These public servants commit their time and energy and provide client-serving actions beyond any reasonable expectations.

Professionalism: A Cure for the Urban Bureaucracy Problem?

As Max Weber described, the job of a bureaucrat is to strictly follow an agency's rules. A **professional**, in contrast, is no mere rule follower but an inner-guided, highly trained public servant who is committed to a higher ethic of service. Rather than simply "go by the book," a professional can be trusted to use his or her discretion wisely.

Professionalization offers a partial cure for the street-level bureaucracy problem. As street-level discretion is unavoidable, a professional is taught to make judgment calls that are in the best interest of the client. Professionalism denotes more than advanced education and training. Professionals adhere to an accepted code of conduct recognized by the profession, placing ethical service above self-interest.

Public health, public education, civil engineering, and social work are all among the urban service fields characterized by a high degree of professionalization. By comparison, police officers and firefighters are semiprofessionals. Police officers, like a great many workers, claim to be professionals and desire the respect, higher pay levels, and freedoms generally accorded to professionals. Yet, while protective officers are expert in their work, they confuse narrow job expertise with the larger perspectives and obligation to society required of professionals. Police officers, for instance, too often abide by an unwritten code that prohibits an officer from "ratting out" a partner by reporting his or her misdoings. The culture of a police department teaches officers to support one another. Such a code of conduct runs contrary to a professional's accountability to the public.[8]

Performance Measurement: Efficiency, Effectiveness, and Equity in Municipal Government

How do citizens and program managers know when a public agency is doing a good job or when changes need to be made? Cities across the country have turned to **performance measurement**, the use of statistical indicators to measure an agency's progress over time and to compare its performance with that of other agencies in similar communities.[9]

What gets measured gets done; hence, agency officials must be careful in choosing what they measure. Agencies must utilize multiple indicators to reveal just how well an agency is meeting various aspects of its assigned mission. A **balanced scorecard** provides indicators that measure an agency's progress in three quite different general performance areas: *efficiency, effectiveness*, and *equity*.[10]

Efficiency measures are concerned with saving money, of getting government performance at a lower cost. Efficiency measures reveal how much it costs the sanitation department to collect a ton of garbage, or how much a city spends to keep a police officer on the beat. As larger cities spend more than smaller cities, an examination of the total spending by an agency does not allow for easy comparison. Hence, efficiency is almost always measured on a "cost per unit" basis. A city can see if it is paying more or less than comparable cities in terms of how much it pays per house inspected or per street mile resurfaced.

But there is always the danger that city officials will rely too heavily on efficiency measures when making program decisions. Efficiency measures emphasize costs but provide no indication of program quality or how effective a program may be in reaching important objectives. Nor do efficiency measures reveal whether government is treating all citizens fairly, an important standard for judging government performance in a democracy.[11]

Effectiveness measures are concerned not with costs but with program objectives. Also known as **outcome measures**, effectiveness indicators provide information on how good a job a program is doing in reaching clients and in solving problems. (See Box 8.1, "The Long Beach Police Department Measures Up.") What percentage of eligible children in a community do Head Start preschool programs serve? Does Head Start increase children's readiness to learn, as seen in test scores and in measures of appropriate social behavior? Does a new reading program actually improve schoolchildren's reading abilities? These are all questions of program effectiveness.

Equity measures seek to ascertain whether programs fairly serve all demographic groups and neighborhoods. Equity, however, is not an easy concept to measure, especially as there are competing definitions of fairness.[12] Some citizens would argue that fairness requires that all clients and neighborhoods receive the same level of service. By this definition, inequity arises when some children have new textbooks and a range of classes and extracurricular activities denied to children attending other schools in the city.

Yet, equity does not always require the equal provision of services. Sometimes, the unequal provision of services can be justified as desirable. Some children have greater needs and receive more extensive tutoring and support services than do other children. This is not very troubling. Similarly, academically gifted children may have specialized science, math, and music and arts classes that are of little interest to other students. Some parents may criticize the diversion of school resources to support such specialized programs; yet other parents will defend the classes as a fair and reasonable response to the needs of gifted students.

The standard of **strict equity** entails giving all citizens the same level of service. Trash, for instance, may be collected in all neighborhoods once a week, regardless of the amounts that property owners pay in taxes and the different service expectations that residents of different neighborhood may have.

Market equity presents a quite different standard, justifying variations in service levels as a response to differences in citizen preferences and the amounts that citizens pay in fees and municipal taxes. Under a standard of market equity, police patrols may be more frequent in the downtown of a city where business owners pay high taxes and expect high-quality protective services. Similarly, a standard of market equity may justify more frequent trash pickup and higher levels of school spending in wealthier neighborhoods where families pay more in property taxes.

The concept of **social equity**, by contrast, justifies spending extra resources in order to help people on the bottom rungs of American society. One variant of social

Box 8.1
The Long Beach Police Department Measures Up

In the early 1990s, the Long Beach (California) Police Department was in fairly bad shape. Long Beach citizens complained of being unsafe and expressed their dissatisfaction with the department's performance. The city spent more on law enforcement than did similar cities and yet was not achieving good results.

The department began to turn things around by emphasizing that its mission was to win citizens' trust and ensure that residents felt safe in the community. The department then developed performance measures (also called **benchmarks**) in different service areas to gauge program effectiveness and indicate just which operations needed improvement. For instance, the department utilized three different measures of neighborhood security: the percentage of citizens who reported in surveys that they frequently observed gang activity, hard statistics on property crimes in a neighborhood, and survey data that reported just how well citizens thought the city responded to reported crimes. The department then targeted a greater commitment of law enforcement resources to those neighborhoods where the data indicated a continuing crime problem.

The department's strategic efforts led to a drop in violent crime and gang-related activity by nearly 40 percent, an improvement far beyond that reported across the nation. Long Beach had begun to turn things around.

Source: Jonathan Walters, *Measuring Up: Governing's Guide to Performance Measurement for Geniuses and Other Public Managers* (Washington, DC: Governing Books, 1998), 13–24.

equity emphasizes **equal results**, targeting assistance and attention to "raise up" school- children, individuals, and neighborhoods with the greatest needs.

The Oregon Benchmarks Report utilizes a balanced scorecard approach in an effort to assure that equity concerns are not overlooked while trying to improve service effectiveness and efficiency. The Oregon Benchmarks program devotes special care to presenting data that document just how well or badly minority communities are progressing in areas such as education and health care.[13]

Good assessment of agency performance almost always includes a measure of citizen satisfaction.[14] Municipal agencies use a number of instruments to gauge citizen satisfaction, including public surveys, user questionnaires, and program evaluation cards filled out by agency clients. An increasingly popular technique entails the use of **focus groups**, in-depth guided discussion that probes the feelings and opinions of a select handful of citizens.[15]

Cities have also turned to **comparative performance measurement**, ranking local service delivery against that of peer cities. Do local housing inspectors perform fewer or more inspections per week as compared to similar cities in a state? How long does it take for a city to issue a building permit, and how does that compare to the performance of other cities?

Municipal departments also use **trained observers** to rate the levels of trash on streets, the physical condition of roads, and the serviceability of playground equipment in local parks.[16] Observers often take photographs to document the physical conditions they report. In New York, the Center on Municipal Government Performance uses state-of-the-art laser technology to provide precise, objective measures ("smoothness scores" and "jolt scores") of the condition of city streets.[17]

Data-driven performance management can be quite sophisticated and complex. New York City Police Chief William Bratton instituted **COMPSTAT**, a series of weekly reports that tracked crime rates on a precinct-by-precinct, and sometimes even on a block-by-block, basis.[18] In departmental meetings conducted under the watchful eyes of the chief or his top assistants, district commanders faced public embarrassment if the data showed that they failed to make improvements. Pushed by "the numbers," district commanders reassigned personnel and rearranged shifts in order to tackle the problems of high-crime areas. They did not wish a repeat of having to defend their unit's poor performance in public, in front of the mayor's top assistants and departmental brass. Bratton was later hired by Los Angeles to see whether his techniques could bring similar reductions in crime to that city.[19]

Baltimore mayor (and later Maryland governor) Martin O'Malley used a quite similar data-driven system, **CitiStat**, with detailed maps that revealed patterns of need and service provision throughout the city. As with COMPSTAT, the data were used as part of a system of "relentless management,"[20] where regularly scheduled meetings of agency heads with mayoral assistants keep constant pressure on the departments to initiate program changes.[21]

Cities and counties across the country have copied the New York and Baltimore systems. San Francisco, St. Louis, Buffalo, Syracuse, Providence, Somerville and Springfield (Massachusetts), Warren (Michigan), and King County (Washington) are a few of the many localities to adopt CitiStat-style systems of data-driven performance.[22] The Atlanta Dashboard system uses departmental data indicators in an effort to force local administrators to initiate corrective action.

But many cities lack the expert staff, resources, and commitment of leadership to implement data-driven performance management systems. Data collection can be time-consuming and expensive. CitiStat requires extensive training to teach managers how to collect and utilize the data. In large cities, a serious commitment to COMPSTAT or CitiStat likely requires the creation of a central data-support office. Cities cannot always make the extensive commitment that COMPSTAT or CitiStat requires.

Data-driven systems like COMPSTAT and CitiStat are no magic bullet that will solve the many problems of urban service provision. In the nation's most distressed cities, modernized data collection and weekly managerial meetings are important, but they cannot manufacture the resources that may be necessary for improved service delivery.[23]

COPRODUCTION AND NEIGHBORHOOD-BASED SERVICE DELIVERY: IMPROVING SERVICES BY PARTNERING WITH CITIZENS

Coproduction entails having citizens work with governmental agencies to provide improved public services.[24] There are numerous instances of citizens joining with municipal agencies to "coproduce" better public service: neighborhood watch programs work with the police to reduce crime; on neighborhood cleanup days, the city hauls away the trash that volunteers pick up from back alleys and vacant lots; community groups help raise the funds and, through their own labor, build new playground equipment at the local park; parents volunteer to assist in school tutoring and student enrichment programs; and environmentalists provide the labor to sort materials in community-based recycling programs.

Coproduction has been a valuable part of local efforts to deal with vacant lots. In Flint, Michigan, when a neighbor complains about the conditions of a vacant lot, the initial reply from the government is: "Would you like to take care of it? We'll help you." Pittsburgh mayor Luke Ravenstahl similarly introduced a "Green Up Pittsburgh" program that provides soil, grass seed, and the advice of a landscape architect to community groups that seek to transform vacant properties into gardens, play spaces, and attractive side lots. The city further provides volunteers with liability assistance and offers help to community groups that wish to gain title to the land.[25]

Coproduction can aid law enforcement efforts. In the Rogers Park neighborhood of Chicago, Operation Beat Feet encouraged "positive loitering" as residents "armed" only with flashlights, cellular phones, and notepads walked nightly rounds, discouraging crime and reporting suspicious activity to the police. In just six months, the program lowered crime in five targeted areas by 33 percent as compared to the prior year. In Detroit, parents and community activists similarly walk the streets the night before Halloween, bringing a virtual end to the reign of "Devil's Night" arson that once plagued the city.[26]

In the fight against AIDS, the city of San Francisco relies on volunteers and nonprofit organizations in the gay community to help with public health education efforts, risk-reduction counseling, and the provision of home-based care.[27] Neighborhood-based organizations also help municipal agencies to reach out and serve Latina women who are the victims of abuse but who may be reluctant to seek help due to language barriers and a distrust of officialdom. Community organizations based in the immigrant community can help win the women's trust and convince them to take advantage of the shelters and the protective services available to them.[28]

BUSINESS IMPROVEMENT DISTRICTS (BIDs)

Businesses, too, have discovered the importance of coproduction, that they can no longer rely solely on overburdened public agencies to provide needed services. Cities across the country have granted local businesses the ability to form a **business improvement district (BID)**, a self-taxing, self-help arrangement where the city collects an additional tax from property owners in a designated area in order to provide the supplemental services that businesses desire.[29] The city collects the additional charge and hands it over to the BID's **district management association**, which then decides how the money is to be spent. Businesses voluntarily create the district, but a BID is *not* a purely voluntary organization. Even property owners who opposed the creation of a BID and its activities must pay the additional assessment or surtax authorized by the BID.

Not surprisingly, BID actions tend to promote an area's business climate, providing the funds to hire additional street security personnel, to improve trash collection and street cleaning, to install new street lamps, and to place signs that will direct tourists to local businesses. BIDs often support local festivals and concerts that will entice visitors to an area.

BIDs are a relatively new and quickly growing phenomenon. At the beginning of the 1990s, there were more than 1,200 BIDs established in cities across the United States. Today, the number is likely closer to 2,000. New York City had 68 BIDs, with a dozen more undergoing planning review.[30] New York Mayor Michael Bloomberg promoted new BIDs as contributing to the economic vitality of commercial districts and their surroundings. Los Angeles had 38 BIDs, most of which focused on increasing public safety in an effort to bring new consumers to graying areas of the city.[31] Atlanta, Baltimore, Boston, Cleveland, Denver, Mesa, Milwaukee, Pasadena, Philadelphia, San Diego, San Francisco, Seattle, and Washington, DC, are only a few of the cities in which BIDs have been established. In Chicago, BIDs are called Special Service Areas.

Each state determines the exact rules for local BID formation and governance. Typically, local business leaders initiate the creation of a BID. A BID is not run by one-person-one-vote voting rules. Instead, votes in a BID are weighted according to the value of an owner's property. The more property an owner has, the greater the vote that he or she can cast at BID meetings. Even the vote to create a BID is weighted according to the *value* of commercial property owned. Citizens residing in the neighborhood do not have a vote on BID creation, even though the BID has the ability to make decisions that will affect the quality of life in the neighborhood.

BIDs of different sizes are formed for different purposes.[32] The largest are **Corporate BIDs** dominated by major national and international businesses. Corporate BIDs are major political actors with budgets that often exceed $1 million. In New York City, the Grand Central Partnership helped to revitalize the area surrounding the famed midtown Manhattan train station. By 2008, the BID covered a seventy-block area and had an operating budget of $13 million.[33] Philadelphia's Center City BID operated over an eighty-block area.

A **Main Street BID** seeks to revitalize declining downtown and older shopping strips in a city, reversing the exodus of retail customers and business to suburbia. Main Street BIDs have budgets that are in the $200,000 to $1 million range and usually cover five to twenty square blocks. Main Street BIDs in Trenton and Seattle were typical, focusing on the promotion and marketing of their areas. In San Diego, BID funds were used to supplement governmental assistance for small business and community development.[34]

The **Community BID** is the smallest type of BID and is usually found in declining neighborhoods. Working in an area that covers only a few square blocks and with budgets of only $200,000 or so, community BIDs lack the ability to finance major capital improvements and business promotional campaigns. Instead, community BIDs tend to focus on improved sanitation services and physical maintenance of the area.[35]

Why do businesses approve BIDs with their ability to levy additional charges? BIDs enable the provision of services beyond what stretched municipal budgets could otherwise afford. The private sector is willing to help pay for the benefits it needs. As one downtown spokeswoman observed: "These aren't like taxes that get lost in the

Box 8.2

The Debate over BIDs in New York and Los Angeles: Or, Should Wall Street Get More Cops?

Business improvement districts have helped revitalize a number of commercial areas. The Times Square BID transformed the image of the once-gritty entertainment and theater district in New York by funding improved trash pickup, graffiti removal, and new safety patrols. Similarly, the Bryant Park Restoration Corporation made numerous improvements in the park adjacent to the New York's central public library (a setting familiar to many non-New Yorkers because the library was featured in such movies as *Ghostbusters* and *Spiderman*), ousting drug users and opening the park to tourists, shoppers, and office workers on their lunch breaks.

In California, BIDs helped to revitalize historic Old Pasadena, Santa Monica's Third Street Promenade, and San Francisco's Union Square. In Los Angeles, the Fashion District BID operates in a 90-block area, emphasizing trash removal, graffiti cleanup, and crime control. In the city's Westwood section, BID-funded jazz concerts, and street festivals have raised the area's profile. Other BIDs worked across the city to improve the image of local shopping strips, including upgrading Ventura Boulevard and the "automobile row" area along Van Nuys Boulevard. In California, business owners turned to BID creation in response to the severe constraints imposed on municipal taxing by Proposition 13 and other tax limitation measures.

Despite their many successes, BIDs have their critics. Los Angeles' first BID, the 1995 Miracle on Broadway, cleaned up overflowing trash cans and improved the aesthetics of the predominantly Latino shopping area. But after only one year, the BID was dismantled, as downtown merchants objected to paying extra for sidewalk sweeping and bicycle cops, services that they thought the city should provide. Similarly, the immigrant entrepreneurs in Los Angeles' Toy Districts decided, after ten years, to abandon their BID as they could no longer afford the special assessment.[1]

In San Francisco, critics charged that the red-and-blue uniformed street "ambassadors" of the Union Square BID harassed the homeless in an attempt to oust them from the city's upscale central shopping area. In New York, the Grand Central Partnership had similarly sought to remove the homeless from the train station and the surrounding area. The Partnership established an outreach program in an effort to move the homeless to shelters and support services. Less commendable, the Partnership's security guards harassed the panhandlers and the homeless. The Grand Central Partnership was even sued for violating federal minimum wage laws; the Partnership had paid homeless workers $1.16 an hour to remove other homeless persons from the ATM-machine vestibules in which they slept.[2]

The Alliance for Downtown New York is a corporate BID that represents the interests of giant global corporations in the Wall Street area of the city. The BID secured the placement a new police substation in Lower Manhattan, despite the fact that the area had one of the lowest rates of street crime in the city. The Alliance offered the city $5 million to help set up and maintain a new substation with 200 officers, with the provision that 40, 50, or more officers would be assigned to patrol the area. Other neighborhoods complained that the new station necessitated the redeployment of officers from other areas of the city with greater rates of crime.

Queens Councilman Sheldon Leffler objected that the affluent Wall Street area was buying a level of police protection denied to poorer neighborhoods: "It raises very disturbing questions about whether city resources are going to be allocated where they're needed or auctioned off to the highest bidder."[3]

[1]Maria Dickerson, "Improvement Districts Spur Revival—and Division," *The Los Angeles Times,* January 20, 1999; Michael Hiltzik, "Landlords' Pullback Puts L.A. Toy District at Risk," *The Los Angeles Times,* December 21, 2009.

[2]Heather Barr, "More Like Disneyland: State Action, 42 U.S.C. 1 1983, and Business Improvement Districts in New York," *Columbia Human Rights Law Review* 28 (Winter 1997); Evelyn Nieves, "Cities Try to Sweep Homeless Out of Sight," *The New York Times,* December 7, 1999.

[3]David Kocieniewski, "Wall St. to Pay to Add a Base for the Police," *The New York Times,* February 17, 1998. Also see Dan Barry, "Mayor Orders Review of Plan for Substation," *The New York Times,* February 19, 1998.

general fund. . . . The money stays inside the business district . . . where businesses can see results."[36]

The increasing importance of BIDs, however, raises questions of power, democracy, and fairness. Given their weighted voting rules, corporate BIDs are often dominated by the big businesses in an area, with little assurance that residential and neighborhood voices are adequately heard. Even the owners of smaller businesses often protest that they are forced to pay additional taxes for services they do not really want. Residents of an area generally have even less of a say in a BID's decisions. BIDs are not general-purpose governments but only associations created for business promotion. As a result, as we have seen, BIDs do not have to meet the one-person-one-vote standard of democratic representation.[37]

Fiscally-strapped cities have begun to turn to BIDs as an important vehicle of service delivery. In Los Angeles, where Proposition 13 and other anti-tax measures have squeezed city finances, the city has increased its reliance on BIDS for effective trash pickup and supplemental security patrols in the downtown.

The proliferation of BIDs raises serious concerns regarding service inequity and urban dualism. Wealthier areas of the city that establish BIDs receive a higher level of services that is denied to poorer areas of the city. (See Box 8.2, "The Debate over BIDs in New York and Los Angeles: Or, Should Wall Street Get More Cops?")

SERVICE CONTRACTING AND PRIVATIZATION

In the search for new ways to improve efficiency and performance, cities have looked to the private sector. Loosely used, the term **privatization** refers to the application of private-sector techniques to public management. More strictly defined, privatization refers to a more extensive transformation: services once provided by governmental agencies are turned over to the private-sector firms and marketlike mechanisms. The privatization movement is driven by the assumption that private firms and private markets can provide services better and cheaper than can government agencies. The

Box 8.3
The Privatization of Policing?

Even a service as seemingly "public" as law enforcement can be privatized or at least partially privatized. There is no reason why protective services must be delivered solely by officers who work directly for the government. Private security firms can be hired to assist in maintaining the safety of downtown entertainment districts and large public housing projects. Communities can hire for-profit firms to manage the local jail.

Privatized policing arrangements are largely driven by the search for efficiency. In an age where local governments have to pick up important homeland security responsibilities and where public resources are stretched thin, cities have looked for ways to carry out their important tasks without making an expensive long-term commitment. Rather than hire new public servants who may earn tenure rights to their jobs under civil service, cities have looked for more flexible options, utilizing private law enforcement firms with contracts that do not have to be renewed if the short-term need soon passes. In the face of budgetary difficulties, police departments in Fresno (California), Mesa (Arizona), and Charlotte (North Carolina) recruited volunteers to respond to low-level calls and to collect evidence and interview witnesses, tasks that were previously performed by salaried police officers.

Critics, however, worry about the loss of public control when private companies are utilized to aid in providing public safety or to run prisons. Private firms may not give their officers the same extensive training that public law enforcement officers received. Private officers and volunteers may also be less committed than public officers to respecting civil rights and civil liberties.

Sources: Jesse McKinley, "Police Departments Turn to Volunteers," *New York Times* March 1, 2011; Brian Forst and Peter K. Manning, *The Privatization of Policing: Two Views* (Washington, DC: Georgetown University Press, 1999); James F. Pastor, *The Privatization of Police in America: An Analysis and Case Study* (Jefferson, NC: McFarland, 2003).

advocates of privatization also seek to enable citizen choice, freeing citizens from their reliance on municipal service provision.

Under **service contracting**, a municipal government enters into a contractual relationship that allows a private firm or nonprofit agency to deliver a service. Local governments contract out a diverse range of services: local governments utilize private haulers to pick up trash, community-based organizations to assist in drug-abuse counseling and operating shelters for the homeless, private janitorial firms to clean governmental offices, and private information technology companies to update a city's data processing systems. New York City turned over the daily management of Central Park to the Central Park Conservancy, a not-for-profit private group that engaged in extensive corporate fund-raising efforts to pay for park improvements.[38] Even certain law enforcement activities can be privatized. (See Box 8.3, "The Privatization of Policing?")

Privatization is based on the distinction between the decision to *provide* a service to the public, and the decision as to who can best *produce* the desired service:

> [T]o provide a service is to decide that a service shall be made available and to arrange for its delivery. This is an integral part of a local government's policy-making process. To deliver a service is to actually produce the service. Although a local government may decide to provide a service, it does not necessarily have to be directly involved in its delivery.[39]

A government agency does not itself have to produce every service the public requires; instead, government can take steps to help assure that such services are provided by private firms and nonprofit organizations. Such arrangements also allow governments to draw on the extensive experience and commitment of nonprofit organizations in working with the elderly, troubled youth, drug users, and the homeless.

THE ADVANTAGES OF PRIVATIZATION

Contracting encourages **competition** that can reduce the costs of service delivery. Private firms that are not modern and efficient will find that they have little chance to submit the winning bid on a contract to perform services for the city. A municipal agency, by contrast, is a **public monopoly**, where workers do not face competition and do not have to perform well in order to keep their civil-service-protected jobs.

Former Indianapolis mayor Stephen Goldsmith argues that competition is the key element by which privatization brings about innovation and efficiency. Privatization without competition will seldom save a city money. A city is likely to receive low bids on a contract only when a number of qualified firms in the city are ready to bid on the contract. A city does not gain any advantages in situations where privatization fails to build a competitive environment, when a private monopoly replaces the public monopoly.[40] Especially in physical and administrative service areas—trash collection, fire protection, automotive fleet maintenance, the upkeep of local parks, and the performance of inspection services—private firms often offer similar or better service at lower cost than do municipal agencies.[41]

A service does not even have to be turned over to a private firm in order to introduce the benefits of competition. Under a process known as **managed competition**, public agencies are allowed to join in the bidding on a contract: the city's contract is not automatically turned over to a private provider. The competitive bidding process and the threat of lost jobs may lead a municipal department to "shape up," redesigning work processes and adopting new efficiency-oriented practices. In Phoenix, a reenergized public sanitation department won back many of the contracts that had previously been contracted out to private haulers. In Indianapolis, the municipal public works department implemented new cost-savings steps and beat out private competitors in those parts of the city where trash collection was put out for bid.[42]

Contracting allows a city to **circumvent the rigidities of civil service personnel rules**. Compared to the public sector, private firms have a greater ability to transfer workers from one division to another and to penalize or dismiss workers who fail to perform effectively. Private firms can also dispense large rewards to top managers for outstanding performance; in public agencies, such awards are severely restricted under civil service rules. Private firms are generally freer than government agencies to utilize part-time employees and to pay workers less in compensation than is the practice in government.

THE DISADVANTAGES AND RISKS OF PRIVATIZATION

The advocates of privatization often present a highly idealized portrait of a private sector that eliminates all waste and excess in the search for efficiency. Yet, as newspaper headlines of corporate scandals have revealed, the performance of private corporations can be marred by **waste, payoffs, skimming**, and **corruption**. In Chicago, service contracting is not simply a means to improve service efficiency: the local political organization also dispensed contracts to its supporters as a form of patronage. (See Box 8.4, "Service Contracting: 'Pin-stripe Patronage' and Corruption in Chicago.")

Privatization does not always save a city money. Contracting often entails **hidden costs**, including the costs that a city incurs in preparing a contract for bid and the costs that the city incurs in having to monitor the work performed by the contractor. The city also faces the potential costs of a service interruption if a contractor is unable to perform as promised or if the city has to dismiss a contractor.[43] Unscrupulous contractors may also attempt to maximize profits by "cutting corners" and lowering service quality.

In some cases, a city may save money in the first year of a contract, but wind up paying additional moneys in the ensuing years. When trying to win the city's business, a private firm may submit a **lowball contract bid**, that is, an unrealistically low bid that does not represent the full cost of services provided over the life of the contract. A city that is dependent on the contractor for continued service provision may have no real choice but to pay the additional overrun costs that a contractor later bills a city.

Bid-rigging, too, can diminish the financial benefits that a city derives from a competitive bidding process.[44] In New York City the privatization of trash hauling did not lower business costs but actually raised costs as "a Mafia-run cartel had rigged prices and denied customers any choice in selecting haulers or in negotiating contracts."[45] Even in the absence of such corruption, the cost savings promised by privatization may disappear in the absence of a sufficient number of qualified firms to establish a competitive bidding environment.

Service contracting can also be seen as **antiunion**. Faced with the prospect of competition from lower-cost nonunion bidders, both municipal workforces and unionized private firms will find it necessary to restrain their own salary and workplace demands. In New York, mayors Rudy Giuliani and Michael Bloomberg turned to the hiring of private cleaning companies in an effort to break the fabled power of the school custodians' union. School custodians were in charge of their building and were often unresponsive to the requests of principals, teachers, parents, and community groups to use school facilities after hours. Giuliani and Bloomberg privatized about a third of the school custodial jobs, using the threat of further privatization to pressure the custodians to accept a reduction in their benefits and job privileges.[46]

Box 8.4
Service Contracting: "Pin-Stripe Patronage" and Corruption in Chicago

Civil service regulations and court rulings prevented Chicago Mayor Richard M. Daley from amassing the large patronage armies of his father, Richard J. Daley, the legendary political "boss" of the city. Instead, Richard M. sought to win the public's favor by demonstrating his ability to manage the city well. Privatization was one of his tools. Daley reduced the size of the city's workforce and increased service efficiency by contracting out various services, including parking meter collections, automobile fleet maintenance, tree stump removal, window cleaning, the towing of abandoned cars, the management of the municipal golf course, and drug addiction treatment.

Yet, his critics took a less charitable view of Richard M. Daley's fondness for contracting. They charged that Daley loyalists steered lucrative contracts to major financial contributors and political friends. The term **pin-stripe patronage** refers to the contracts for legal work and other business services that were awarded the administration's political friends wearing good suits.

At its worst, the award of contracts was plagued by blatant corruption. The Hired Truck Scandal revealed that the city paid bills for work that was never performed. Operation Incubator, a federal investigation, uncovered a system in which municipal officials took bribes when deciding just which firms would win the contracts to collect water bills and unpaid parking tickets.

Sources: Rowan A. Miranda, "Privatization in Chicago's City Government," in *Research in Urban Policy,* vol. 4, ed. Kenneth K. Wong (Greenwich, CT: JAI Press, 1992); Thomas J. Gradel, Dick Simpson, and Andris Zimelis, "Curing Corruption in Illinois: Anti-Corruption Report Number 1," University of Illinois at Chicago, Department of Political Science, February 3, 2009, www.ilcampaign.org/docs/Anti-corruptionReport.pdf.

THE PRIVATE MANAGEMENT OF PUBLIC SCHOOLS

A number of states and cities have turned to private management firms for the day-to-day administration of troubled local schools. Private management firms have greater freedom to act on curriculum and personnel matters, especially when compared to public school systems that are ensnared in a myriad of state regulations and labor-union job protections. Private management firms are also likely to borrow cost-savings techniques from the private sector. Most significantly, the states hope that a private management agency will shake up school operations and establish a "culture of achievement"[47] in failing schools. Yet, the record shows that privately managed public schools do not consistently produce the results that privatization enthusiasts promise.

Miami was the first city to contract with a private firm, Educational Alternatives, Inc. (EAI), to take over the operations of a troubled public school. EAI developed an individualized learning plan for each student. It subcontracted maintenance and building repair tasks to partner firms, allowing principals and educators to devote greater attention to their teaching mission. EAI promised that it would create a "dream school" with the latest in computers and innovative math and reading programs. But sixty-one teachers soon filed a complaint charging that EAI forced them to work a longer school day with no extra pay, a significant part of EAI's strategy for achieving better results without raising the costs of education.[48]

Baltimore in 1992 signed a five-year contract with EAI to run nine of its schools. Two years later, Hartford, Connecticut, turned over all thirty-two city schools. But Baltimore, Hartford, and Miami-Dade County all eventually decided not to renew their contracts with EAI. The introduction of private management was a quite tumultuous undertaking that did not produce the dramatic improvements in student test scores that had been promised.

The continuing conflict between EAI and the teachers' unions also impeded reform. The teachers' unions fought against what they saw as privatization's all-out assault on teacher tenure and efforts to replace teachers with lower-cost instructional personnel. In Baltimore, EAI hired college students at $7-an-hour to work as teacher aides, replacing the $13-an-hour positions previously held by union members.[49] In Hartford, teachers schooled on Apple computers even fought against EAI's efforts to put IBM PCs in school computer labs. According to EAI, the teachers were reluctant to adapt and provide students with the job skills demanded by the business world.[50]

In Baltimore, BUILD, a local Alinsky-style organization, opposed a style of instruction that seemed to prepare children to be little more than cogs in the workplace. Outspoken members of the African American community were also critical of EAI's decision to turn school operations over to a firm headed by a white outsider.[51]

In the face of strong political opposition, EAI accepted a number of contract provisions that it disliked, including provisions that limited the firm's ability to dismiss problem teachers and to replace them with educators attuned to EAI's mission. Given the controversies it faced in Philadelphia and other cities, EAI eventually decided to withdraw from the inner city; the company announced that in the future it would manage only schools in "less political and less volatile" suburban districts. However, TesseracT (the new name that EAI assumed) continued to face financial difficulties and eventually was forced to lay off staff, file for bankruptcy, and even close a few of its schools in Arizona and New Jersey.[52]

In the nation's most extensive experiment with the private management of public schools, the State of Pennsylvania in 2002 turned over forty-five Philadelphia elementary and middle schools to three for-profit educational companies—Edison Schools (the nation's largest private educational management organization), Victory Schools, and Chancellor Beacon Academies—and five nonprofit organizations. Chancellor Beacon Academies did not perform well, and the school district cancelled its contract with the academies after only a single year.

The management team introduced a new curriculum, and the schools also received an infusion of new resources. But the changes led to few educational gains. The number of Philadelphia students reaching math and English proficiency levels increased in the first year but not in the years that followed. Students in the city's most troubled schools reported the least gain.[53] In some cases, the gains in student achievement in the Edison-run schools actually lagged behind the gains reported by the remaining public schools in the city.[54]

In 2008, Philadelphia decided to bring its experiment with private school management to an end. The government reestablished municipal control over six schools that had been privately managed, and the school district indicated its intention to terminate its relationship with Edison.

This short review shows that private management, despite the claims of privatization enthusiasts, provides no magic bullet that will cure the ills of public education. The track record of privately managed public schools is most uneven. While a number of EAI elementary schools reported gains in reading and math scores,[55] others did not. In Baltimore, Philadelphia, Miami, and other cities, the private management produced no clear and consistent gains in student test scores.

SCHOOL CHOICE: VOUCHERS, TAX CREDITS, AND CHARTER SCHOOLS

A VARIETY OF SCHOOL CHOICE PROGRAMS

A variety of **school choice programs** seek to give parents greater ability to decide just which school their child will attend, empowering them to find a school with a curriculum and an approach that matches the student's particular interests. School choice programs seek to liberate parents and students from dependence on the local public school.

The most radical choice advocates argue for a system of **school vouchers**, under which students (or their parents) receive a certificate that can be used to help pay tuition at a school of their choice. Despite the rhetoric of choice, however, a system of vouchers does not allow every student the free ability to choose schools. The **monetary size of the voucher** is crucial to determining how much choice parents and students are truly given. A large voucher allows a student a greater choice of schools. Yet, as choice advocates often seek to contain school spending, such generous vouchers are rarely given. Instead, vouchers tend to cover only part of the costs of a private education. Such vouchers give a limited range of choices to working-class and poor families who lack the ability to pay for the portion of tuition and fees not covered by the voucher.

A voucher program's **accompanying regulations** also help to determine how much choice a student actually possesses. Regulations can reduce some of the unfairness and discriminations of an unregulated or free-market approach to vouchers. A school that has total freedom to set its own admissions criteria, for instance, may engage in a process known as **creaming**, where a school may admit only the most capable voucher students (the "cream of the crop"), leaving other students with no real alternative but to attend the more troubled public schools. Eligibility provisions, too, also determine just who benefits from a voucher program. Voucher programs in Cleveland and Milwaukee are largely targeted on poorer children in the city to help them escape failing schools. A voucher plan that dispensed assistance more broadly would have a vastly different impact, enabling middle-class students to flee racially mixed schools.[56]

Florida and Texas have used **publicly and privately funded scholarships** to increase the options available to students from low-income families. In 1999, Florida created a system of state-funded "opportunity" scholarships—a voucher-style program to help students pay private school tuition. Public schools that received failing performance grades by the state year after year were required to initiate improvements or else face a reduction of state aid, since their students would be allowed to enroll elsewhere with the assistance of opportunity scholarships.

Despite the great publicity it received, the Florida Opportunity Scholarship program did not create very much choice. The state legislature failed to provide the level of funding that would allow large numbers of students to leave failing schools. In fact, the program was paying the private school tuition of only 730 students at the time the state supreme court struck down the program for having violated a provision in the Florida constitution requiring the state to maintain an efficient system of public schools.[57]

Tax deductions and **tax credits** are other tools that seek to enable greater school choice. Yet, such programs often have a pernicious class bias, as they wind up subsidizing the education decisions of the middle class while providing only the most minimal assistance to the poor. Such a bias is clearly evident in the national system of **Education Savings Accounts (ESA)** which allows parents to set aside up to $2,000 a year in interest-free accounts for a child's K–12 tuition. Middle- and upper-income families enjoy the tax benefits accorded the investment of money in educational accounts. Such a tax incentive, however, does little to help poorer families that lack the resources to set aside money in tuition accounts. A promise of tax credits is also of no benefit to parents who are so poor that they have little or no tax liability.

Defenders of the public schools caution that there is no need to resort to educational vouchers and tax credits. Instead, a public school district can offer increased choice to students simply by establishing its own system of **specialized schools** and **minischools**, with each school offering a distinctive curriculum.

In more recent years, states and cities have also turned to charter schools, a reform that seems to offer a middle ground between voucher schools and traditional public education. A **charter school** is an innovative school established (i.e., "chartered") under the sponsorship of an authorized governing body (such as a state university or community college).[58] Governmental regulations regarding curriculum and various facets of school operation are relaxed in order to give each charter school the freedom to develop curriculum, disciplinary policies, and other policies and practices that best fit the school's unique mission. Still, as charter schools are still public schools, they do not possess the full freedoms enjoyed by voucher-funded private schools. Numerous state rules and regulations still apply to charter schools, including regulations that limit the ability of charter schools to abridge teacher tenure.

The Critical Issue of Student Achievement

Study after study has shown that vouchers and other choice programs have, at best, only the most marginal impact on improving student performance. Empirical studies led the prestigious Carnegie Foundation to conclude that the movement for school choice has been guided more by ideology than by evidence, that "many of the claims for school choice have been based more on speculation than experience."[59] Yet, choice advocates continue to find pieces of evidence to support the program, such as data from Milwaukee showing that voucher students enjoy higher graduation rates than nonvoucher students.[60]

The Carnegie Foundation further warned that choice programs may exacerbate **urban dualism**, widening the gap between the haves and have-nots of American society. In Massachusetts, 135 students left the city of Brockton and transferred to neighboring Avon under a state-created choice program. The students who changed schools were pleased with the program. But the picture was "far grimmer for the 14,500 students left behind in Brockton" as the transfers led to a loss of nearly $1 million in state aid in Brockton, contributing to the layoff of 200 teachers.[61] Choice programs enable more-capable students and the children of more-vigilant parents to escape troubled schools. But other children are left behind in **dumping-ground schools** with even less funding and even lower prospects of student success than before.

There is no clear evidence that choice plans promote voluntary racial integration, as voucher theorists contend. In some cities, choice programs have had the opposite effect, facilitating "white flight" from schools undergoing racial change. In Cleveland, vouchers did little to increase racial integration in suburban schools, as suburban districts refused to participate in the program and admit voucher students.[62] Voucher programs that allow tuition **add-ons**—families can use their own money to supplement the amount provided by a voucher—have the potential to exacerbate the class and racial stratification of schools.

Many of the above-mentioned problems, however, are minimized when a voucher or choice program is tightly targeted. In Milwaukee and Cleveland, where voucher participation is restricted to the inner-city poor, vouchers do not add greatly to white flight. Instead, vouchers in these cities enable some minority students to attend classes in less stratified, church-related parochial schools.[63]

Do School Vouchers Violate the Constitution?

In Cleveland and Milwaukee, large numbers of students use government-funded vouchers to enroll in **parochial schools** (the Catholic-run schools in the inner city). Critics argued that such aid is a violation of the constitutional requirement for the separation of church and state.

A sharply divided U.S. Supreme Court in 2002 decided the question, ruling in ***Zelman v. Simmons-Harris***[64] that the Cleveland program's inclusion of parochial schools was constitutionally permissible. According to the Court, the voucher program did *not* violate the United States Constitution's First Amendment prohibition against the state establishment of religion. Even though many families used the assistance to enroll their children in parochial schools, the Court did not see the program as providing state support of religious instruction. Instead, the Court viewed the Cleveland voucher program as "neutral" in terms of its respect toward religion. The voucher program had a clear secular purpose—to assist children trapped in failing public schools: it did not purposely seek to advance religious instruction. Nor did the government provide aid directly to church schools; rather, parents freely chose which schools their children would attend.

Dissenters responded that the Court was blind to the clear subsidies that the voucher program provided for the teaching of religion. At the time of the decision, 96 percent of the state-provided voucher funds were spent in Cleveland's parochial schools, schools that taught religious doctrine.

THE EVIDENCE FROM MILWAUKEE'S LOW-INCOME SCHOOL VOUCHER PLAN

In 1990, the State of Wisconsin enacted the first—and largest—school voucher program in the nation. In the 2007–2008 school year, approximately 20,000 Milwaukee students used vouchers (set at the time at $6,607 per child) to attend private and parochial schools instead of the city's regular public schools.[65]

The Milwaukee program is highly targeted: vouchers are given only to students whose families are poor or near the poverty line. The tight targeting also serves to limit state expenditures. State regulations on school admissions also seek to avoid selection bias and creaming, efforts by receiving schools to admit only the best students. Schools that accepted vouchers were prohibited from admitting students on the basis of a student's prior educational or behavioral record.

Evaluations of the Milwaukee program show that it has had mixed results. On the plus side, the vouchers were utilized by students who had been performing poorly in the public schools. The program enhanced the options available to poor students and parents. African American parents expressed their satisfaction with a program that enabled their children to escape problem schools.[66] As the parent of a seventh-grade Milwaukee voucher student explained, "As soon as I came here it was a big change. Here teachers care about you. . . . [In public schools] the teachers were too busy to help."[67] The program did not advance racial integration; nor did it lead to higher levels of racial segregation, as opponents had feared.

Yet voucher students showed few gains on standardized tests.[68] The small edge that the voucher students exhibited was a product of self-selection class: the children of more- concerned parents had enrolled in the voucher schools and of course did better than the children of less-involved parents. Quite surprisingly, approximately half of the students in the program chose not to reenroll for the second year, indicating a fair degree of dissatisfaction with the program.[69] As the Carnegie Foundation summarized, the Milwaukee experience "failed to demonstrate that vouchers can, in and of themselves, spark school improvement."[70]

Voucher advocates respond that it often takes years for the new schools to shake off students' bad habits. By their fourth year of participation, voucher students begin to show moderate achievement gains.[71]

The creation of the voucher program did lead Milwaukee public schools to initiate a number of limited reforms of its own in an attempt to stem the outflow of students to voucher academies. Yet, they did not constitute a revolution that shook up public school operations. The Milwaukee teachers' union blocked attempts to modify seniority rules, close schools, and strengthen the process for evaluating teachers.[72]

In sum, the Milwaukee system of targeted vouchers offers aggrieved parents and their children an alternative to inner-city public schools. Yet, the Milwaukee experience also illustrates that a voucher program poses no clear solution to the problems of poor student achievement.

CHARTER SCHOOLS: A MIDDLE WAY?

Given the numerous criticisms of voucher programs, school reformers in many cities have turned their attention to a less revolutionary alternative, charter schools. A **charter school** is established and funded by the state but run by an independent group that is given greater free rein to make innovative choices in curriculum and other matters of school operations. The administrators of a charter school are freed from many of the rules and regulations that constrain the operation of regular public schools.[73] Quite unlike a system of school vouchers, the choice of schools offered students is limited to the innovative schools that the state has chartered.

A charter school does not charge tuition. Instead, each charter school receives state aid based on the number of pupils enrolled. In many states the amount is roughly equivalent to the student-based aid that the state would provide a regular public school. Some states also provide grants to assist the start-up of charter schools.

Charter schools are popular because of their smaller-size classes, their emphasis on academics, and their efforts at curriculum reform and innovative teaching. Many charter schools make a concerted effort to involve families in the educational process. A charter school may also have a unique specialization—instruction in science, the arts, military-like discipline, or specialized ethnic history.

Charter schools represent a moderate form of choice, a means of creating alternatives to conventional public schools while maintaining state authority:

> In some ways, charter schools are the middle-way response in the twenty-plus year arguments over school choice. While they are not the free-range schools of choice that some voucher proponents have advocated (. . . charter schools are still moderately to heavily regulated), neither are they the traditional, shop-worn school down the street.[74]

The educational establishment has come to accept state-authorized charter schools as a preferable alternative to vouchers. Teacher unions and local school boards, however, also press for state regulations to "cap" the number of charter schools that can be created, to limit funding for charter schools, and to prohibit for-profit educational firms with little experience from managing charter schools.[75] In Los Angeles, public school teachers threatened litigation in their efforts to block charter-school takeovers by outside groups.[76] Kansas law allows only local school boards to authorize the creation of a charter school. Arizona, in contrast, allows a wider range of entities to create charter schools.[77] Arizona, California, Colorado, Florida, Michigan, North Carolina, and Texas allow the relatively easy formation of new charter schools.[78]

The number of charter schools has grown rapidly. There were 250 charter schools in 1995. By the 2008–2009 school year, the number had grown to 4,624. The states with the largest number of charter schools were Arizona (523), California (771), Florida (375), Texas (354), and Michigan (270).[79]

Like a program of school vouchers, charter schools have the potential to create a competitive environment that can lead conventional public schools to reform their

Charter Schools: First Lady Michelle Obama attends the Cinqo de Mayo celebration at the Latin American Montessori Bilingual Charter School in Washington, D.C., 2009. Charter schools offer students a more specialized curriculum than that found in regular public classrooms. Some of the more traditional members of the school establishment resented President Barack Obama's support of charter schools. http://commons.wikimedia.org/wiki/File:Michelle_Obama_at_Latin_American_Montessori_Bilingual_Public_Charter_School_5-4-09_2.jpg.

curriculum and practices. Yet, data from Texas show that the effect of a charter school on its more conventional neighbors is far less than is imagined.[80] In Arizona, the competition from charter schools has had only a very limited effect on pushing public schools to make their own improvements.[81] More traditional public school officials resist charter-style changes.

CHARTER SCHOOLS AND RACE

Do charter schools offer hope to racial minorities whose children are stuck in underperforming inner-city schools? Or do charter schools exacerbate "white flight," worsening racial segregation?

Enrollment data show that charter schools serve inner-city, low-income, and racial minority students. Nationwide, about half of the students in charter schools come from minority backgrounds.[82] Numerous inner-city charter academies offer college prep courses and specialized programs in industrial training and the creative arts.

Yet, in some metropolitan areas, the existence of charter schools enables white families to avoid sending their children to schools with concentrations of racial minorities.[83] In Pontiac, Michigan, and the inner-ring Detroit suburb of Ferndale, the creation of charter schools undercut the local district's ability to comply with federal school-desegregation orders.[84]

In Arizona, too, the creation of charter schools diminished racial integration, as students chose to attend charter schools that were less racially integrated than the district schools the students had exited.[85] Similarly, in Durham, North Carolina, school choice programs enabled more-advantaged students to move to less racially integrated schools.

Charter schools provide educational alternatives demanded by inner-city students and their parents. Overall, charter schools do not have a great influence on the racial balance of big-city schools.[86]

CHARTER SCHOOLS ASSESSED

In some communities, the growth of charter academies raises questions concerning the separation of church and state. A growing number of charter schools are "quasi-religious" schools, despite requirements that they provide a nonsectarian education.[87] The National Heritage Associates, founded by J.C. Huizenga, a wealthy devout Christian, creates charter schools with a stress on morals, values, and character development consistent with a Christian education, even though the schools disavow an explicitly religious curriculum.[88] In New York City and Washington, DC, low-enrollment Catholic schools converted to charter schools. They maintained much of their previous staff and, in classroom instruction, continued to stress the importance of faith and Catholic values—but not the recitation of prayer.[89]

In the important area of student performance, charter schools do not live up to the promises made by their supporters, as one quite extensive examination of charter academies in Washington, DC, underscored.[90] The results of the first national assessment of reading and math scores were particularly worrisome. Students in charter schools actually lagged behind the gains that were being achieved by students attending conventional public schools. The Department of Education released the data with little fanfare and tried to bury the disappointing evidence amid a mountain of data.[91] A RAND Corporation analysis of charter schools in eight states similarly found that chartering had little positive impact on student performance.[92]

Despite the disappointing results reported in most studies, there are other studies that point to the successes achieved by charter schools, especially in Milwaukee, a city that has charter academies as well as voucher schools and regular public schools. Milwaukee's, charter academies provided specialized education services to at-risk students. The charter schools also outperformed the city's regular public schools.[93] Yet, parental satisfaction with the charter schools diminished over time, as the new schools could not remedy the many educational difficulties that their children confronted.[94]

In sum, charter schools have a moderate effect on education. While some perform well, others do not. On the other hand, charter schools do not represent the dangers that their critics often assume. Especially when their number is capped by state law, charter schools do not pose an extensive threat to conventional public schools. Nor have charter schools served as a vehicle for white flight.[95]

CONCLUSION: IMPROVING PUBLIC SERVICES

Coproduction, neighborhood-based delivery systems, contracting out, vouchers, tax credits, and school choice are all strategies that seek to improve local services or otherwise allow citizens to make an "end run" around irresponsive and ineffective municipal systems The new public management borrows management practices from the private sector. Too often, however, the quest for bureaucratic reform has been driven by the goal of cost reduction, with no similar concern given to assuring the equitable delivery of public services. The reformers hope to replace a public monopoly with a marketlike system of competition. Competition, they hope, will drive cost efficiency.

New mechanisms for public choice have brought much-needed change to public education. Yet, the advocates of public choice strategies—private management of public schools, vouchers, charter schools, and tax credits—have clearly oversold what privatization can accomplish. The more revolutionary systems seldom deliver the results—especially the gains in student achievement—promised by their supporters. The more radical reforms are often driven by ideological groups that are hostile to public bureaucracy and critical of committing more and more taxpayer dollars to support public education.

Public–private partnerships, neighborhood-based service provision, privatization, and choice programs are all efforts to improve urban service delivery and increase citizen satisfaction. Yet, bureaucratic reforms and restructuring cannot by themselves be expected to solve the urban crisis. Oftentimes, service problems are the result of a city's fiscal position, the inability of a city to raise the necessary funds to support quality services for its people.

As we discuss in the next two chapters, cities are parts of larger metropolitan systems. At times, the effort to combat urban ills will require concerted action by neighboring governments. In the face of federal and state budget cutbacks, cities and their administrative leaders will find that they have no real alternative but to find ways to work together for cost savings and more effective joint problem solving.

NOTES

1. Theodore J. Lowi, "Machine Politics—Old and New," *Public Interest* (Fall 1967): 86.
2. Sam Whimster, ed., *The Essential Weber: A Reader* (London and New York: Routledge, 2004), 245–247.
3. Sandra J. Clark, Martha R. Burt, Margaret M. Schulte, and Karen Maguire, "Coordinated Community Responses to Domestic Violence in Six Communities: Beyond the Justice System," research report (Washington, DC: Urban Institute, October 1996), www.urban.org/publications/406727.html.
4. Michael Lipsky, *Street-Level Bureaucracy: Dilemma of the Individual in Public Services* (New York: Russell Sage Foundation, 1980); Janet Coble Vinzant and Lane Crothers, *Street-Level Leadership: Discretion and Legitimacy in Front-Line Public Service* (Washington, DC: Georgetown University Press, 1998).
5. Clark et al., "Coordinated Community Responses to Domestic Violence in Six Communities."
6. Peter Hupe and Michael Hill, "Street-Level Bureaucracy and Public Accountability," *Public Administration Review* 83, no. 2 (2007): 279–299.
7. Ibid.

8. Samuel Walker, *The New World of Police Accountability* (Thousand Oaks, CA: Sage, 2005), 22–26.

9. David N. Ammons, *Leading Performance Management in Local Government* (Washington, DC: International City/County Management Association, 2008); Patricia de Lancer Julnes and Marc Holzer, eds., *Performance Measurement: Building Theory, Improving Practice* (Armonk, NY: M.E. Sharpe, 2008); Patricia Keehley and Neil N. Abercrombie, *Benchmarking in the Public and Nonprofit Sectors: Best Practices for Achieving Performance Breakthroughs,* 2d ed. (San Francisco: Jossey-Bass, 2008).

10. Harry P. Hatry, *Performance Measurement: Getting Results*, 2d ed. (Washington, DC: Urban Institute, 2007) urges managers and citizens to pay greater attention to outcome measures (indicators of a program's reach and effectiveness) as opposed to input measures that merely indicate the resources (i.e., budgetary dollars or number of personnel). Output measures seek to ascertain just what has and has not been accomplished by the money spent on a program.

11. Beryl A. Radin, *Challenging the Performance Movement: Accountability, Complexity, and Democratic Values* (Washington, DC: Georgetown University Press, 2006), 91–102.

12. James H. Svara and James R. Brunet, "Filling the Skeletal Pillar: Addressing Social Equity in Introductory Courses in Public Administration," *Journal of Public Affairs Education* 10, no. 2 (2004): 99–109, discuss various definitions of the concept of "social equity. Deborah Stone, *Policy Paradox: The Art of Political Decision Making*, rev. ed. (New York: Norton, 2002), 39–85, presents competing definitions of the term equity. She also challenges the quite common assertion that public policy can advance equity goals only by sacrificing efficiency.

13. Radin, *Challenging the Performance Movement*, 100–102.

14. Kathe Callahan, "Performance Measurement and Citizen Participation," in *Public Productivity Handbook*, rev. ed., ed. Marc Holzer and Seok Hwan-Lee (New York: Marcel Dekker, 2004), 31–42; Thomas I. Miller, Michelle M. Kobayashi, and Shannon E. Hayden, *Citizen Surveys for Local Government: A Comprehensive Guide to Making Them Matter* (Washington, DC: International City/County Management Association, 2008).

15. Robert Godenkoff, "Using Focus Groups," in *Handbook of Practical Program Evaluation,* ed. Joseph S. Wholey, Harry P. Hatry, and Kathryn E. Newcomer (San Francisco: Jossey-Bass, 2004), 340–362; and Richard A. Krueger and Mary Anne Casey, *Focus Groups: A Practical Guide for Applied Research,* 4th ed. (Thousand Oaks, CA: Sage, 2009).

16. John M. Greiner, "Trained Observer Ratings," in Wholey, Hatry, and Newcomer, *Handbook of Practical Program Evaluation,* 211–256.

17. The Fund for the City of New York, Center on Municipal Government Performance, *How Smooth Are New York City's Streets?* 2008, http://venus.fcny.org/cmgp/streets/pages/indexb.htm.

18. William J. Bratton and Sean W. Malinowski, "Police Performance Management in Practice: Taking COMPSTAT to the Next Level," *Policing* 2, no. 3 (January 2008): 259–265.

19. See the COMPSTAT section of the official Web site of the Los Angeles Police Department, www.lapdonline.org/crime_maps_and_COMPSTAT/content_basic_view/6363.

20. Paul D. Epstein, Paul M. Coates, and Lyle D. Wray, with David Swain, *Results that Matter: Improving Communities by Engaging Citizens, Measuring Performance, and Getting Things Done* (San Francisco: Jossey-Bass, 2006), 53.

21. Robert D. Behn, "What All Mayors Would Like to Know About Baltimore's CitiStat Performance Strategy," report of the IBM Center for the Business of Government, 2008, www.businessofgovernment.org/report/what-all-mayors-would-know-about-baltimore%E2%80%99s-citistat-performance-strategy.

22. Teresita Perez and Reese Rushing, "The CitiStat Model" (Washington, DC: Center for American Progress, 2007), www.americanprogress.org/issues/2007/04/pdf/citistat_report.pdf; Robert D. Behn, "The Varieties of CitiStat," *Public Administration Review* 66, no. 3 (2006): 332–340.

23. Beth Weitzman, Diana Silver, and Caitlynn Braill, "Efforts to Improve Public Policy and Programs through Data Practice: Experiences in 15 Distressed American Cities," *Public Administration Review* 66, no. 3 (2006): 386–399.

24. Tony Bovaird, "Beyond Engagement and Participation: User and Community Coproduction of Public Services," *Public Administration Review* 67, no. 5 (2007): 246–260.

25. Remarks of Daniel Kildee, former treasurer of Genesee County (Flint), Michigan, and Kim Graziani, director of neighborhood initiatives, Pittsburgh, at the Conference on Reclaiming Vacant Properties, Cleveland, Ohio, October 14, 2010.

26. Wesley G. Skogan and Susan M. Hartnett, *Community Policing, Chicago Style* (New York: Oxford University Press, 1997), 8 and 173.

27. Anne Elder and Ira Cohen, "Major Cities and Disease Crises: A Comparative Perspective," paper presented at the annual meeting of the Midwest Political Science Association, Chicago, April 14–16, 1988. See also P. Arno, "The Nonprofit Sector's Response to the AIDS Epidemic: Community-Based Services in San Francisco," *American Journal of Public Health* 76 (1986): 1325–1330.

28. Anna M. Santiago and Merry Morash, "Strategies for Serving Latina Battered Women," in *Gender in Urban Research*, Urban Affairs Annual Review, vol. 42, ed. Judith A. Garber and Robyne S. Turner (Thousand Oaks, CA; Sage, 1995), 228–233.

29. Lawrence O. Houstoun Jr., *Business Improvement Districts*, 2d ed. (Washington, DC: Urban Land Institute, 2003); Jerry Mitchell, *Business Improvement Districts and the Shape of American Cities* (Albany: State University of New York Press, 2008).

30. New York City, Department of Small Business Services, *Fiscal Year 2008 Annual Report Summary: 64 Business Improvement Districts*, www.nyc.gov/html/sbs/html/neighborhood/bid.shtml.

31. Los Angeles BID Consortium, "The State of Los Angeles' Business Improvement Districts: Why BIDs Matter," 2009, www.centralcityeast.org/pdf/WhyBIDsMatter.pdf.

32. Edward T. Rogowsky and Jill Simone Gross, "To BID or Not to BID?" *Metropolitics* 1, no. 4 (Spring 1998): 7–8; Jill Simone Gross, "Business Improvement Districts in New York City's Low-Income and High-Income Neighborhoods," *Economic Development Quarterly* 19, no. 2 (2005): 174–189. These two articles provide the basis for much of our discussion of the various types of BIDs.

33. Grand Central Partnership, "About Us" (n.d.), www.grandcentralpartnership.org/who_we_are/about.asp; and Grand Central Partnership 2008 Annual Report, p. 13, www.grandcentralpartnership.org/pdfs/GCP2008AnnualReport.pdf.

34. Robert J. Stokes, "Business Improvement Districts and Small Business Advocacy: The Case of San Diego's Citywide BID Program," *Economic Development Quarterly* 21, no. 3 (2007): 278–291.

35. Jill Simone Gross, "Business Improvement Districts in New York City's Low-Income and High-Income Neighborhoods," *Economic Development Quarterly* 19, no. 2 (May 2005): 174–189.

36. Maria Dickerson, "Improvement Districts Spur Revival—and Division," *Los Angeles Times,* January 20, 1999.

37. Mike Muller, "Business Improvement Districts," *Gotham Gazette*, October 2006, www.gothamgazette.com/article/communitydevelopment/20061019/20/2005.

38. Douglas Martin, "Management of Central Park Is Going Private," *New York Times,* February 12, 1998.

39. Carl F. Valente and Lydia D. Manchester, *Rethinking Local Services: Examining Alternative Delivery Approaches* (Washington, DC: International City Management Association, 1984), xi. Ronald J. Oakerson, *Governing Local Public Economies: Creating the Civic Metropolis* (Oakland, CA: Institute for Contemporary Studies Press, 1999), 7–9, explains the distinction between the provision and the production of urban services.

40. Stephen Goldsmith, *The Twenty-First Century City: Resurrecting Urban America* (Lanham, MD: Rowman and Littlefield, 1999), esp. 18–19.

41. E.S. Savas, *Privatization in the City: Success, Failures, Lessons* (Washington, DC: CQ Press, 2005), esp. chap. 6.

42. David Osborne and Peter Plastrik, *The Reinventor's Fieldbook: Tools for Transforming Your Government* (San Francisco: Jossey-Bass, 2000), 183–187; Jeffrey D. Greene, *Cities and Privatization: Prospects for the New Century* (Upper Saddle River, NJ: Prentice Hall, 2002), 42–43; Goldsmith, *The Twenty-First Century City*, 96–99.

43. Kelly LeRoux, *Service Contracting: A Local Government Guide* (Washington, DC: ICMA Press, 2007) details the work that a government still incurs when contracting out a service. The city must determine the scope of the work to be contracted out, prepare a Request for Proposals, circulate the bid document, establish the criteria by which the bids will be rated, select a panel to evaluate the bids, formulate the legal documents that will govern the city's relationship with the winner, arrange for insurance, monitor contract performance, intervene to deal with poor performance, and, upon the end of the contract, decide whether to renew the contract or to make a change in service delivery.

44. Elliott Sclar, *The Privatization of Public Service: Lessons from Case Studies* (Washington, DC: Economic Policy Institute, 1997).

45. Selwyn Raab, "Cheaper Trash Pickup With New York's Crackdown on Mob Control," *New York Times,* May 11, 1998.

46. Elissa Gootman, "School Custodians Object as City Hires Private Firms," *New York Times,* September 26, 2003. Elissa Gootman, "Education Department Plans Nearly 500 Job Cuts," *New York Times,* December 9, 2003.

47. Brian P. Gill et al., *Inspiration, Perspiration, and Time: Operations and Achievements in Edison Schools* (Santa Monica, CA: RAND Corporation, 2005).

48. Jodi Mailander, "Teachers Dislike Pay, Workload at 'Dream School,'" *Miami Herald,* December 18, 1996.

49. See James G. Cibulka, "The NEA and School Choice," 165–166, and William Lowe Boyd, David N. Plank, and Gary Sykes, "Teachers Unions in Hard Times," 204–206, in *Conflicting Mission? Teachers, Unions, and Educational Reform,* ed. Tom Loveless (Washington, DC: Brookings Institution Press, 2000).

50. George Judson, "Hartford to End Private Management of Schools, Citing Struggles Over Finances," *New York Times,* January 24, 1996; idem, "Private Business, Public Schools: Why Hartford Experiment Failed," *New York Times,* March 11, 1996.

51. Marion Orr, "The Challenge of School Reform in Baltimore: Race, Jobs, and Politics," in *Changing Urban Education,* ed. Clarence N. Stone (Lawrence: University of Kansas Press, 1998), 106–113.

52. "TesseracT Assures Parents: Schools Will Stay Open," *School Reform News* (a publication of The Heartland Institute), April 1, 2000.

53. Brian Gill, Ron Zimmer, Jolley Christman, and Suzanne Blanc, "School Restructuring, Private Management, and Student Achievement in Philadelphia" (Santa Monica, CA: RAND Corporation, 2007), http://www.rand.org/pubs/monographs/MG533.html. A quite different study reports that the evidence on achievement scores is mixed but on the whole still favorable to the management of public schools by for-profit firms; see Paul E. Peterson and Matthew M. Chingos, "For-Profit and Nonprofit: Management in Philadelphia Schools," *Education Next* (Spring 2009): 64–70, http://educationnext.org/for-profit-and-nonprofit-management-in-philadelphia-schools/educationnext.org/files/ednext_20092_64.pdf.

54. Vaughan Byrnes, "Getting a Feel for the Market: The Use of Privatized School Management in Philadelphia," *American Journal of Education* 115 (May 2009): 437–455.

55. John E. Chubb, "The Performance of Privately Managed Schools: An Early Look at the Edison Project" in *Learning from School Choice,* ed. Paul E. Peterson and Bryan C. Hassel (Washington, DC: Brookings Institution Press, 1998).

56. John F. Witte, *The Market Approach to Education: An Analysis of America's First Voucher Program* (Princeton, NJ: Princeton University Press, 2000), 205.

57. Sam Dillon, "Florida Supreme Court Blocks School Vouchers," *New York Times,* January 6, 2006.

58. Sandra Vergari, ed., *The Charter School Landscape* (Pittsburgh, PA: University of Pittsburgh Press, 2002).

59. Ernest L. Boyer, "Foreword," to The Carnegie Foundation for the Advancement of Teaching, "School Choice: A Special Report" (Princeton, NJ: Carnegie Foundation, 1992), xv. For a competing collection of studies that present a more positive assessment of school vouchers, see William G. Howell

and Paul E. Peterson, *The Education Gap: Vouchers and Urban Schools,* rev. ed. (Washington, DC: Brookings Institution Press, 2002).

60. John R. Warren, "Graduation Rates for Choice and Public School Students in Milwaukee," report issued by School Choice Wisconsin, Milwaukee, January 2008, www.heartland.org/custom/semod_policybot/pdf/22908.pdf.

61. Carnegie Foundation for the Advancement of Teaching, "School Choice: A Special Report," 58.

62. Richard Rothstein, "Failed Schools? The Meaning Is Unclear," *New York Times,* July 3, 2002.

63. Brian P. Gill, P. Michael Timpane, Karen E. Ross, and Dominic J. Brewer, *Rhetoric Versus Reality: What We Know and What We Need to Know About Vouchers and Charter Schools* (New York: RAND Education, 2001), reviews the effect of school choice programs on racial integration.

64. *Zelman v. Simmons-Harris*, 536 U.S. 639 (2002).

65. John F. Witte, Joshua M. Cowen, David J. Fleming, and Patrick J. Wolf, "The Second Year of the Longitudinal Educational Growth Study of the Milwaukee Parental Choice (Voucher) Program," paper prepared for the conference on School Choice and School Improvement: Research in State, District and Community Contexts, Vanderbilt University, Nashville, October 25–27, 2009, www.vanderbilt.edu/schoolchoice/conference/papers/Witte_etal_COMPLETE.pdf.

66. Howell and Peterson, *The Education Gap*, 168–184; Witte, *The Market Approach to Education*, 117–118; Patrick J. McGuinn, "Race, School Vouchers, and Urban Politics: the Disconnect Between African-American Elite and Mass Opinion," paper presented at the annual meeting of the American Political Science Association, San Francisco, August 30–September 2, 2001.

67. For the words of parents who express their profound thanks for choice programs, see Peterson, "School Choice: A Report Card," 17–19.

68. Carnegie Foundation, "School Choice: A Special Report," 70; Witte, *The Market Approach to Education*, 119–143.

69. Witte, *The Market Approach to Education*.

70. Carnegie Foundation, "School Choice: A Special Report," 73.

71. Jay P. Greene, Paul E. Peterson, and Jiangtao Du, "School Choice in Milwaukee: A Randomized Experiment," in *Learning from School Choice,* ed. Paul E. Peterson and Bryan C. Hassel (Washington, DC: Brookings Institution Press, 1998), 338 and 345.

72. Frederick M. Hess, "Hints of the Pick-Axe: Competition and Public Schooling in Milwaukee," in *Charters, Vouchers, and Public Education*, ed. Paul E. Peterson and David E. Campbell (Washington, DC: Brookings Institution Press, 2001), 173–175; Frederick M. Hess, *Revolution at the Margins: The Impact of Competition on Urban School Systems* (Washington, DC: Brookings Institution Press, 2002), 17–18 and 197–208; Martin Carnoy et al., *Vouchers and Public School Performance: A Case Study of the Milwaukee Parental Choice Program* (Madison: University of Wisconsin Economic Policy Institute, 2007).

73. Paul T. Hill, ed., *Charter Schools against the Odds: An Assessment of the Koret Task Force on K–12 Education* (Stanford, CA: Hoover Institution Press, 2006), 1. A copy of the book is available online at www.hoover.org/publications/books/8322.

74. John F. Witte, Arnold F. Shober, Paul A. Schlomer, Pär Jason Engle, "The Political Economy of School Choice," La Follette School of Public Affairs Working Paper no. 2004–002. University of Wisconsin-Madison (August 2004): 4–5, www.lafollette.wisc.edu/publications/workingpapers/witte2004–002.pdf.

75. Hill, *Charter Schools against the Odds*.

76. Howard Blume, "Teachers Union Files Lawsuit over Charter Takeovers," *Los Angeles Times,* December 22, 2009; Howard Blume, "Teachers Seek Control at Up-for-bid L.A. Unified Schools," *Los Angeles Times,* January 2, 2010.

77. Brian P. Gill, P. Michael Timpane, Karen E. Ross, and Dominic J. Brewer, *Rhetoric Versus Reality: What We Know and What We Need to Know About Vouchers and Charter Schools* (Santa Monica, CA: RAND Corporation, 2001), 54–55.

78. Pearl R. Kane and Christopher J. Lauricella, "Assessing the Growth and Potential of Charter

Schools," in *Privatizing Education: Can the Marketplace Deliver Choice, Efficiency, Equity, and Social Cohesion?* ed. Henry M. Levin (Boulder, CO: Westview Press, 2001), 207.

79. Center for Education Reform, "National Charter School & Enrollment Statistics 2009," www.edreform.com/_upload/CER_charter_numbers.pdf.

80. Amy Brandon and Gregory Weiher, "The Impact of Competition: Charter Schools and Public Schools in Texas," paper presented at the annual meeting of the Midwest Political Science Association, Chicago, April 12, 2007, www.allacademic.com/meta/p198562_index.html.

81. Robert Maranto, Scott Milliman, Frederick Hess, and April Gresham, "Do Charter Schools Improve District Schools? Three Approaches to the Question," in *School Choice in the Real World: Lessons from Arizona Charter Schools*, ed. Maranto, Milliman, Hess, and Gresham (Boulder, CO: Westview Press, 1999), 129–141.

82. Peterson, "School Choice: A Report Card," 10–11.

83. Robert Bifulco, Helen F. Ladd, and Stephen L. Ross, "Public School Choice and Integration: Evidence from Durham, North Carolina," *Social Science Research* 38, no. 1 (2009): 71–85.

84. Tamara Audie, "Desegregation an Issue in Charter School Plan," *Detroit Free Press,* September 3, 1998.

85. David R. Garcia, "The Impact of School Choice on Racial Segregation in Charter Schools," *Educational Policy* 22, no. 6 (2008): 805–829.

86. Ron Zimmer et al., *Charter Schools in Eight States: Effects on Achievement, Attainment, Integration, and Competition* (Washington, DC: RAND Corporation, 2009), 12–19, www.rand.org/pubs/monographs/2009/RAND_MG869.pdf.

87. Peter Schrag, "The Voucher Seduction," *American Prospect* 11, no. 1 (November 23, 1999): 52.

88. Peggy Walsh-Sarnecki, "National Heritage-run Charter Schools Making Profits," *Manatee-Bradenton-Sarasota Herald Today,* Knight Ridder wire story, January 15, 2003.

89. Javier C. Hernandez, "Secular Education, Catholic Values," *New York Times,* March 8, 2009.

90. Jack Buckley and Mark Schneider, *Charter Schools: Hope or Hype?* (Princeton, NJ: Princeton University Press, 2007).

91. President George W. Bush was an ardent supporter of public schools. The Department of Education was reluctant to release the results of a study that undermined the president's agenda for charter schools. See Diana Jean Schemo, "Nation's Charter Schools Lagging Behind, U.S. Test Scores Reveal," *New York Times,* August 17, 2004.

92. Zimmer et al., *Charter Schools in Eight States,* esp. 35–39.

93. John F. Witte, David L. Weimer, Paul A. Schlomer, Arnold F. Shober, "The Performance of Charter Schools in Wisconsin," University of Wisconsin-Madison La Follette School of Public Affairs (2004), www.lafollette.wisc.edu/wcss/docs/persum.doc.

94. Buckley and Schneider, *Charter Schools: Hope or Hype?* chap. 10.

95. Jeffrey R. Henig, *Spin Cycle—How Research Is Used in Public Policy Debates: The Case of Charter Schools* (New York: Russell Sage Foundation, 2008), 6–7.

9 Suburban Politics and Metropolitan America

The United States is a suburban nation: its people live a suburban way of life.[1] Since the 1960s, the population of suburbia has exceeded that of central cities. As we saw in Chapter 3, even gentrification, the much celebrated "return" to the cities, represents only a very small trend that does not begin to counterbalance the continuing outmigration to the suburbs.

Between 2000 and 2009, outer suburban areas in the United States grew at three times the rate of central cities and inner suburbs. The nation's fastest-growing communities are on the edges of metropolitan regions: North Las Vegas and Henderson (Nevada), Victorville (sixty miles northeast of Los Angeles), McKinney and Denton (outside of Dallas), and Gilbert and Chandler (outside of Phoenix). McKinney doubled its population in just seven years! Riverside and San Bernardino (outside of Los Angeles), Clark (Nevada), and Maricopa (Arizona) are suburban counties experiencing similarly explosive growth rates.[2]

Although it is seldom recognized, major **boomburbs**—rapidly growing suburbs—are equivalent in size to older core cities. Mesa (Arizona) has a larger population than Minneapolis, Miami, or St. Louis; Arlington (Texas) has surpassed Pittsburgh. Noteworthy boomburbs include Anaheim, Riverside, Santa Ana, San Bernardino, Chula Vista, and Fremont (all in California); Glendale, Scottsdale, and Tempe (Arizona); Arlington (Texas); and Aurora (Colorado). Boomburbs are especially prevalent in the Southwest where limited availability of water serves to concentrate patterns of suburban development.[3] Naperville (Illinois), west of Chicago, is the rare exception—a rapidly growing major suburb in the Midwest.

Relatively few suburbs, however, exhibit the explosive growth of boomburbs. In fact, a number of suburbs are beginning to show signs of weakness. As the 2000 Census revealed, more than one-third of U.S. suburbs experienced no significant population growth during the preceding decade. A number of suburbs actually lost population as younger families sought more modern homes on the metropolitan periphery. In the Northeast and the Midwest, once prestigious inner-ring suburbs of Cleveland, Detroit, Buffalo, St. Louis, Pittsburgh, and Philadelphia suffered many of the same social and economic ills that plagued central cities. The crash of the housing market in the early 2000s also slowed suburban growth in numerous metropolitan areas.[4]

This chapter examines the evolving suburban landscape, with special attention given to how local zoning and land-use practices have shaped suburban growth. We finish by assessing two contemporary movements—Smart Growth and New Urbanism—that promise to build a "better" and more sustainable urban America.

THE HETEROGENEITY OF SUBURBIA

Although television and popular movies largely present suburbia as a homogeneous string of more privileged white, middle-and upper-class **bedroom** or **dormitory communities** (see Box 9.1, "Television and Hollywood's Schizophrenic View of Suburbia"), suburbia contains quite a diverse expanse of communities, many of which do not fit the bedroom community stereotype. Even in the 1950s, when suburban communities were just beginning to blossom, **blue-collar and industrial suburbs** centered on manufacturing plants did not fit the upper-status stereotype, such as that in television shows like *Mad Men.*[5] *Mad Men*, however, does accurately portray the "familial" ideal that was so much a part of suburbia, an ideal that had no room for independent working women, single mothers, gays, and lesbians.[6]

The "myth of the suburban monolith" is clearly dated.[7] Contemporary suburbia encompasses a wide variety of communities: affluent bedroom or dormitory residential suburbs; **privatopias** or **common-interest developments** with security-controlled gated entrances and home-owner associations;[8] industrial suburbs centered around factories; lower-middle-class **bedroom-developing suburbs**[9] that lack the tax base to provide for quality schools and to keep up with the costs necessitated by rapid growth; far-flung **exurbs** and **boomburbs** located at some distance from the metropolitan center; **minority-dominated suburbs** such as Prince George's County, Maryland (outside of Washington, DC), and East Chicago Heights; and declining inner-ring suburbs with vacant storefronts and a stock of housing no longer attractive to a new generation of homebuyers.[10] **Disaster suburbs**—East St. Louis (Illinois), Compton (California), and Camden (New Jersey, just across the river from Philadelphia)—are not all that different from the troubled central cities they border.

Edge cities—suburban concentrations of office towers, research parks, college campuses, shopping gallerias, and entertainment complexes—are the new centers of life in metropolitan areas, as found in Valley Forge and King of Prussia (outside of Philadelphia), Monroeville (Pittsburgh), Towson (Baltimore), Bloomington (Minneapolis/St. Paul), La Jolla (San Diego), Bellevue (Seattle), Tempe/Scottsdale (Phoenix), North Atlanta, North Dallas, and the Houston Galleria, to name only a few. The New York region has various concentrations of edge-city development: Morristown (New Jersey); the Route 1 corridor by Princeton (New Jersey); Huntington, Long Island, and White Plains (New York) and Stamford (Connecticut).[11] But even the concept of edge cities does not fully capture the evolving suburban form. In **edgeless cities**, sprawl extends beyond the concentrated nodes of edge cities, taking the form of unglamorous strip malls and clusters of offices that are spread along highway access roads and interchanges. As seen in the chaotic sprawl of offices in central New Jersey,

Box 9.1

Television and Hollywood's Schizophrenic View of Suburbia

From the 1950s through the 1980s, television presented a fairy-tale portrait of suburbia as a string of well-to-do bedroom communities. *The Donna Reed Show, Father Knows Best, Leave It to Beaver*, and *The Dick Van Dyke Show* featured well-dressed mothers happily tending to their children and single-family homes, waiting for their husbands to return from work. Hollywood movies such as *Miracle on 34th Street* (1947; remade in 1994) presented a very similar view of suburbia as the American Dream: A little girl gets her Christmas wish; with the help of Santa, she leaves crowded New York City for a huge suburban home with a fireplace and a large backyard.

Hollywood, however, never fully embraced suburbia. More critical movies revealed the underside of life in suburban communities that existed beneath the public veneer of normalcy. *Rebel Without a Cause* (1955), *The Man in the Gray Flannel Suit* (1956), *Peyton Place* (1957), *The Graduate* (1967), and *American Beauty* (1999) all attacked the materialism, conformity, sterility, and hypocrisy of suburban lives. *The Stepford Wives* (1975; remade 2004) attacked the isolation of suburban lives, presenting the "ideal" suburban woman as a robot with no mind of her own. Numerous films presented husbands and wives as seeking to escape from the boredom of suburban living through alcohol and meaningless sexual affairs, a theme also picked up by television's *Desperate Housewives.*

In *Edward Scissorhands* (1990), Tim Burton's charming take on the Frankenstein tale, the boy/monster (played by Johnny Depp) represents everyone who has ever felt out of place in the enforced conformity of suburbia. In *Pleasantville* (1998), life in 1950s-1960s suburbia is so mind-numbingly dull and colorless that portions of the film are shot in black and white. In *The Truman Show* (1998), the normalcy of suburban life is depicted as ordered and antiseptic, so much so that Truman Burbank (Jim Carrey) actually believes that he lives in an ideal suburban community when, in fact, he has spent his entire life on a huge, fabricated, television stage set.

Do Americans share elite Hollywood's distaste for suburbia? Not really. Polls show that most residents are satisfied with life in the suburbs, a view that is reflected in a countercurrent of films that present a much more affectionate portrait of suburbia. Steven Spielberg's *E.T.: The Extra-Terrestrial* (1982) reveals a suburbia of family love and contentment, a place where children grow up in relative safety and with a brimming self-confidence.

Ferris Bueller's Day Off (1986) is the rare movie that mixes both positive and negative assessments of suburbia. A hip, fast-talking high-school student (played by Matthew Broderick) must cut classes in order to taste the vitality of life that can only be found in the big city, Chicago. The father of his best friend is so blinded by the trappings of suburban materialism that he cares more for his luxury sports car than for his son. Yet, the film is no caustic, antisuburban diatribe. Bueller clearly enjoys the privileges of being a teenager who lives in, and goes to schools in, a top-end, North Shore community. Life in the suburbs is quite good, even though the city beckons with the enticements of ethnic diversity and adventure.

Television and Hollywood have largely presented a stereotype of suburbia as a collection of upscale residential communities. With rare exceptions, television and film fail to show the diversity of suburbs and the people who reside there. *American Beauty*, to its credit, revealed a suburbia that has increasingly become home to same-sex couples. *E.T.* and *Close Encounters of the Third Kind* (1977), focusing on the actions of single mothers, revealed a transformed suburbia where the two-parent family is no longer the norm.

Sources: Robert Beuka, *SuburbiaNation: Reading Suburban Landscape in Twentieth-Century American Fiction and Film* (New York: Palgrave Macmillan, 2004); Douglas Muzzio and Thomas Halper, "Pleasantville? The Suburb and Its Representation in American Movies," *Urban Affairs Review* 37, no. 4 (March 2002): 542–574; and Stanley J. Solomon, "Images of Suburban Life in American Films," in *Westchester: The American Suburb*, ed. Roger Panetta (New York: Fordham University Press; and Yonkers, NY: Hudson River Museum, 2006), 411–441.

edgeless development can spill over hundreds of square miles, eating up green space, wetlands, and agricultural acreage.[12]

In Florida, Arizona, and southern California, gated housing communities and "strips" of low-rise offices make for a suburban landscape that differs markedly from the **first suburbs** or inner-ring communities of the Northeast and the Midwest. New outer-rim development often lacks the sidewalks, walkable central business districts, and density of residential population that typify America's first suburbs. Many inner-ring suburbs have to cope with the costs of an aging infrastructure and a permanently weak housing market, as buyers do not value houses, built in an earlier era, that have no attached garage, only a tiny backyard, and maybe only a single bathroom.

Continued growth has brought a new diversity to the population of suburbia. While Hispanics and African Americans continue to be underrepresented in suburbia, recent decades have seen a substantial increase in minority suburbanization.[13] In numerous metropolitan areas, however, African Americans and Hispanics are predominantly found in declining industrial suburbs and "spillover" communities adjacent to the central city. In such regions, racial minorities live in a suburbia that is quite different from the suburbia enjoyed by whites. Yet, the pattern varies greatly from one metropolitan area to the next. The suburbs of Washington, DC, and Atlanta are significantly stratified by race. But in greater Los Angeles, San Diego, and Phoenix, there appear to be fewer barriers to black suburbanization. In these western metropolises, the African American population is not concentrated in only a small handful of suburbs.[14]

The new immigration from abroad has made suburbia increasingly multiclass, multiethnic, and multiracial, home to East Asians, South Asians, and Hispanics. **Melting-pot suburbs**, especially in the South and the West, are population centers of new arrivals from Asia and Latin America.[15] A majority of the Asian and Latino populations in the United States reside in suburbs, not in the central city.[16] California's Orange County, the home of Disneyland, was once the iconic image of white, -middle-class suburbia. Today, Orange County is the hub of southern California's Chinese and Vietnamese populations, with a "Little Saigon" that advertises itself as the "Capital of Vietnamese America."[17] In northern California, Cupertino, the home of Apple computers, has a population that is half Asian American.[18] On the East Coast, Prince William County, once a center of white-flight suburbanization outside of Washington, DC, has become the most ethnically diverse county in Virginia. The growing African American, Hispanic, and Asian populations have, in the words of one local official, made Prince William "a totally different place" than it was thirty years ago.[19] The term **cosmoburb** refers to an upscale, thriving suburb—Irvine, Fremont, Sunnyvale, Cupertino, and Davis (California), Naperville (Illinois), Plano (Texas), and Bellevue (Washington)—with an ethnically heterogeneous population.[20]

The gay and lesbian population of suburbia has also increased over the years, a reflection, perhaps, of the affluence, education, and tolerance of many suburban communities.[21] Lesbian couples raising children are especially likely to value suburban homes and schools.[22]

Suburbia is also a site of individual poverty that belies the myth of universal suburban affluence. Nationally speaking, half of all people below the poverty line live in the suburbs.[23] In the Great Recession of the first decade of the twenty-first century, poverty rates in the suburbs increased dramatically and began to approach the levels found in central cities.[24] Lacking effective mass transit systems, many suburbs are ill-equipped to deal with the rise in poverty: the suburban poor have great difficulty in relying on public transit to go to work.[25]

Is It Race or Income that Determines Where People Live? The Evidence on Discrimination in Metropolitan Housing Markets

What accounts for the continuing racial imbalances of suburbia? Contrary to the widely held belief, suburban housing patterns are not simply a reflection of group differences in buying power.[26] In greater St. Louis, Kansas City, and Detroit, blacks and whites of equal income, education, and professional status live in different areas.[27] If economic factors alone explained residential location, each Chicago suburban county would have about three to eight times the number of African American families than actually live there.[28]

Nor does voluntary choice fully explain why black and white Americans live in different communities. Survey after survey shows that most African Americans prefer to live in mixed, as opposed to all-black, neighborhoods. African Americans and whites both value communities with high-quality, single-family, detached homes. African Americans do not choose self-segregation. The preferences of white residents, by contrast, appear to be a much more important factor in maintaining community segregation.[29]

For many decades, in a process known as **racial steering**, real estate agents and home loan officers helped to direct white and minority home seekers to different communities. A real estate agent would show a prospective white buyer a home in certain communities while showing a minority buyer houses in other communities.

Does racial steering continue today? Federal **fair housing laws** have had a great influence and have virtually eliminated the most blatant discriminatory real estate and rental practices. Yet, more subtle variants of racial steering are not easily detected and fought.

African Americans do not have the same housing search experiences as whites do. A real estate agent may show fewer homes in predominantly white neighborhoods to an African American buyer than to white buyers. Real estate personnel and institutional lenders may also present minority buyers with less help in arranging the financing for a home in a racially incompatible area.[30] Racial profiling continues to affect the award of property insurance necessary for a home loan.[31] In some cases, real estate and home insurance agents ascertain a caller's race from the sound of their voice over the phone, leading to follow-up questions that affect the terms and rates of a home loan.[32]

When the more subtle forms of racial steering occur, the victimized party seldom reports the act of discrimination. How can he or she know just what homes are being shown and what financing information is being provided to other prospective home buyers? Individual home seekers also seldom have the money to pursue fair housing enforcement through the courts.

Housing discrimination is primarily detected through a housing audit process known as **paired testing**, where closely matched white and minority individuals pose as home seekers in order to compare the treatment they receive from landlords, real estate agents, and financial institutions. Evidence from more than 2,000 paired tests conducted in twenty major metropolitan areas (during 2000 and 2001) points to the continued existence of the more subtle forms of racial steering:

> [I]n roughly one of five visits to a real estate or rental agent, black and Hispanic customers were denied some of the information and assistance that comparable white customers received as a matter of course. Whites were more likely to find out about available houses and apartments, more likely to be given the opportunity to inspect these units, more likely to be offered favorable financial terms, more likely to be steered toward homes for sale in predominantly white neighborhoods, and more likely to receive assistance and encouragement in their housing search.[33]

As Shanna Smith and Cathy Cloud conclude, "While not the exclusive cause of segregation, discriminatory real estate practices clearly contribute to continued patterns of racial and ethnic segregation in the United States."[34]

SCHOOLS AND SUBURBIA: RECENT TRENDS

Schools are at the center of suburban lives and often the focal point of suburban politics. Parents often defend their choice of suburban residence by pointing to the local schools and the quality education that living in a "good" suburb offers children. In this section, we take a brief look at two key issues that have the potential to "threaten" suburban school systems: the prospects of school funding reform and the prospects for increasing racial integration.

WHY SCHOOL FINANCE REFORM IS SO DIFFICULT TO BRING ABOUT

In the vast majority of communities, school funding is heavily reliant on the local property tax. Such local-based financing leads to great inequalities in the money spent on behalf of a child's education. Richer districts can spend on educational activities that are denied to children in poorer communities.

Over the past decades, citizen-initiated lawsuits resulted in judicial decisions that forced state governments to reduce the interdistrict inequalities in school spending. The states responded by increasing the level of state aid for education, reducing a school's reliance on the local property tax base. State aid to schools now surpasses the local-based contribution, with the national government playing only a minor role in school funding. In 2007–2008, the states provided 48 percent of the funds for K–12 education, local governments accounted for 43 percent, and the federal government only 8 percent.[35]

Yet, despite the rise in state aid, school finance equalization is far from complete, and local wealth and property taxes still help to determine the total money available to a school. A community with high property values—with expensive homes and significant industrial and commercial facilities—can even levy a low tax rate and still yield vast sums of money for its schools. In contrast, property-poor districts cannot come up with similar funds even when they impose much higher rates of school taxes on their citizens.

The nationwide campaign for school finance equalization was sparked by a 1970s case that dealt with the outrage of parents in Baldwin Park, a low-income suburb of Los Angeles. They were paying twice the tax rate of exclusive Beverly Hills; yet, property-poor Baldwin Hills had the ability to spend only less than half of what Beverly Hills spent per school child. The California Supreme Court in ***Serrano v. Priest*** (1971) ruled that such unequal school spending violated the equal protection clauses of both the federal and state constitutions.[36] The Serrano victory led parents in other states to initiate similar lawsuits.

However, the school finance reform movement suffered a major setback when the United States Supreme Court ruled 5–4 in ***Rodriguez v. San Antonio*** (1973) that reliance on local property taxes for school funding did not violate a person's "equal protection" rights guaranteed by the Fourteenth Amendment of the U.S. Constitution.[37] As "education" is nowhere mentioned in the U.S. Constitution, the Court did not consider education to be a "fundamental right" deserving of special federal protection. The Court was also reluctant to order the equalization of school spending, as a number of experts contended that money was of no great importance, that school spending was less critical to student learning than were influences such as parental expectations and student peer pressure.

Advocates of more equal school funding continued the fight in state courts, pressing claims based on the provisions of state constitutions. In California, Texas, New Jersey, Kentucky, and a whole host of other states, courts found that the specific language of state constitutions made the provision of a "thorough and efficient" system of education a state responsibility, leading the courts to order state legislatures to take action to reduce school finance disparities.

The taxpayers' rebellion, however, put a new barrier in the path of school funding reform. State legislators were reluctant to levy new taxes that would anger suburban parents who were already quite satisfied with the education their children received. In California, voter-imposed initiatives sharply curtailed the ability of local school districts to raise money. Faced with outraged parents, the State of California stepped in and assumed primary responsibility for funding schools, bringing a new level of equality to school spending across the state.[38] Critics charged that, in California and other states, much of the new parity was achieved by a process of **equalizing down**, where wealthier suburbs faced new limits on the amounts of money that they could raise on behalf of schoolchildren.[39]

Despite state equalization efforts, school spending continues to vary greatly from district to district. In the greater Dallas area, Denton spent $13,286 per student in 2004–2005; Grand Prairie spent only $7,597.[40] Compared to Grand Prairie, Denton had an additional $100,000 per year to spend in support of each class of twenty students. Given these disparities, it comes as no surprise that the residents of property-rich suburbs continue to oppose meaningful school finance reform. When it comes to the public schools, the residents of more advantaged communities do not wish to change a system that allows them to outspend their neighbors.

THE SCHOOLS: INTEGRATION OR RESEGREGATION?

Suburbs generally do not have to participate in efforts aimed at the racial integration of a region's public schools. In its all-important 1974 ***Milliken v. Bradley*** decision,[41] the U.S. Supreme Court ruled that the busing of students across district lines is not required, even if it is the only means capable of desegregating central-city schools. Suburban residence can offer a family an escape from major school integration efforts.

A suburb can be forced to participate in a desegregation plan only if it is first proved that the suburb intentionally undertook segregative actions. However, "intent" is near impossible to prove. Suburbanites contend that there is no racial motivation behind school districts with populations that are overwhelmingly white; rather, racial imbalances are merely the reflection of housing patterns in the metropolis.

Since the 1990s, the Supreme Court has given local districts new leeway to abandon those desegregation efforts that were previously put in place. In its 1991 ***Oklahoma City* decision**, in a situation where a school district had been found guilty of past discrimination, the Supreme Court even allowed the district to terminate desegregation efforts that had been attempted for a "reasonable" period of time. In DeKalb County, Georgia, the Court's decision placed severe limits on metropolitan desegregation plans, even in instances where "white flight" to the suburbs undermined court-ordered efforts to integrate central-city schools. Charlotte, Seattle, Denver, Kansas City, Minneapolis, Indianapolis, Cleveland, Pittsburgh, Buffalo, Dallas, Austin, Savannah, Nashville, Norfolk, and Wilmington (Delaware) are among the areas that took advantage of the Supreme Court's more relaxed approach and terminated or diminished their metropolitan school desegregation efforts.[42] In Charlotte-Mecklenburg, North Carolina, leaders in the African American community accepted the reality of resegregation and turned their energies to securing additional resources for central-city schools.[43]

In Denver, the termination of desegregation efforts led to the increased isolation of Latino students. Seventy percent of Latino students in Denver attend "intensely segregated" schools that have a student population that is more than 90 percent minority.[44] As the Civil Rights Project concluded in its review of the national situation, "suburban school districts remain segregated," and a growing **resegregation** of classrooms limits the interaction that African American, Latino, and Caucasian students have with one another.[45]

SUBURBAN LAND USE AND EXCLUSION

ZONING POWERS AND SUBURBAN EXCLUSION

Suburban jurisdictions use zoning and land-use ordinances to determine the location of housing and business activities. These actions help to determine which types of people can afford to live in the community. **Exclusionary zoning** refers to those zoning and land-use measures that serve to restrict entry by people who are less well-off and people who may be of a different race than existing community residents.

Of course, there are quite legitimate reasons for zoning, and not all zoning actions are exclusionary in their impact or intent. Planning and zoning serve important purposes, for instance, promoting community livability by separating manufacturing activity from residential areas. Land-use plans also protect a community from over-development and can promote public safety. The absence of strong land-use regulations contributed to the lethality of wildfires in Oakland Hills in the San Francisco Bay Area region, as there were no zoning regulations that prohibited new residential construction in tinderbox woodland areas.[46]

Suburbanites use zoning powers to "keep out" unwanted growth, traffic congestion, and crime. In better-off communities, residents rely on zoning to prevent the "citification" of a community. By keeping out lower-class citizens, exclusionary ordinances also help to protect the substantial equity that owners have invested in their homes:

> Suburban home owners believe that such [low-density] zoning will maximize the value of their homes. Open-space, low-density zoning adds to existing home values in many ways. Open space may be a substitute for parks and viewscapes. Low density may keep congestion down, at least within one's own community. Larger lots may price out supposedly undesirable residents and promote own-lot privacy. Less development means fewer substitutes for existing housing and thus the possibility of larger capital gains when the home is sold. . . . Few public officials are so stupid as to say that they do not really care about preserving farmland but rather just want to keep out the denizens of public housing.[47]

Suburbanites fear that a relaxation of zoning ordinances will lead to an increase in local tax rates, as the existing residents of a community will wind up helping to pay for the public schooling and other costly services provided to low- and moderate-income newcomers.

Suburbanites seldom admit it, but the demand for exclusion can also reflect racist, nativist, and classist sentiments. A review of the history of local land-use controls points to the racial and ethnic motivation underlying those controls:

> Land use regulations were therefore initially designed in part to separate people by ethnicity; in other words, they were meant to construct an American system of apartheid. It is

> therefore only natural to suspect that land use regulations might still be complicit in the construction and maintenance of racial and ethnic segregation, even though they have many other overt objectives.[48]

In Los Angeles's San Gabriel Valley, the residents of Monterey Park, San Gabriel, Arcadia, and Alhambra organized "slow-growth" campaigns in an effort to limit the influx of Latino, Chinese, and Vietnamese newcomers.[49] In well-to-do Scottsdale, outside of Phoenix, the development of gated communities serves to signify residents' membership in an upscale, exclusive community that is separate from the lower-status outside world.[50]

THE CONSTITUTIONALITY OF ZONING AND EXCLUSIONARY PRACTICES

Many Americans believe that an owner has the unlimited liberty to use a piece of property in any way that he or she sees fit. The Supreme Court, however, has ruled to the contrary, upholding the constitutionality of local zoning codes that restrict the use of property. Expressed as far back as 1926 in the ***Euclid* case** (*Village of Euclid, Ohio, v. Ambler Realty Co.*),[51] the Supreme Court views zoning as a legitimate exercise of the state's **police powers** to protect the public well-being against unwanted noise, congestion, and changes in a community's character.

Advocates for the poor and racial minorities contend that more affluent suburbs do not use zoning simply in an effort to maintain public health and safety and to eliminate nuisances. Suburban communities also employ zoning as a means of keeping out less-advantaged people.

The U.S. Constitution does not bar discrimination on the basis of income or buying power. There is no constitutional violation per se when a poor or middle-class family is unable to "buy into" a wealthier community. The courts will strike down a local zoning ordinance only if a litigant can prove that the community's intent to discriminate was racial, not economic, in nature.

The Supreme Court's 1977 ***Arlington Heights* decision** upheld the ability of suburbs to enact exclusionary land-use policies.[52] A church group had sought to build subsidized housing units in Arlington Heights, an affluent, overwhelmingly white suburb northwest of Chicago. But the existing local zoning laws prohibited multifamily housing throughout most of the suburb. The Supreme Court upheld the zoning restrictions, observing that a community may use its zoning powers to preserve a peaceable environment, promote orderly land development, and safeguard local property values. The plaintiffs were able to show that the zoning regulations served to keep less-well-off minority citizens from being able to move into Arlington Heights. But, according to the Court, proof of a discriminatory effect was not enough: the housing advocates would have to show that the zoning and land-use regulations were not enacted for legitimate purposes but had a clear intent to discriminate.

The significance of the *Arlington Heights* ruling cannot be overstated. Suburbs are generally under no obligation to modify exclusionary zoning and land-use ordinances in order to promote racial and class integration. As historian Charles Lamb has observed, the Court

> transformed the vision of low-income suburban housing into a pipe dream in *Arlington Heights*. Its policy prevents federal judges from inferring intent from disproportionate impact . . . and therefore makes a finding of racial discrimination very difficult to prove. . . . The fundamental problem with this approach, however, is all too obvious: local legislators and administrators are too politically conscious to exhibit their racial prejudices openly.[53]

A suburb's legal counsel will always argue that exclusionary ordinances reflect no racial intent but are simply tools to preserve local housing values and promote a community's tranquil, congestion-free ambiance.

The Technique of Suburban Exclusion

The overwhelming majority of suburbs refuse to build subsidized low-income housing within their borders. Beyond that, suburbs possess a variety of additional tools that they can use to effectively limit the housing opportunities available to poor and working-class citizens.

Suburban zoning and land-use plans can **prohibit the construction of multifamily housing**, effectively pricing the community beyond the means of people who can only afford apartments, condominiums, and town houses. More exclusive suburbs also drive up the price of entry to their community through **large-lot zoning**, a requirement that homes be built on no less than a half acre, one acre, or even two acres of land. Zoning ordinances that require homes to be built on an acre or more of land clearly are not intended to protect against nuisance land uses; rather, such ordinances seek to restrict entry into a community to only people who can afford the high price of large-lot homes.[54]

Minimum room/space requirements beyond those necessitated by concerns for health and safety, also act to increase the price of building and buying a home. **Regulations for the use of expensive construction technologies and materials** further add to home prices, requiring, for instance, that homes be built piece by piece on-site without the use of labor-saving, preassembled modular components. Construction regulations can require the use of expensive copper pipes instead of plastic pipes.

Suburban municipalities can also charge thousands of dollars in **developer fees** and **access charges** that a developer will pass on to homebuyers. These fees burden new homeowners not just with the usual property taxes but with additional payments for new streets, sewers, and schools, services that are provided to other community residents who do not have to pay additional fees.

A **moratorium on the extension of sewer and water lines** effectively limits the supply of land available for new home construction. The designation of **agricultural preserves** and **open-space** or **green-space areas** similarly limits the land available for new home construction. In New Jersey, suburban communities did not buy natural areas simply to promote open-space preservation; instead, local officials acquired land parcels that were targeted for development and that were already serviced by sewers and other infrastructure.[55] In such cases, suburban officials and residents continue to deny exclusionary intent and instead claim that their actions are motivated by concerns for the natural environment. (See Box 9.2, "Should Environmentalists Oppose Suburban Housing Development? Is There an 'Environmental Protection Hustle'?")

Box 9.2

Should Environmentalists Oppose Suburban Housing Development? Is There an "Environmental Protection Hustle"?

Suburbanites have learned to dress up their exclusionary preferences in the more respectable language of environmentalism, justifying limitations on local growth as a means of protecting valuable green space and unique natural areas. In *The Environmental Protection Hustle,* Bernard Frieden attempts to expose the inconsistencies of such arguments. He uses case studies of development in the San Francisco Bay region to show that environmentalists have too often become the unwitting allies of suburban exclusionists.

In one case, environmentalists stopped the construction of 2,200 affordable town home and condominium units in the foothills outside Oakland. They rejected a project that had considerable environmental merits, as the project emphasized compact development and devoted 480 acres of open space to public use. By contrast, the community forced the adoption of a compromise plan that wound up building 300 expensive estate homes spread throughout the foothills. The new plan did not dedicate land for public recreational space.[1]

Overregulation drives up the costs of development, posing new barriers to home buying by racial minorities, working-class families, and newly marrieds who seek a suburban home. Research from Wisconsin indicates that reducing minimum lot-size requirements and other zoning restrictions could, in some cases, lower the costs of new suburban homes by as much as 50 percent.[2] Other studies report substantial but lesser savings.

Environmental activists respond that Frieden and other housing advocates fail to give adequate consideration to environmental concerns, including the importance of limiting development in ecologically fragile foothills or along an imperiled coastline. Property developers already possess significant influence in the developmental arena, having made substantial campaign contributions to elected officials. Environmentalists warn of the potential dangers of exacerbating this power imbalance still further if growth advocates are able to use the affordable housing arguments to justify questionable development plans.

[1]Bernard J. Frieden, *The Environmental Protection Hustle* (Cambridge, MA: MIT Press, 1979), pp. 23–24, 38–41, and 52–59.

[2]Mary K. Schuetz and Sammis White, *Identifying and Mitigating Regulatory Barriers to Affordable Housing in Waukesha County, Wisconsin* (Milwaukee: University of Wisconsin-Milwaukee Urban Research Center, 1992), Table 2, reprinted in Mark Edward Brown, "Subdivision Sprawl in Southeastern Wisconsin: Planning, Politics, and the Lack of Affordable Housing," in *Suburban Sprawl: Culture, Theory, and Politics,* ed. Matthew J. Lindstrom and Hugh Bartling (Lanham, MD: Rowman and Littlefield, 2003), p. 263.

Suburban jurisdictions can also defeat new development projects through a **strategy of delays** and constantly **shifting development standards**. When a developer meets one set of conditions, a city council or planning commission can stall a project by imposing newer and even more expensive ones. A developer can go to court to challenge the imposition of new requirements. But judicial action takes quite a bit of time and can be expensive. Good business sense will simply lead developers to cede to exclusionary pressures. Developers will be reluctant to propose mixed-income home construction in communities where the prospects of government-imposed delays and court fights serve to make such development an unwise gamble.

In some cases, suburbs enact **limited-growth** and **no-growth ordinances**. Ramapo, a town in Rockland County about thirty-five miles outside New York City, gained fame for its policy of slow-growth zoning. The municipality issued permits for new residential development only in instances where the required municipal services were readily available and a building proposal was especially meritorious. Decades later, in a more precarious economy, Ramapo's leaders finally decided to relax the municipality's stringent slow-growth measures, as the regulations appeared to be driving jobs and new economic development to nearby jurisdictions.[56] Petaluma (California), Boulder (Colorado), and Livermore (California) are other communities that set an annual quota or otherwise limit the construction of new residential dwellings.

Under **ballot-box planning**, citizen groups use the tools of direct democracy in order to slow growth. Voters in cities as well as suburbs have turned to the ballot box in an effort to limit growth. In San Francisco and in southern California communities from San Bernardino to San Diego County, citizens have used the initiative and referendum processes to restrict new construction. Voters in Cape Cod, Massachusetts, similarly endorsed a development moratorium. In Portland, Maine, voters approved a measure to preserve the city's waterfront for marine uses, limiting new residential development and the threat of "creeping condominiumism."[57]

CAN THE COURTS "OPEN" THE SUBURBS? NEW JERSEY'S MOUNT LAUREL DECISIONS

Activists seeking to "open" the suburbs have turned to litigation in state courts, arguing that exclusionary practices violate state constitutions and statutes. But even where such lawsuits succeed, they seldom have the great impact that their supporters desire.

In New Jersey, open-suburbs advocates seemingly won a major victory when the state supreme court, in a series of rulings known as the ***Mount Laurel* decisions**, struck down the exclusionary practices of a broad range of communities. The New Jersey court ruled that, under the state's constitution, Mount Laurel township (a New Jersey suburb of Camden and Philadelphia) and all growing communities in the state were obliged to allow the construction of a "fair share" of a region's low- and moderate-income housing units.[58]

The 1975 decision had little immediate impact. Suburban communities simply dragged their feet and rezoned as few parcels of land as possible, producing no real increase in the availability of affordable housing.

After eight years, the court again intervened.[59] The court encouraged developers to challenge exclusionary practices in court. In instances where local ordinances were found to improperly obstruct new home building efforts, developers would win the right to construct homes at higher densities than a community normally allows. The New Jersey Supreme Court set up a special system of housing courts to expedite the legal cases brought by developers.

Suburbanites were outraged by the judiciary's actions. The state's governor and legislature responded by passing laws that undercut the open-suburbs thrust of the *Mount Laurel* rulings. A new state statute abolished the special housing courts, creating in its place an appointed Council on Affordable Housing. Despite its name, the council did not seek to promote affordable housing but more typically reduced the number of affordable units that a suburb was otherwise required to build. The suburbs were also allowed to reserve a number of the new units for established residents and the elderly, reducing the number of units for newcomers. Most significantly, the new legislation reduced the number of affordable units that a suburb had to build within its borders. A community could meet half of its fair-share obligation by helping to pay for subsidized housing in troubled cities like Newark, Paterson, and Jersey City. Suburban Wayne Township in 1993 gave $8 million to low-income Paterson in order to escape the burden of having to build nearly 500 units of affordable housing within its own borders.[60]

The *Mount Laurel* decisions did eventually lead suburbs like Mount Laurel to build a few more units for working- and lower-middle-class people. The system of intermunicipal agreements also gave Newark and other fiscally strapped core cities much-needed assistance for constructing and maintaining low-income housing. Between 1987 and 1996, intermunicipal agreements led to the transfer of more than $92 million and the construction of 4,700 units of affordable housing.[61]

Yet, overall, the *Mount Laurel* decisions reveal the limited ability of the judiciary, acting top-down, to open the suburbs in terms of class and race.[62] Eighty percent of the units built as a result of *Mount Laurel* were owner-occupied, not rental units. The new condominiums, town houses, and garden apartments seldom went to central-city residents and the poor. Instead, suburbs gave the affordable units to the grown children of suburban residents, essential public service workers (the police, fire, and hospital personnel that suburban communities need), divorced mothers, and rising middle-class young couples—not the poor.[63] The intermunicipal transfer of funds helped to provide low-income housing in the central cities; it did not open the suburbs.

INCLUSIONARY APPROACHES

Massachusetts's Chapter 40B **Anti-Snob Zoning law** allows the state to invalidate local land-use controls that unreasonably interfere with the construction of low- and moderate-income housing. Offending municipalities can also be denied development-related assistance. The Massachusetts law seeks to ensure that at least 10 percent of the housing stock in each local community is within the financial reach of working-class and poorer families. Connecticut, Rhode Island, and New Hampshire have similar state ordinances.

Anti-snob zoning laws work. They lead to the construction of affordable housing units in municipalities that would otherwise have zoned out such construction.[64] Yet, the requirements of the Massachusetts law, which are seemingly tough, are not aggressively enforced. Suburbanites bitterly object that the law interferes with their ability to control the character of their communities, allowing developers too great an ability to bypass local zoning restrictions. In 2001, Governor Jane Swift responded to the complaints, giving localities new authority to reject large projects that are out of character with their communities.[65]

Montgomery County (Maryland) and Orange County (California) are among the few local governments to have initiated **inclusionary programs**, relaxing zoning ordinances, modifying building codes, and providing financial assistance to developers in an effort to encourage the construction of multifamily and affordable housing units.[66] **Density bonuses** incentivize the construction of affordable units, allowing a developer to build a greater number of housing units than is normally permitted—in return for a signed agreement that sets aside a specified number of the units for low- and moderate-income families.

SUBURBAN AUTONOMY AND METROPOLITAN FRAGMENTATION

The concept of a **metropolitan area** denotes the economic and social **interdependence** of communities in a region. No community—city or suburb—is an island unto itself; instead, each community is dependent on the existence, actions, and resources of its neighbors. Even the most affluent suburb needs the support functions provided by other jurisdictions in the metropolis. Central cities and inner-ring suburbs provide the warehousing, distribution, and manufacturing that support economic activity throughout the region. Core cities and declining suburbs also house many of a region's low-wage manual and service workers.

The economic dependence of even far-off exurbs on their regional neighbors is readily observable in traffic patterns. The streets of Moreno Valley, located seventy miles outside of downtown Los Angeles, are relatively empty during weekday working hours as one-third of the exurb's workers have ventured off to jobs elsewhere in Los Angeles, Riverside, and Orange counties.[67]

Metropolitan fragmentation denotes the lack of a broad, overarching body capable of governing the socially and economically interconnected metropolis; instead, the region is divided into many smaller pieces with governmental authority parceled out to autonomous local bodies. Governmental powers in the metropolis are exercised by hundreds of—and, in some major metropolitan areas, more than a thousand—independent cities, towns, villages, townships, counties, special authorities, and narrow-purposed service districts. The Greater New York metropolitan area sprawls into three states and is governed by a confusing array of more than 2,000 separate units of government, including cities, villages, towns, townships, boroughs, 31 counties, more than 740 special districts (each responsible for providing a service like water or parks), and numerous special authorities and regional multistate agencies.[68]

With such a large number of governing bodies, effective, coordinated regional action proves immensely difficult, if not impossible, to undertake. Each locality and special service district looks first to its own interests. Local jurisdictions and narrow-focused agencies do not have to give great consideration to the impacts that their actions will have on neighboring jurisdictions or even on the natural environment of the larger region.

Metropolitan fragmentation imposes obstacles to the effective provision of public services across political and administrative boundaries. No metropolitan area can develop an effective system of regional mass transit when bus and rail service stop at the edge of a community where local residents are unwilling to support the service. The provision of emergency medical services is impeded when a community's ambulances are not permitted to cross a political boundary line in response to a call for service.

Metropolitan fragmentation results in the costly **overlap** and **duplication of services**, as key facilities in a region are not centrally coordinated or planned.[69] Some services in the metropolis are overprovided, as each community has its own fire station and hospital, and, of course, the local hospital must have its own CAT scan equipment, despite the expense. The taxpayer shoulders the costs. Metropolitan fragmentation also impedes the realization of **economies of scale**, where cost savings and volume discounts can be gained through the larger-scale provision of a service.

The fragmented metropolis also serves to maintain the racial segregation of public schools. The Detroit metropolitan area has "115 separate school districts empowered to erect walls around themselves."[70]

Metropolitan fragmentation adds to suburban sprawl, compounding environmental problems and adding to the costs of providing the region's built infrastructure. According to one estimate, the Salt Lake City region would save $4.5 billion in transportation, water, sewer, and utility investments if it could override local decisions and contain sprawled growth.[71]

Smart Growth: Protecting the Natural Environment

Local Autonomy and Suburban Sprawl

Suburban sprawl adversely affects sustainability.[72] Automobile commuting uses nonrenewalable energy, producing tailpipe emissions that degrade air quality and greenhouse gases that contribute to global warming. Runoff from roadways, parking lots, and the paved surfaces of suburbia allows oil, road salts, and other contaminants to flow into lakes and streams. The impermeable surfaces of suburbia's roads and parking lots interfere with the groundwater seepage necessary to replenish aquifers. Sprawl eats up greenfields and wetlands, destroying animal habitats and diminishing biodiversity. Sprawl also results in the loss of agricultural acreage. In Wisconsin, new subdivisions on the edge of the greater Milwaukee area have driven up land prices, prompting the sale of farmland for nonfarm uses.[73]

In the fragmented metropolis, localities pursue developmental decisions that exacerbate sprawl. A community on the metropolitan rim that gains substantial tax revenues from a new regional shopping mall will often show little regard for the project's effect in terms of lost wetlands, increased storm-water runoff, and heightened air pollution resulting from lengthened automobile trips. Upscale inner-ring suburbs enact land-use restrictions to limit commercial development and preserve the community's peaceful style of life. Such policies also lead developers to "head for the more rural areas in search of more buildable land."[74]

Urban sprawl also raises concerns about racial equity and environmental justice.[75]

Sprawled development often adds to problems of metropolitan school segregation. The concentrations of employment in edge cities and edgeless development often put jobs geographically out of the reach of the inner-city poor. Sprawl also increases the reliance on automobiles and trucks, with diesel emissions leading to emphysema and related health problems among the children and the elderly who live in the poor neighborhoods through which traffic is funneled.[76]

POLICIES FOR SMART GROWTH

Can urban sprawl be contained? Twenty or so states pursue **sustainable development** or **Smart Growth** policies that emphasize compact and transit-oriented development, construction steered to infill sites, and other practices that seek to minimize the stress that growth places on the natural environment.

Florida has a program of statewide growth management intended to ward off the spread of development into the Everglades and fragile coastal areas. The State of Florida requires localities to develop comprehensive development plans that allow new development only in areas where the necessary supporting infrastructure is already in place. But localities, seeking the benefits of growth, have found ways around the restrictions imposed by Florida's Growth Management Act. The act does not fully constrain sprawl. Substantial new growth has occurred in suburban rim areas where sufficient highway capacity was previously built.[77]

Maryland adopted its renowned Smart Growth legislation as the state faced the prospect of lost farmland and green space with the expected arrival of more than a million new residents by the year 2020. Another half million residents were expected to leave central cities and move to the metropolitan rim, further adding to the pressure for sprawled development. If left undirected, new suburban growth threatened to drain the life out of Baltimore and inner-ring communities while requiring taxpayers to bear the costs of new sewers, roads, and other infrastructure.

Maryland's Smart Growth Areas Act, adopted in 1997, seeks to direct state support for highways, sewage treatment, housing, and other infrastructure to already-developed areas, including existing communities in need of redevelopment. Large-lot subdivisions and greenfield areas do not qualify for priority funding.[78] New Jersey established similar priorities in 1998, prioritizing state aid to development projects where the local infrastructure was already in place.[79]

Smart Growth strategies have received substantial acclaim but nonetheless have been only moderately successful, at best, in curbing sprawled development: "Despite the rhetoric, smart growth still means that growth will happen in the suburbs and on the periphery."[80] The Maryland and New Jersey strategies spurn a strong-state regulatory approach that would prohibit new development in green areas; instead, the state offers various subsidies in its attempt to steer growth to already-built-up areas. Self-interested local governments pursuing new growth projects can simply ignore the state incentives. In Maryland, developers have won local approval to build thousands of new housing units in areas that the state had not designated for growth. More exclusive communities similarly continue to zone out multifamily housing, driving new development to the urban periphery. Suburban citizens refuse to surrender their autonomy, their ability to control the density of development in, and the future growth of, their communities.[81]

THE PORTLAND URBAN GROWTH BOUNDARY

In contrast to Maryland's strategy of incentives, the State of Oregon adopted a more direct, regulatory approach to growth management. During the 1970s, the Oregon legislature enacted a series of strong planning laws, including the requirement that Portland and other cities formulate growth boundaries. A Portland **Urban Growth Boundary (UGB)** was created to prevent new residential development in the region from encroaching on farmland in the Willamette Valley. Developers are permitted to build new housing only inside, not outside, the designated growth boundary. By drawing a line beyond which new development would not be allowed, the UGB averted new sprawl while promoting infill development that strengthened Portland's neighborhoods and the region's older suburbs.[82]

The UGB has clearly succeeded in its major goals. In the 1988–1990 period, over 90 percent of single-family homes and 99 percent of multifamily development occurred within the boundary.[83] In terms of sprawl, the Portland metropolitan area was the eighth lowest of eighty-three metropolitan areas.[84] The UGB reinforced patterns of compact development, and, as a result, Portlanders drive less and enjoy cleaner air than do the residents of similar communities in other states.

Yet, the Portland regulatory approach has its downside: home seekers are able to buy less house for their money. Builders construct town houses and relatively small homes or "skinny houses" that are "shoehorned" onto small plots of land inside the growth boundary. The homes often have relatively tiny backyards and no side yards.

Critics charge that the UGB diminishes the supply of developable land and thereby drives up the costs of housing. Yet, the evidence on this point is not as clear as the critics contend. As Denver and Salt Lake City, two cities with no growth boundary, experienced a similar rapid escalation in home prices, the extent to which the UGB deserves the blame for Portland's home-price inflation is unclear. Home prices in Portland and elsewhere soared in the 1990s as a result of rapid job and wage growth; good wages, not the UGB, seem to bear the burden for the Portland area's high home prices.[85]

The UGB also does not impede new home construction as sharply as its critics contend. The growth boundary was initially drawn to include sufficient space within it for new development. Housing densities within the boundary were increased to allow for new construction. In 2002, Portland's Metro Council expanded the boundary by nearly 18,000 acres, a 7 percent increase, to ensure a continuing supply of land for residential purposes.[86]

Portland planners have taken additional steps to promote the construction of a mix of housing types and to further ensure that housing will remain within the price reach of working- and middle-class families. Oregon state law prohibits communities in the region from capping housing construction. The state also requires all jurisdictions in the greater Portland area to rezone land so that apartments and multifamily homes will constitute half or more of all new housing.[87]

The Urban Growth Boundary promotes compact development. Orenco Station, Portland. Courtesy of user About-movies from Wikimedia Commons. http://commons.wikimedia.org/wiki/File:HillsboroOrencoStation.JPG.

"New Urbanism": Can We Build Better Suburbs?

The New Urbanism shares a lot in common with Smart Growth. The **New Urbanism (NU)** is a movement of designers, developers, and urban planners who have reacted against the environmental costs of sprawled suburban development and the disappearing sense of "community" in contemporary suburbs. The New Urbanism seeks to build new-style communities that are ecologically sustainable and that provide an antidote to the isolation and anomie of life in automobile-dominated suburbia. The New Urbanism "is arguably the most influential movement in city design in the last half-century."[88]

The Guiding Principles of the New Urbanism

New Urbanists seek to get Americans out of their cars and back on the street and in touch with their neighbors. Conventional suburbs, designed for the convenience of the automobile, place nearly insurmountable barriers in the way of walking. Homes are located far from commercial destinations. High schools and office centers are situated on virtual islands surrounded by acres of parking that are almost untraversable on foot. Fast highway approaches and access ramps make it nearly impossible for pedestrians to cross the street. The workers in a suburban office tower who go out for lunch often find that they have no real alternative but to drive from one parking lot to another. The highway- and parking-dominated landscape of suburbia makes suburbia "an incredibly boring place to walk."[89]

NU seeks compact development, minimizing the acreage lost to roadways, access ramps, and the sea of parking lots that surround shopping centers, malls, and office gallerias. New Urbanists emphasize walkability, with homes built close to sidewalks and located within a five-minute walk to schools, convenience stores, and other neighborhood focal points. Attractive, retro-style town centers with cafés and interesting shops and window displays serve to promote pedestrian traffic. Townhomes and garden apartments are part of NU communities, providing the population densities to support neighborhood schools and town centers.

Front porches on homes help to restore the "eyes" that watch over streets, helping to make them safe and free of crime. **Traffic-calming measures**, such as low speed limits, traffic bumps, and the preservation of on-street parallel parking, all serve to protect pedestrians, enhancing walkability. Tree-lined walkways and bike paths provide pleasant alternatives to the automobile. Stores (and, oftentimes, houses as well) are located one abutting the next in order to reduce walking distances. Where central facilities require automobile access, parking is pushed to rear garages so that a pedestrian-friendly shopping environment is maintained.

New Urbanists emphasize diversity as opposed to the homogeneity that more conventional suburbs enforce through zoning. NU mixes visually attractive apartments and townhomes with single-family homes. Where government monies for subsidized housing are available, New Urbanists seek to "blend in" the subsidized units so that, from the outside, they are not readily distinguishable from market-rate housing.

New Urbanism is not solely a suburban movement. Its principles have also been applied to center-city shopping districts in an effort to bring twenty-four-hour-a-day life back to a city's downtown. The Department of Housing and Urban Development's (HUD) **HOPE VI** program has adopted a number of New Urbanism design elements in an effort to create more attractive and habitable public housing environments. In Chicago, Atlanta, Baltimore, Charlotte, New Orleans, and numerous other cities, HOPE VI helped to demolish some of the nation's worst high-rise public housing structures, replacing them with low-rise housing units built according to NU principles.[90]

THE LIMITED NATURE OF THE NEW URBANISM REVOLUTION

The New Urbanism's singular achievement has been the building of more aesthetic and walkable communities, an alternative to automobile-centered suburbia. New Urbanism features have also been incorporated into the lively faux-urban shopping–entertainment villages that are more attractive and lively than the older generation of indoor shopping malls they replaced.[91] Yet, despite theses laudable successes, the New Urbanism will not substantially alter the face of suburbia or contain sprawl.[92] The New Urbanism cannot undo patterns of land use that have taken root over the years. Most Americans will continue to seek homes with multi-car garages and spacious side yards and backyards.

NU communities have failed to produce the mix of uses and population that is an inherent part of the NU vision. In the absence of public subsidies, NU developers have been unable to include housing units for the poor. Despite its physical design, an NU community that lacks population diversity is not greatly different from a conventional suburb.[93] As one critic has observed, the New Urbanism may have succeeded only in building "a slightly reconfigured suburb," an "automobile-oriented subdivision dressed up to look like a small pre-car-centered town."[94]

CONCLUSION: TOWARD A WORKABLE REGIONALISM?

Suburban communities jealously guard their autonomy, especially their control over schools, zoning, and land-use powers. The school finance reform, fair housing, and "open suburbs" movements all seek to address some of the equity problems that derive from suburban development. Smart Growth and New Urbanism seek to address questions of sustainability, providing compact communities and viable alternatives to the automobile-dominated, sprawled development of suburbia. Yet, in a free society, the growth of suburbia will continue. None of the movements reviewed in this chapter are likely to promote a radical redirection in suburban development.

Urban economist Anthony Downs has observed that "the long-run welfare of suburban residents is still closely linked to how well central cities and their residents perform significant social and economic functions in each metropolitan area. The belief among suburbanites that they are independent of central cities is a delusion."[95]

In a global economy, a core city's health and vitality continue to determine how potential investors view a region. Investors from overseas, in particular, do not always easily distinguish a suburb from its central city. The future economic development and well-being of a region's suburbs is often more intertwined with the region's core city than suburban residents recognize.

Can cities and suburbs cooperate effectively in promoting job growth, environmental protection, and the cost-efficient delivery of public services? Just what are the prospects for effective interlocal and regional action in the fragmented metropolis? The answer to these questions is the subject of our next chapter.

NOTES

1. Robert A. Beauregard, *When America Became Suburban* (Minneapolis: University of Minnesota Press, 2006), ix and 14.

2. Alan Berube et al., *State of Metropolitan America: On the Front Lines of Demographic Transformation* (Washington, DC: Brookings Institution Press, 2010), 7, www.brookings.edu/~/media/Files/Programs/Metro/state_of_metro_america/metro_america_report.pdf; U.S. Census Bureau press release CB08–106, July 10, 2008, www.census.gov/Press-Release/www/releases/archives/population/012242.html.

3. Robert E. Lang and Jennifer E. LeFurgy, *Boomburbs: The Rise of America's Accidental Cities* (Washington, DC: Brookings Institution Press, 2007); idem, "Boomburb 'Buildout': The Future of Development in Large, Fast-Growing Suburbs," *Urban Affairs Review* 42, no. 4 (May 2007): 533–552.

4. William H. Lucy and David L. Phillips, "Suburbs and the Census: Patterns of Growth and Decline," report of the Brookings Institution Center on Urban and Metropolitan Policy (Washington, DC, 2001); William H. Lucy and David L. Phillips, *Confronting Suburban Decline: Strategic Planning for Metropolitan Renewal* (Washington, DC: Island Press, 2000); U.S. Census Bureau, Population Estimates Program (2004); Berube et al., *State of Metropolitan America*, 9.

5. For good examples of the 1950s literature that portrayed suburbia as a stream of bedroom communities,

see William H. Whyte Jr., *The Organization Man* (New York: Simon and Schuster, 1956); David Riesman, *The Lonely Crowd* (Garden City, NY: Doubleday, 1957); and J. Seeley, R. Sim, and E. Loosley, *Crestwood Heights* (New York: Basic Books, 1956). Bennett M. Berger's *Working-Class Suburb* (Berkeley: University of California Press, 1960) was a noteworthy exception, a book that detailed life in a blue-collar suburban community. Robert Lewis, ed., *Manufacturing Suburbs: Building Work and Home on the Metropolitan Fringe* (Philadelphia: Temple University Press, 2004) provides an overview of industrial suburbs.

6. Lynn M. Appleton, "The Gender Regimes of American Cities," in *Gender in Urban Research,* Urban Affairs Annual Review, vol. 42, ed. Judith A. Garber and Robyne S. Turner (Thousand Oaks, CA: Sage, 1995), 44–59; Stephanie Coontz, "Why 'Mad Men' Is TV's Most Feminist Show," *Washington Post,* October 10, 2010.

7. Myron Orfield, *American Metropolitics: The New Suburban Reality* (Washington, DC: Brookings Institution Press, 2002), 28.

8. Evan McKenzie, *Privatopia: Homeowner Associations and the Rise of Residential Private Government* (New Haven, CT: Yale University Press, 1994).

9. Orfield, *American Metropolitics*, 2–3.

10. See Robert Puentes and Myron Orfield, "Valuing America's First Suburbs: A Policy Agenda for Older Suburbs in the Midwest," report of the Brookings Institution Center on Urban and Metropolitan Policy, Washington, DC, 2002, www.brookings.edu/reports/2002/04metropolitanpolicy_puentes.aspx.

11. Joel Garreau, *Edge City: Life on the New Frontier* (New York: Doubleday, 1991).

12. Robert E. Lang, *Edgeless Cities: Exploring the Elusive Metropolis* (Washington, DC: Brookings Institution Press, 2003).

13. The 2000 Census shows that racial and ethnic minorities constitute 27 percent of the population of suburbia, up from 19 percent just ten years previous. The all-white suburb has virtually disappeared from the suburban landscape. See William H. Frey, "Melting Pot Suburbs: A Census 2000 Study of Suburban Diversity," report of the Brookings Institution Center on Urban and Metropolitan Policy, Washington, DC, 2001, http://www.brookings.edu/reports/2001/06demographics_frey.aspx. See also Valerie C. Johnson, *Black Power in the Suburbs: The Myth or Reality of African American Suburban Political Incorporation* (Albany: State University of New York Press, 2002).

14. Thomas I. Phelan and Mark Schneider, "Race, Ethnicity, and Class in American Suburbs," *Urban Affairs Review* 31, no. 5 (May 1996): 307–309.

15. William H. Frey, "Melting Pot Suburbs: A Study of Suburban Diversity" in *Redefining Urban and Suburban America: Evidence from Census 2000*, vol. 1, ed. Bruce Katz and Robert E. Lang (Washington, DC: Brookings Institution Press, 2003), 155.

16. Roberto Suro and Audrey Singer, "Latino Growth in Metropolitan America: Changing Patterns, New Locations," report of the Brookings Institution Center on Urban and Metropolitan Policy, Washington, DC, 2002, www.brookings.edu/reports/2002/07demographics_suro.aspx; Frey, "Melting Pot Suburbs."

17. Karin Aguilar-San Juan, "Staying Vietnamese: Community and Place in Orange County and Boston," *City and Community* 4, no. 1 (2005): 37–65. Mike Davis, "Behind the Orange Curtain," *Nation,* October 31, 1994, 485–490, provides a somewhat dated but provocative description of racial and ethnic conflict in a changing Orange County.

18. Patricia Leigh Brown, "In One Suburb, Local Politics with Asian Roots," *Washington Post,* January 3, 2004.

19. Nick Miroff, "Diversity Blooms in Outer Suburbs," *Washington Post,* November 3, 2008.

20. Lang and LeFurgy, *Boomburbs*, 66–69; Paul L. Knox, *Metroburbia USA* (New Brunswick, NJ: Rutgers University Press, 2008), 55–57.

21. G. Scott Thomas, *The United States of Suburbia: How the Suburbs Took Control of America and What They Plan to Do with It* (Amherst, NY: Prometheus Books, 1998), 165, presents brief polling evidence showing that suburbia is relatively liberal on the issue of gay rights.

22. U.S. Census Bureau, "Census 2000 Special Reports" (February 2003), www.census.gov/prod/2003pubs/censr-5.pdf. Gay and lesbian voters living in the suburbs are somewhat more conser-

vative on fiscal and social matters and are less politicized by "gay rights" issues than are their city counterparts. For further discussion, see Robert W. Bailey, *Gay Politics, Urban Politics: Identity and Economics in the Urban Setting* (New York: Columbia University Press, 1999), 120–123.

23. Alan Berube and William H. Frey, "A Decade of Mixed Blessings: Urban and Suburban Poverty in Census 2000," report of the Brookings Institution Center on Urban and Metropolitan Policy (Washington, DC, 2002).

24. Elizabeth Kneebone and Emily Garr, "The Suburbanization of Poverty: Trends in Metropolitan America, 2000 to 2008" (Washington, DC: Brookings Institution), Metropolitan Opportunity Series no. 48, 2010, www.brookings.edu/~/media/Files/rc/papers/2010/0120_poverty_kneebone/0120_poverty_paper.pdf; Scott W. Allard and Benjamin Ross, "Strained Suburbs: The Social Service Challenges of Rising Suburban Poverty" (Washington, DC: Brookings Institution), Metropolitan Opportunity Series no. 8, 2010), www.brookings.edu/~/media/Files/rc/reports/2010/1007_suburban_poverty_allard_roth/1007_suburban_poverty_allard_roth.pdf.

25. Yonah Freemark, "As Suburban Poverty Grows, U.S. Fails to Respond Adequately," *Next American City,* October 12, 2010, http://americancity.org/columns/entry/2670/.

26. Casey J. Dawkins, "Recent Evidence on the Continuing Causes of Black-White Residential Segregation," *Journal of Urban Affairs* 26, no. 3 (2004): 379–400.

27. John E. Farley, "Race Still Matters: The Minimal Role of Income and Housing Cost as Causes of Housing Segregation in St. Louis, 1990," *Urban Affairs Review* 31, no. 2 (November 1995): 244–254; Joe T. Darden, "Choosing Neighbors and Neighborhoods: The Role of Race in Preference," in *Divided Neighborhoods: Changing Patterns of Racial Segregation,* ed. Gary A. Tobin (Newbury Park, CA: Sage, 1987), 16–20; and Joe T. Darden, "African American Residential Segregation: An Examination of Race and Class in Metropolitan Detroit," in *Residential Apartheid: The American Legacy*, ed. Robert D. Bullard, J. Eugene Grisby III, and Charles Lee (Los Angeles: University of California Center for African American Studies, 1994), 82–94.

28. John F. Kain, 'The Extent and Causes of Racial Residential Segregation," paper prepared for a conference on "Civil Rights in the Eighties," Chicago Urban League, June 15, 1984, tables 1 and 2. This paper is cited by Gary Orfield, "Ghettoization and Its Alternatives," in *The New Urban Reality*, ed. Paul E. Peterson (Washington, DC: Brookings Institution Press, 1985), 168.

29. Ingrid Gould Ellen, "Continuing Isolation: Segregation in America Today," in *Segregation: The Rising Costs for America*, ed. James H. Carr and Nandinee Kutty (New York: Routledge, 2008), 265–271.

30. Gregory D. Squires, Samantha Friedman, and Catherine E. Saidat, "Experiencing Residential Segregation: A Contemporary Study of Washington, DC," in *Desegregating the City: Ghettos, Enclaves, and Inequality,* ed. David P. Varady (Albany: State University of New York Press, 2005), 127–144; George Galster and Erin Godfrey, "By Word and by Deed: Racial Steering by Real Estate Agents in the U.S. in 2000," *Journal of the American Planning Association* 71, no. 3 (Summer 2005): 251–268; Margery Austin Turner and Stephen L. Ross, "How Discrimination Affects the Search for Housing," in *The Geography of Opportunity: Race and Housing Choice in Metropolitan America*, ed. Xavier de Souza Briggs (Washington, DC: Brookings Institution Press, 2005), 81–100.

31. Gregory D. Squires and Charis E. Kubrin, *Privileged Places: Race, Residence, and the Structure of Opportunity* (Boulder, CO: Lynne Rienner, 2006), 69–93.

32. Gregory D. Squires and Jan Chadwick, "Linguistic Profiling: A Continuing Tradition of Discrimination in the Home Insurance Industry?" *Urban Affairs Review* 41, no. 3 (January 2006): 400–415. In contrast, Meena Bavan, "Does Housing Discrimination Exist Based on the 'Color' of an Individual's Voice?" *Cityscape* 9, no. 1 (2007): 109–130, finds that there is no real evidence of "linguistic profiling," at least when it comes to the success that members of different racial groups had in using the telephone to arrange appointments with real estate agents.

33. Turner and Ross, "How Discrimination Affects the Search for Housing," 86.

34. Shanna L. Smith and Cathy Cloud, "Welcome to the Neighborhood? The Persistence of Discrimination and Segregation," in *The Integraton Debate: Competing Futures for American Cities*, ed. Chester Hartman and Gregory D. Squires (New York: Routledge, 2010), p. 18.

35. U.S. Census Bureau, *Public Education Finances 2008* (Washington, DC: Government Printing Office, 2010), xi.

36. *Serrano v. Priest,* 5 Cal. 3d 584,487 (1971). See also Jonathan Kozol, *Savage Inequalities* (New York: Crown, 1991), 214 and 220.

37. *Rodriguez v. San Antonio Independent School District* 411 U.S. 1 (1973). See also Kozol, *Savage Inequalities*, 214–219.

38. Michael W. Kirst, "The Evolution of California's State School Finance System and Implications from Other States," Stanford University Institute for Research on Education Policy and Practice, March 2007.

39. William A. Fischel, *The Homevoter Hypothesis: How Home Values Influence Local Government Taxation, School Finance, and Land-Use Policies* (Cambridge, MA: Harvard University Press, 2001), 131–133 and 140–143.

40. Texas Education Agency reports, as compiled by Dallas Indicators, www.dallasindicators.org/Education/PublicSupportforEducation/PerstudentspendingonK12publiceducation/tabid/569/language/en-US/Default.aspx.

41. *Milliken v. Bradley*, 418 U.S. 717 (1974).

42. Sue Anne Presley, "Charlotte Schools Scramble as Busing Ends," *Washington Post,* November 18, 1999; Laurent Belsie, "School Busing: An Era in Decline," *Christian Science Monitor*, February 2, 1999; John Charles Boger and Gary Orfield, eds., *School Resegregation: Must the South Turn Back?* (Chapel Hill: University of North Carolina Press, 2005).

43. Stephen Samuel Smith, "Hugh Governs? Regime and Education Policy in Charlotte, North Carolina," *Journal of Urban Affairs* 19, no. 3 (1997): 247–274; Megan Twohey, "Desegregation Is Dead," *National Journal*, September 18, 1999, 2614–2620.

44. Chungmei Lee, "Denver Public Schools: Resegregation, Latino Style," report of the Civil Rights Project, Harvard University, January 2006.

45. The quotation is from Gary Orfield, "Schools More Separate: Consequences of a Decade of Resegregation," report of the Civil Rights Project, Harvard University, July 17, 2001. See also Erika Frankenberg and Chungmei Lee, "Race in American Public Schools: Rapidly Resegregating School Districts," report of the Civil Rights Project, Harvard University, August 8, 2002.

46. Jane Gross, "Politicians, Amid Ruins, Talk of Laws," *New York Times,* October 23, 1991; and Robert Reinhold, "Building on Sand: Pain Repays Reckless California," *New York Times,* October 28, 1991.

47. Fischel, *The Homevoter Hypothesis*, 230.

48. Rolf Pendall, Arthur C. Nelson, Casey J. Dawkins, and Gerritt J. Knapp, "Connecting Smart Growth, Housing Affordability, and Racial Equality," in de Souza Briggs, *The Geography of Opportunity*, 222.

49. Mike Davis, *City of Quartz* (New York: Random House, 1990), 206–209.

50. Kevin Romig, "The Upper Sonoran Lifestyle: Gated Communities in Scottsdale, Arizona," *City and Community* 4, no. 1 (2005): 67–86.

51. *Village of Euclid, Ohio, v. Ambler Realty Co.,* 272 U.S. 365 (1926). Robert H. Nelson, *Private Neighborhoods and the Transformation of Local Government* (Washington, DC: Urban Institute, 2005), 139–152, argues that contemporary communities are no longer concerned with safeguarding against nuisance and incompatible uses of land; instead, communities primarily use zoning for exclusionary purposes to maintain income and class segregation, thereby preserving property values.

52. *Arlington Heights v. Metropolitan Housing Development Corporation*, 429 U.S. 252 (1977).

53. Charles M. Lamb, *Housing Segregation in America since 1960* (Cambridge, UK and New York: Cambridge University Press, 2005), 220–224.

54. Nelson, *Private Neighborhoods and the Transformation of Local Government,* 144–146.

55. Stephan Schmidt and Kurt Paulsen, "Is Open-Space Preservation a Form of Exclusionary Zoning? The Evolution of Municipal Open-Space Policies in New Jersey," *Urban Affairs Review* 45, no. 1 (2009): 111–112.

56. Alexander Garvin, *The American City: What Works, What Doesn't,* 2d ed. (New York: McGraw-Hill, 2002), 454.

57. Roger W. Caves, *Land Use Planning: The Ballot Box Revolution* (Newbury Park, CA: Sage, 1992). The "creeping condominiumism" remark appears on p. 133. See also Mai Thi Nguyen, "Local Growth Control at the Ballot Box: Real Effects or Symbolic Politics?" *Journal of Urban Affairs* 29, no. 2 (2007): 129–147.

58. *Southern Burlington County NAACP v. Township of Mount Laurel* 67 N.J. 151,336 A. 2d 713 (1975). Charles M. Haar, *Suburbs Under Siege: Race, Space, and Audacious Judges* (Princeton, NJ: Princeton University Press, 1996) presents an in-depth discussion of the *Mount Laurel* decisions and offers the *Mount Laurel* approach as a model for the judicial attack on exclusionary practices.

59. *Burlington County NAACP v. Township of Mount Laurel,* 92N.J. 158, 336A. 2d 390 (1983).

60. Patrick Field, Jennifer Gilbert, and Michael Wheeler, "Trading the Poor: Intermunicipal Housing Negotiation in New Jersey," *Harvard Negotiation Law Review* (Spring 1997): 1–33.

61. David L. Kirp, John P. Dwyer, and Larry A. Rosenthal, *Our Town: Race, Housing, and the Soul of Suburbia* (New Brunswick, NJ: Rutgers University Press, 1995), 175, present a detailed discussion of the Mount Laurel decisions and their impact.

62. Gerald Benjamin and Richard P. Nathan, *Regionalism and Realism: A Study of Governments in the New York Metropolitan Area* (Washington, DC: Brookings Institution Press, 2001), 193–201.

63. Allan Mallach, "The Rise and Fall of Inclusionary Housing in New Jersey: Social Policy, Judicial Mandates, and the Realities of the Real Estate Marketplace," paper presented at the annual meeting of the Urban Affairs Association, March 16, 1996.

64. Spencer M. Cowan, "Anti-Snob Land-Use Laws, Suburban Exclusion, and Housing Opportunity," *Journal of Urban Affairs* 82, no. 3 (2006): 295–313.

65. Gretchen Weismann, "More than Shelter: Housing the People of Greater Boston," in *Governing Greater Boston: The Policy and Politics of Place*, ed. Charles C. Euchner (Cambridge, MA: Harvard University's Rappaport Institute for Greater Boston, 2002), 143–145.

66. Gerrit-Jan Knaap, Antonio Bento, and Scott Lowe, "Housing Market Impacts of Inclusionary Zoning," report prepared for the National Center for Smart Growth Research and Education, University of Maryland, 2008; Jenny Schuetz, Rachel Meltzer, and Vicky Been, "31 Flavors of Inclusionary Zoning: Comparing Policies from San Francisco, Washington, DC and Boston," Furman Center for Real Estate and Urban Policy Working Paper 08–02, New York University, 2008, http://furmancenter.org/files/publications/31flavorsofIZ9–9-08.pdf.

67. William Fulton, *The Reluctant Metropolis* (Baltimore: Johns Hopkins University Press, 2001), 2–4.

68. Benjamin and Nathan, *Regionalism and Realism*, 3–26.

69. Robert W. Burchell et al., *Sprawl Costs* (Washington, DC: American Planning Association, 2005) provides detailed estimates of the extensive costs of sprawls.

70. David Rusk, "Growth Management: The Core Regional Issue," in *Reflections on Regionalism*, ed. Bruce Katz (Washington, DC: Brookings Institution Press, 2000), 88.

71. American Planning Association, *Planning for Smart Growth: 2002 State of the States* (Washington, DC: APA, 2002), as cited in Bruce Katz, "Smart Growth: Future of the American Metropolis?" report of the Centre for Analysis of Social Exclusion, London School of Economics, 2002, 17. Available from the Brookings Institution Center on Urban and Metropolitan Policy, Washington, DC, www.brookings.edu/dybdocroot/es/urban/publications/20021104katzlse2.htm.

72. David J. Cieslewicz, "The Environmental Impacts of Sprawl," in *Urban Sprawl: Causes, Consequences, and Policy Responses,* ed. Gregory D. Squires (Washington, DC: Urban Institute Press, 2002), 23–38; Kahn, *Green Cities*, 110–129; Sarah Gardner, "The Impact of Sprawl on the Environment and Human Health," in *Urban Sprawl: A Comprehensive Reference Guide*, ed. David C. Soule (Westport, CT: Greenwood Press, 2006), 240–259.

73. Mark Edward Brown, "Subdivision Sprawl in Southeastern Wisconsin: Planning, Politics, and

the Lack of Affordable Housing," in *Suburban Sprawl: Culture, Theory, and Politics,* ed. Matthew J. Lindstrom and Hugh Bartling (Lanham, MD: Rowman and Littlefield, 2003), 263.

74. Fischel, *The Homevoter Hypothesis*, 230. See also Matthew E. Kahn, *Green Cities: Urban Growth and the Environment* (Washington, DC: Brookings Institution Press, 2006), 127–129.

75. Robert D. Bullard, "Smart Growth Meets Environmental Justice," in *Growing Smarter: Achieving Livable Communities, Environmental Justice, and Regional Equity,* ed. Robert D. Bullard (Cambridge, MA: MIT Press, 2007), 23–50.

76. Swati R. Prakash, "Beyond Dirty Diesels: Clean and Just Transportation in Northern Manhattan," in Bullard, *Growing Smarter*, 273–298.

77. Peter Calthorpe and William Fulton, *The Regional City: Planning for the End of Sprawl* (Washington, DC: Island Press, 2001). See also Robyne S. Turner, "New Rules for the Growth Game: The Use of Rational State Standards in Land Use Policy," *Journal of Urban Affairs* 12, no. 1 (1990): 35–47.

78. Richard Moe and Carter Wilkie, *Changing Places: Rebuilding Community in the Age of Sprawl* (New York: Owl Books/Henry Holt, 1997), 253; Calthorpe and Fulton, *The Regional City*, 188–190; James R. Cohen, "Maryland's 'Smart Growth': Using Incentives to Combat Sprawl," in *Urban Sprawl: Causes, Consequences, and Policy Responses,* ed. Gregory D. Squires (Washington, DC: Urban Institute Press, 2002), 293–324.

79. Katz, "Smart Growth: Future of the American Metropolis?" 18.

80. Christopher G. Boone and Ali Modarres, *City and Environment* (Philadelphia: Temple University Press, 2006), 181. See also Jerry Anthony, "Do State Growth Management Regulations Reduce Sprawl?" *Urban Affairs Review* 39, no. 3 (January 2004): 376–397.

81. Anthony Downs, "Smart Growth: Why We Discuss It More Than We Do It," *Journal of the American Planning Association* 71, no. 4 (Autumn 2005): 367–378.

82. It should also be noted that more than one study has found that urban growth boundaries and other "urban containment" strategies have an impact on reducing residential racial segregation in a metropolis. See Arthur C. Nelson, Thomas W. Sanchez, and Casey J. Dawkins, "The Effect of Urban Containment and Mandatory Housing Elements on Racial Segregation in U.S. Metropolitan Areas, 1990–2000," *Journal of Urban Affairs* 26, no. 3 (2004): 339–350.

83. Nancy Chapman and Hollie Lund, "Housing Density and Livability in Portland," in *The Portland Edge: Challenges and Successes in Growing Communities,* ed. Connie P. Ozawa (Washington, DC: Island Press, 2004), 210.

84. Reid Ewing, Rolf Pendall, and Don Chen, *Measuring Sprawl and Its Impact* (Washington, DC: Smart Growth America, 2002), www.smartgrowthamerica.org/sprawlindex/sprawlindex.html. See also Carl Abbott, "Planning a Sustainable City: The Promise and Performance of Portland's Growth Boundary," in *Urban Sprawl: Causes, Consequences, and Policy Responses,* ed. Gregory D. Squires (Washington, DC: Urban Institute Press, 2002), 207–235.

85. Arthur C. Nelson, Rolf Pendall, Casey J. Dawkins, and Gerritt J. Knapp, "The Link Between Growth Management and Housing Affordability: The Academic Evidence," discussion paper prepared for the Brookings Institution Center on Urban and Metropolitan Policy (Washington, DC, 2002), www.brookings.edu/dybdocroot/es/urban/publications/growthmanagexsum.htm.

86. Ethan Seltzer, "It's Not an Experiment: Regional Planning at Metro, 1990 to the Present," in Ozawa, *The Portland Edge*, 50.

87. Rolf Pendall et al., "Connecting Smart Growth, Housing Affordability, and Racial Equity," in de Souza Briggs, *The Geography of Opportunity*, 237–239; Anthony Downs, ed., *Growth Management and Affordable Housing* (Washington, DC: Brookings Institution Press, 2004), 9 and 18.

88. Alex Marshall, *How Cities Work: Suburbs, Sprawl, and the Roads Not Taken* (Austin: University of Texas Press, 2000), xix. For a good review of the guiding principles of the New Urbanism, see: Andres Duany, Elizabeth Plater-Zyberk, and Jeff Speck, *Suburban Nation: The Rise of Sprawl and the Decline of the American Dream* (New York: North Point Press, 2000); Congress for the New Urbanism, *Charter of the New Urbanism* (New York: McGraw-Hill, 2000); Calthorpe and Fulton, *The Regional City;* and Paul Crawford, *Codifying the New Urbanism* (Chicago: American Planning Association, 2004).

89. Duany Plater-Zyberk, and Speck, *Suburban Nation*, 30.

90. Calthorpe and Fulton, *The Regional City*, 253–265; Janet L. Smith, "HOPE VI and the New Urbanism: Eliminating Low-Income Housing to Make Mixed-income Communities," *Planner's Network* 151 (Spring 2002): 22–25; James R. Elliott, Kevin F. Gotham, and Melinda J. Milligan, "Framing the Urban: Struggles over HOPE VI and New Urbanism in a Historic City," *City and Community* 3, no. 4 (2004): 373–394.

91. Ellen Dunham-Jones and June Williamson, *Retrofitting Suburbia: Urban Design Solutions for Redesigning Suburbs* (Hoboken, NJ: Wiley, 2009), 112–134; Lee S. Sobel, Ellen Greenberg, and Steven Bodzin, eds., *Greyfields into Goldfields: Dead Malls Become Living Neighborhoods* (San Francisco: Congress for a New Urbanism, 2002).

92. Myron A. Levine, "The New Urbanism: A Limited Revolution," in *Redefining Suburban Studies: Searching for New Paradigms,* ed. Daniel Rubey (Hempstead, NY: National Center for Suburban Studies at Hofstra University, 2009), 25–30.

93. Jill L. Grant, "Two Sides of a Coin? New Urbanism and Gated Communities," *Housing Policy Debate* 18, no. 3 (2007): 481–501.

94. Marshall, *How Cities Work*, xx and 6. See also Alex Krieger, "Arguing the 'Against' Position: New Urbanism as a Means of Building and Rebuilding Our Cities," in *The Seaside Debates: A Critique of the New Urbanism,* ed. Todd W. Bressi (New York: Rizzoli, 2002), 51–58.

95. Anthony Downs, *New Visions for Metropolitan America* (Washington, DC: Brookings Institution Press, 1994), 52.

10 Regional Governance in a Global Age

As we saw in Chapter 9, governing power in a metropolitan area can be fragmented among hundreds—in some cases, even thousands—of autonomous and often overlapping governmental bodies. Municipalities, villages, townships, counties, various narrow-purpose governments (including school districts, community college districts, library districts, park districts, fire districts, and water and sewer districts), broader multifunctional districts, and regional planning boards and authorities each have a part of the power needed to govern the metropolis. The existence of so many independent bodies undermines the possibility of comprehensive, coordinated regional action.

In the fragmented metropolis, each jurisdiction and decision-making body can pursue its own interests, with little regard for neighboring communities or the good of the region as a whole. Wealthier suburbs, for instance, adopt exclusionary zoning ordinances that worsen urban sprawl by driving multifamily housing and commercial developments to the edges of the metropolis. Suburban prohibitions on multifamily housing and SROs (single-room occupancy hotels) lock out the homeless and the poor, burdening other communities with the responsibility of taking care of people in need.

The fragmentation of the metropolis continues to obstruct the development of a unified mass transit that can capably serve all the communities of the San Francisco Bay area. For decades, San Mateo and Marin counties would not accept a plan that outlined their contributions to the Bay Area Rapid Transit (BART) system. As a result, BART rail was not extended into these populous parts of the metropolis. For a quarter of a century, BART rail did not even serve the region's airport, located south of San Francisco in San Mateo County. Decades of contentious interlocal haggling over routes and funding mechanisms also impeded the extension of BART rail service across the bay to communities in the I-580 corridor. Even today, the region has no integrated transportation system; instead, a rider may have to switch from a local bus to Caltrain to BART to San Francisco's Muni, transfers that discourage ridership by lengthening commuting times and requiring the payment of multiple fares. The region's various autonomous bus and rail systems have not even been able to come to an agreement to offer riders the convenience of a single transit pass that would be good for rides anywhere in the Bay Area.

The BART tale of fragmentation is not unique. In Georgia, voters in suburban Cobb County blocked the extension of the Metropolitan Atlanta Regional Transit Agency (MARTA) rail service. In the Dallas-Fort Worth metroplex, suburban objections to new taxes similarly thwarted the extension of Dallas Area Rapid Transit (DART) light-rail service to populous Arlington—the home of the University of Texas-Arlington—and other up-county communities.

As we shall see, reform efforts, with rare exceptions, have largely failed in creating strong regional governments with the authority to plan and legislate for an entire urban region. The movement toward metropolitan government has stalled amid fierce suburban opposition and the defense of local autonomy. Even where new metropolitan governing arrangements are created, they seldom possess the extensive powers that metropolitan reformers advocate. In Jacksonville, Nashville, Baton Rouge, Lexington, Louisville, Indianapolis, Miami, Portland (Oregon), Seattle, and the Minneapolis-St. Paul "Twin Cities" area, regional governing arrangements fall far short of the metropolitan government ideal.

However, as this chapter describes, while measures aimed at revolutionizing metropolitan government seldom succeed, more partial and limited forms of regional cooperation are possible and, in fact, are quite commonplace. Globalization has added to the pressure for regional action. Communities that work cooperatively find that they enjoy improved chances of putting together proposals that can "win" the location of attractive new businesses.

OLD-STYLE METROPOLITANISM

Old-style metropolitan restructuring emphasized efforts to redraw local borders in order to create governments with the authority to act effectively over a larger geographical area. Annexation continues to be the most commonplace means of realigning local borders. For a while, efforts to consolidate or merge city and county government also had great popularity. In the 1950s and 1960s, metropolitan reformers also argued for plans that would create new metropolitan governments with the authority to govern multicounty metropolitan areas.

ANNEXATION

Under **annexation**, a municipality extends its boundaries outward, absorbing neighboring territory. Through the nineteenth century and much of the twentieth century, cities grew considerably as a result of annexation. Chicago expanded to the south, capturing Hyde Park and industrial Pullman, and to the north, absorbing Rogers Park and other bungalow neighborhoods. Los Angeles, in a brief ten-year period, from 1915 to 1925, mushroomed to nearly four times its size, expanding its geographical area from 108 to 415 square miles. Los Angeles pursued an aggressive policy of **water imperialism**, refusing to supply water to outlying communities unless they accepted incorporation into the city. (See Box 10.1, "Urban Films: *Chinatown* and

Box 10.1
Urban Films: *Chinatown* and the Story of Los Angeles Water Imperialism

In the arid West, water is a scare resource. Los Angeles in the early twentieth century used its control over water supply as a weapon of territorial expansion. The city forced other communities to consent to annexation in exchange for water.

The power play of municipal water politics provides the backdrop for Roman Polanski's 1974 *cinema noir* classic, *Chinatown*, a film that received eleven Academy Award nominations. The film, despite its name, is not really about the city's Chinese enclave. Instead, the movie presents a fictionalized recounting of the efforts by Los Angeles water chief William Mulholland to construct the Owens Valley aqueduct, a project that, in 1913, brought water from over 200 miles away to Los Angeles. In a desert region, Los Angeles needed to control such a water supply in order to provide for the city's future growth. Control over water enabled L.A. to annex communities in the water-starved San Fernando Valley. The region's orchard growers and ranchers, however, were unhappy with the changes being forced upon them; they charged that Los Angeles had stolen the water from the Owens River and was using it for extortion. In the 1920s, angry protestors dynamited sections of the new aqueduct.

In *Chinatown*, private detective Jake Gittes (played by Jack Nicholson) explores the mystery of why Los Angeles is secretly dumping water at a time when fruit growers and urban dwellers are both suffering from drought conditions. Gittes is shot at by resentful Valley farmers. Gittes uncovers a cesspool of corruption; the city's growth machine, including its leading newspaper, has whipped up a frenzy over water in order to win approval for the city's efforts to gain control over the Owens River water supply, to make possible the dynamic growth of Los Angeles. The film, of course, distorts a number of the events that took place and exaggerates the sinister motives behind them in order to "amp up" the drama of a classic detective story.

Note: For a recounting of the story of Los Angeles water expansionism, and the Owens Valley water controversy—and their assessment of how these events are portrayed in the film *Chinatown*—see: John Walton, "Film Mystery as Urban History: The Case of *Chinatown*," in *Cinema and the City: Film and Urban Society in a Global Context*, ed. Mark Shiel and Tony Fitzmaurice (Oxford, UK: Blackwell, 2001), pp. 46–58; William Fulton, *The Reluctant Metropolis: The Politics of Urban Growth in Los Angeles* (Baltimore: Johns Hopkins University Press, 2001), pp. 44 and 104–106; and, Gary D. Libecap, *Owens Valley Revisited: A Reassessment of the West's First Great Water Transfer* (Stanford, CA: Stanford University Press, 2007).

the Story of Los Angeles Water Imperialism.") Other cities lacked similar leverage over surrounding areas. New Jersey's major cities are typical of the Northeast and the Midwest. Newark and Jersey City lacked control over the region's water supply and hence could not force growing suburban areas to accept annexation.[1]

Each state has the authority to determine just when a local annexation can take place and just what procedures must be followed. State law is generally permissive in allowing cities to annex **unincorporated areas** that have not yet formed their own municipal governments under state law. State laws also generally permit a municipal-

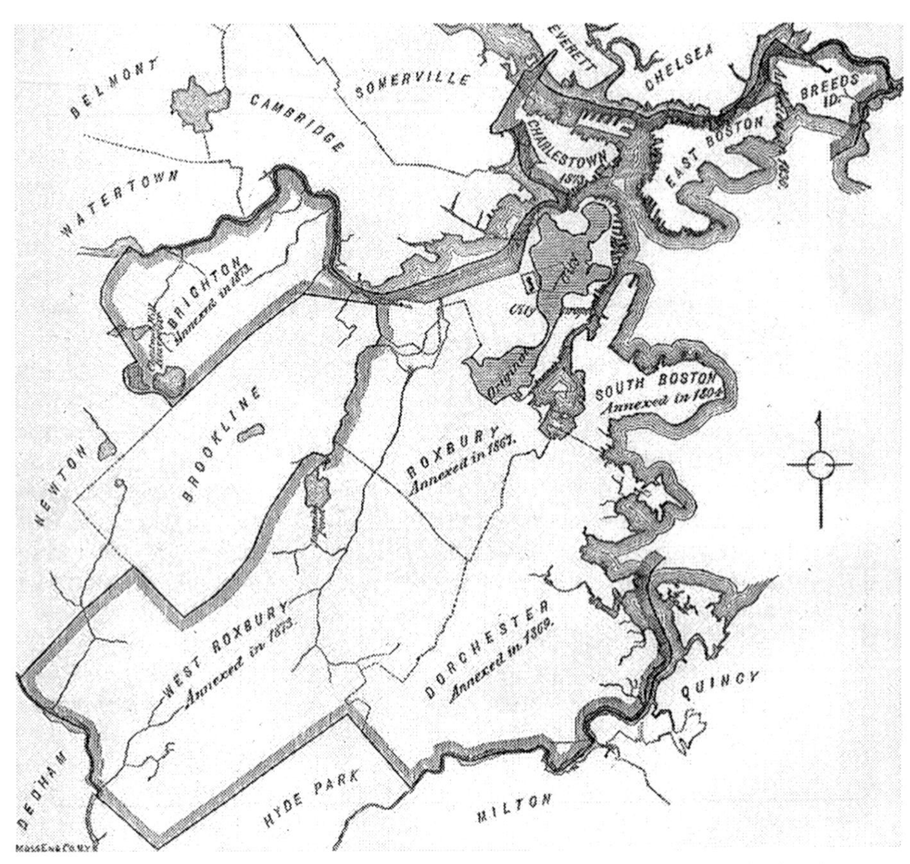

Boston Annexations,1880. By the beginning of the twentieth century, Boston had taken its present-day shape, having grown through the annexation of Roxbury, Dorchester, East Boston, and other surrounding areas. Brookline, however, spurned annexation and remains outside of Boston. Today, Boston is landlocked by already incorporated areas and no longer can expand via annexation. http://commons.wikimedia.org/wiki/File:Boston_annexations_1880.jpg.

ity to annex small parcels of land that are critical to a city's economic development efforts. Under certain conditions, a city can annex (or a state-established boundary commission can approve the annexation of) a relatively small geographical area with only a tiny population without first having to secure the consent of voters in the area to be annexed. The owner of a factory in an unincorporated part of a county may even request such an annexation, discovering that plans for the plant's expansion require a greater level of water, sewage service, and fire protection that only a neighboring city has the capacity to provide.

Cities have much less ability to annex larger land areas, areas with a population of any substantial size, and already-incorporated entities. Twenty-eight states require local consent before such annexations can proceed.[2] Typically, state law requires **dual approval**: both the larger municipality and the area to be annexed must agree to the annexation. Los Angeles, San Francisco, Chicago, Detroit, St. Louis, Milwaukee, Pittsburgh, Cleveland, Boston, and Baltimore are all **landlocked cities** completely

Box 10.2
The End of the Age of Annexation: A Look at Texas

The bitter controversy surrounding the largest annexation in Texas history led the state legislature to place substantial roadblocks in the path of future annexations. In 1996, Houston annexed upscale Kingwood, with its 50,000 residents and large homes. Two decades before, the developers of the then-new Kingwood subdivision had agreed to the future annexation of the area in return for the sewer and water extensions that the city provided the development. When that day finally came, Kingwood residents were not willing to abide by an agreement that a developer had made two decades previously, before homeowners had even moved into the community.

In the "Mother of All Annexation Battles," Kingwood citizens showed up by the busload at the state capitol to protest. They were joined by the suburban residents from other metropolitan areas who feared the possible annexation of their communities. Interestingly, even leaders of Houston's African American community also attacked the Kingwood annexation, a move that added thousands of white voters to the city's voting rolls, diluting the power that black voters had gained in Houston.

The protests could not halt the Kingwood annexation. But they did lead the State of Texas to rewrite its annexation laws, making large-scale annexations exceedingly more difficult and time-consuming. City of Houston officials began to slow annexation, fearing that continued expansionism would lead the state to impose new curbs that would tighten the fiscal noose around the city.

In Houston, the age of annexation had come to an end. With major annexations no longer that feasible, Houston officials began to invest their energies in arranging new efforts at regional cooperation and collaboration.

Sources: Scott N. Houston, "Municipal Annexation in Texas: 'Is It Really All that Complicated?'" (paper presented to the Texas Municipal League Annexation Workshop, Plano, Texas, September 26, 2003), www.tml.org/legal_pdf/AnnexationUT2003.pdf. See also Myron Orfield, *American Metropolitics: The New Suburban Reality* (Washington, DC: The Brookings Institution Press, 2002), p. 135; and Juliet F. Gainsborough, "Bridging the City-Suburb Divide; States and the Politics of Regional Cooperation," *Journal of Urban Affairs* 23, 5 (2001): 503–04.

surrounded by already-incorporated suburban municipalities. These central cities no longer have any real prospect of expanding through annexation.

For most of the twentieth century, Sunbelt states were quite permissive, even allowing major annexations. In the 1970s alone, Houston gained over 200,000 new residents as a result of annexations. San Antonio, Portland (Oregon), Charlotte, and Phoenix were other national annexation leaders.[3] Texas state law even allowed cities to unilaterally annex an abutting area with a population as large as 5,000 residents, if the larger city was already providing water and sewer service to the developing community.

Local economic elites pushed for annexations that would assist economic development ventures. Albuquerque in the 1950s and early 1960s seized sparsely populated acreage at the request of developers who knew that the extension of municipal services would be essential to their ability to build and market new residential subdivisions.[4] Houston and Denver annexed the acreage necessary to construct new international airports.

Annexation is one key to a central city's good fiscal health. David Rusk, the former mayor of Albuquerque, uses the term **elastic cities** to refer to cities such as Albuquerque, Charlotte, Houston, and San Antonio that have been able to use annexation to capture much of the tax base of new suburban development. In contrast, Hartford, Cleveland, and Detroit and other landlocked and **inelastic** cities of the Frostbelt continued to suffer steep decline, since they could not tap into the new economic growth taking place on the city's edge.[5] Columbus, Ohio, is the rare example of a Frostbelt city that was able to use its control over water and sewer hookups to force annexation. Columbus grew from 39 square miles in 1950 to 210 square miles in 2000, absorbing sizable areas of new rim development. As a result, Columbus, whatever its problems, was able to maintain a much better fiscal position than landlocked Cleveland and Cincinnati.

In recent years, however, even in the Sunbelt, the wave of annexations has receded. Cities like Charlotte and Oklahoma City have already swallowed up easily annexed land parcels.[6] Suburban resistance to annexation has also stiffened, leading state legislatures to revise state codes to make future annexations more difficult to achieve. (See Box 10.2, "The End of the Age of Annexation: A Look at Texas.") Only in the West have a number of cities, especially smaller cities, continued to grow via annexation.[7]

City–County Consolidation

Under **city–county consolidation**, a city merges with its surrounding county to form a single government; the city and county are no longer separate entities with separate legislatures and separate administrative departments. A complete consolidation would entail the elimination of all municipalities in the county, with the county becoming the sole general-purpose local government. Contemporary city–county consolidations in the United States, however, are never complete. Instead, numerous suburban governments and other local governing bodies continue their existence despite the merger of a county and its central city.

The movement toward city–county consolidation has clearly slowed (see Table 10.1). The 2001 merger of Louisville and Jefferson County is the only city–county consolidation to take place in the forty-plus years since the 1969 merger of Indianapolis with Marion County. Local citizens—especially suburban citizens—oppose consolidation as a denial of small-scale, accessible government.

A half-century ago, the residents of some of the developing suburbs actually welcomed consolidation as a way to tap into the superior levels of municipal services provided by the established city. In the 1960s, homeowners in the quickly developing rim areas of Nashville and Jacksonville turned to consolidation as a means of gaining paved streets, curbs, gutters, and other municipal improvements. Today, however, suburban residents tend to view such merger plans not as a help but as a threat.

Consolidation can alter the local balance of power. Business interests in Nashville, Jacksonville, and other cities looked to metropolitan restructuring as a way to wrest power away from conservative municipal officials who would not provide financial support for

Table 10.1

City–County Consolidations

Year	City–County	State
1805	New Orleans–Orleans Parish	Louisiana
1821	Boston–Suffolk County	Massachusetts
1821	Nantucket–Nantucket County	Massachusetts
1854	Philadelphia–Philadelphia County	Pennsylvania
1856	San Francisco–San Francisco County	California
1874	New York (Manhattan)–New York County	New York
1984	New York–Bronx and Staten Island	New York
1898	New York–Brooklyn, Queens, and Richmond County	New York
1904	Denver–Arapahoe County	Colorado
1907	Honolulu–Honolulu County	Hawaii
1947	Baton Rouge–East Baton Rouge Parish	Louisiana
1952	Hamilton and Phoebus–Elizabeth City County	Virginia
1957	Newport News–Warwick City County	Virginia
1962	Nashville–Davidson County	Tennessee
1962	Chesapeake–South Norfolk–Norfolk County	Virginia
1962	Virginia Beach–Princess Anne County	Virginia
1967	Jacksonville–Duval County	Florida
1969	Indianapolis–Marion County	Indiana
1969	Carson City–Ormsby County	Nevada
1969	Juneau and Douglas–Greater Juneau Borough	Alaska
1970	Columbus–Muscogee County	Georgia
1971	Holland and Whaleyville–Nansemond County	Virginia
1971	Sitka–Greater Sitka Borough	Alaska
1972	Lexington–Fayette County	Kentucky
1972	Suffolk–Nansemond County	Virginia
1975	Anchorage, Glen Alps, and Girdwood–Greater Anchorage	Alaska
1976	Anaconda–Deer Lodge County	Montana
1976	Butte–Silver Bow County	Montana
1984	Houma–Terrebonne County	Louisiana
1988	Lynchburg–Moore County	Tennessee
1992	Athens–Clarke County	Georgia
1992	Lafayette–Lafayette Parish	Louisiana
1995	Augusta–Richmond County	Georgia
1997	Kansas City (KS)–Wyandotte County	Kansas
2001	Hartsville–Trousdale County	Tennessee
2001	Louisville–Jefferson County	Kentucky
2002	Haines City–Haines Borough	Alaska
2003	Cusseta City–Chattahoochee County	Georgia
2006	Georgetown–Quitman County	Georgia
2007	Tribune–Greeley County	Kansas
2008	Statenville–Echols County	Georgia

Sources: National Association of Counties, Research Division, "Research Brief," 1999; National Association of Counties, "City-County Consolidation Proposals," 2007; Jacqueline Byers, "City-County Consolidation Proposals," a list prepared for the National Association of Counties (2010), www.naco.org/Counties/Documents/CityCountyConsolidationProposals.pdf.

downtown renewal projects. In Indiana, Republican leaders used the creation of Unigov, the merger of Indianapolis and Marion County, to extend their party's control over the city into the coming decades. (See Box 10.3, "Indianapolis: Unigov or Unigrab?")

City–county consolidation also diminishes the prospect of African American control of city hall. At the time of the Jacksonville–Duval County merger, for instance, African Americans made up 40 percent of the central city but only one-fourth of the population of the merged city–county.[8]

Indianapolis' Unigov: Creating a Powerful Engine for Economic Development

In 1969, the Indiana state legislature merged the City of Indianapolis and Marion County to form **Unigov**, a "unified" system of government. As Indiana lacks a strong home-rule tradition, the state legislature was able to order the merger without having to gain explicit approval from the affected local governments.

Local business leaders saw the merger as a means to energize the city, enabling Indianapolis to escape its "Indiana-no-place" image. Overnight, the merger made Indianapolis "major league"; civic leaders claimed that, in terms of population, Indianapolis was the twelfth largest city in the nation (1990 figures). Extending the city's boundaries also increased the assessed total value of property in the city, increasing the amounts of money that the city, under state law, could borrow to support downtown redevelopment and other growth projects.[9]

The merger created a county government with a greater capacity to act cohesively in promoting downtown revitalization and regional economic development. Unigov's mayor presides over what is arguably the strongest regional planning and economic development department in the entire country.[10] The economic team steered new investment to Indianapolis' center, something that the leaders of the old city could not do. The county's suburbs could no longer launch their own development efforts that would undermine downtown revitalization. Unigov planners persuaded the developers of Market Square Arena to locate their new sports facility in the center of the city rather than along an interstate highway. Unigov officials similarly convinced American United Life to abandon plans for a suburban headquarters and instead build a thirty-eight-story downtown office tower, the tallest building in the state, that brought an estimated 1,500 employees into the heart of the city. Unigov's ability to speak with one voice also helped the region win the ninety-three-city national competition for an $800 million United Airlines maintenance facility.[11]

The renaissance of Indianapolis's central core stands as evidence of Unigov's success. Indianapolis built a new professional football and basketball arena and new facilities for amateur tennis, swimming, bicycle racing, and track and field. Indianapolis became the self-proclaimed amateur sports capital of the United States and the home of the National Collegiate Athletic Association. Unigov's success in promoting downtown revitalization compares quite favorably to the situation in Cleveland, where leaders in a politically fragmented region could not organize a similar joint commitment to center-city renewal.[12]

Yet, despite its noteworthy achievements, Unigov also suffers serious limitations and criticisms. Confined to the borders of Marion County, Unigov cannot control

Box 10.3

Indianapolis: Unigov or Unigrab?

The creation of Unigov was motivated by partisan concerns, not just by the need to strengthen planning and economic development in Indiana's capital region. Indiana Democrats charged the state's Republican-controlled legislature with a power grab so brazen that Democrats referred to the move not as Unigov but as "Unigrab." Demographic trends indicated that if Indianapolis' boundaries were left unchanged, the Democrats would soon gain electoral control of the city as a result of the city's growing number of the poor and racial minority voters. But Unigov changed the city's boundaries, effectively adding thousands of suburban residents—a Republican voting bloc—who would help determine the selection of the Unigov mayor and council.

The results of post-consolidation elections underscore the political success of the Republican strategy. In 1975, Republican votes from the suburbs provided their party's mayoral candidate, William Hudnut, with his margin of victory, despite the Democrats having won the "old city" by 17,500 votes. In 1991, Republican Stephen Goldsmith similarly won Unigov's mayoralty, despite Democrats having won the old city by 15,000 votes. It was not until 1999, thirty years after the creation of Unigov, that a Democrat, Bart Peterson, was at long last elected mayor.

Source: The vote tallies are from William Blomquist, "Metropolitan Organization and Local Politics: The Indianapolis-Marion County Experience" (paper presented at the annual meeting of the Midwest Political Science Association, Chicago, April 9–11, 1992).

development in the far parts of a metropolitan region that lie beyond the county's borders. Unigov has also had far less success in social policy than in economic development. While Unigov's efforts have sparked a downtown renewal, the consolidated government has done much less to reverse the decline of Indianapolis' poorer neighborhoods.

The creation of a countywide governing system did not bring about an equalization of services. In fact, the name "Unigov" is actually a misnomer, as government in the county is not really unified. Post-consolidation Marion County has six municipal corporations, nine townships, and more than 100 separate taxing units (including school districts). In 2009, Unigov's mayor, Greg Ballard, called for further governmental consolidation and streamlining efforts,[13] a proposal that the area's townships vigorously opposed.

The existence of separate taxing and service districts not only allowed for continued inequalities in service provision but also meant that center-city district residents were burdened with the costs of paying for the new sports facilities that the residents of outlying service and taxing districts did not have to pay.[14] Nor did unification lead to the racial integration of the region's public schools, for the obvious reason that school districts were intentionally left out of the consolidation plan. Any proposed consolidation that threatened the local control of schools and raised the prospects of racial integration was doomed to failure.

Louisville: Was the Merger Really Necessary?

Louisville's 2001 merger with surrounding Jefferson County gained the city instant national prestige. Louisville's boosters claimed that the city jumped from number sixty-four to become the sixteenth largest city in the nation in terms of population.[15] Civic pride was one factor that drove the consolidation effort. Without the merger, Lexington-Fayette was soon likely to surpass Louisville as Kentucky's most populous city. Advocates further argued that the merger would provide the regional leadership necessary to reverse the decline of the core-city area.

Much like Indianapolis' Unigov, the consolidation of governments in Louisville-Jefferson County was incomplete. While the city of Louisville was removed from the map, eighty-four smaller suburban municipalities continue to maintain their independent existence postconsolidation.[16]

Critics argue that the Louisville consolidation was not all that necessary. Studies across the nation have shown that city–county consolidations seldom produce significant gains in service efficiency, economic development, and racial desegregation.[17] In Louisville, as in other regions, existing interlocal arrangements allow for cooperative action when economies of scale are obvious. In Louisville, city-suburban cooperation went even further. The 1986 Louisville-Jefferson County Compact not only reduced interlocal competition for new economic development but also provided for limited tax sharing, redistributing over $5 million a year in fiscal assistance to the city.[18] Louisville's suburbs had agreed to the compact as a means of warding off possible annexation by the city.[19]

The region's growth elites had argued that metropolitan reform would promote economic development in Louisville.[20] While the new Metro government did help to facilitate new investment in both the downtown and the suburbs, it brought little new investment and revitalization to inner-city residential neighborhoods where community projects failed to excite the region's growth coalition.[21] The existence of numerous service and taxing districts meant that there was no influx of suburban resources to help battle inner-city ills: the residents of Louisville's troubled inner-city neighborhoods were "just as poor after consolidation as before."[22] The merger, however, did adversely affect the prospects of black electoral power. African Americans, 34 percent of the old city's population, won less than a quarter (6 of 26) of the initial elections to the Metro Louisville council.

Overall, data show that the creation of Louisville's Metro had only limited economic effects, that merger was no "breakthrough" event that jump-started the local economy in the city and the region. The years immediately following consolidation saw no sharp escalation in employment, payrolls, or other measures of economic growth.[23]

MIAMI'S TWO-TIERED SYSTEM

Created in 1957, Miami's **two-tiered system** of metropolitan government was once hailed as a model for urban regions across the nation. The new model assigned a number of important planning responsibilities to a strengthened Dade County government while local governments continued to perform other municipal functions. There was no consolidation of governmental units, and no local government faded from existence. Instead, Metro-Dade was given new authority and additional resources to tackle problems that were regional in scope.

The creation of Metro-Dade led to improvements in areas such as mass transit, highway construction, countywide land-use planning, social service provision, voter registration, and countywide tax assessment and administration. Metro-Dade brought a new professionalization to municipal government, an upgrading that posed quite a contrast to the episodes of corruption, maladministration, and patronage abuses that continued to plague the city of Miami, Hialeah, and other municipalities in the region.

But over the half century since Metro-Dade's creation, no U.S. region has copied the two-tiered model, a reflection of the strong political opposition to such major metropolitan restructuring. It is even doubtful that the two-tiered system could be created today in the Miami area. Over the years, Dade County's more wealthy communities—Miami Beach, Surfside, Golden Beach, Bal Harbour, and North Bay Village—have repeatedly attempted, without success, to secede from the arrangement. Hundreds of lawsuits have also been filed in an attempt to diminish the authority of the regional government.[24]

Like Indianapolis' Unigov, Metro-Dade is also limited in terms of its geographic reach. As the governing arrangement for only a single county, Metro-Dade lacks the ability to plan or control development in a growing region that spills into neighboring Broward (Fort Lauderdale), Monroe, and Palm Beach counties.

Creating New Metropolitan Governments: Portland and Minnesota's Twin Cities

The Greater Portland (Oregon) Metropolitan Service District and the Twin Cities (Minneapolis-St. Paul) Metropolitan Council are the most prominent examples of the three-tiered approach to metropolitan government, which adds a new regional government atop the existing municipal and county levels of government.

Portland

The Portland Metropolitan Service District (commonly called "Metro") is unique as it is the only directly elected multicounty regional government in the United States. Metro's authority cuts across the region's twenty-four cities and three counties.

Oregon state law gives Metro real authority in areas such as land use, environmental protection, and transportation planning. Oregon law mandates that local land-use and zoning regulations comply with the overall framework set by Metro. As we saw in Chapter 9, Metro sets the region's urban growth boundary. Metro has sought to "build up" as opposed to "build out" the Portland area, with planning efforts that promote downtown revitalization and infill projects as an alternative to sprawl. Portland planners have also channeled new development to growth nodes along light-rail lines.

Oregon state law also gives Metro the responsibility to formulate an affordable housing plan that details how each of the district's twenty-four cities will accept their proportionate share of low- and moderate-income housing units. Metro's actions in this area have led to the greater availability of apartments and small-lot housing in Portland's suburbs than is typical of suburbs in the United States.

While Portland has arguably the most powerful metropolitan government in the nation, in important ways its authority is still quite limited. Metro "is at once path-breaking as a mode of regional governance yet benign in its functions."[25] Metro's "budget is piddling by comparison to many other governmental units."[26] Existing municipalities, not Metro, retain responsibility for most service provision. Metro's greatest successes have come in the provision of physical infrastructure and maintenance of quality-of-life and environmental concerns. Metro has been much less active in social policy and racial integration matters.[27]

The Twin Cities Met Council

In 1969 the Minnesota state legislature created the Twin Cities Metropolitan Council in order to cope with the rapid growth taking place in the seven-county capital region. Over the years, the Met Council, the region's planning organization, has gained additional powers in areas such as sewers, wastewater management, open space protection, transportation, airport construction, and the development of stadiums and sports facilities. The Met Council can also levy property taxes and issue bonds, important financial powers that are seldom given to the regional planning bodies found in other U.S. metropolitan areas.

The Met Council formulates a **metropolitan development guide**, a "blueprint" or "binding plan" that designates certain areas of the county for concentrated development while safeguarding farmland and other areas from development incursions and sprawl. The Met Council also serves as the region's housing authority and has even enjoyed a certain limited success in dispersing subsidized housing units into the suburbs.[28]

Unlike Portland's Metro and Indianapolis' Unigov, however, the members of the Twin Cities Met Council are not elected, but are appointed by the governor. Appointment rather than election places an important limitation on the Met Council's power, denying it the legitimacy, visibility, and leadership potential that derives from popular election. Various members of the Met Council felt that they had little alternative but to approve the construction of the suburban Mall of America despite the adverse effects that the megamall might have on older shopping centers in the region; the Met Council lacked the political independence to challenge a project favored by the governor.[29]

The Met Council has also been quite restrained in its efforts to push the development of affordable housing in the region's better-off suburbs. Despite the goals set by metropolitan housing plans, more affluent suburbs have still been able to use exclusionary zoning ordinances to keep out low-income housing.[30] Lacking political support for "fair-share" housing efforts, the Met Council turned to a policy of noninterference, seeking the construction of public housing only in communities willing to accept new units. In 1986, the council even defined houses costing $120,000 as "affordable," enabling virtually all communities in the region to meet their assigned affordable-housing goals without really opening their communities to families in need.[31]

Indoor Amusement Park at The Mall of America, The Twin Cities. The Met Council had no ability to challenge the building of the suburban Mall of America, a mega economic development project that had the backing of the state's governor and other pro-growth officials. Copyright © Jeremy Noble. http://commons.wikimedia.org/wiki/File:Mall_of_America-2005-05-29.jpg.

The Twin Cities area has also gained renown for its system of **regional tax-base sharing**, another initiative enacted by the Minnesota state legislature. Under the state's tax-base sharing or **fiscal disparities** law, 40 percent of the net value of all new construction does not go to the local government in which the development is sited. Instead, those revenues are placed in a pool for distribution to localities throughout the region according to their population and need.

Tax-base sharing has smoothed out some of the inequalities of local tax bases in the Twin Cities region, providing additional assistance to the poorer communities, especially to blue-collar suburbs. The region's two major cities, however, have not always gained money from tax-base sharing. In more recent years, Minneapolis has been the site of substantial new downtown development and, as a result, has contributed to the pool of money that is redistributed to other communities.[32]

No community likes to share tax revenues with its neighbors, and the region's better-off suburbs have bitterly attacked the plan. (See Box 10.4, "Jesse 'The Body' Ventura Views Regional Government.") The program, however, continues to maintain the support of the Minnesota legislature, despite constant calls for the law's repeal.

Box 10.4

Jesse "The Body" Ventura Views Regional Government

In 1998, Minnesotans elected the former professional wrestler, Jesse "The Body" Ventura, as governor. Ventura was not just a pro-wrestling and television personality, he had also served as mayor of Brooklyn Park, a Twin Cities suburb, rising to power as an antitax populist highly critical of big government. Brooklyn Park's so-called Legion of Doom vigorously opposed both taxes and requirements that communities build low-income housing.

Throughout his political career, Ventura was a sharp critic of tax-base sharing and other efforts at regionalism. But as mayor of Brooklyn Park, a low-property-value suburb that received much-needed tax-sharing funds, Ventura came to see some value in the regional mechanisms he previously scorned.

When he later moved to affluent Maple Grove and began his career as a radio talk-show host, Ventura once again emerged as an outspoken critic of regionalism. He sharply castigated the fiscal disparities law and tax-base-sharing efforts promoted by state legislator Myron Orfield:

> Representative Myron "the Communist" Orfield, his latest wealth-sharing strategy, I mean this guy really needs to go to China. I mean I think he'd be most happy there. Oh Myron, Myron, Myron. You never realized the communists folded for a reason. You didn't figure it out, did you Myron?[1]

On his radio show, Ventura continued to talk about abolishing the Met Council. But, as governor, he came to see the value of Met Council actions in the effort to avert Los Angeles-style sprawl, to "protect what we love about Minnesota."[2] He made the Met Council the lead agency in implementing the state's Smart Growth and multimodal transportation initiatives.

Still, Ventura favored the creation of a less bureaucratic and less didactic Met Council. He wanted a regional body that would be flexible and open to working in partnership with suburban communities, not one that imposed unwanted social policies on localities.[3]

[1]Myron Orfield, *Metropolitics: A Regional Agenda for Community and Stability* (Washington, DC: Brookings Institution Press, 1997), 109–110. The quotation appears on page 149.

[2]Governor Jesse Ventura, address to the "Growing Smart in Minnesota Conference," June 11, 1999.

[3]Ted Mondale and William Fulton, "Managing Metropolitan Growth: Reflections on the Twin Cities Experience," case study prepared for the Brookings Institution Center on Urban and Metropolitan Policy, Washington, DC, September 2003.

Whatever its limitations, the Twin Cities Met Council, like Portland's Metro, represents the most expansive model of multicounty regional government in the United States. Regional government faces strong opposition. Were they not already in existence, it is highly questionable whether the Minnesota state government would today be willing to vote for the creation of the Met Council and regional tax-base sharing.[33]

IS METROPOLITAN GOVERNMENT DESIRABLE? TWO SCHOOLS OF THOUGHT

There are two sharply contrasting schools of thought regarding the desirability of metropolitan restructuring. **Metropolitanists** seek a centralized government that can provide more efficient, uniform, and equitable service provision across the metropolis. Environmentalists argue for a strong regional system that would constrain the self-seeking actions of localities that promote sprawl. Metropolitanists also point to **economies of scale** or the cost savings that are gained when bulk purchases are made or when services are provided on a large-scale basis. A regional police or fire force, for instance, would allow for the closing of duplicate local police and fire stations.

Polycentrists, in contrast, doubt that metropolitan government is an ideal worth pursuing. They see great virtue in having a multitude of local governments in a region and are critical of proposals that would place greater powers in the hands of centralized metropolitan bodies. Smaller-scale governments offer citizens increased accessibility and responsiveness. Polycentrists also argue that small-scale service provision may oftentimes prove to be more cost-effective than having services provided on a metropolitan basis.

PUBLIC CHOICE THEORY: DEFENDING THE POLYCENTRIC METROPOLIS

Polycentrism is rooted in **public choice theory**, which argues that individuals vary in their demand for services and the level of taxes they are willing to pay. A single centralized government providing a uniform set of services throughout a region cannot possibly respond to the great variety of citizen preferences. The smaller-scale governments of metropolitan fragmentation, in contrast, allow citizens to choose from a greater range of service and taxing "packages," maximizing overall citizen satisfaction. Citizens who desire finely maintained public parks and high-quality recreational services can choose to live in a community that offers such high-level amenities at a higher rate of taxation. Citizens who do not wish to pay high taxes can choose to reside in another community that keeps taxes low and focuses almost exclusively on the provision of basic municipal services.

Polycentrists also reject the metropolitanists' contention that bigger is better, that a metropolitan government saves taxpayer money by taking advantage of economies of scale. Public choice theorists argue that economies of scale seldom exist. Instead, urban service delivery is often characterized by **diseconomies of scale**, where the large size of an organization leads to waste and inefficiency. Polycentrists argue that large-scale metropolitan governments will tend to be bloated, wasteful, bureaucratized, and unresponsive to citizens.

Evidence from past city-county mergers shows that major political consolidations seldom produce the cost savings that metropolitanists predict. Where savings do result, they tend to be concentrated in a few administrative areas. The cost savings gained from consolidation also fade over time as service providers tend to "level up" municipal wages and benefits across the region to the highest levels found in the metropolis.[34] In a consolidated system, it is difficult for municipal officials to justify giving lower remuneration to a firefighter or bus driver in one part of the region when higher pay and benefits are offered to similar workers in other parts of the region.

Public choice theory applies market theories in defense of the fragmented or polycentric metropolis.[35] Public choice theorists contend that **interlocal competition** for businesses and more desirable residents spurs communities to place greater emphasis on efficient service delivery. To attract good businesses and residents, municipal leaders have to search for new ways to provide high-quality services while keeping taxes low.

Polycentrists further argue that even where economies of scale can be found, there is no need to create a centralized metropolitan government. Instead, local communities voluntarily join in cooperative service arrangements that save money.

Criticisms of Public Choice's Defense of the Fragmented Metropolis

Public choice theorists have constructed a highly articulate defense of the fragmented metropolis. They have also pointed to a number of shortcomings in the metropolitan government ideal. Yet, the public choice theory suffers shortcomings of its own.

While bigger is often bureaucratic, there are also times when consolidation does actually produce new efficiencies and cost savings. The consolidation movement achieved its greatest success in the area of public education, where mergers slashed the number of school districts in the United States from 117,000 (in 1940) to just 14,200 (in 2005).[36] Consolidation eliminated thousands of tiny school districts that were too small to take advantage of volume discounts in purchasing and other economies of scale. The mergers allowed for the elimination of redundant administrative positions. Medium-size and large school districts also had the ability to offer students a variety of specialized programs that the tiny districts could not offer.[37]

Not all citizens have the ability to choose a community in which they would like to live. In fact, the choices exercised by more privileged residents can reduce the choices available to the working class and the poor. Exclusionary zoning and land-use regulations in upscale suburbs limit the free-market production of rental units and other forms of affordable housing, denying working- and even lower-middle-class families the opportunity to move into the communities they prefer.

Interlocal competition also does not always lead lagging communities to upgrade their performance, as public choice theorists assert. A region's more distressed communities may simply lack the resources necessary to make much-needed alterations in service provision. In such cases, "competition feeds upon itself and makes the competitive more competitive, and the noncompetitive more noncompetitive."[38]

Public choice theorists correctly point out that extensive intergovernmental cooperation already exists in metropolitan areas. Yet, jurisdictions cooperate only when they find it to their mutual advantage to do so. There is little voluntary resource sharing and joint action in combating such serious social problems as the isolation of the poor or the racial imbalance of public school systems. Nor, as we have already seen, do communities always find it in their self-interest to cooperate in the pursuit of environmentally sound, sustainable patterns of development.

REGIONAL COOPERATION, OLD STYLE

As public choice theorists have underscored, regional action does not require the creation of a metropolitan government. Instead, a variety of interlocal cooperative arrangements offer flexible responses to regional problems.

INFORMAL COOPERATION AND JOINT POWERS AGREEMENTS

Informal cooperation occurs when two or more localities share equipment or work together to improve a service, with no agreement spelled out in writing. Casual arrangements, however, often evolve into a formalized **joint powers agreement**, a legally binding arrangement that spells out each community's contribution, say, to support a shared firefighters' training center. Many metropolitan areas have fairly simple joint powers agreements that allow residents to patronize the libraries of neighboring communities. In other cases, a joint powers agreement can be quite complex and detailed. The agreement between Dallas and Fort Worth that sets the terms for the financing and operations of the region's international airport runs well over 100 pages.[39]

Mutual aid agreements, where localities commit to helping one another in times of emergency, are typified by the compact of Thornton and Westminster, Colorado, to back up each other's computer system in the event of a disaster.[40] The inadequacy of the New York region's immediate response to the attacks on the World Trade Center underscores the importance of mutual aid agreements. Prior to the 9/11 attacks, neighboring jurisdictions were leery about entering into agreements with an agency as huge as the Fire Department of New York (FDNY). As a result, on 9/11 the FDNY had no clear procedures or practiced routines in place to direct the utilization of first responders and reinforcements from Nassau and Westchester counties and other communities in the region; the initial resonse to the emergency was poorly coordinated.[41]

Informal understandings provide the basis for interlocal action across national borders, where the intricacies of international law may preclude cities from signing formal agreements. San Diego (California) and Tijuana (Mexico) have responded to their mutual dependency with innovative, often informal, measures of cross-border collaboration. (See Box 10. 5, "San Diego and Tijuana: Collaboration in a Cross-Border Metropolis.") Nongovernmental organizations have similarly demanded that law-enforcement agencies in El Paso (Texas) extend their assistance across the border to help officials combat the growing problem of femicides—the murder of hundreds of women—and the escalating drug-gang violence in Ciudad Juárez (Mexico).[42]

INTERGOVERNMENTAL SERVICE CONTRACTING

A municipality does not always have to provide a service with its own workers: where state law allows, a locality can sign an **intergovernmental service contract**, agreeing to buy a service provided by another city or a county. Contracting allows municipalities to "pool" their resources and share in the bulk purchasing discounts and other economies of scale that a large jurisdiction enjoys. Smaller communities contract for

Box 10.5

San Diego and Tijuana: Collaboration in a Cross-Border Metropolis

Over the years, cooperation between San Diego, California, and Tijuana, Mexico, has become increasingly commonplace. Officials from the two cities meet to coordinate disaster response plans, to regulate traffic, to share intelligence on street gangs, to arrange ride-along exchanges for police officers, and to promote the economic development of the region, tourism, and even recycling.

Local law-enforcement agencies work, often informally, with their counterparts across the border. Under Mexico's centralized political system, municipalities generally lack the authority to enter into formal joint efforts to combat drug trafficking and to maintain homeland security.[1] The United States Constitution bars state and local governments from negotiating their own agreements with foreign nations. As a result, in policing and other service areas, many of the collaborative efforts by Tijuana and San Diego are limited to informal understandings.

The interdependence of two cities, however, does at times require joint action that extends beyond informal understandings. The commitments of extensive sums of money to construct a light-rail system to connect the two downtowns necessitated a binding cooperative arrangement. The Agreement on Binational Cooperation formalized a number of joint cross-border actions. San Diego residents pressed for the construction of new sewage facilities to lessen untreated effluent from Tijuana that washes up on California beaches. Local officials have also discussed the construction of an international airport that would straddle the border.

[1]José María Ramos, "Managing Transborder Cooperation on Public Security: The Tijuana-San Diego Region," University of California, San Diego, Center for U.S.-Mexican Studies, October 2003, http://repositories.cdlib.org/usmex/ramos/.

services that they could not possibly afford to provide on their own. Many suburbs, for instance, purchase their water from a central-city municipal system.

The **Lakewood Plan** is perhaps the most expansive variant of intergovernmental service contracting in the United States. The Lakewood Plan offers communities in Los Angeles County an extremely large "menu" of services that they can choose to purchase from the county. Under the Lakewood Plan, a municipality may decide not to maintain a municipal police force, and instead arrange to have the county provide police services, with a legally binding contract specifying the frequency of patrols, the number of officers in each patrol car, and the price that the city will pay for the service. The plan takes its name from the city of Lakewood, which incorporated in 1954 and became the first community to contract with the county for law enforcement and other services. (See Box 10.6, "The Lakewood Plan: Cure or Contributor to Metropolitan Fragmentation?")

Communities in Los Angeles County routinely contract with the county for service provision. Smaller communities may even choose to purchase nearly all of their services from the county, maintaining only a skeletal municipal workforce of their own. In 2010, the city of Maywood, a poor Latino community southeast of

Box 10.6

The Lakewood Plan: Cure or Contributor to Metropolitan Fragmentation?

Under the Lakewood Plan, a municipality can contract to have Los Angeles County provide a large range of municipal services. The arrangement offers communities—especially smaller communities—the ability to secure high-quality, professional services and to save money by taking advantage of economies of scale. But the Lakewood Plan, especially in its early years, also catalyzed a rash of new municipal incorporations (where previously unincorporated areas become official communities recognized under state law), exacerbating metropolitan fragmentation by increasing the number of autonomous governmental entities in the region. Residents incorporated the City of Lakewood, and turned to the county for service provision, as a means of warding off annexation by the neighboring city of Long Beach.

The Lakewood Plan led to the creation of a number of **minimal cities**—small, independent suburban jurisdictions that bought most of their services from the county. The new municipalities became centers of "white flight" as residents sought escape from the region's troubled core cities. The newly established suburbs used their zoning and land-use powers to exclude low-income and renter populations. Rancho Palos Verdes enacted land-use regulations that blocked new development, thereby preserving the community's exclusive, estate-like character.

Business interests engineered a number of the early municipal incorporations, with the new communities relying on the county for service provision. Chief executive officers saw incorporation as a more desirable alternative to annexation by a neighboring city, as the latter move would have raised taxes on a business' extensive property holdings. The strange names of a number of the newly created Lakewood communities reflect their industrial and commercial roots. The City of Industry was created as a tax island to shelter the railroad yards, factories, and warehouses within its borders. In order to meet the minimum population of 500 required for incorporation, the city had to count the 169 patients and 31 employees of a local psychiatric sanitarium! At the time it was incorporated, the town had only 624 residents. In the year 2000, tiny Industry still had a population of only 777. The City of Industry levies no taxes on industrial or residential property.

The City of Commerce was similarly created as a tax haven for railroad and industrial property that faced the threat of higher levels of taxation that would accompany annexation. The City of Dairy Valley was a **tax island** created to protect large agricultural land holdings. As Dairy Valley grew, the community changed its name to Cerritos, but only after agricultural interests had profited by selling their acreage to developers.

Sources: Gary J. Miller, *Cities by Contract: The Politics of Municipal Incorporation* (Cambridge, MA: MIT Press, 1981); Christopher G. Boone and Ali Modarres, "Creating a Toxic Neighborhood in Los Angeles County: A Historical Examination of Environmental Inequity," *Urban Affairs Review* 35, no. 2 (November 1999): 163–187; William A. Fischel, *The Homevoter Hypothesis: How Home Values Influence Local Government Taxation, School Finance, and Land-Use Policies* (Cambridge, MA: Harvard University Press, 2001), 221–228.

Los Angeles, in the face of mounting budget shortfalls, dismissed its entire municipal workforce—police officers, school-crossing guards, and other public workers. Maywood outsourced law enforcement to the Los Angeles County Sheriff's Department and signed other contracts to have other municipal services provided by a neighboring community and by private firms.[43]

Councils of Governments and Regional Planning Councils

A **council of governments (COG)** is a voluntary association of the top-elected official of each municipality in a region. To a great degree, a COG is a "United Nations" of the cities and suburbs in a region. A council of governments provides a forum for members to discuss matters of common interest. The COG's staff helps to identify potential solutions to regional problems. But, much like the United Nations, the COG possesses little authority to enforce action on unwilling members.

COGs are found in metropolises across the United States. Noteworthy COGs include the Metropolitan Washington Council of Governments, the Baltimore Metropolitan Council (BMC), the Association of Bay Area Governments (ABAG) in greater San Francisco, the Southern California Association of Governments (SCAG), the San Diego Association of Governments (SANDAG), the Houston-Galveston Area Council, and the Southeast Michigan Council of Governments (SEMCOG) in the greater Detroit area.

A **regional planning council (RPC)** is a staff-dominated organization that is quite similar to a COG, but without the region's mayors and city managers assembling to direct the organization's activities. Instead, an appointed executive director determines the areas of RPC research and planning activities.

COGs and RPCS are weak regional organizations. First and foremost, these bodies are only advisory: they possess no legislative power, no ability to raise money through taxes, and no authority to force local governments to follow a regional plan. In the greater Chicago area, the Northeastern Illinois Planning Commission has been unable to impose any serious constraints on the continued growth of suburban communities.[44] Governments in a region often ignore COG recommendations. When more aggressive COGs such as SCAG and ABAG push **fair-share housing** plans, suburban jurisdictions often remain out of compliance, failing to meet the targets set for them by the region's affordable housing plan.[45] At times, disgruntled members even threaten to pull out of a COG. In southern California, Orange County officials seriously discussed withdrawing from SCAG.[46]

COGs shy away from recommending controversial courses of action, especially in housing and social policy, that may estrange member municipalities. COGs cannot afford to offend dues-paying members. COGs survive by helping member governments, by providing technical assistance to communities, and by aiding members in their applications for federal and state grants.[47]

Regional planning bodies, though, have gained prominence in one important program area, transportation planning. Under the federal government's **Intermodal Surface Transportation and Efficiency Act (ISTEA**, commonly pronounced "Ice Tea" and later revised as **TEA-21**, the Transportation Equity Act for the 21st Century), a COG or RPC may serve as the **Metropolitan Planning Organization (MPO)**, "a voice for metropolitan areas"[48] in planning balanced transportation systems for a better environment. MPOs can even take a portion of the funds that were previously devoted to highways and instead use the money to support the extension of commuter rail and bus routes. In Salt Lake City, Denver, Dallas, Charlotte, Las Vegas, San Jose, and San Diego, MPOs used the ISTEA/TEA-21 process to increase the funding of light-rail systems.[49] But in other metropolitan areas, weak and understaffed COGs have not been able to fight state highway departments and the many advocates of continued highway construction.[50]

Even in the area of transportation planning, their singular area of authority, COGs and MPOs are reluctant to alienate members. The Baltimore Metropolitan Council (BMC) sought to avoid hard choices on transportation projects that would alienate members; instead, the BMC helped members to pursue federal funding for their "wish lists" of transportation projects.[51]

COGs are not directly elected and, as a result, lack the legitimacy that derives from popular election. As an intergovernmental organization, COGs do not abide by one-person-one-vote rules; instead, each member jurisdiction, regardless of size, has a single vote. Such a voting system underrepresents a region's more populous cities and suburbs.[52]

SPECIAL DISTRICTS

There are nearly 90,000 units of local government in the United States (see Table 10.2). Most are narrow-purpose **special districts**, autonomous bodies that provide a single specific service (such as drainage and flood control, solid waste management, fire protection, water supply, community college administration, or assisted housing) or a set of related services. Special districts lack the visibility of general-purpose cities, counties, villages, and townships, the bodies that most Americans generally think about when they discuss "local government."

Over half of the units of local government in the United States are school districts and other special districts. In 2007, there were over 37,000 special districts, of which more than 90 percent handled only a single function.[53] Another 13,000 independent local school districts were responsible for K–12 education.

The size of a special district can vary considerably by service function. Special districts for libraries, fire protection, and local recreation often have quite small service areas. By contrast, the Metropolitan Sanitary District of Greater Chicago and the Forest Preserve District of Cook County each serves a geographical area larger than the city of Chicago.

The majority of special districts, including independent school districts, have the authority to levy taxes. Others can impose user fees and charges. As a result of the voter-imposed restrictions that limit taxing and borrowing by cities and other general-purpose local governments, special districts have gained a new prominence in providing local services, picking up some of the slack in public service provision.

Special districts can cross normal local political borders, allowing for the capture of economies of scale by providing services over a larger area. In some cases, spe-

Table 10.2

Number of Local Governmental Units in the United States

Type of government	1952	1962	1972	1982	1992	2002	2007
County	3,052	3,043	3,044	3,041	3,043	3,034	3,033
Municipal	16,807	18,000	18,517	19,076	19,279	19,429	19,492
Town/Township	17,202	17,142	16,991	16,734	16,656	16,504	16,519
School district	67,355	34,678	15,781	14,851	14,422	13,506	13,051
Special district	12,340	18,323	23,885	28,078	31,555	35,052	37,381
Total number of local governments	116,756	91,186	78,218	81,780	84,955	87,525	89,478

Source: U.S. Department of Commerce, Bureau of the Census, 2002 Census of Governments, GC02–1(P), and 2007 Census of Governments IGC07(1)-1.

cial districts can even help address issues of service equity. Suburban taxpayers, for instance, help to fund the Milwaukee Technical College, a special-district institution that disproportionately serves central-city residents.[54]

Yet, the existence of so many special districts can also compound problems of governmental fragmentation. The existence of numerous independent bodies adds to the difficulties of service coordination in the metropolis. Special districts are also relatively **invisible and unaccountable government**. Newspapers and television devote little coverage to district boards. Most citizens are unaware of the existence of, and cannot name the officials in charge of, community college districts, sewer and water districts, and other specialized units of local government. Private developers and real estate interests have been able to dominate the boards of urban fringe districts that provide the funding for new sewers, water mains, and other infrastructure improvements necessary for new development on the edges of a metropolis. Developers use these districts to support growth projects and shield them from oversight and control by general-purposed governments.[55] (See Box 10.7, "Does Walt Disney World have Its Own Government?") The invisibility of special districts raises important questions regarding their lack of democracy and accountability.[56]

Regional Districts and Authorities

State law can establish **regional districts and authorities** that are more powerful, metropolitan-wide variants of the special district. The Bay Area Rapid Transit District, the Southern California Metropolitan Water District, the Massachusetts Bay Transit Authority, the Chicago Metropolitan Sanitary District, and the Seattle Port District are all important regional districts.

The Port Authority of New York and New Jersey possesses broad powers in a number of service areas, with policy responsibilities that go well beyond maintaining the freight terminals and shipping facilities in the New York–New Jersey region. The Port Authority is involved in highway and bridge construction, commuter rail and airport operations, the maintenance of a giant bus terminal in midtown Manhattan, and regional planning. As we saw in Chapter 1, the Port Authority built the original

Box 10.7

Does Walt Disney World Have Its Own Government?

When the Disney Corporation sought to build Walt Disney World, one of its first actions was to get the Florida legislature to create a forty-square-mile special district, the Reedy Creek Improvement District. The 1967 establishment of the special district essentially meant that Disney would not have to ask the elected officials of Orlando, Kissimmee, or any other municipality for approval of its development plans. Within the forty-square-mile zone of the Reedy Creek Improvement District, Disney effectively assumed the powers of local government, with the ability to make decisions concerning land use, building codes, police and fire service, drainage, sewer line extensions, and other infrastructure investment. As a unit of local government, Disney was even able to issue public bonds, borrowing money at low cost to finance its theme-park-centered development. Having gained control of its own special local government, the Disney Corporation did not have to worry that local political actors, not loyal to the Disney vision, would impose unwanted taxes, impact fees, environmental safeguards, and requirements for subsidized housing.

Disney officials dominated the Reedy Creek District, which had a relatively small residential population. When the Disney Corporation launched an effort to build the new residential town of Celebration, Florida, it made sure to de-annex or detach the development site from the Reedy Creek District. The new homeowners in Celebration would not be permitted to have a say over Disney's affairs and plans for expansion.

Sources: Richard Foglesong, "When Disney Comes to Town," in *The Politics of Urban America: A Reader,* ed. Dennis R. Judd and Paul P. Kantor (Boston: Allyn and Bacon, 1998), 238–241 and Richard E. Foglesong, *Married to the Mouse: Walt Disney World and Orlando* (New Haven, CT: Yale University Press, 2003).

World Trade Center and was a major player in the post-9/11 reconstruction efforts at Ground Zero.

Regional districts and authorities get important things done but raise important questions of accountability. To whom do these districts answer? Regional authorities "are frequently as accountable to bond buyers as to the localities and the citizen consumers."[57] During the 1970s, the directors of the Port Authority of New York and New Jersey neglected the region's ailing commuter rail system, which was deemed a never-ending "bad" investment, and instead continued to promote road construction.[58]

Despite its responsibilities for regional planning, the Port Authority provides only a weak vehicle of metropolitan cooperation.[59] The Port Authority could not get state and local governments in the New York–New Jersey region to respect the "nonaggression pact" to which state and local officials had earlier agreed. The governments had promised that they would not offer tax incentives and other subsidies in an effort to lure businesses away from neighboring communities. The agreement, however, proved short-lived. New York officials were outraged when the State of New Jersey offered to help pay for the cross-river relocation of over 1,000 First Chicago Trust jobs from the corporation's offices in Lower Manhattan.[60]

STRENGTHENED COUNTY GOVERNMENT

Counties were once America's "forgotten governments"[61]—viewed as backward, rural-oriented, and understaffed entities generally incapable of effective action. In more recent years, however, this view has changed considerably. Urban and suburban counties have modernized their structures and improved their problem-solving abilities. They have tapped new sources of revenue, restructured their operations to provide stronger executive leadership, and assumed new service responsibilities in law enforcement, social services, housing assistance, workforce training, and economic development.[62]

But even a strengthened and modernized urban county faces a very important limitation when it comes to regional action. No county can govern beyond its borders. In the more than 150 metropolitan areas that spill over two or more counties, even a reinvigorated county government can provide, at best, only a subregional basis for metropolitan action.

TOWARD A NEW REGIONALISM: REGIONAL GOVERN*ANCE*, NOT REGIONAL GOVERN*MENT*

Clearly, the large variety of informal and formal cooperative arrangements has enabled improved and more cost-efficient service delivery in the metropolis. Still, such vehicles of cooperation are limited and do not provide for the more extensive collaborative arrangements that would enable communities in a region to compete more effectively with other regions around the world. Business executives and local economic development officials have come to recognize the importance of mobilizing economic efforts that transcend local political borders. Communities that join together in designing plans that meet the needs of business will find that they enjoy greater success in attracting new jobs and development. Regions that fail to practice such collaboration will suffer continued economic decline.

New Regionalism denotes the move toward intergovernmental collaborations that extend beyond the more formalized structures of cooperation described above. The Allegheny Conference on Community Development, Cleveland Tomorrow, and the Greater Houston Partnership are a few of the more noteworthy new-style **public–private partnerships**—where business leaders and local officials have created new forums for regional economic action.[63]

The Allegheny Conference brought together private, nonprofit, and public institutions in an effort to "re-vision" a Pittsburgh region not as a declining center of an aging steel manufacturing industry but as an important high-tech and office-headquarters city in a postindustrial global economy. Private-sector groups helped to underwrite a planning process that overcame the severe political fragmentation of a region that has over 300 units of government in Allegheny County alone.[64] The Greater Pittsburgh Chamber of Commerce and other industrial councils launched a second public–private umbrella organization, the Pittsburgh Regional Alliance, to further enhance collaboration for economic development.[65] Across the continent, the San Diego Regional Economic Development Corporation and BIOCOM (an industry association) joined with local governments, the San Diego Association of Governments, and the region's universities in a similar public–private effort to direct the transformation of the region's post–Cold War economy, seeking to replace defense-related manufacturing with new biotechnology and biomedical jobs.[66]

New Regionalists contend that "regional cooperation makes for optimal economic growth."[67] A private employer does not look at what an individual municipality can provide but at whether or not the region can offer the quality labor, transportation, and infrastructure essential for a firm's continued growth. A high-tech firm, for instance, will choose to locate its headquarters in a well-to-do technoburb only if it is reasonably certain that transportation arrangements and education and job training efforts will allow the firm to draw qualified workers from surrounding communities.

A region stands its greatest chances of winning a major new corporation if it can present a clear plan for "holistic economic development,"[68] a multifaceted strategy that details how the various communities in the region will work together to provide the transportation, quality labor, infrastructure improvements, and workforce housing that meet a firm's needs.

Standing alone, no city or suburb can provide the airports, universities, land, transportation, material resources, and trained labor force demanded by businesses.[69] Indeed, the United States can be viewed as being made up of a number of **local economic regions** where the "economic fates and fortunes of cities and suburbs are inextricably interwoven."[70] As Theodore Hershberg has observed, "The most important lesson that the global economy teaches is that regions—not cities or counties—will be the units of economic competition."[71]

When the Boeing Corporation announced that it was moving its headquarters out of Seattle, its officers announced that the corporation wanted to relocate in a culturally diverse community with a probusiness environment. Rather than receive development proposals from thousands of communities across the United States, Boeing requested that communities in the Denver, Dallas-Fort Worth, and Chicago metropolitan areas come up with joint regional proposals that would meet Boeing's needs. Compared to Denver and Dallas, the greater Chicago area lacked a strong tradition of interlocal collaboration, and individual localities initially (but unsuccessfully) attempted to approach Boeing on their own. Governor George Ryan and Chicago Mayor Richard M. Daley quickly acted to impose regional discipline, organizing a Blue Ribbon Commission that put together the joint incentive package that brought Boeing's headquarters to Chicago.[72]

The Boeing case study illustrates the New Regionalism, where ad hoc public–private partnerships emerge and cross existing political boundaries in order to "win" the competition for economic development. The old-style means of regional cooperation discussed earlier in this chapter were largely focused on achieving cost savings and economies of scale. The New Regionalism, in contrast, is focused less on efficiency and more on joint undertakings for economic development.

The New Regionalism emphasizes **gover*nance***, not govern*ment*.[73] As evident in the competition for Boeing, New Regionalism efforts do not entail the creation of new bodies of metropolitan government. Instead, New Regionalism seeks pragmatic solutions, ad hoc and less rule-bound means of cooperation outside the structures of government. New Regionalism seeks to get things done—gover*nance*—without creating new units of govern*ment*.

But even supporters of the New Regionalism recognize a potential danger in creating new action-oriented forums, outside of government, that are so greatly influenced by business actors. The business-led partnerships can act as **shadow governments**, making important decisions regarding future investment in a region, with no clear accountability to the public. Such regional collaborations often lack the full insistence on transparency and public participation that is necessary to ensure that public–private partnerships do not narrowly reflect the interests of the business community.[74]

MOVING BEYOND BUSINESS-LED REGIONALISM: BUILDING CREATIVE REGIONAL ALLIANCES

Can New Regionalism extend to policy areas beyond economic development? Myron Orfield argues that creative alliance building can lead to regional action even in areas such as social and environmental policy. Orfield argues that central cities, declining inner-ring suburbs, and rapidly growing middle-income suburbs (growing communities that can ill afford the costs of new roads and schools) will jointly share in the benefits of actions that redirect economic development, school aid, and various other subsidies away from a region's "favored quarter" of wealthier communities.[75]

Smart Growth, for instance, can use the goal of green space and farmland preservation to bring together a coalition of central cities, inner-ring suburbs, environmentalists, and agriculture interests. In Ohio, the First Suburbs Consortium joined with farmers to support an Agricultural Preservation Act to preserve farmland by limiting sprawl development, development that drains the vitality of older communities.[76] In greater Portland, Oregon, environmentalists, farmers, downtown business interests, and neighborhood activists all came together to support growth management measures that preserved green space and agricultural acreage by directing investment toward already built-up areas.[77]

Church groups and nonprofit associations can add a "justice" dimension to New Regional action. In the mid-1990s, church congregations and religious organizations pushed the Minnesota state legislature for regional fair-share-housing and social justice legislation.[78] In northwest Indiana, an interfaith federation cut across racial and jurisdictional lines in order to block plans to relocate the county's juvenile courts outside the troubled city of Gary.[79]

Such creative city–suburban coalitions, however, are difficult to build and maintain. The residents and leaders of many older suburbs and quickly growing edge communities continue to be leery about entering into an alliance with central cities. Local communities also view one another more as competitors than as partners.[80] Outside the economic development arena, the achievements of the New Regionalism have been relatively minimal.

CONCLUSION: GOVERNING REGIONS IN A GLOBAL AGE

City–county consolidation and the creation of a strong metropolitan government are not politically viable options in most metropolitan areas. Suburbanites and local officials oppose major political restructuring: suburbanites are unwilling to surrender local autonomy for the vague promise of cost savings. Public choice theorists doubt the merits of metropolitan restructuring. They point out that in Athens–Clarke County (Georgia), Carson City–Ormsby County (Nevada), and Kansas City–Wyandotte County (Kansas), consolidation brought no great savings.[81] Racial minorities often object that metropolitan reform will effectively take power away from them just as their numbers have grown sufficiently large to gain electoral control of the central city.

While consolidation seldom yields clear and consistent cost savings, the evidence reveals that consolidation does have a somewhat stronger impact on promoting local economic fortunes.[82] The creation of Unigov was a key factor in spurring the rebirth of downtown Indianapolis and the economic growth of the region. Yet, Unigov is in many aspects exceptional. Consolidations in greater Louisville and in other areas across the United States have had much more modest impacts on economic growth.

The promise of new jobs just may convince citizens of the necessity of metropolitan action. The merger of Kansas City, Kansas, with Wyandotte County was driven by a concern for the region's economic future. The failure of city and county efforts in the mid-1990s to land a NASCAR racetrack, a project that was seen as vital to the region's economy, led voters to surmount the usual barriers and accept consolidation. Consolidated Kansas City eventually won the NASCAR tourist facility it so greatly valued.[83]

Where metropolitan restructuring is impossible to achieve, regional governance provides an important substitute. Various cooperative arrangements allow local governments to transcend borders, take advantage of economies of scale, and secure more professional service provision. In more recent years, business associations have been the primary drivers in the economic development-oriented New Regionalism that crosses local borders.

But the private-led nature of the New Regionalism raises important questions of democracy and accountability, questions that are also raised concerning the operations of special districts and metropolitan authorities. Just who is, and is not, represented in these decision-making bodies? Developers and major corporations often enjoy privileged access to special districts, regional planning commissions, and business-led associations. Neighborhood groups, in contrast, face great difficulty in mobilization efforts aimed at pressuring seemingly distant regional bodies and quasi-governmental associations. Working through quasi-governmental organizations, suburban leaders have gained a say over the operations of museums, educational enrichment programs, and health programs, reshaping them to serve the needs of suburban constituencies as opposed to central-city populations.[84] Latino and African American activists have been hesitant to embrace the New Regionalism banner, fearing that a business-led regionalism will be insensitive to many of the concerns of minority communities.[85]

Procedures for transparency, public elections, and citizen participation are necessary to ensure the democratic nature and legitimacy of regional bodies. The active involvement of community-based organizations and church groups can add a degree of balance to a metropolitan agenda that too often is shaped by a region's growth coalition.

Around the world, the competitive pressures of globalization have led localities in a region to work together to provide the infrastructure and other support services necessary to attract new private investment.[86] In a global age, the economic competition is no longer simply between cities in a region but between city-regions. Cities and suburbs are increasingly finding that they must work together collaboratively in order to remain competitive. In a global postindustrial age, communities in a metropolis engage in collaborative as well as competitive actions.

NOTES

1. Richardson Dilworth, *The Urban Origins of Suburban Autonomy* (Cambridge, MA: Harvard University Press, 2005), 108–193.

2. Rex L. Facer II, "Annexation and State Law in the United States," *Urban Affairs Review* 41, no. 5 (2006): 701.

3. Joel Miller, "Annexations and Boundary Changes in the 1980s and 1990–1991," *Municipal Year Book 1993* (Washington, DC: International City/County Management Association 1993), 104; Juliet F. Gainsborough, "Bridging the City-Suburb Divide: States and the Politics of Regional Cooperation," *Journal of Urban Affairs* 23, no. 5 (2001): 503–504.

4. Howard N. Rabinowitz, "Albuquerque: City at a Crossroads," in *Sunbelt Cities: Politics and Growth Since World War II,* ed. Richard M. Bernard and Bradley R. Rice (Austin: University of Texas Press, 1983), 258–259.

5. David Rusk, *Inside Game/Outside Game: Winning Strategies for Saving Urban America* (Washington, DC: Brookings Institution Press, 1999), 3–10 and 126–145; idem, "Annexation and the Fiscal Fate of Cities," report of the Brookings Institution, Metropolitan Policy Program, Washington, DC, August 2006, www.brookings.edu/reports/2006/08metropolitanpolicy_rusk.aspx.

6. Timothy D. Mead, "Governing Charlotte-Mecklenburg," *State and Local Government Review* 32, no. 3 (Fall 2000): 194.

7. David Y. Miller, *The Regional Governing of Metropolitan Areas* (Boulder, CO; Westview Press, 2002), 120–122.

8. Bert Swanson, "Jacksonville: Consolidation and Regional Governance," in *Regional Politics: America in a Post-City Age,* Urban Affairs Annual Review, vol. 45, ed. H.V. Savitch and Ronald K. Vogel (Thousand Oaks, CA: Sage, 1996), 239–240; and Bert E. Swanson, "Quandaries of Pragmatic Reform: A Reassessment of the Jacksonville Experience," *State and Local Government Review* 32, no. 3 (Fall 2000): 227–238.

9. Mark Rosentraub, "City-County Consolidation and the Rebuilding of Image: The Fiscal Lessons from Indianapolis's UniGov Program," *State and Local Government Review* 32, no. 3 (Fall 2000): 180–191.

10. C. James Owen and York Willbern, *Governing Metropolitan Indianapolis: The Politics of Unigov* (Berkeley: University of California Press, 1985), 1–2.

11. C. James Owen, "Indianapolis Unigov: A Focus on Restructured Executive Authority," paper presented at the annual meeting of the Urban Affairs Association, Indianapolis, April 22–24, 1993. Indianapolis Mayor Stephen Goldsmith describes his success in building regional cooperation for economic development in *The Twenty-First Century City: Resurrecting Urban America* (Lanham, MD: Rowman and Littlefield, 1999), 75–94; figures on the airport, p. 36.

12. Suzanne M. Leland and Mark S. Rosentraub, "Consolidated and Fragmented Governments and Regional Cooperation: Surprising Lessons from Charlotte, Cleveland, Indianapolis, and Wyandotte/

Kansas City, Kansas," in *Governing Metropolitan Regions in the 21st Century*, ed. Donald Phares (Armonk, NY: M.E. Sharpe, 2009), 143–163.

13. Mayor Greg Ballard, speech to the Rotary Club of Indianapolis, January 28, 2009, www.insideindianabusiness.com/newsitem.asp?ID=33672. The establishment and continued existence of numerous taxing and service zones are notable features of a number of consolidations, including Baton Route–East Baton Rouge. See G. Ross Stephens and Nelson Wikstrom, *Metropolitan Government and Governance* (New York: Oxford University Press, 2000), 69.

14. Rosentraub, "City-County Consolidation and the Rebuilding of Image."

15. "Beyond Merger: A Competitive Vision for the Regional City of Louisville," report of the Brookings Institution Center for Urban and Metropolitan Policy, Washington, DC, July 2002, www.brookings.edu/reports/2002/07louisville.aspx.

16. Hank V. Savitch, Ronald K. Vogel, and Lin Ye, "Beyond the Rhetoric: Lessons from Louisville's Consolidation," *American Review of Public Administration* 40, no. 1 (2010): 3–28.

17. Richard C. Feiock, "Do Consolidation Entrepreneurs Make a Deal with the Devil?" in *City-County Consolidation and Its Alternatives,* ed. Jered B. Carr and Richard C. Feiock (Armonk, NY: M.E. Sharpe, 2004), 39–52. For a more complete discussion of the national evidence on consolidation and its impacts, see Suzanne M. Leland and Kurt Thomas, eds., *City-County Consolidation: Promises Made, Promises Kept?* (Washington, DC: Georgetown University Press, 2010).

18. H.V. Savitch and Ronald K. Vogel, "Metropolitan Consolidation versus Metropolitan Governance in Louisville," *State and Local Government Review* 32, no. 3 (Fall 2000): 201. This paragraph relies on pp. 198–212, and the authors' argument for a "New Regionalism" based on innovative forms of interlocal cooperation instead of the creation of new metropolitan government plans.

19. H.V. Savitch and Ronald K. Vogel, "Suburbs Without a City: Power and City-County Consolidation," *Urban Affairs Review* 39, no. 6 (2004): 758–790; H.V. Savitch, Takashi Tsukamoto, and Ronald K. Vogel, "Civic Culture and Corporate Regime in Louisville," *Journal of Urban Affairs* 30, no. 4 (2008): 441.

20. Suzanne Leland and Kurt Thurmaier, "When Efficiency Is Unbelievable: Normative Lessons from 30 Years of City-County Consolidations," *Public Administration Review* 65, no. 4 (July/August 2005): 475–489.

21. Joseph Gerth, "Merger: One Year Later," *(Louisville) Courier-Journal,* December 22, 2003; Savitch and Vogel, "Suburbs Without a City."

22. Savitch and Vogel, "Metropolitan Consolidation versus Metropolitan Governance in Louisville," 210.

23. Savitch, Vogel, and Ye, "Beyond the Rhetoric: Lessons from Louisville's Consolidation."

24. Raymond A. Mohl, "Miami: The Ethnic Cauldron," in Bernard and Rice, *Sunbelt Cities,* 82–83.

25. Arthur C. Nelson, "Portland: The Metropolitan Umbrella," in Savitch and Vogel, *Regional Politics: America in a Post-City Age,* 253.

26. Nelson, "Portland: The Metropolitan Umbrella," 263. See also pp. 263–220 for a further discussion of Metro's limitations.

27. Christopher Leo, "Regional Growth Management Regime: The Case of Portland, Oregon," *Journal of Urban Affairs* 20, no. 4 (1998): 363–394, esp. 366–367 and 370.

28. Judith A. Martin, "In Fits and Starts: The Twin Cities Metropolitan Framework," in *Metropolitan Governance: American/Canadian Intergovernmental Perspectives,* ed. Donald N. Rothblatt and Andrew Sancton (Berkeley, CA: Institute of Governmental Studies Press, 1993), 229–230.

29. Ibid., 233–236; John J. Harrigan, "Governance in Transition: Regime Under Pressure in the Twin Cities," paper presented at the annual meeting of the American Political Science Association, New York, September 2, 1994.

30. Harrigan, "Governance in Transition."

31. Edward G. Goetz, *Clearing the Way: Deconcentrating the Poor in Urban America* (Washington, DC: Urban Institute Press, 2003), 98–99 and 189–190; Edward G. Goetz, Karen Chapple, and Barbara

Lukermann, "Enabling Exclusion," *Journal of Planning Education and Research* 22, no. 3 (2003): 213–225; Edward Goetz, "Fair-share or Status Quo? The Twin Cities Livable Communities Act," *Journal of Planning Education and Research* 20 (2000): 37–51.

32. Martin, "In Fits and Starts," 228; and Myron Orfield, *Metropolitics: A Regional Approach for Community and Stability* (Washington, DC: Brookings Institution Press, 1997), 109–111.

33. Remarks of George Latimer, former mayor of St. Paul, Minnesota, to the annual conference of the National Civic League, Denver, Colorado, October 27, 1989.

34. Dagney Faulk and Michael Hicks, "Local Government Reform in Indiana," Ball State University, Miller College of Business, Center for Business and Economic Research, 2009, http://cms.bsu.edu/Academics/CentersandInstitutes/BBR/~/media/995AFE81828E409193E6C8273059A552.ashx; Leland and Thurmaier, "When Efficiency Is Unbelievable"; and Suzanne Leland and Kurt Thurmaier, "City-County Consolidation: Do Governments Actually Deliver on Their Promises?" paper presented at the annual meeting of the Urban Affairs Association, Chicago, Spring 2009; and Leland and Thurmaier, *City-County Consolidation: Promises Made, Promises Kept?*

35. For classic statements of public choice theory applied to metropolitan areas, see: Vincent Ostrom, Charles Tiebout, and Robert Warren, "The Organization of Government in Metropolitan Areas," *American Political Science Review* 55 (December 1961): 831–842; Robert L. Bish, *The Public Economy of Metropolitan Areas* (Chicago: Markham, 1971); Robert L. Bish and Vincent Ostrom, *Understanding Urban Government: Metropolitan Reform Reconsidered* (Washington, DC: American Enterprise Institute, 1973); and Vincent Ostrom and Elinor Ostrom, "Public Choice: A Different Approach to the Study of Public Administration," *Public Administration Review* 31 (March/April 1971): 203–216. More readable overviews of the public choice debate are provided by Stephens and Wikstrom, *Metropolitan Government and Governance*, 105–121; and Kathryn A. Foster, *The Political Economy of Special-Purpose Governments* (Washington, DC: Georgetown University Press, 1997), 35–41.

36. William Duncombe, "Strategies to Improve Efficiency: School District Consolidation and Alternative Cost-Sharing Strategies," presented at the Conference on School Finance and Governance in Providence Rhode Island, November 13, 2007.

37. All of these successes were gained in school consolidation in Pennsylvania. See Standard & Poor's, *Study of the Cost-effectiveness of Consolidating Pennsylvania Districts* (New York: Standard & Poor's School Evaluation Services, 2007).

38. Miller, *The Regional Governing of Metropolitan America,* 143.

39. Patricia S. Atkins, "Local Intergovernmental Agreements: Strategies for Cooperation," *MIS Report* (Washington DC: International City/County Management Association, 1997), 2–3.

40. Atkins, "Local Intergovernmental Agreements: Strategies for Cooperation," 5.

41. Donald F. Kettl, *System Under Stress: Homeland Security and American Politics* (Washington. DC: CQ Press, 2003), 30–31 and 63–66.

42. Kathleen Staudt, *Violence and Activism at the Border: Gender, Fear, and Everyday Life in Ciudad Juárez* (Austin: University of Texas Press, 2008).

43. David Streitfeld, "A City Outsources Everything. Sky Doesn't Fall," *New York Times,* July 19, 2010; Ruben Vives, Jeff Gottlieb, and Hector Becerra, "Maywood to Hire Others to Run the City," *Los Angeles Times,* June 23, 2010.

44. Wim Wiewel and Kimberly Schaffer, "Learning to Think as a Region: Connecting Suburban Sprawl and City Poverty," *European Planning Studies* 9, no. 5 (2001): 608.

45. Tony Barboza, "Irvine Is Told to Accommodate 35,000 Homes in 7 Years," *Los Angeles Times,* July 25, 2007; Paul G. Lewis, *California's Housing Element Law: The Issue of Local Noncompliance* (San Francisco: Public Policy Institute of California, 2003), www.ppic.org/content/pubs/report/R_203PLR.pdf.

46. William Fulton, *The Reluctant Metropolis* (Baltimore: Johns Hopkins University Press, 2001), 162–167.

47. J.H. Svara, "Setting a Regional Agenda for Councils of Government in North Carolina," paper presented at the annual meeting of the Urban Affairs Association, Cleveland, April 1992; Donald F.

Norris, "Killing a COG: The Death and Reincarnation of the Baltimore Regional Council of Governments," *Journal of Urban Affairs* 16 (1994): 157–158.

48. Bruce Katz, Robert Puentes, and Scott Bernstein, "TEA-21 Reauthorization: Getting Transportation Right for Metropolitan America," paper prepared for the Brookings Institution Center on Urban and Metropolitan Policy, Washington, DC, March 2003, p. 4, www.brookings.edu/es/urban/publications/tea21.htm. The MPO process is also part of the 2005 Safe, Accountable, Flexible, Efficient Transportation Act: A Legacy for Users (SAFETEA-LU), which succeeded TEA-21.

49. Katz, Puentes, and Bernstein, "TEA-21 Reauthorization," 4. See also Thomas A. Horan, Hank Dittmar, and Daniel R. Jordan, "ISTEA and the New Era in Transportation Policy: Sustainable Communities from a Federal Initiative," in *Toward Sustainable Communities: Transition and Transformations in Environmental Policy*, ed. Daniel A. Mazmanian and Michael E. Kraft (Cambridge, MA: MIT Press, 1999), 217–245.

50. Bruce Katz, Robert Puentes, and Scott Bernstein, "Getting Transportation Right for Metropolitan America," in *Taking the High Road: A Metropolitan Agenda for Transportation Reform,* ed. Katz and Puentes (Washington, DC: Brookings Institution Press, 2005), 21–25.

51. Donald F. Norris and Carl W. Stenberg, "Governmental Fragmentation and Metropolitan Government: Does Less Mean More? The Case of the Baltimore Region," in Phares, *Governing Metropolitan Regions in the 21st Century*, 132–133.

52. Thomas W. Sanchez and James F. Wolf, "Environmental Justice and Transportation Equity: A Review of MPOs," in *Growing Smarter: Achieving Livable Communities, Environmental Justice, and Regional Equity*, ed. Robert D. Bullard (Cambridge, MA: MIT Press, 2007), 249–271.

53. U.S. Census Bureau, "2002 Census of Governments," GC02–1(P), July 2002, www.census.gov/govs/cog/2002COGprelim_report.pdf.

54. Brett W. Hawkins and Rebecca M. Hendrick, "Do Metropolitan Special Districts Reinforce Sociospatial Inequalities? A Study of Sewerage and Technical Education in Milwaukee County," *Publius: Journal of Federalism* 27, no. 1 (Winter 1997): 135–143.

55. Kathryn A. Foster, *The Political Economy of Special-Purpose Governments* (Washington, DC: Georgetown University Press, 1999), 103–104; Nancy Burns, *The Formation of American Local Governments: Private Values in Public Institutions* (New York: Oxford University Press, 1994), 4–6, 14–15, 25–32, and 114–117.

56. Some special districts, of course, do take steps to consult the people they serve, using surveys, focus groups, and various other methods to engage citizens. See Tanya Heikkila and Kimberley Roussin Isett, "Citizen Involvement and Performance Management in Special-Purpose Governments," *Public Administration Review* 67, no. 2 (March/April 2007): 238–248.

57. David Walker, "Snow White and the 17 Dwarfs: From Metro Cooperation to Governance," *National Civil Review* 76 (January/February 1987). See also Dennis R. Judd and James M. Smith, "The New Ecology of Urban Governance: Special-Purpose Authorities and Urban Development," in *Governing Cities in a Global Era: Urban Innovation, Competition, and Democratic Reform*, ed. Robin Hambleton and Jill Simone Gross (New York: Palgrave Macmillan, 2007), 151–160.

58. Jamieson Doig, *Empire on the Hudson: Entrepreneurial Vision and Political Power at the Port of New York Authority* (New York: Columbia University Press, 2002), 379–386 and 397–402; Benjamin and Nathan, *Regionalism and Realism*, 126–134.

59. Susan Fainstein, "The Port Authority of New York and New Jersey and the Rebuilding of the World Trade Center," paper presented at the annual meeting of the Urban Affairs Association, Washington, DC, April 1, 2004. See also Bruce Berg and Paul Kantor, "New York: The Politics of Conflict and Avoidance," in Savitch and Vogel, *Regional Politics: America in a Post-City Age*, 39.

60. Bruce Berg and Paul Kantor, "New York: The Politics of Conflict and Avoidance," in Savitch and Vogel, *Regional Politics: America in a Post-City Age*, 39–50.

61. Vincent L. Marando and Robert D. Thomas, *The Forgotten Governments: County Commissioners as Policy Makers* (Gainesville: Florida Atlantic University/University Presses of Florida, 1977).

62. Linda Lobao and David S. Kraybill, "The Emerging Roles of County Governments in Metro-

politan and Nonmetropolitan Areas: Findings From a National Survey," *Public Administration Review* 19, no. 3 (August 2005): 245–259.

63. Norman Krumholz, "Regionalism Redux," *Public Administration Review* 57, no. 1 (1997): 88.

64. Louise Jezierski, "Pittsburgh: Partnerships in a Regional City," in Savitch and Vogel, *Regional Politics: America in a Post-City Age*, 159–181; H.V. Savitch and Ronald K. Vogel, "Perspectives for the Present and Lessons for the Future," in ibid., 292.

65. Bill Barnes, "Broad Cooperation among Organizations Aids Pittsburgh's Development Scene," *Nation's Cities Weekly*, February 15, 1999.

66. Barry Bluestone, Joan Fitzgerald, David Perry, and Martin Jaffe, "The New Metropolitan Alliances: Regional Collaboration for Economic Development," report prepared for CEOs for Cities, Boston, 2002, www.ceosforcities.org/research/2002/regional_alliances/Metro%20Report.pdf.

67. Krumholz, "Regionalism Redux," 84.

68. Beverly A. Cigler, "Economic Development in Metropolitan Areas," in *Urban and Regional Policies for Metropolitan Livability,* ed. David K. Hamilton and Patricia S. Atkins (Armonk, NY: M.E. Sharpe, 2008), 296–323, here 311.

69. Savitch and Vogel, *Regional Politics: America in a Post-City Age*.

70. William R. Barnes and Larry C. Ledebur, *Local Economies: The U.S. Common Market of Local Economic Regions* (Washington, DC: National League of Cities, 1994), 11.

71. Theodore Hershberg, "Regional Imperatives of Global Competition," in *Planning for a New Century,* ed. Jonathan Barnett (Washington, DC: Island Press, 2001), 13.

72. Joel Rast and Virginia Cohen, "When Boeing Landed in Chicago: Lessons for Regional Economic Development," paper presented at the annual meeting of the Urban Affairs Association, Washington, DC, April 2, 2004.

73. Neal R. Peirce, with Curtis W. Johnson and R. Stuart Hall, *Citistates* (Washington, DC: Seven Locks Press, 1993), 322–323; Hambleton and Gross, *Governing Cities in a Global Era.*

74. Judd and Smith, "The New Ecology of Urban Governance: Special-Purpose Authorities and Urban Development," 151–161. Jonathan S. Davies, "Against 'Partnership': Toward a Local Challenge to Global Neoliberalism," raises many of the same concerns in his study of the new public-private development bodies in England and Scotland; see Hambleton and Gross, *Governing Cities in a Global Era*, 199–210.

75. Myron Orfield, *Metropolitics: A Regional Agenda for Community and Stability* (Washington, DC: Brookings Institution, 1997, 1998), 104–172.

76. David Rusk, "The Exploding Metropolis: Why Growth Management Makes Sense," *Brookings Review* 16, no. 4 (Fall 1998): 13–16. See also Robert Puentes and Myron Orfield, "Valuing America's First Suburbs: A Policy Agenda for Older Suburbs in the Midwest," report of The Brookings Institution Center for Urban Affairs, Washington, DC, April 2002, www.brookings.edu/dybdocroot/es/urban/firstsuburbs/firstsuburbsexsum.htm.

77. Christopher Leo, "Regional Growth Management Regime: The Case of Portland, Oregon," *Journal of Urban Affairs* 20, no. 4 (1998): 376–382.

78. Orfield, *Metropolitics*, 129–131, 140–141 and 169–170.

79. Rusk, *Inside Game/Outside Game*, 278.

80. Victoria Gordon, "Partners or Competitors? Perceptions of Regional Economic Development Cooperation in Illinois," *Economic Development Quarterly* 21, no. 1 (February 2007): 60–78.

81. The arguments in this paragraph and the next paragraph are based on Leland and Thurmaier, "When Efficiency is Unbelievable"; and idem, "City-County Consolidation: Do Governments Actually Deliver on Their Promises?"

82. In addition to the work of Leland and Thurmaier, see: Patricia S. Atkins, "Metropolitan Forms, Fiscal Efficiency, and Other Bottom Lines," in Hamilton and Atkins, *Urban and Regional Policies for Metropolitan Livability,* 78–79; and Samuel R. Staley, "The Effects of City-County Consolidation: A Review of the Recent Academic Literature," report prepared by the Indiana Policy Review Foundation

for the Marion County Consolidation Study Commission of the Indiana General Assembly, November 16, 2005, www.in.gov/legislative/interim/committee/2005/committees/prelim/MCCC02.pdf.

83. Suzanne M. Leland, "Kansas City/Wyandotte County, Kansas," in Leland and Thurmaier, *Case Studies of City-County Consolidation*, 266.

84. Carolyn Adams, "How the Suburbs Are Reshaping the City: A Philadelphia Case Study" (paper presented at the annual meeting of the Urban Affairs Association, New Orleans, March 17, 2011).

85. Joel Rast, "Environmental Justice and the New Regionalism," *Journal of Planning Education and Research* 25, no. 3 (2006): 249–263.

86. Robin Hambleton and Jill Simone Gross, "From Governance to Governing," in Hambleton and Gross, *Governing Cities in a Global Era,* 213–224, esp. 220.

11 The Intergovernmental City

State and National Policy

No city is an island. Cities exist in an **intergovernmental system** where they are greatly affected by the actions of the national government and state governments. The federal and state governments provide considerable fiscal assistance to cities and suburbs. Federal and state regulations also impose costly service obligations on cities and suburbs. Each state essentially determines the powers that its municipalities possess.

This chapter begins by describing the constitutional underpinnings and evolution of the American intergovernmental system. As we shall see, in a system of **cooperative federalism**, the national government, the states, and localities share responsibility for fighting urban ills.

Critics argue that the national government's policy reach has expanded too far, producing a top-heavy system overloaded with wasteful programs and bureaucratic rules and regulations that stifle subnational initiative. Republican administrations in Washington, beginning with the presidency of Richard Nixon, pursued a **New Federalism** designed to reduce the program authority of the national government by returning decision-making power to states and localities. Even Bill Clinton and Barack Obama, Democratic presidents committed to having the federal government play an active role in combating urban problems, found it prudent to respect the public's New Federalism sensibilities.

The Constitutional Basis for Federal Urban Programs

Does the U.S. Constitution permit the national government to play an active role in urban policy? Critics of the central government argue that the Constitution gives primacy in the domestic arena to the states, not to the central government. These critics view the Constitution as having established a system of **dual federalism**, giving the national government and the states distinctly different areas of authority. According to this perspective, the national government is limited to the few **expressed powers** (also called **delegated powers** or **enumerated powers**) explicitly listed for it in

Article I, Section 8 of the Constitution, including the powers to coin money, regulate interstate commerce, raise an army, declare war, enter into treaties with other nations, and establish post offices. All other policy areas, according to the doctrine dual federalists, fall under the **reserved powers** given to the states by the **Tenth Amendment**, which reads:

> The powers not delegated to the United States by the Constitution, nor prohibited by it to the States, are reserved to the States respectively, or to the people.

Under dual federalism, the states, not the central government, are the dominant actors when it comes to making policy decisions that affect the health of cities.

But the doctrine of dual federalism is dated; it does not describe the governmental system of the United States as it has taken shape over the past two centuries, especially as the system has evolved in the eighty-plus years since the Great Depression. Nor do the dual federalists take note of provisions of the Constitution that enable the central government to take extensive action in the domestic arena. The national governments and the states do not have totally separate areas of responsibility; rather, the national government and the states share responsibility for building roads, providing health care and quality education, preventing disease, maintaining the security of key facilities, and combating a whole host of other domestic problems.

The United States has a **federal system** of government where a central government with meaningful powers exists alongside the states. The framers of the Constitution assembled in Philadelphia to create a governmental system with a stronger center than the one that existed under the Articles of Confederation. The inability of the government to function under the Articles convinced the Framers of the dangers inherent in too-weak government. The framers of the Constitution were concerned with protecting individual rights and liberties from too-strong government, but they threw out the prior system of **federation**, where the states were the most important entities and the central government lacked meaningful decision-making authority.

Over more than two centuries of U.S. history, the balance of power in the federal system has shifted. As the nation grew and matured, American citizens came to expect that the central government would act to protect their rights and would enact programs that would make their lives better. In the midst of the Great Depression of the 1930s, Americans demanded that the national government step in to provide jobs and relief. Americans today continue to approve of the extended reach of the central government in areas such as environmental protection, the provision of Social Security and Medicare for the elderly, research to assist disease prevention, and the protection of children. In the first decade of the twenty-first century, in the midst of a troubled economy and a home foreclosure crisis, Americans expected the national government to take effective action to protect their jobs, homes, and communities. Americans do not believe that these policy areas are the exclusive realm of the fifty states.

As Supreme Court decisions have made clear, the U.S. Constitution does indeed permit the national government to play an expansive role in domestic policy. The national government is not confined only to a few specified roles and forced to serve as a junior partner to the states. The Tenth Amendment, which seemingly tilts power toward the states, is counterbalanced by the Constitution's **supremacy clause**, which declares that the laws passed by Congress shall be the supreme law of the land. The Constitution's **interstate commerce clause** also gives the national government the authority to act in a broad range of actions that affect commerce, including education, job training, local economic development, environmental protection, and even maintaining the health of citizens and workers.

After the list of enumerated powers given the national government, Article I, Section 8 of the Constitution contains important language, the **necessary and proper clause**, which declares that the national government has the right "to make all laws which shall be necessary and proper for carrying into execution the foregoing powers." This wording means that the national government is not limited to only those very few actions that are specifically spelled out or enumerated in the Constitution. Rather, the necessary and proper clause indicates that the federal government possesses a whole host of unstated but **implied powers** that are related to the broad functions enumerated for the central government. In essence, the necessary and proper clause can be viewed as an **elastic clause** that vastly stretches the list of powers given the federal government, narrowing the area of authority reserved for the states by the Tenth Amendment.

Americans welcomed the extended reach of the national government as Franklin Delano Roosevelt's New Deal sought to combat the Great Depression. A second surge in national government action commenced in the 1960s with President Lyndon Johnson's War on Poverty and Great Society programs. The federal government took strong civil-rights-oriented actions to ensure that all citizens received the "equal protection of the laws," as guaranteed by the **Fourteenth Amendment** of the Constitution. In the 1970s, the national government assumed greater responsibility for environmental protection. The Supreme Court decisions declared that the central government's reach was constitutionally allowable and was not barred by the Tenth Amendment.[1]

In the late 1970s and the 1980s, Republican victories in presidential elections led to new appointments to the Supreme Court that produced a moderate shift in the Court's rulings on federalism, but only to a very small degree. The Republican-era Court exhibited a renewed interest in respecting the position of the states in a federal system. In ***United States v. Lopez*** (1995),[2] the Court invalidated the Gun Free School Zones Act because Congress had made no attempt whatsoever to show how the prohibition of firearms in school zones was related to interstate commerce. For the first time since 1936, the Supreme Court struck down an act of Congress for falling outside the scope of the national government's power to regulate interstate commerce.[3]

Two years later, in ***Printz v. United States***,[4] the Supreme Court again referred to the doctrine of federalism in striking down a provision of the Brady Handgun Prevention Act. A local sheriff had objected to the act's requirement that law-enforcement officials conduct background checks on handgun buyers. The Court ruled that, under their "retained authority," the states "remain independent and autonomous within their proper sphere of authority." State and local officers cannot be "dragooned" into administering federal law.[5]

"Better Housing: The Solution to Infant Mortality in the Slums": As this 1930s federal publication reveals, advocates saw federal programs in support of government-built public housing as an important housing reform, a means of providing much improved living environments, especially when compared to the dilapidated, rat-infested firetraps the new housing replaced. From the Library of Congress, Prints and Photographs Division, Washington, DC, 20540 USA. http://www.loc.gov/pictures/resource/cph.3f05647/.

In ***United States v. Morrison*** (2000),[6] the Supreme Court again recognized the existence of a boundary that separates national and state authority. The Court voided a provision of the federal Violence Against Women Act that allowed victims of rape to sue their attackers in federal court as opposed to state courts. *Morrison*, like *Lopez* and *Printz*, breathed new life into the concept that a federal system does indeed impose some outer limit on the federal government's claim of powers.[7]

Yet, it would be a clear misreading of these decisions to portray the Republican-era judiciary as having demolished the system of cooperative federalism and returned the nation to the old system of dual federalism.[8] The rulings in *Lopez, Printz*, and *Morrison* concerned only a select few programs. The Supreme Court left the national government's reach in the great realm of domestic policy largely untouched. When Congress corrected the specific flaws that the Court had found in the programs, the reconstituted programs were allowed to proceed. Overall, the Supreme Court did little to roll back the scope of central government authority in domestic affairs. In *Gonzales v. Raich* (2005), the Supreme Court reaffirmed the expansive scope of the central government's authority under the interstate commerce clause, recognizing the right of the federal government to criminalize marijuana sales. The federal prohibition on marijuana is a legitimate exercise of its power to regulate interstate commerce. Under the doctrine of national supremacy, federal law supersedes state laws that permit the sale of marijuana for medical purposes.[9]

GRANTS-IN-AID: THE BASIS OF COOPERATIVE FEDERALISM

The intergovernmental system is built around money, or, more precisely, the transfer of money. A **grant-in-aid** is a transfer of money from one level of government to another to accomplish specified purposes. In 2007, annual federal grants to states and localities approached $450 billion and accounted for about 28 percent of state and local expenditures.[10] Accompanying rules and regulations attempt to constrain recipient governments in the use of program funds.

The federal grant system has produced a number of admirable results. Federal assistance reduced the gross state-to-state and city-to-city inequities that once plagued the nation in areas such as health care, income assistance, and social services. Federal grants helped to upgrade municipal services and local physical infrastructure, establishing a more uniform level of service provision to citizens no matter where they lived. Federal grants and regulations helped to spur state and local action in the area of pollution reduction. Federal assistance provided for important advances in numerous other policy areas, including Head Start preschool programs, special education, child nutrition, the protection of homeland security, and the construction of hospitals, mass transit, and solid waste disposal facilities, to name only a few.

Cities and counties are active lobbyists in the intergovernmental system. The lobbying efforts of the U.S. Conference of Mayors, the National League of Cities (NLC), and the National Association of Counties (NACO)[11] seek to expand the levels of federal assistance to cities and counties. These and similar associations of state governments are often referred to as **public interest groups** (or **PIGs**, for short). The PIGs lobby for continued increases in federal program assistance and for a relaxation of program rules in order to permit greater subnational flexibility. A number of big cities and states also maintain their own individual offices in Washington, offices that provide valuable assistance when a city applies for a grant and seeks to win federal program dollars.

TYPES OF GRANTS

Broadly speaking, there are two general types of federal grants to states and cities. **Categorical grants** seek to achieve very specific program objectives and have accompanying rules that sharply constrain how states and localities can spend program funds. Categorical grants seek to limit subnational flexibility. A municipality that receives a categorical grant to upgrade its police communications equipment, for instance, must use program funds only for that purpose; it cannot use the grant money for any other police or nonpolice purpose.

Block grants, by contrast, allow greater program flexibility, giving recipient governments greater discretion to decide just how to spend federal aid dollars within a broad functional or program area. The Comprehensive Employment Training Act (CETA), a very well-known block grant of the 1970s, gave local governments significant leeway to design their own job-training efforts. The Energy Efficiency and Conservation Block Grant program similarly allows communities to come up with a wide variety of approaches in their efforts to reduce fossil fuel emissions, promote energy-wise transportation, and minimize energy waste.

As part of their New Federalism, Republican presidents looked toward block grants as a tool to increase subnational program authority. Block grants were also a key part of the late-1990s welfare reform efforts that gave states and localities new leeway to experiment with a variety of welfare-to-work transition programs. George W. Bush proposed block grants to give the states greater freedom in such programs as Head Start, Medicaid, assisted housing, and child protective services.[12]

President Richard Nixon introduced the first truly significant block grants with the purpose of increasing state and local power when administering federally funded programs. In more recent years, Republican policymakers have modified the block grant approach, turning to **new-style block grants** that seek to cut public spending. Budget cutters argue that states and localities can get by with less aid, as the conversion to block grants gives subnational governments the freedom to discover new cost-saving ways to run public programs.[13]

President Barack Obama utilized both categorical grants and block grants in his economic stimulus program. Categorical grant "strings" required state and local governments to spend the stimulus money quickly on highway construction, mass transit improvements, and other "shovel ready" infrastructure projects that would produce immediate job creation. Program strings also sought to target assistance to children at risk, to K–12 education programs, to higher education, and to communities with the greatest needs. Yet, the American Recovery and Reinvestment Act (ARRA) also gave states and localities considerable discretion to design their own recovery and job-creation projects. The ARRA included funding for the Energy Efficiency and Conservation Block Grant program, which allowed states and cities to develop their own projects to reduce energy consumption and fossil-fuel emissions.[14]

Federal grants can also be classified as either *formula grants* or *project grants*. **Formula grants** distribute money in relatively automatic fashion to all eligible states and local governments; statistical criteria determine just how much money is dispensed to a jurisdiction. The size of the grant may be determined by formula factors such as a jurisdiction's population, per capita income, poverty rate, tax effort, age of the local housing stock, or daily school attendance. The Energy Efficiency and Conservation Block Grant program relied on a formula to distribute funds to every city with a population of 35,000 or more and to every county with a population greater than 200,000.

Formula grants are popular as they ease some of the administrative burdens placed on states and cities. Because a formula determines just how much assistance a state or locality will receive, a municipality does not have to spend a lot of time completing detailed applications and competing with other jurisdictions for a program award. Instead, a city files a relatively simple application and receives its share of program monies.

Project grants, in contrast, are competitive and not at all automatic. Project grants do not dispense money to all jurisdictions. Instead, eligible jurisdictions must submit an application that details just how they plan to use the program's award. Only the "winning" applications are funded. The Obama administration relied on the competitive offering of Race to the Top grants to catalyze states to come up with creative and effective K–12 educational strategies. The Obama administration similarly awarded Neighborhood Stabilization Program 2 (NSP2) funds on a competitive basis, to spur cities to find new ways to deal with their vacant properties. Local officials often complain that the competitive nature of project grants interferes with effective program planning, as no city can ever be sure that it will win the funds necessary to support a local project.

PROBLEMS WITH THE GRANT SYSTEM

Most federal aid to states and cities is given in the form of categorical grants, not block grants. Narrow-purpose grants and their accompanying regulations seek to ensure that recipient governments use the program monies for the stated program objectives and do not shift the money to other purposes. States and localities complain about the **lack of flexibility** of a federal aid system that relies so heavily on categorical grants. Cities resent the fact that they are often unable to shift program monies to higher-priority needs.

Categorical grants often contain **matching requirements** that a recipient government spend some of its own money on a program as a condition of receiving federal funds. The federal government uses such matching stipulations to force state and localities to contribute monetarily to problem-solving efforts, rather than stick the national government with the entire cost of a program. Matching requirements, however, can **distort subnational program priorities**, as state legislatures and city councils begin to shift their own spending toward projects that offer generous federal matching assistance, ignoring more pressing needs where spending fails to generate additional federal assistance.

Project grants also result in a **grantsmanship game**. A city or suburb can increase its chances of winning federal money by hiring professional staff members who are expert in the art of filing grant applications. Not all communities have the ability to compete effectively in such an expensive "game."

Block grants are very popular because they seek to increase the authority of state and local officials who would seem to be in a good position to judge a locality's needs. Yet, the history of block grants reveals that subnational governments cannot always be trusted to act wisely. (See Box 11.1, "Can the Cities Be Trusted? The Case of Community Development Block Grants.")

The phrase "cooperative federalism" is actually a bit misleading as it seems to imply that the state, local, and national governments are harmoniously working together in joint action in the pursuit of shared goals. In reality, the partnerships can be quite quarrelsome and unwieldy, since the different partners each see problems somewhat differently. In an effort to control program implementation, the central government has increased the number of program rules and regulations that seek to

Box 11.1

Can the Cities Be Trusted?
The Case of Community Development Block Grants

Do state and local governments act responsibly in their exercise of program discretion? The history of the **Community Development Block Grant (CDBG)** program, the largest federal aid program to cities, raises some doubts.

Enacted in 1974, the CDBG program combined a number of urban renewal, urban parks, and Model Cities social services programs into a single block grant. The grant consolidation gave cities a new freedom to use the funds that had previously been segregated by project area. The discretion allowed cities, however, was not complete. The Democratic Congress succeeded in listing certain priorities: eliminating slums and blight, aiding low- and moderate-income families, and meeting urgent community needs. While Republicans gave maximum deference to local wishes, Democrats in Washington sought to ensure that local officials would not use their newfound freedom to slight poorer neighborhoods.

How wise were local governments in their exercise of CDBG discretion? In Bridgeport, Connecticut, city officials made little attempt to target community development spending in the city's neediest areas. Instead, municipal leaders decided to spend a sizable chunk of CDBG funds for parks development, with most of the investment going to the improvement of recreational facilities in the better-off parts of town. The city council even earmarked funds for new tennis courts on the city's affluent north side. The city council also acted to ensure that a portion of CDBG monies was spent on parks development in all neighborhoods, thereby allowing each council member to claim political credit with their voters. Bridgeport officials largely ignored low- and moderate-income housing and instead allocated CDBG funds to help build an upscale pier and marina project. The federal Department of Housing and Urban Development eventually ruled the marina project as ineligible.

Was the Bridgeport experience unique? Unfortunately, no. While many localities use their community development assistance wisely, devoting a sizable portion to aiding poorer neighborhoods, the misuse and lack of targeting of CDBG funds was a phenomenon found nationwide. City councils spent CDBG funds on projects that were popular with local constituencies, not on programs that served poorer neighborhoods. Cities favored economic and physical development projects and ignored social services.

When Democrats returned to power, the federal government responded to the abuses by tightening program rules and oversight. The tightening of program rules seeks to ensure that local governments meet a program's declared objectives. Such tightening of rules, however, also represents a **creeping categorization** of block grants that diminishes the degree of subnational program flexibility that was so much a part of the original block grant idea.

Sources: Donald F. Kettl, *Government By Proxy: (Mis?)Managing Federal Programs* (Washington, DC: CQ Press, 1988), 54–66. Kenneth Finegold, Laura Wherry, and Stephanie Schardin, "Block Grants: Historical Overview and Lessons Learned," Urban Institute project on Assessing the New Federalism, Washington, DC, April 2004, www.urban.org/UploadedPDF/310991_A-63.pdf.

constrain local actions. Local officials protest that a system of voluntary cooperative federalism has been supplanted by a less gentle **regulatory federalism** or **coercive federalism**, where the national government often mandates (i.e., requires) local action and threatens to withhold assistance in cases where subnational actors refuse to comply with central directives.[15]

Yet, while federal aid conditions are quite real, local officials often exaggerate the national government's ability to dictate program administration. Local officials do not cede to every demand of federal program overseers. The federal government has no power to demote or dismiss uncooperative state and local officials. Nor can federal officials even easily cut off assistance in cases of state and local noncompliance, as such sanctions will hurt citizens who are dependent on the services supported by intergovernmental assistance. Categorical grants offers an "**illusion of federal control**,"[16] since subnational officials often retain considerable leeway in deciding how joint programs are administered.

UNFUNDED MANDATES

An **unfunded federal mandate** is an order or regulation by a higher level of government or the court system that requires a state and locality to undertake an action but does not provide the funding to fully pay for the action. The Clean Air Act, the Clean Water Act, the Endangered Species Act, the Fair Labor Standards Act, the Americans with Disabilities Act, federal historic preservation, national standards for foster care, requirements for brownfields cleanup, and the Homeland Security Act are only a few of the vast number of federal programs that impose costly requirements on states and localities. The states complain that they have been saddled with more than $29 billion in mandated costs in just a single year (2004).[17] Even Republican presidents, despite their criticisms of power in Washington, have added to the mandate burden imposed on states and localities. George W. Bush relied on mandates in a number of service areas, including school achievement testing, homeland security, and emergency management.[18]

In the mid-1990s, the Congress responded to state and local complaints by passing the **Unfunded Mandates Relief Act (UMRA)**. The new law required the Congress to pay fully for any new mandate that had an annual cost in excess of $50 million. Despite UMRA, "the march of mandates"[19] continues, as the legislation was riddled with numerous loopholes.[20] Most significantly, the Unfunded Mandates Relief Act does not apply to existing programs where the costs of required state and local action dramatically increase each year. The federal government, also, has not fully compensated localities for the training exercises and policing and protection services required as part of the homeland defense.

The **Individuals with Disabilities Education Act (IWDEA)** imposed new financial obligations on the states and localities. The **No Child Left Behind Act (NCLB)** burdened local school districts with the costs of administering tests and remedial education programs. The State of Connecticut sued the federal Department of Education, claiming that No Child Left Behind imposed a $40 million burden on the state.[21] The Office of Management and Budget (OMB) ruled that IWDEA and NCLB were grant-in-aid offerings and technically not mandates subject to the constraints imposed by UMRA. The OMB argued that the states and cities had applied for grants money and agreed to comply with accompanying program rules. States and local officials responded that such fine distinctions are absurd, that they have no real choice but to take federal aid even when accompanying rules force them to undertake unwanted and costly actions.[22]

While the states complain about federal mandates, the state governments themselves often impose costly service responsibilities on municipalities.[23] State mandates range from something as small as regulations governing the safety of playground equipment to something as large as requirements for the local provision of special education. The Connecticut Conference of Municipalities claims that the state's statutes impose more than 1,200 mandates on local governments.[24]

National Policy Toward Cities

The Traditional Democratic Approach: Targeted Programs and the Impossible Dream of National Urban Policy

Can the Federal Government Target Urban Aid? The Model Cities Experience

Democrats tend to favor **targeted urban policies** that focus aid on big cities and communities in need. But the contemporary Congress, with growing numbers of members elected from suburban and Sunbelt districts, has little interest in passing highly targeted urban aid and economic development programs.

The near impossibility of enacting effective, coherent urban policies was clearly apparent even as early as the 1960s when Democratic President Lyndon Johnson pursued a **War on Poverty** to combat destitution in both urban and rural areas. Johnson's policy advisers recognized that uprooting poverty was no easy task; effective antipoverty action would require simultaneous measures taken on a broad range of fronts, including education, social work, job training, and child care. Johnson's planners proposed the creation of a **Model Cities program** where a handful of communities would be chosen to demonstrate just what could be accomplished by concentrating resources in a coordinated, multifaceted, multiagency attack on poverty.

But members of Congress would not vote for a program that focused so many resources on a select few cities. The president's advisory task force tried to anticipate legislators' needs by broadening the program to create sixty-six model cities across the nation. But even that was not enough to accommodate localist-oriented legislators; Congress spread Model Cities money to 140 communities. Powerful congressional committee and subcommittee chairs assured that their states and districts would share in the program's benefits. As a result, Model Cities were created in unlikely states such as Maine, Tennessee, Kentucky, and Montana.[25] With program funds spread so thinly, no critical mass of monies existed to allow an effective multipronged attack on poverty in any of the Model Cities. The parochialism of Congress had undermined the entire Model Cities concept.

Why the United States Has No National Urban Policy

On the campaign trail in 1976, Jimmy Carter pledged to the nation's mayors that he would be the first president in the nation's history to adopt an explicit national policy to help cities. After his election, the mayors pressured Carter to deliver on his promise. Carter's *New Partnership to Preserve America's Communities* sought to target financial assistance and job creation to those communities that most needed the help. As the centerpiece of his **National Urban Policy**, Carter's proposed **National Development Bank** sought to offer grants, loan guarantees, and other means of financing as an incentive to induce businesses to locate or expand in distressed communities. The National Development bank was originally conceived as an Urban Bank or "Urbank," but the policy's strategists changed its name and broadened its focus in an effort to win greater support in Congress.

For all the publicity it received, the Nation Urban Policy went virtually nowhere. Congress defeated the National Development Bank and public works and fiscal assistance programs that sought to provide relief to the nation's most distressed communities. Representatives from the suburbs and the Sunbelt would not vote for programs that offered few benefits to their districts. Carter proposed to target the local job-creation assistance dispensed by the Department of Commerce's Economic Development Administration (EDA). But Congress moved in the exact opposite direction, redefining "distress" so broadly that 90 percent of the nation's population lived in areas eligible to apply for EDA assistance.

Carter's notion of a coherent, targeted national urban policy had smashed head-on against a constituent-protectionist Congress. The policy failure had a profound affect on future presidents. Carter was the first, and last, president to announce an explicit policy to help cities.

THE REPUBLICAN APPROACH: NEW FEDERALISM—DECENTRALIZATION, DEVOLUTION, AND CUTBACKS

Revenue Sharing

President Richard M. Nixon relied on two innovative tools—general revenue sharing and block grants—in his New Federalism effort to increase state and local power in implementing intergovernmental programs. **Revenue sharing** provided all fifty states and nearly every city and county in the nation with virtually no-strings-attached money to be spent however the recipient desired. The cities loved the program, which, despite its popularity, suffered a number of criticisms and had only a short life.

Big-city mayors complained that revenue sharing allowed wealthy communities such as Scarsdale (New York), Grosse Pointe (Michigan), Palm Beach (Florida), and Palm Springs (California) to build new tennis courts while distressed cities like Detroit and St. Louis lacked the ability to maintain basic municipal services. Across the country, local officials also spent the shared revenues on politically popular causes, lowering property taxes and increasing law enforcement; little of the money was spent on social programs to help the poor.[26]

As federal budget deficits climbed, "budget hawks" questioned whether the national government could afford to share revenues so freely with the states and cities. In 1980, Congress terminated the state portion of revenue sharing. Six years later, President Ronald Reagan ended the local portion. Reagan argued that revenue sharing was wasteful, that it led local communities to overspend on projects they would not normally fund.

Block Grants

Block grants, the New Federalism grant-in-aid innovation that we reviewed earlier in this chapter, have had a more enduring impact on the intergovernmental system.[27] Nixon merged numerous narrow-based categorical grants into a few broader block grants in order to increase the program flexibility available to states and cities. Democrats in Congress, however, feared state and local officials would slight the needs of poor and minority neighborhoods. As a result, Congress added "strings" to the new block grants, provisions requiring citizen participation and that a sizable portion of program monies be spent on low- and moderate-income communities. Republicans favored program rules to curb overspending by localities and wasteful practices in program administration.[28]

Unlike Nixon, Ronald Reagan did not simply seek to give state and local officials greater flexibility in administering intergovernmental programs. Reagan's larger goal was to cut federal domestic spending: "In short, Reagan did not aim simply at decategorizing the system; he ultimately sought to defund it."[29] For Reagan and his Republican successors, block grants were an acceptable "transitional device," a "halfway house" on the road to withdrawing federal support from unessential policy areas."[30]

Reagan brought a halt to new subsidized housing construction. He terminated the Urban Development Action Grant (UDAG) program, a tool that had aided downtown revitalization. Reagan forced drastic reductions in other urban programs: in real-dollar terms, he cut one-third of Community Development Block Grant money, half of mass-transit aid, and two-thirds of federal assistance for employment and training.[31]

Demetrios Caraley characterized the Ronald Reagan–George H.W. Bush era as "Washington Abandons Cities."[32] During the first ten years of the Reagan and Bush administrations, cities lost nearly 46 percent ($26 billion) in aid. Much-troubled Detroit lost more than half its federal assistance[33] under "fend-for-yourself federalism."[34] Distressed cities responded by reducing critical services, including job training, subsidized day care for the poor, bridge replacement, and sewer upgrading.[35]

George W. Bush (2000–2008) used block grants in an effort to provide states and localities greater room for policy innovations that would help reform welfare, child care, health services, job training, and public housing assistance.[36] Unlike Reagan. Bush did not slash domestic spending, but instead sought to make programs work better. The Cato Institute, a conservative think tank, decried that "Bush Is No Reagan."[37]

Bush supported the continuation of the Low-Income Housing Tax Credit (LIHTC), an expensive program of tax incentives that spurred private investors to support the low-income housing efforts of community development corporations[38] (see Chapter 7). A self-styled "compassionate conservative," Bush's **faith-based initiatives** sought to channel a greater portion of federal program assistance to church-related organizations willing to play an active role in running homeless shelters, tutoring disadvantaged children, fighting substance abuse, and aiding prisoner reentry. President Bush lauded **Habitat for Humanity** for its efforts, rooted in biblical teachings, to build homes for poor families, a program that more ideological conservatives attacked as welfarism in disguise.[39]

THE DEMOCRATIC "THIRD WAY": THE PRAGMATIC APPROACHES OF BILL CLINTON AND BARACK OBAMA

Clinton's "Stealth" Urban Policy

Bill Clinton was a **New Democrat** who sought an alternative to the big-government "old" Democratic approaches of the past. The disastrous defeat of his national health-care bill in his first year in office only served to reinforce his sense of caution in advancing major domestic programs. Midway through his first term in office, Clinton was confronted by a new obstacle, a Republican-controlled Congress intent on checking domestic initiatives.

Clinton resorted to a **refrigerator list strategy**,[40] emphasizing a series of small but politically popular programs that had an appeal to middle-class voters. He called for the federal government to fund 100,000 local police officers as well as after-school and summer programs aimed at reducing youth crime. He proposed brownfields revitalization programs that attracted the support of environmentalists.

Clinton practiced a **stealth urban policy**, pursuing urban goals through "nonurban" means.[41] The president did not talk explicitly about cities; instead, Clinton rallied people around the banner of heightened law enforcement, advances in schooling, brownfields reclamation, and "ending welfare as we know it." Clinton sought targets of opportunity, taking advantage of Congress' willingness to expand the highly popular Head Start, child nutrition, and violence-against-women programs. He secured new levels of assistance for job training, housing vouchers, and day care, all with the announced goal of moving people from welfare to work.

Clinton's expansion of the **Earned Income Tax Credit (EITC)** provides an illustration of the stealth urban policy approach. The EITC provides millions of dollars in income assistance to the working poor, giving low-income workers a refundable tax credit, that is, extra money in their paychecks. Clinton increased EITC eligibility and benefits. A working mother with two children could receive as much as $3,370 annually in income assistance; families earning as much as $27,000 received smaller income supplements. The expansion of EITC helped cities, as that is where concentrations of the working poor are found. In 1998 alone, the EITC pumped an estimated $737 million into the economy of the greater Chicago area, with 60 percent going to families residing in the central city.[42]

As a provision embedded in the tax code, the EITC enjoyed a number of distinct political advantages as compared to direct-spending urban programs. A tax benefit given only to people who worked, EITC was not a program that could be easily attacked as welfare or a reward for indolence.

Clinton succeeded by pursuing a number of relatively small **urban policy pieces**, not a bold, holistic vision of national urban policy. Clinton's welfare reform, day care, EITC, and Moving to Opportunity (MTO) housing programs all provided aid directly to *people*, not to urban *places*. Only the Clinton empowerment zone program explicitly attempted to target aid to distressed communities.[43]

Barack Obama: Pragmatism, with Extra Aid Targeted to Places in Need

Barack Obama came to the presidency in the midst of twin national crises: an economic recession that seemed to continue without end, and the collapse of the housing finance industry that resulted in home foreclosures across the nation. In important ways, Obama followed the same pragmatic urban approach set forth by Bill Clinton. He did not announce an explicit national urban policy but instead sought to aid cities through a variety of programs aimed at larger problems, measures aimed at rescuing the nation from its economic and housing miseries. Even Obama's initiatives for neighborhood revitalization were framed as part of a larger strategy for dealing with the collapse of the housing finance system; Obama's program offered relief to troubled homeowners in the suburbs of Las Vegas and Phoenix as well as in central cities like Cleveland.

In three important ways, however, the Obama approach differed from the Clinton approach to cities:

1. The economic and housing crises opened a window of opportunity for Obama to initiate **major new spending initiatives** costing hundreds of billions of dollars. The **American Recovery and Revitalization Act of 2009 (ARRA)**, a $780 billion package of new spending and tax cuts, was the centerpiece of the Obama **economic stimulus program**. In response to the foreclosure crisis, Obama announced a $247 billion plan under which the government would help buy the "toxic" assets of banks, freeing up the capital that banks could use to make new loans.[44] The programs contained tens of billions of dollars of aid that states, cities, and nonprofit organizations could use to combat urban ills. Contrary to often repeated words of Bill Clinton, the age of big government was not yet entirely over.

2. The Obama programs exhibited emphasized **spatial targeting**, with a **place-conscious approach** that gave extra assistance to the nation's most troubled neighborhoods.[45] The Office of Management and Budget, the White House Domestic Policy Council, and the National Economic Council all issued directives instructing federal departments and agencies to develop "effective place-based policies" when submitting their annual budget requests.[46] The president himself called for agencies to work together to build **regional innovation clusters** that would be able to compete in a global economy.

3. Obama utilized a series of **competitive grants** in an effort to stimulate the formation of public–private partnerships and intercommunity problem-solving efforts. The competitive approach rewarded applications that reflected a collaborative approach

to problem solving by public, private, and nonprofit organizations. The **Race to the Top** program sought to have states and localities attempt to out-do one another in their efforts to win federal assistance for school reform. The Choice Neighborhoods Program (discussed below) similarly offered competitive awards "to communities whose proposals make a convincing case that the housing redevelopment will catalyze and leverage lasting neighborhood revitalization, including better schools, grocery stores, and parks."[47]

ARRA emphasized **shovel-ready projects** for immediate job creation, providing support for street resurfacing, bridge repairs, modernized sewers and wastewater treatment, the upgrading of bus and subway systems, and a variety of other municipal infrastructure and transportation projects. The Obama administration even funded track improvements for new high-speed intercity rail service, a project that the administration argued was essential to future economic growth. The newly elected Republican governors of Florida, Ohio, and New Jersey, however, returned the federal money, observing that the development of high-speed rail was not worth the additional costs that state taxpayers would have to bear.

As ARRA sought to create jobs as quickly as possible, it did not have an explicit urban focus. Federal assistance for highway and infrastructure improvements went to the suburbs and rural areas, not just to central cities. Still, municipalities received a substantial portion of ARRA monies.

The Obama administration offered a number of place-based programs targeted on communities in need of assistance:

- **Recovery Zone Bonds**, created under ARRA, made low-interest-rate financing available for new economic development projects in communities that suffered high rates of poverty, joblessness, and home foreclosures.
- The **Neighborhood Stabilization Program (NSP1)**, established by the Housing and Economic Recovery Act of 2008 just before Obama assumed office, set aside $3.9 billion to combat property foreclosures and to inject new investment capital into troubled neighborhoods. The next year, ARRA provided an additional $2 billion for a second round, known as **NSP2**. Compared to the first-round of NSP funds, NSP2 gave a greater share of assistance to hard-hit sections of Cleveland and Detroit and other cities where the tide of boarded-up properties posed a threat to a neighborhood's viability. NSP also provided aid to Sunbelt communities where extensive defaults created virtual ghost towns, where new condominium and vacation-villa developments were barely populated, and where work had stopped mid-construction. Phoenix, Las Vegas, Miami, and Sacramento and Riverside (California) were among the communities where once-hot property markets had given way to a sharp spike in home foreclosures.[48] NSP2 funds were dispensed on a competitive basis, to spur the formation of local consortiums of nonprofit and governmental organizations that would work together to acquire, fix up, and resell abandoned properties.
- The **Hardest Hit Fund** delivered extra assistance to ten states (Arizona, California, Florida, Michigan, Nevada, North Carolina, Ohio, Oregon, Rhode Island,

and South Carolina) that suffered a steep decline in housing prices or continuing high levels of unemployment. The aid allowed states to develop their own programs to assist low-income homebuyers and to help owners who faced possible eviction because they had fallen behind on their mortgage payments.

- The **Promise Neighborhoods Program**, part of the White House Neighborhood Revitalization Initiative, sought to assist high-risk communities as they began to develop programs similar to the **Harlem Children's Zone**, the famed program in New York City that provided for the health, safety, nurturing, and education of children from birth to college.
- The **Choice Neighborhoods Program**, also part of the Neighborhood Revitalization Initiative, sought to strengthen areas that surrounded public housing projects and other areas that had a large concentration of distressed subsidized housing. Just as the HOPE VI program (initiated by President George H.W. Bush) had torn down the nation's worst public housing towers and attempted to build new mixed-income developments, the Choice Neighborhoods Program, too, sought to strengthen neighborhoods by bringing mixed-income communities into areas that, for too long, had been zones of concentrated poverty.
- The **First Look Program**, the outcome of a 2010 agreement negotiated with top mortgage firms, gave cities and nonprofit groups a right of first refusal, that is, up to two weeks to decide to buy select foreclosed properties critical to a neighborhood's revival, before the properties are put up for sale on the open market. The program allowed cities the opportunity to gain control of strategic land parcels key to the future development of a neighborhood.

The Obama approach provided an infusion of resources to communities trying to stave off decline. Still, more liberal activists scorned Obama, just as they had previously scorned Clinton, for being too cautious and for lacking a bold vision in combating urban ills. Liberals pointed out that the Obama initiatives provided nowhere near the resources that major cities required to stem the flood of boarded-up properties and promote neighborhood reinvestment.[49] Liberals were especially angered when Obama's 2012 budget, a response to the drastic deficit reduction initiatives proposed by a Republican-controlled House of Representatives, embraced sizable cuts in domestic programs, including reductions in home heating assistance and the CDBG program.

Other critics attacked Obama for giving vast sums of bailout money directly to the banks instead of simply giving assistance directly to homeowners who faced difficulties in meeting their monthly mortgage obligations. In receipt of federal "bailout" money, banks and other lending institutions felt no great urgency to take new steps to ease the credit crunch that constricted home loans or to restructure mortgage repayment schedules in order to allow homeowners facing difficulty to remain in their homes.[50]

Conservative critics, of course, made a quite different argument, that most of Obama's placed-based and social spending was a waste of taxpayer money. These critics argued that the entire history of federal urban programs showed a paucity of achievements despite the substantial sums spent on place-based assistance.[51] Suburban

HOPE VI and the Demolition of Rockwell Gardens Public Housing on Chicago's West Side: Chicago and other cities used federal HOPE VI assistance to tear down the worst-off public housing towers, which were replaced, in part, by low-rise, mixed-income housing built according to New Urbanism design principles. The new units were certainly better physically, than the old units they replaced. But the income mixing seldom generated the sense of community that the planners had envisioned. Copyright © Paul Goyette. http://commons.wikimedia.org/wiki/File:Demolition_of_Rockwell_Gardens.jpg.

officials also charged that HUD's efforts to target NSP funds to neighborhoods with the greatest need ignored the needs of suburban areas that, too, were affected by the wave of property foreclosures.[52]

THE IMPORTANCE OF STATE ACTION

The national government lacks the resources to tackle urban ills on its own. The states, with their resources and constitutional position, play a critical role in urban affairs. A state can set a limit on how much a city may tax or borrow. State law can be permissive or restrictive when it comes to annexations, local service contracting, and arrangements for interlocal cooperation. As we saw in Chapter 9, state-enacted Smart Growth and growth management measures can help to contain sprawl and promote the infill development of core cities and older suburbs.

The states, not the national government, play the more important role in K–12 education. Each state establishes a formula to assist local school funding. A state, if it so wishes, can redraw school district lines, force the consolidation of smaller school districts, or establish a program of charter schools or school vouchers. A number of states have passed **educational bankruptcy laws** that authorize the takeover or restructuring of failing urban schools. In New York, Los Angeles, Chicago, Baltimore,

Boston, Cleveland, Detroit, Harrisburg, Hartford, New Haven, Providence, Trenton, and Oakland, state governments overrode the authority of local school boards, in some cases giving the mayor new authority to appoint board members and take other steps necessary to shake up underperforming schools.[53] State governments assumed responsibility for running troubled school districts in Compton (California), Lawrence (Massachusetts), Providence, Newark, and Jersey City.

The most dramatic instance of state action came when Pennsylvania in 2002 took charge of Philadelphia's 200,000-student school system with its history of fiscal problems and poor student performance. The governor appointed a new School Reform Board that placed the management of elementary and middle schools in the hands of nonprofit agencies. A new core curriculum and other reforms led to an increase in student proficiency scores.[54]

State action can give a city greater authority in responding to the problem of vacant properties. State statutes determine the extent to which a municipality can exercise eminent domain powers and otherwise acquire tax-delinquent properties in **land banking** efforts. When given land banking authority, a city can control the disposition of blighted properties, as opposed to letting financial speculators pick up vacant properties at rock-bottom prices, skim the profits, and run the properties into the ground. A city or county can use land banking as a tool to stem the spread of blight by assuring that vacant properties will be maintained and used in ways that add to a neighborhood's livability. (See Box 11.2, "Land Banks: Flint, Cleveland, Baltimore, and Atlanta Respond to Property Abandonment.") State action can clear a property of delinquent taxes and all liens, so a good buyer can get a property free and clear of entanglements.[55]

Pennsylvania's innovative Tax Increment Financing Guarantee Program encourages lenders to invest in brownfields reclamation projects. Pennsylvania established a state fund to take some of the risk out of financing inner-city redevelopment projects. The state government helps to promote new development by promises to reimburse creditors in cases where a local project fails to produce the revenues necessary to repay bondholders.[56]

The states have come to recognize that their economic futures are to a great extent intertwined with the fate of their major cities. A blighted city can drag down the image and economic competitiveness of an entire state. The State of New Jersey found that it could not afford to ignore the bleak conditions of much-troubled Newark. The state provided over $100 million in funds and loans—twice the amount garnered by corporate and philanthropic giving—to build a world-class performing arts center in Newark.[57] The arts-based strategy was aimed at jump-starting Newark's rebirth and raising the state's international profile.

States are extremely interested in economic development. New state action authorizing local land banking indicates that the states are also willing to help fight other deep-seated urban problems. Yet, in other important policy areas, especially the taxing and bonding authority permitted municipalities, state policy too often continues to reflect a mistrust of cities and their officials.[58] Even advocates of the New Federalism have recognized that the states have not always had an exemplary record in responding to the needs of big cities and racial minorities.[59] In Louisiana, state officials intervened

Box 11.2

Land Banks: Flint, Cleveland, Baltimore, and Atlanta Respond to Property Abandonment

Can cities find opportunity in abandoned and tax-foreclosed properties? Some states have given cities and counties the ability to create a **land bank** in order to "gain control" over the disposition of vacant lots and structures, properties that, in cases of continued neglect, will lead to the quick decline of a neighborhood. Land banking enables a city or county to acquire, hold, and develop properties when landlords fail to pay property taxes or meet their legal requirements regarding the maintenance of vacant buildings.

Land banking legislation allows a city to coordinate property development in an attempt to stabilize conditions in, and maybe even upgrade, a distressed neighborhood. Without a land bank, a city or county typically seizes a tax-delinquent property and quickly auctions it off in an effort to recoup a minimal amount of money for the public treasury. In too many instances, however, such auction sales prove to be shortsighted as they set in motion a process that accelerates a neighborhood's decline. Speculators often buy the properties at low auction prices. These absentee buyers do not intend to make repairs or meet the other obligations of ownership. Instead, they simply hope to "flip" a property, selling it to make a quick profit. If a property cannot be sold quickly, they simply hold on to it, board it up, and let it decline. Rather than allow a distressed property to fall into the hands of speculators, land banking authority enables a city or county to acquire and hold on to an abandoned property (metaphorically putting the property in a "bank"), assuring that the property is properly maintained and eventually put to a more positive use.

Land banking allows a city or county to engage in **greening strategies** to make a neighborhood more attractive to residents. A government can offer vacant lots at virtually no cost to the owners of abutting properties who will maintain the addition as a green side lot or garden, with the city aiding in landscaping and reseeding. Neighborhood groups can maintain community playgrounds and gardens. In some cases, the city can use the new land for parks extensions. Where funds permit, a city can demolish vacant, dilapidated structures and turn the property into a community asset. Cleveland has targeted vacant property acquisition and upgrading not to the city's hardest hit areas but to neighborhoods that still have market viability, where a green lot can add to community livability and help spur development. For cities that have lost substantial population, land banking and greening strategies may represent the only viable approaches for maintaining property values in core communities, turning nuisance properties into neighborhood assets.

A city can even use land banking as part of an ambitious program of neighborhood transformation. Developers are more willing to invest and build in a core neighborhood if they can be assured that other properties in the area will be maintained and similarly upgraded. Land banking allows the city to hold and assemble properties that can then be offered to a developer for a large-scale project.

Under Michigan Public Act 123, Genesee County Treasurer Dale Kildee took control over every new piece of land entering Flint's foreclosure system, preventing, as he phrased it, the "late-night infomercial speculators" from taking ownership and spreading further ruin in the city's neighborhoods. From 2003 through the beginning of 2009, Genesee County took charge of some 7,400 properties—12 percent of all land in Flint—and demolished over 1,000 abandoned homes. In a city that had lost vast numbers of residents and jobs, land banking was part of the municipal effort to repurpose land and "shrink" the city's footprint.

Can other cities copy Flint and gain control over property development in troubled neighborhoods? State law determines whether and under what conditions a locality can acquire and hold on to a nuisance property. State law also determines whether or not a city can use eminent domain powers to acquire a land parcel needed as part of an economic or neighborhood renewal project.

Changes in state statutes are also necessary to streamline excessively lengthy tax foreclosure processes. In Michigan, tax foreclosure on a property used to take from four to seven years, that is, until Public Act 123 fast-tracked the process, shortening foreclosure proceedings to just a year or two. Ohio House Bill 294 similarly streamlined the tax foreclosure process so that it now typically takes a city only four months, not two years, to gain control of an abandoned property.

By the first decade of the twenty-first century, eight states—Georgia, Indiana, Kentucky, Maryland, Michigan, Missouri, Ohio, and Texas—allowed municipal land banks. The cities of St. Louis, Cleveland, Louisville, Atlanta, and Flint all made extensive use of land bank authority in their efforts to stem neighborhood decline and put an end to the spread of blight caused by the home foreclosure crisis.

Sources: "Genesee County Land Bank," presentation by Genesee County Treasurer Dan Kildee to the Revitalizing Older Cities Capitol Hill Urban Summit, organized by the Northeast-Midwest Institute, Washington, DC, February 12, 2009; Frank S. Alexander, *Land Bank Authorities: A Guide for the Creation and Operation of Local Land Banks,* a publication of the Local Initiatives Support Corporation, April 2005; "State Policy Toolkit: State Land Bank Enabling Legislation," a publication of the Restoring Prosperity Initiative, 2008, www.restoringprosperity.org/wp-content/uploads/2008/09/land-bank-policy-package-pdf.pdf; and Sage Computing, Inc., "Revitalizing Foreclosed Properties with Land Banks," prepared for the U.S. Department of Housing and Urban Development, August 2009.

in New Orleans's affairs primarily to support economic growth projects. In the years preceding Hurricane Katrina, state policymakers made little concerted effort to address the needs of the Crescent City's poorer neighborhoods.[60]

Much like the United States Congress, the state legislatures often reflect the policy concerns of electorates dominated by middle-class suburban (and sometimes rural) constituencies. State programs provide disproportionate funding to suburban and rural roadways while failing to provide for urban transportation needs.[61]

Even **state enterprise zone programs**, often justified as a way to bring new jobs to economically troubled areas, lack targeting. Enterprise zones offer extensive tax breaks and other inducements in an attempt to lure businesses to distressed communities. Yet, many states create enterprise zones in areas that exhibit no obvious distress.[62] A number of states make only the most minimal attempt to target zone creation to communities in need. Illinois, Ohio, and Texas designated hundreds of enterprise zones; Louisiana created over 1,700 spread throughout the state! Arkansas declared the entire state an enterprise zone.[63] Such broad-scale creation of enterprise zones may attract business to a state, but it does little to help cities in need. When so many enterprise zones exist or an entire state is an enterprise zone, a business has little incentive to choose a location in a troubled city or suburb; instead, a business can locate in a fairly well-off community and still gain the program's various tax incentives and subsidies.[64]

CONCLUSION: URBAN POLICY IN AN ANTI-URBAN POLICY AGE

The American antigovernment attitude undermines the ability of the national government to pursue a strong, sustained, and coordinated urban policy. The New Federalism is rooted in the public's distrust of "big government" programs that are viewed as wasteful, inflexible, inefficient, overly complex.[65] Local officials, too, chafe at the constraints and costs of federal rules.

National programs, however, also serve important public purposes, aiding local as well as national economic development, promoting equity, preventing discrimination, and providing assistance to communities and people in need. In a suburban age, however, the U.S. Congress has little inclination to commit to a national urban policy or even to target assistance to communities in need.

The political logic that guides state and national legislators leads to a **spread effect,** where legislatures spend program monies widely, allowing each legislator to claim electoral credit for funding of local projects. Resources spread so widely, by definition, undermine targeted, coherent action. Even in the crucially important policy area of homeland security, Congress spread the political "pork" of antiterrorism spending, giving every state and virtually every congressional district a share of homeland security assistance. According to one estimate, three-fourths of the funds for homeland security were allocated without regard to a jurisdiction's risk of attack! New York City, a prime target of terrorism, received less homeland security assistance per capita than did a number of small states.[66]

The New Federalism started out as a Republican effort to decentralize decision-making power. The Reagan administration went further, arguing that programs aimed at reviving cities do not contribute to the national economy. The Reagan–Bush era saw sharp reductions in federal assistance to cities. Republican presidents and congressional majorities have pursued budget reductions and shrinkage of government, not just program decentralization. Democratic presidents, too, have been constrained in although to a lesser degree, by the public's New Federalism, antigovernment sentiment.

The Obama administration launched programs of assistance that were explicitly targeted to troubled communities. Reflecting his past as a community organizer, Obama did not abandon central cities and core-city neighborhoods. His critics charged that such policy efforts were a waste of money, that spatially based assistance cannot reverse the choices that businesses and residents have made to leave declining communities. Yet, the record shows that spatially focused programs have succeeded in providing job training and improving the housing conditions for the urban poor who are left behind. Assistance targeted to core communities is also critical for dealing with vacant properties, preventing the further decline of housing values and the spread of blight to surrounding areas. As one analysis of the Obama policy concluded, "Recent experience offers some basis for optimism that well-conceived and well-implemented investments can catalyze meaningful improvements, not just for places, but for the people who live in them."[67]

Barack Obama, like Bill Clinton before him, did not announce a Marshall Plan of aid for cities; neither announced the sort of well-funded, strong national urban policy that liberals often urge. Instead, Obama, like Clinton, chose a more pragmatic path, pursuing "politically possible" programs in an anti-urban age where population and power have shifted to suburbia and the Sunbelt.

Yet, the end of National Urban Policy does not mean the end of effective national and state urban actions. Smaller, well-crafted and important urban programs are politically possible, especially if the programs promise to aid middle-class families and not just the poor. Obama and Clinton both recognized the necessity of advancing program initiatives that were not exclusively urban in nature or narrowly focused on conditions in the inner city. In an anti-urban age, an effective urban policy must offer assistance to suburban and Sunbelt communities while giving disproportionate aid to cities and communities with the greatest need.

NOTES

1. During the New Deal, the Supreme Court declared that the Tenth Amendment was only a "truism" which stated the obvious but not very meaningful proposition that "all is retained which has not yet been surrendered." See *United States v. Darby*, 312 U.S. 100 (1941).

2. *United States v. Lopez*, 514 U.S. 549 (1995).

3. Charles Wise, "Judicial Federalism: The Resurgence of the Supreme Court's Role in the Protection of State Sovereignty," *Public Administration Review* 58, no. 2 (March/April 1998): 96.

4. *Printz v. United States* 117 S. Ct. 2365 (1997).

5. See the discussion by Wise, "Judicial Federalism," 97.

6. *United States v. Morrison* 120 S. Ct. 1740 (2000).

7. Timothy J. Conlan and Francois Vergniolle De Chantal, "The Rehnquist Court and Contemporary American Federalism," *Political Science Quarterly* 116, no. 2 (Summer 2001): 253–275; John Dinan and Dale Krane, "The State of American Federalism, 2005: Federalism Resurfaces in the Political Debate," *Publius: Journal of Federalism* 36, no. 3 (Summer 2006): 327–374.

8. See the Supreme Court's seemingly inconsistent rulings in: *National League of Cities v. Usery,* 426 U.S. 833 (1976); *Garcia v. San Antonio Metropolitan Transportation Authority,* 464 U.S. 546 (1985); and *South Carolina v. Baker*, 108 S. Ct. 1935 (1988). The *South Carolina v. Baker* case dealt with the technical question of whether the national government could mandate the exact form that state and local bonds must take in order to earn federal tax-exempt status. The larger question was whether the national government could impose rules on state and local financing, a matter crucial to subnational authority. The Supreme Court ruled that the Constitution posed no limits to the actions of the national government in this area.

9. Troy E. Smith, "Intergovernmental Lobbying: How Opportunistic Actors Create a Less Structured and Balanced Federal System," in *Intergovernmental Management in the 21st Century,* ed. Timothy J. Conlan and Paul L. Posner (Washington, DC: Brookings Institution Press, 2008), 312. For further discussion of the significance of *Gonzales v. Raich*, 125 S.Ct. 2195 (2005) and its effect on legitimizing the expansive reach of the national government in domestic affairs, see Ilya Somin, "Gonzales v. Raich: Federalism as a Casualty of the War on Drugs," *Cornell Journal of Law and Public Policy* 15, no. 3 (Summer 2006): 507–550; also available as George Mason Law and Economics Research Paper no. 06–31, http://ssrn.com/abstract=916965.

10. U.S. Census Bureau, *The 2009 Statistical Abstract: The National Data Book,* tables 414 and 415; www.census.gov/compendia/statab/tables/09s0414.pdf and www.census.gov/compendia/statab/tables/09s0415.pdf.

11. In addition to the three organizations mentioned in the paragraph, the ranks of the public interest groups (PIGs) also include the International City/County Management Association (ICMA), the National Governors Association (NGA), the National Conference of State Legislatures (NCSL), and the Council of State Governments (CSG). For a further description of intergovernmental lobbying and its impact on the federal system, see Smith, "Intergovernmental Lobbying," 321–329.

12. See the Brookings Institution Public Forum on "Block Grants: Past, Present, and Prospects," Washington, DC, October 13, 2003. Transcript available at: www.brookings.edu/comm/events/20031015.htm. John Dinan and Shama Damkhar, "The State of American Federalism 2008–2009: The Presidential Election, The Economic Downturn, and the Consequences for Federalism," *Publius: Journal of Federalism* 39, no. 3 (2009): 369–407.

13. Carl W. Stenberg, "Block Grants and Devolution: A Future Tool?" in Conlan and Posner, *Intergovernmental Management in the 21st Century,* 271.

14. Dinan and Damkhar, "The State of American Federalism 2008–2009," 376.

15. Timothy J. Conlan, "Between a Rock and a Hard Place: The Evolution of American Federalism," in Conlan and Posner, *Intergovernmental Management in the 21st Century*, 33–34.

16. Charles J. Orlebeke, "The Evolution of Low-Income Housing Policy, 1949 to 1989," *Housing Policy Debate* 11, no. 2 (2000): 505–506.

17. "50-State Update: Analysis Details State Costs of Federal Mandates," National Conference of State Legislatures press release, NCSL News, April 7, 2004; updated May 12, 2004, www.ncsl.org/programs/press/2004/pr040407.htm.

18. Paul Posner, "The Politics of Coercive Federalism in the Bush Era," *Publius: Journal of Federalism* 37, no. 3 (2007): 390–412; Posner, "Mandates: The Politics of Coercive Federalism," in Conlan and Posner, *Intergovernmental Management in the 21st Century,* 286–309.

19. Paul L. Posner, "Unfunded Mandate Reform Act: 1996 and Beyond," *Publius: Journal of Federalism* 27 (1997): 59 and 69.

20. Paul L. Posner, *The Politics of Unfunded Mandates* (Washington, DC: Georgetown University Press, 1998); Janet M. Kelly, "The Unfunded Mandate Reform Act: Working Well for No Good Reason," *Government Finance Review* 19, no. 1 (February 2003): 28–30.

21. Associated Press, "Connecticut Lawsuit says 'No Child Left Behind' Is Illegal," *Los Angeles Times,* August 23, 2005.

22. Molly Stauffer and Carl Tubbesing, "The Mandate Monster: Unfunded Federal Mandates Are Back, and They Are Costing States Millions," *State Legislatures* (May 2004): 23; David S. Broder, "President's Unfunded Mandates Criticized," *Washington Post,* March 11, 2004.

23. G. Ross Stephens and Nelson Wikstrom, *American Intergovernmental Relations: A Fragmented Federal Polity* (New York: Oxford University Press, 2007), 197–199.

24. Connecticut Conference of Municipalities, "CT Mandate Watch—2010," www.ccm-ct.org/advocacy/mandates/.

25. Bernard Frieden and Marshall Kaplan, *The Politics of Neglect* (Cambridge, MA: MIT Press, 1975); Benjamin Kleinberg, *Urban America in Transformation: Perspectives on Urban Policy and Development* (Thousand Oaks, CA: Sage, 1995), 175–184.

26. Bruce A. Wallin, *From Revenue Sharing to Deficit Sharing* (Washington, DC: Georgetown University Press, 1998), 56–95 and 137–139.

27. Donna Milam Handley, "Strengthening the Intergovernmental Grant System: Long-Term Lessons for the Federal-Local Relationship," *Public Administration Review* 68, no. 1 (January/February 2008): 126–136.

28. See, for instance, Colleen M. Grogan and Elizabeth Rigby, "Federalism, Partisan Politics, and Shifting Support for State Flexibility: The Case of the U.S. State Children's Health Insurance Program," *Publius: Journal of Federalism* 39, no. 1 (Winter 2009): 47–69.

29. Kleinberg, *Urban America in Transformation*, 229.

30. Timothy Conlan, *New Federalism: Intergovernmental Reform from Nixon to Reagan* (Washington DC: Brookings Institution Press, 1988), 160.

31. U.S. Conference of Mayors, figures cited by Peter Eisinger, "City Politics in an Era of Federal Devolution," *Urban Affairs Review* 33, no. 3 (January 1998): 311.

32. Demetrios Caraley, "Washington Abandons Cities," *Political Science Quarterly* 107, no. 1 (1992): 1–30.

33. Carol F. Steinbach, "Shelter-skelter," *National Journal*, April 8, 1989, 851–855.

34. John Shannon, "The Return to Fend-For-Yourself Federalism: The Reagan Mark," *Intergovernmental Perspective* 13, no. 3/4 (Summer–Fall 1987), cited in John D. Donahue, *Disunited States* (New York: Basic Books, 1997), 29.

35. George E. Peterson and Carol W. Lewis, eds., *Reagan and the Cities* (Washington, DC: Urban Institute Press, 1986).

36. Pietro S. Nivola, Jennifer L. Noyes, and Isabel V. Sawhill, "Waive of the Future? Federalism and the Next Phase of Welfare Reform," Brookings Institution Policy Brief no. 29, Washington, DC, 2004, www.brookings.edu/es/research/projects/wrb/publications/pb/pb29.htm; and Jill Khadduri, "Should the Housing Voucher Program Become a State-Administered Block Grant?" *Housing Policy Debate* 14, no. 3 (2003): 235–269, www.fanniemaefoundation.org/programs/hpd/pdf/hpd_1403_khadduri.pdf; Margery Austin Turner and Susan Popkin, "Comment on Jill Khadduri's 'Should the Housing Voucher Program Become a State-Administered Block Grant?' A Housing Block Grant Is a Bad Idea," *Housing Policy Debate* 14, no. 3 (2003): 271–281, www.fanniemaefoundation.org/programs/hpd/pdf/hpd_1403_turner.pdf; and Barbara Sard and Will Fischer, "Passing the Buck: The Administration's Flexible Voucher Program Would Compel Housing Agencies to Impose Deep Cuts in 2005 and Subsequent Years," report of the Center on Budget and Policy Priorities, March 16, 2004, www.cbpp.org/3–16–04hous.htm; and John Dinan, "The State of American Federalism 2007–2008: Resurgent State Influence in the National Policy Process and Continued State Policy Innovation," *Publius: Journal of Federalism* 38, no. 3 (Summer 2008): 381–415.

37. Veronique de Rugy and Tad DeHaven, *Cato Institute Tax & Budget Bulletin*, no. 16, August 2003. See also J. Edwin Benton, "George W. Bush's Federal Aid Legacy," *Publius: Journal of Federalism* 37, no. 3 (Summer 2007): 371–389.

38. Kirk McClure, "The Low-Income Housing Tax Credit as an Aid to Housing Finance: How Well Has It Worked?" *Housing Policy Debate* 11, no. 1 (2000): 91–114; Lance Freeman, "Siting Affordable Housing: Location and Neighborhood Trends of Low Income Housing Tax Credit Developments in the 1990s," report of the Brookings Institution Center on Urban and Metropolitan Policy, Washington, DC, April 2004, www.brookings.edu/urban/publications/20040405_freeman.htm; and Alex F. Schwartz, *Housing Policy in the United States* (New York: Routledge, 2006), 76–99 and 83–99.

39. R. Allen Hays, "Habitat for Humanity: Building Social Capital through Faith Based Service," *Journal of Urban Affairs* 24, nos. 3 and 4 (2003): 247–269. For a more general discussion and assessment of Bush's faith-based initiatives, see: Amy E. Black, Douglas L. Koopman, and David K. Ryden, *Of Little Faith: The Politics of George W. Bush's Faith-Based Initiatives* (Washington, DC: Georgetown University Press, 2004); Jo Renee Formicola, Mary C. Segers, and Paul Weber, *Faith-Based Initiatives and the Bush Administration: The Good, the Bad, and the Ugly* (Lanham, MD: Rowman and Littlefield, 2003); Sheila Suess Kennedy and Wolfgang Beilefeld, *Charitable Choice at Work: Evaluating Faith-Based Jobs Programs in the States* (Washington, DC: Georgetown University Press, 2006); and Richard M. Clerkin and Kristen A. Grønbjerg, "The Capacities and Challenges of Faith-Based Human Service Organizations," *Public Administration Review* 67, no. 1 (February 2007): 115–126.

40. Robert J. Waste, *Independent Cities: Rethinking U.S. Urban Policy* (New York: Oxford University Press, 1998), 90.

41. Myron A. Levine, "Urban Policy in America: The Clinton Approach," *Local Economy* 9 (November 1994): 278–281.

42. Alan Berube and Thacher Tiffany, "The 'State' of Low-Wage Workers: How the EITC Benefits

Urban and Rural Communities in the 50 States," study of the Brookings Institution, Washington, DC, February 2004, www.brookings.edu/es/urban/publications/eitc/20040203_berube.htm. See also Alan Berube and Benjamin Forman, "Rewarding Work: the Impact of the Earned Income Tax Credit in Greater Chicago," study of the Brookings Institution Center on Urban and Metropolitan Policy, Washington, DC, November 2001, www.brookings.edu/es/urban/eitc/chicago.pdf.

43. Marilyn Gittell, Kathe Newman, Janice Bockmeyer, and Robert Lindsay, "Expanding Civic Opportunity: Urban Empowerment Zones," *Urban Affairs Review* 33, no. 4 (March 1998): 530–558; Deirdre Oakley and Hi-Shien Tsao, "A New Way of Revitalizing Distressed Urban Communities? Assessing the Impact of the Federal Empowerment Zone Program," *Journal of Urban Affairs* 28, no. 5 (2006): 443–471.

44. Sheryl Gay Stolberg and Edmund L. Andrews, "$275 Billion Plan Seeks to Address Housing Crisis," *New York Times*, February 18, 2009; U.S. Department of Treasury, "Homeowner Affordability and Stability Plan: Executive Summary," February 18, 2009, www.ustreas.gov/press/releases/tg33.htm.

45. "The White House Neighborhood Revitalization Initiative," www.whitehouse.gov/sites/default/files/nri_description.pdf.

46. See, for instance, White House, "Memorandum for the Heads of Executive Departments; Subject: Developing Effective Place-Based Policies for the FY 2012 Budget," June 21, 2010.

47. Manuel Pastor and Margery Austin Turner, "Reducing Poverty and Economic Distress after ARRA: Potential Roles for Place-Conscious Strategies," paper prepared by the Urban Institute for the Georgetown University and Urban Institute Conference on Reducing Poverty and Economic Distress after ARRA, Washington, DC, January 15, 2010, www.law.georgetown.edu/povertyandinequality/documents/ReducingPovertyandEconomicDistressafterARRA.pdf.

48. Dan Immergluck, "The Foreclosure Crisis, Foreclosed Properties, and Federal Policy: Some Implications for Housing and Community Development Planning," *Journal of the American Planning Association* 75, no. 4 (2009): 408.

49. See, for instance, Paul Kantor, "City Futures: Politics, Economic Crisis, and the American Model of Urban Development," *Urban Research and Practice* 3, no. 1 (March 2010): 1–11; and Matt Chaban, "Can Obama's Office of Urban Affairs Carrion?" *Architect's Newspaper*, June 2, 2010, http://archpaper.com/e-board_rev.asp?News_ID=4588.

50. John B. Judis, "Foreclosure? For Shame: Obama Is Making a Historic Mistake," *New Republic*, October 21, 2010.

51. Economist Edward L. Glaeser, "Can Buffalo Ever Come Back?" *City Journal* 17, no. 4 (Summer 2007): 95–99, also makes the argument for people-based programs—for education programs that would allow workers to move to areas of job growth, instead of spatially-oriented programs that attempt to restore places that residents and businesses no longer value.

52. Juan-Pablo Velez, "Suburbs United in Quest of Federal Housing Aid, but Are Shut Out," *New York Times*, May 7, 2010.

53. Kenneth K. Wong, Francis X. Shen, Dorothea Anagnostopoulos, and Stacey Rutledge, *The Education Mayor: Improving America's Schools* (Washington, DC: Georgetown University Press, 2007). For a readable overview of the actions taken by the states to increase the mayor's control over failing school systems, see Frederick M. Hess, "Assessing the Case for Mayoral Control of Urban Schools," *AEI (American Enterprise Institute) Online*, 4 (August 2008), www.aei.org/outlook/28511. For an analysis of mayoral takeover efforts, see Joseph P. Viteritti, ed., *When Mayors Take Charge: School Governance in the City* (Washington, DC: Brookings Institution Press, 2009).

54. Brian Gill, Ron Zimmer, Jolley Christman, and Suzanne Blanc, "State Takeover, School Restructuring, Private Management, and Student Achievement in Philadelphia," report of RAND Education, Santa Monica, CA, 2007, www.rand.org/pubs/monographs/2007/RAND_MG533.pdf.

55. Jim Rokakis, Cuyahoga County (Ohio) treasurer, remarks at the Reclaiming Vacant Properties Conference, Cleveland, Ohio, October 14, 2010.

56. Evans Paull, "Vacant Properties, TIFs, and What's Working Now," presentation to the Reclaiming Vacant Properties Conference, Cleveland, Ohio, October 14, 2010.

57. Elizabeth Strom, "Let's Put on a Show! Performing Arts and Urban Revitalization in Newark, New Jersey," *Journal of Urban Affairs* 21, no. 4 (1999): 423–435.

58. Gerald E. Frug and David J. Barron, *City Bound: How States Stifle Urban Innovation* (Ithaca, NY: Cornell University Press, 2008).

59. John A. Ferejohn and Barry R. Weingast, eds., *The New Federalism: Can the States Be Trusted?* (Stanford, CA: Hoover Institution Press, 1997).

60. Peter Burns and Matthew O. Thomas, "Governors and the Development Regime in New Orleans," *Urban Affairs Review* 39, no. 6 (2004): 791–812.

61. Edward Hill et al., "Slanted Pavement: How Ohio's Highway Spending Shortchanges Cities and Suburbs," in *Taking the High Road: A Metropolitan Agenda for Transit Reform*, ed. Bruce Katz and Robert Puentes (Washington, DC: Brookings Institution Press, 2005), 101–135.

62. Gary Sands, Laura A. Reese, and Heather L. Kahn, "Implementing Tax Abatements in Michigan: A Study of Best Practices," *Economic Development Quarterly* 20, no. 1 (February 2006): 44–58.

63. Robert T. Greenbaum, "Siting It Right: Do States Target Economic Distress When Designating Enterprise Zones?" *Economic Development Quarterly* 18, no. 1 (February 2004): 70.

64. Alan H. Peters and Peter S. Fisher, *Enterprise Zones: Have They Worked?* (Kalamazoo, MI: Upjohn Institute, 2002), 218–219; Jim F. Couch and J. Douglas Barrett, "Alabama's Enterprise Zones: Designed to Aid the Needy?" *Public Finance Review* 32, no. 1 (January 2004): 65–81; Robert C. Turner and Mark K. Cassell. "When Do States Pursue Targeted Economic Development Policies? The Adoption and Expansion of State Enterprise Zone Programs," *Social Science Quarterly* 88, no. 1 (March 2007): 86–103.

65. John Kincaid and Richard L. Cole, "Public Opinion on Issues of Federalism in 2007: A Bush Plus?" *Publius: Journal of Federalism* 38, no. 3 (Summer 2008): 469–487.

66. Hillary Rodham Clinton, "Give New York Its Fair Share of Homeland Money," *New York Times,* August 22, 2004. See also Sewell Chan, "Bloomberg Criticizes Security Fund Distribution," *New York Times,* January 9, 2007; and Peter Eisinger, "Imperfect Federalism: The Intergovernmental Partnership for Homeland Security," *Public Administration Review* 66, no. 4 (July 2006): 537–545.

67. Pastor and Turner, "Reducing Poverty and Economic Distress after ARRA," 3.

12 The Future of Urban America

In a global age, cities devote considerable effort to the pursuit of jobs and new economic development. Yet, urban politics is not solely about economic development. In the United States, questions of class and racial equity continue to define the urban arena. While the more blatant forms of racial steering and housing discrimination have disappeared, urban ghettoes have not. New patterns of school segregation (or, more strictly speaking, resegregation) are emerging. African Americans have also gained entrance to inner-ring suburban communities that differ markedly from the "suburbia" in which white Americans live.

In an age of limited public resources, municipal leaders are also preoccupied with strategies to improve local service effectiveness and efficiency. Governmental officials have no choice but to do more with less.

Concern for the urban future also entails a new awareness of the importance of *sustainability*, the need to promote patterns of growth and development that minimize resource depletion and environmental harm. Across the nation, cities and suburbs have adopted "green" policies to reduce energy consumption, reuse recycled building materials, preserve wetlands, minimize water runoff and soil contamination, and ensure that the decisions made today do not adversely affect the quality of life for future generations.

"Shrinking" cities that have lost substantial population have adopted "greening" strategies, for turning vacant lots into green areas that promote natural drainage and flood control while adding to community livability. Atlanta has committed more than $2.8 billion to the Atlanta BeltLine, an effort to transform underutilized and abandoned rail property surrounding the core of the city into a twenty-two-mile extension of parks, greenways, and mass transit that will connect forty-five city neighborhoods to one another. The project will make Atlanta a more livable city. Civic leaders hope that such green development will also attract new economic investment to the city.[1]

We conclude this book by discussing the future of cities and suburbs as policymakers attempt to balance economic development with concerns for equity, service effectiveness and efficiency, and a sustainable urban future.

THE EMPHASIS ON ECONOMIC DEVELOPMENT

U.S. cities have always been concerned with their economic development. Early New York City, Buffalo, Chicago, and Dayton constructed canals to promote trade. In the age of the big-city political machines, party bosses supported growth projects that enabled them to dispense valuable contracts, franchises, and job patronage to their loyal supporters. In Houston, Los Angeles, Long Beach, and other Sunbelt cities, local leaders expanded port facilities and shipping channels, built new airports, and otherwise provided the infrastructure necessary for business growth and local prosperity.[2]

While U.S. cities throughout their history have always pursued growth, concern for economic development did not dominate the local agenda to the extent that it does today. For nearly a hundred years, the battle between the machine and reformers defined local politics. Beginning in the 1960s, social, antipoverty, community action, community control, school busing, and law-and-order programs dominated national, state, and local agendas as governments attempted to find a solution to the "urban crisis" and the wave of riots that spread across the nation. None of these programs had economic development at their heart. Beginning in the mid-1970s, after New York City's and Cleveland's flirtation with bankruptcy, concerns about the big-city fiscal crisis and cutback management dominated the urban agenda. Rising voter anti-tax sentiment reinforced municipal belt-tightening. Once again, questions of urban local economic development did not dominate urban affairs.

By the 1990s, however, postindustrial restructuring had undermined local economies, leading local leaders to give new urgency to economic development and job creation. With globalized competition adding to cities' fiscal insecurity, economic development gained a near-hegemonic position in the municipal arena. Only the most affluent communities could be selective in seizing new opportunities for economic growth. Today, local economic initiatives are a normal part of municipal government, an activity as commonplace as street cleaning and the provision of police and fire service.

Cities across the nation offer improved infrastructure, tax concessions, and other subsidies in their attempt to attract and retain businesses. Cities established **tax increment financing (TIF) districts** to help pay for the improvements demanded by business. When a TIF district is created in a designated area in a city, the gains in property tax revenues from business expansion are plowed back into the district, helping to pay for physical improvements made in the district. Politicians see TIFs as an attractive "self-financing" means of development. The revenues yielded from a project are used to pay off the obligations that were incurred when the city borrowed money to begin work on the project. Businesses find TIF districts quite attractive as the additional taxes they pay are dedicated to the improvements they desire. Dallas created a 9.5-mile-long TIF district in the Skillman corridor, northeast of the downtown, to promote commercial renewal around the newly opened stations of the DART light-rail system.[3]

But TIFs also have problems. Business expansion in a TIF does not yield additional tax revenues that can be used to finance service improvements in other neighborhoods or to support the provision of public education. A city's schools gain little when the tax revenues received from new development are dedicated to repaying debt and financing infrastructure improvements inside the TIF district.[4]

Numerous economists argue that TIFs and other tax abatements are wasteful, that they have only a minor influence on business-siting decisions. Tax rates are less critical to business location than are matters of transportation, accessibility to suppliers and markets, and the quality of the local labor force.[5] Yet, despite the findings of numerous academic studies, local officials continue to offer prospective businesses a seemingly endless array of tax concessions and subsidies. Local officials feel that they are in a competitive race and that they have no choice but to match what other communities are offering. Few elected officeholders want to risk being blamed for the relocation of a prominent business or the loss of the city's professional baseball or football team.

TIFs and other tax concessions awarded to businesses serve to reduce the net revenues that a city gains from a project. When the revenues do not cover the full costs to a city of promoting a new sports arena, convention center, or other development project, the city's taxpayers—residents, small businesses, and businesses located in other parts of the city—wind up paying the difference. School systems find that the revenues available for education are diminished when a city awards tax abatements to industrial and commercial property.

In an intensely competitive environment, cities increasingly find that a strategy based on tax cuts and other business subsidies is no longer sufficient to win the "job wars." A city's offer of tax concessions are easily matched by other cities. A city that invests heavily to expand "Wi-Fi" coverage may find that it gains very little, because hundreds of other communities have done the same.

Improved roads, telecommunications, and transportation infrastructure are the **hard factors** that affect private investment. Numerous studies, however, also highlight the critical importance of **soft factors** that a city can use to help attract employers. Businesses are drawn to communities with good schools, a capable workforce, plentiful parks and recreational facilities, interesting arts and cultural programs, and a pleasant living environment. As the success of Seattle and Portland attests, an excellent local **quality of life** helps to make a region attractive to upscale employers and "creative" workforces.[6]

The "shadow governments" of special districts, regional authorities, and business-led public–private partnerships possess the ability to subsidize new development projects. These bodies often possess eminent domain authority as well. The shadow governments "get things done," working with minimal citizen participation and minimal scrutiny from the press.[7] In some cities, their actions have led to a countermobilization by homeowner associations, anti-tax forces, environmental organizations, and minority groups. Particularly in the Sunbelt, neighborhood and taxpayer groups have turned to the voter initiative and referendum processes in an effort to check the growth-oriented actions of shadow governments.

Do cities have any real choice but to give into the demands of growth forces? Certain policies can reduce the economic stranglehold that business seems to have on the local arena. Federal revenue sharing, metropolitan tax-base sharing, and state assumption of a greater share of local school expenditures would mitigate some of the fiscal pressures that lead localities to woo new development. Strict land-use regulation, statutes that limit condominium conversion and displacement, and plant-closing laws can all serve to constrain the dislocations of unfettered free-market growth.[8] In the privatist United States, however, few cities will adopt such solutions.

Instead, the local love affair with economic development will likely continue. Laws for greater transparency, public participation, the provision of affordable housing, environmental protection and "green" construction, and even campaign finance reform can all add a measure of balance to a decision-making process that is too often dominated by developers, corporate interests, local chambers of commerce, and other members of the local growth coalition.

The Future of Minority Empowerment

The New Style of African American and Latino Politics

Nearly half of the U.S. cities with populations exceeding 100,000 are "majority minority": African Americans, Hispanics, and Asians make up the majority of the populations of these cities.[9] The Hispanic urban population grew by 46 percent in just ten years, a product of both immigration and high birthrates.[10] Latinos make up nearly a quarter of the population of the 100 largest cities in the United States. In recent years, the Latino population has reached virtual numerical parity with the African American population. In the Southwest, the Latino "sleeping giant" is just beginning to waken to its potential voting and political power.[11] The potential for Latino power, however, is diminished by poor rates of voting turnout that are lower than those of whites and African Americans.[12]

As African Americans and Latinos have gained power in city hall, the more militant rhetoric of earlier generations has given way to the more pragmatic concerns of governance. Black and Latino mayors have had to be concerned with improving the quality of municipal services, finding new managerial efficiencies in city government, and forging new partnerships with private-sector and nonprofit groups in order to bring new jobs and revitalization back to the inner city.

In Newark, New Jersey, the governing approach of Rhodes Scholar and Yale Law–educated Mayor Cory Booker contrasts markedly with the parochialism and machine-style excesses of his predecessor, Sharpe James. Booker has reached out to business chief executive officers and the heads of nonprofit foundations in order to gain the resources for charter schools, parks renovation, jobs fairs, and even the purchase of new police equipment.[13] In economically distressed Youngstown, Ohio, Jay Williams, the city's first African American mayor, has similarly relied on a soft-spoken approach as he has built partnerships with businesses, nonprofit foundations, and the local university.[14] Latino leaders, too, have come to recognize the importance of a politics of "accommodation" as well as "recognition."[15] Yet, in both the African American and Latino communities, more activist local leaders criticize the compromises that are made when black and Latino mayors govern as the head of multiracial coalitions. Latino governing officials have been criticized for a pragmatism that is "more an achievement of the conservative middle class than of the masses."[16]

Progressives often call for African Americans and Latinos to unite in a biracial coalition in their mutual quest for power. Yet, the formation of a biracial alliance often proves quite difficult, as blacks and Latinos do not share a common identity.[17] In Miami and Los Angeles, black and Hispanic voters are polarized, with the two groups seeing themselves as competitors for the same slice of the urban political and economic pie.[18] Public opinion data from California reveal that Latinos tend to align with whites, and not with African Americans, on major public policy questions.[19]

Yet, with special care and the proper leadership skills, a biracial—even a multi-racial—coalition can emerge. Antonio Villaraigosa, a Latino, won the Los Angeles mayoralty in 2005, gaining nearly half of the votes cast by the city's black citizens who were upset that the incumbent mayor had ousted Bernard Parks, the city's African American police chief.[20]

Limits on Racial Preferences for Minority Economic Empowerment

During the age of the political machine, city bosses steered jobs and benefits to various ethnic constituencies. Today, where blacks and Latinos control city hall in many big cities, their leaders have only a limited ability to do the same. The U.S. Supreme Court has placed sharp restrictions on **contract compliance** programs, the affirmative-action-style preferences used to give city contracts to minority-owned firms and to businesses that agree to racial hiring targets.

African Americans constitute more than half of the population Richmond, Virginia, the former capital of the Confederacy. When whites controlled the city government, very few African American-owned firms received contracts from the city; in fact, less than 1 percent of the city's contracting business was awarded to black-owned firms. When African Americans finally gained electoral power, one of their first actions was to correct this vast imbalance. They established a **minority set-aside program**, specifying that at least 30 percent of the total dollar amount of municipal contracts be awarded to minority firms.

The city's business community was split in its reaction to the program. The more pragmatic white business leaders recognized the advantages of pursuing development projects with the backing of black elected officials who could show their supporters how new development was bringing jobs to the black community. Contract compliance set-asides were the "glue" that allowed African Americans and whites to agree on economic development initiatives.[21] But the white owners of other businesses, especially in the construction trades; objected that the requirements amounted to reverse discrimination they argued that the city should simply award a contract to whichever qualified firm submitted the lowest bid, with no added requirements for hiring on the basis of race.

The U.S. Supreme Court, in ***Richmond v. Croson*** (1989), struck down the City of Richmond's contract compliance program as a noxious racial classification. According to the decision, a city cannot simply refer to broad societal discrimination in the past to justify its use of a system of racial preferences. A city can use such a system of preferences only if it first presents clear evidence that the municipality itself had engaged in unconstitutional discrimination in the particular service area in question. **Disparity studies**—statistical analyses pointing to the difference between the percentage of minority businesses in a market area and the percentage of city contracts they received—are an important first step in documenting that a pattern of discrimination *may* exist. The Supreme Court further ruled that an acceptable minority set-aside program must be **narrowly tailored**: the program cannot offer preferences to all minority groups but only to individuals and groups proven to have suffered actual discrimination by the city.[22]

Croson posed difficult requirements for a city to meet if it wished to use racial preferences. Many cities simply gave up, substantially reducing or ending their contract compliance efforts. Relatively few cities were willing to assume the costs of preparing the detailed racial disparity studies necessary to justify minority preferences. Cities were also hesitant to continue contracting practices that could embroil the city in costly legal challenges brought by white-owned firms.[23]

RESEGREGATION AND THE PUBLIC SCHOOLS

In the 1950s, the Supreme Court declared as unconstitutional the **de jure segregation** of public schools, the racial segregation of schools mandated by state law. The Court, however, has not taken similar action against **de facto segregation**, the racial imbalances in school enrollments that are not ordered by state law but are the consequence of residential patterns; blacks and whites tend to live in different areas. In fact, the Court's 1975 ***Milliken v. Bradley*** decision effectively brought metropolitan school desegregation efforts to a halt. In striking down a busing program that encompassed Detroit and its nearby suburbs, the Court ruled that no suburb has to participate in a plan to correct the de facto segregation of metropolitan schools. The *Milliken* decision "sent the unmistakable message—urban apartheid would not be overcome through judicial decree."[24]

Over the ensuing decades, the Supreme Court continued to beat a retreat from earlier court-ordered school integration orders. The Court allowed DeKalb County (Georgia), Kansas City (Missouri), Charlotte-Mecklenburg (North Carolina), and a whole host of other cities across the nation, in both the North and the South, to terminate desegregation plans. The Court allowed school systems to curtail integration measures that had been tried for a substantial period of time, even when the city had not yet succeeded in producing integrated classrooms. City after city ended major desegregation efforts, and the percentage of students attending racially integrated schools fell.[25]

School officials turned to voluntary techniques—most notably **magnet schools** with their enriched curriculums and the promise of a safe school environment—in an effort to persuade parents to voluntarily send their children to a school other than their neighborhood school. Such voluntary programs produced only a limited number of racially integrated classrooms. But here, too, the Supreme Court eventually intervened, ruling in 2007 that districts could not use race as a factor in the selection of students for a magnet school. The Court ruled that a city may establish a magnet school; however, no city can use a race-conscious selection system in seeking to promote racial balance in the school's enrollment.[26] Once again, Supreme Court rulings limited local desegregation efforts.

Polling data reveal that African Americans have come to accept the permanence of de facto segregation.[27] Many minority parents see little worth in carrying on a fight for desegregation that just cannot be won. Instead, African American parents, especially middle- and upper-class parents whose children attend integrated schools, have turned their efforts to improving the quality of the schools their children attend rather than continuing the fight for citywide school integration.[28]

URBAN POLICY IN A SUBURBAN AGE

THE END OF URBAN POLICY?

Numerous urban scholars have called for an explicit, comprehensive policy to alleviate urban ills: "Only a total rethinking of the nation's priorities and a reinvestment in social and human capital can transform urban life."[29] In a suburban nation, however, such sweeping national urban policy is not politically possible. The call for a national urban policy has little resonance outside of academic circles.[30]

The 2008 election of Barack Obama brought a new optimism, a sense that the federal government would adopt strong policies of benefit to cities. Obama's outlook was shaped by the years he spent as a community organizer on the poor South Side of Chicago. As president, he created a White House Office of Urban Affairs to give new priority to, and to coordinate, urban policies. He also appointed Shaun Donovan as Secretary of the Department of Housing and Urban Development (HUD). Donovan, who, having served as the housing commissioner for New York City and as deputy assistant secretary for multifamily housing at HUD, possessed great familiarity with urban programs. Obama's Recovery Act programs offered cities much-needed assistance for street reconstruction, transportation, and other infrastructure projects. Faced with the spread of foreclosed home loans and vacant properties, the president initiated various efforts to spur new home loans and to restructure mortgages so that homeowners facing difficulty would not be forced out of their homes. The president's Neighborhood Initiatives also gave core-city neighborhoods—in the Sunbelt as well as the Frostbelt—special assistance in repurposing vacant properties.

Yet, as expansive as these efforts were, Obama's urban actions were still sharply constrained. Obama recognized that most Americans do not live in cities and were not willing to support a high visibility program that focuses resources on cities. Republican victories in the 2010 midterm elections and their proposals to make vast cuts in domestic programs only underscored that the dream of national urban policy was just that, a dream.

URBAN POLICY FOR AN ANTI-URBAN AGE: EIGHT SUGGESTIONS FOR HOW TO BUILD A REALISTIC URBAN POLICY

In an age where there is no broad public support for an explicit national urban policy, the advocates of cities will find their greatest chances of success if they pursue "nonurban programs"[31] which, as a side product, provide substantial aid to cities and distressed communities. The eight suggestions listed below provide tactical advice for enacting a pragmatic urban policy, for finding urban programs in an age that is not conducive to strong urban policy:

1. Emphasize a program's benefits for America's middle class

In a middle-class nation, advocates need to stress the benefits that programs will bring to the middle class, not to central cities and the poor. Educational reforms, for instance, not only help the inner-city poor but also empower middle-class parents who are dissatisfied with underperforming public schools. Programs aimed at repurposing vacant properties do not simply concentrate assistance to inner-city sections of Cleveland, Detroit, Baltimore, and other distressed Frostbelt cities. Vacant properties programs also provide extensive aid to California, Florida, Nevada, and Arizona, states that suffered some of the highest rates of foreclosures in the country as buyers could not meet the monthly mortgage obligations they incurred in buying large suburban homes, condominiums, and homes in retirement communities.

2. Tie program benefits to participation in the workplace

Americans are hostile to "welfare." However, a public generally opposed to welfare still gives its support to assistance programs that emphasize workforce participation, job training, and the transition from welfare to work.[32] The provision of day care, too, can be justified as part of a program than enables poor women to leave welfare and return to work.

3. Pursue "race-neutral" and universal programs

Americans as a whole disapprove of programs that give benefits to the members of a specific racial group while denying the same benefits to members of other racial and ethnic groups. Americans give greater support to **race-neutral programs** that promise assistance to all people in need, irrespective of race or ethnicity. Affirmative action programs remain highly controversial. Programs that provide opportunity to the economically disadvantaged, irrespective of skin color, are less so.

The American public endorses education and job-training programs that promise assistance to all citizens in need, not just to racial minorities.[33] Head Start enjoys overwhelming popularity because it serves all children in need; still, the program delivers disproportionate benefits to inner-city communities, the sites where large numbers of poor people live.

4. Spread benefits! Target when possible! Target within universalism!

As we have just discussed, programs that **spread benefits** have the potential to garner broad public support. Yet, such programs suffer an overwhelming drawback: high cost! The wide spread of program benefits also dilutes the assistance provided to people and communities most in need. As a consequence, many urban advocates argue for the exact opposite approach, programs that **target benefits** by concentrating a program's limited resources on the most needy residents and distressed inner-city communities. But as we have seen throughout this book, targeted urban policy, however rational in theory, is extremely difficult to achieve politically.

A mixed approach actually provides the most satisfactory strategy. Theda Skocpol calls for **targeting within universalism**: a program can define program eligibility quite broadly, allowing the participation of a great many communities, while allocating a higher level of benefits and additional services to poorer people and communities in need.[34]

The Community Development Block Grant (CDBG) program provides a good example of targeting within universalism. The CDBG program delivers assistance annually to nearly 1,200 communities. Yet, the CDBG aid formula ensures that aid is disproportionately given to the nation's big cities and to smaller jurisdictions with the greatest need.

5. Look to the tax code!

Bill Clinton expanded the **Earned Income Tax Credit (EITC)**, a program of wage supplements to the working poor. In doing so, he faced virtually none of the harsh debate that accompanies proposals to expand "welfare" programs. As EITC benefits go only to low-income workers—and not to nonworkers—the change could not easily be attacked as an expansion of welfare. Clinton understood that Americans would accept a program that gave assistance to people who held jobs but who still faced difficulties in "getting by." Clinton also recognized that, embedded in a complex and difficult-to-understand tax code, EITC expansion enjoyed a certain measure of political insulation. Administered through the tax code, EITC expansion flew "under the political radar."

Another tax code program, the **Low Income Housing Tax Credit (LIHTC)**, has become arguably the nation's most important program for the construction of housing for families in need. In terms of **tax expenditures**, the money lost to the public treasury as a result of the program's tax provisions, the LIHTC cost $19.6 billion over just a five-year period (1998–2002).[35] As a program administered through the tax code, with developers receiving the tax credits to construct affordable housing, the LIHTC escapes much of the controversy that usually erupts when the government announces more direct efforts to build subsidized housing. The LIHTC even has a better record than other federal subsidized housing programs when it comes to building low-income housing units in the suburbs.[36]

6. Emphasize the win–win benefits of regional cooperation, especially for job creation and economic development

The prominence of economic development concerns opens the door to a potentially fruitful area of interlocal collaboration. No city or suburb has the ability to "go it alone" in the interregional and global competition for attractive businesses. Cities and suburbs can share in the benefits from joint efforts that draw investors to a region. Cities and suburbs enjoy their best chances of attracting a major firm to a region when they cooperate in providing the roads, sewers, water, and other infrastructure improvements demanded by a major new employer.

Businesses seek the advantages of locating in an **industrial cluster** where they have close proximity to similar businesses and shared support services. An industrial cluster is regional in nature and spills over local boundaries. No single city or suburb acting on its own possesses the ability to establish an industrial cluster.

Cities and suburbs enter into numerous intergovernmental arrangements for mutual cost savings and enhanced service provision. Economic development is the next wave of regionalism. Still, state and national incentives will likely be necessary to get communities to overcome past antagonisms and collaborate more extensively with one another.

The ISTEA/NEXTEA/TEA-21 program provides a model for what higher levels of government can do to promote regional cooperation. New levels of regional collaboration in public transportation were achieved when the federal government required the establishment of metropolitan planning organizations (usually referred to as MPOs) as a condition for receiving federal assistance.

The Obama administration in 2010 similarly awarded $100 million in **Sustainable Communities regional planning grants**[37] to promote collaborative action in land use, development planning, and job creation beyond the functional area of transportation. Minnesota's Twin Cities received money to plan the development of new communities along transit lines. Austin and ten surrounding communities received funds to connect new housing with schools and transportation.[38] The awards were quite small in terms of the actual dollars spent, and no recipient received the necessary funding to fully implement the proposed projects. Still, the New Sustainable Communities Planning grants represent the federal government's renewed interest in promoting long-term regional planning and smart growth, an approach that had been abandoned under Republican pressure in the 1960s.

The states, too, have shown a new interest in promoting regionalism. New Jersey, New York, and Ohio are among the states that have begun to consider incentives for interlocal collaboration. Yet, the programs often lack follow-through. State legislatures are interested in promoting joint local actions that will save money but are fearful of incurring the wrath of suburban voters by pushing regionalism too far.[39]

Too often, efforts at regional action are focused narrowly on cost-savings measures or are dominated by the growth-oriented priorities of local business leaders. Church organizations, nonprofit groups, and environmental organizations have an important role to play in pushing for regional collaborations that will advance more equitable social and housing policy and protect the natural environment.

7. Build cities bottom-up through Community Development Corporations, nonprofits, and community-based organizations

Urban affairs journalist Neal Peirce observes that the hope for the urban future lies largely with Community Development Corporations (CDCs), mutual housing associations, land trusts, reinvestment corporations, and a myriad of disparate civic, neighborhood, and corporate and citizen-volunteer organizations.[40] State and federal policy can nurture and build on the problem-solving energies of the tens of thousands of nonprofit and community organizations that exist in urban and suburban America. An urban policy approach that works through community, faith-based, and other nonprofit organizations also has the potential to gain greater local legitimacy and acceptance. The bottom-up approach is flexible: nonprofit and community organizations know a neighborhood's needs, having worked in an area for a number of years.

CDCs have demonstrated an impressive ability to leverage resources in constructing and rehabilitating low-income housing, in providing job training for low-income residents, in building neighborhood-based health-care centers, and in building a community's "social capital."[41] But CDCs do not work in isolation. Their work requires the financial support of corporate philanthropy, nonprofit foundations, and government agencies. Three key federal programs—the Low Income Housing Tax Credit (LIHTC) program, the Community Development Block Grant program, and the HOME Investment Partnership—have helped to fuel much of the bottom-up revitalization activity in lower-income neighborhoods since the 1990s. The LIHTC program was especially important in providing the financial incentives that led corporations to invest as partners in CDC low-income housing construction and rehabilitation. The LIHTC example illustrates how the government can use a system of tax credits to catalyze private and nonprofit action in rebuilding America's communities.[42]

8. Focus on powerful emotional symbols and "deserving" constituencies: education, children, the elderly, women, and the environment

The American public continues to support domestic initiatives focused on children and education. Children are a particularly sympathetic constituency. Head Start and the Supplemental Food Program for Women, Infants, and Children continued to grow even during years when more general welfare programs were scaled back. The public also considers education to be a worthwhile public investment that provides individual opportunity and the nation's long-term economic growth.

Spending for education can also be sold as an alternative to welfare. If schools do their jobs and children learn and grow to become productive citizens, there will be less future need for expensive social welfare and correctional programs.

The elderly are another sympathetic constituency. Communities build subsidized housing for the elderly even when they oppose construction for the nonelderly poor. The elderly also vote, giving policymakers further incentive to respond to their needs. Programs aimed at helping veterans, families on the street, battered women, the homeless, and people with AIDS also enjoy considerable public support.

Environmentalism is another powerful symbol that can be used to mobilize support for urban-related programs. Regional growth management can be justified in terms of saving green space and farmland. "Smart Growth" can be creatively framed: it does not have to be sold as a program designed to promote center-city revitalization. Program initiatives targeted at sustainable growth, the cleanup of toxic brownfields, and the "greening" of abandoned properties can attract the support of environmentalists who might otherwise be uninterested in urban revitalization.

TOWARD SUSTAINABLE CITIES

Critics often misrepresent *sustainable development* as "no growth" environmental extremism. Yet, the truth is that **sustainable development** *does* seek new growth, growth that is guided by practices that will minimize the adverse effects of development on the natural environment: "Reduced to its most basic tenets, sustainable urbanism is *walkable and transit-served urbanism integrated with high-performance buildings and high-performance infrastructure*."[43]

Concerns for sustainability have gained new prominence in urban affairs. Cities have even had to address sustainability questions as part of their applications to host the Olympic Games. New York, Madrid, and London all boasted of their "green" bids for the 2012 Olympics, as did Chicago in its bid for the 2016 games. New York's application emphasized the creation of new parkland, reliance on mass transit, and the design of a sustainable "urban village." London's winning bid for 2012 promised a 25 percent gain in the energy efficiency of the Olympic Village, increased reliance on renewable sources, reduced water consumption, the use of recycled materials from demolished buildings, reliance on low-carbon-emission mass transit, and the dedication of new bicycling and walking paths.[44]

THE SUSTAINABILITY TRIANGLE

Concern for the natural environment is only the first of the three legs of the **sustainable development triangle**. Green policies will not be politically sustainable unless they also meet the economic and social needs of urban populations, the other two legs of the triangle.

Voters are not focused narrowly on the ecology. They will not approve of environmental measures that interfere with job growth, economic prosperity, and housing affordability. Requirements for citizen participation help to ensure that decisions made to protect the environment do not adversely affect the job and housing prospects of poorer and working-class citizens in the metropolis.

The sustainability triangle points to the importance of actions that Portland has taken to address some of the criticisms of the region's Urban Growth Boundary (UGB). Critics contend that the boundary restricts housing supply in the region, leading to an inflation of home prices that serves to deny home-ownership opportunities to newly marrieds, younger families, working-class citizens, and minorities. Portland, however, has sought to offset such adverse effects through regulations and incentives for developers to include affordable units in new residential developments. The city also expanded the boundaries of the UGB to allow new construction, a move intended to increase housing supply and reduce the pressures that might lead to home price inflation.

SMART GROWTH, COMPACT CITIES, AND TRANSIT-ORIENTED DEVELOPMENT

Chapters 9 and 10 reviewed a number of state growth-management efforts, including Smart Growth programs and the imposition of urban growth boundaries. New

Urbanism, too, as we saw, seeks compact development as an alternative to energy-intensive urban sprawl. All of these efforts aim to guide growth in order to preserve green space and agricultural land while promoting the population densities for mass transit, bicycling, and even walking.[45] Compact development also lessens the acreage devoted to roadways and parking lots, reducing the runoff of contaminants contributing to the pollution of streams and rivers.

GREEN CONSTRUCTION

By 2009, more than 138 U.S. communities with populations of 50,000 or greater had green building ordinances to promote sustainable practices.[46] Green cities condition the issuance of a building permit on a developer's willingness to meet or surpass the federal government's **Energy Star standards** and the home construction industry's **LEED (Leadership in Energy and Environmental Design) standards** for energy efficiency, reduced water use, and the use of recycled building materials in construction.[47] Incentives for reducing the square footage of a structure and requirements for a tight building "envelope" (i.e., a downsized building footprint) allow for reduced energy consumption. Cities use regulations and incentives to promote passive solar heating (i.e., the use of skylights and windows that take advantage of sunlight), natural ventilation, low-flow toilets, and energy-efficient heating systems and appliances in new construction. European-style **passive houses** are fully insulated with ventilation systems that recycle heat so thoroughly that homeowners pay extremely low winter heating bills.[48]

Chicago, Portland (Oregon), and Dayton are only a few of the more noteworthy cities to promote **green roofs**, which cover the tops of buildings with a layer of grass or vegetation.[49] A green roof provides the natural insulation of a structure, saving on energy costs. Green roofs in a city retain rainwater, reducing storm-water runoff and the flow of pollutants downstream. Green roofs also reduce the "heat island effect," where a city's downtown becomes warmer than surrounding areas, suffered during summer months.

Green cities reduce storm-water runoff by narrowing the widths of new streets and through measures that incentivize the use of **porous surfaces** instead of impervious concrete in parking lots and public plazas. Porous paving materials permit water to seep into the ground below, allowing the soil to filter contaminants while minimizing the pollution that occurs when storm water is piped through sewers into nearby rivers and streams. **Green dividers**, strips of trees and low-lying grassy areas between aisles of a parking lot, also help minimize water runoff. Municipal building codes can reward developers for site design plans that include **rain gardens**, low-lying landscaped areas that capture and absorb storm water.[50] Cleveland, New Orleans, and other "shrinking cities" have adopted **greening strategies** to turn large swaths of vacant property into green swales that aid in storm-water retention, minimizing flooding and downstream pollution.[51]

GREEN PROMOTION AND PRACTICES AT CITY HALL

Through its own actions, a local government can promote model sustainable practices. The City of Chicago placed a green roof atop its 100-year-old city hall, a demonstration project intended to show builders how such an investment can reduce energy costs. Milwaukee similarly put a green roof on its local library. Local governments promote mass transit usage by distributing reduced-cost transit passes to city workers and putting an end to free employee parking at city hall. Numerous cities make fuel efficiency an important factor in vehicle procurement.

Portland and Seattle are among the national leaders in the use of **performance indicators** to measure environmental progress. The collected data do not merely sit on the shelf. Instead, the data are integrated into a system of **performance management** where managers and even activist local and neighborhood groups are given the information that they need to demand that municipal agencies live up to the environmental standards that the city has promised.

SUSTAINABLE URBAN DEVELOPMENT: FIVE CITIES

What do sustainable cities look like? A brief look at Chattanooga, Austin, Boulder, Portland (Oregon) and Seattle[52] gives some indication as to how cities can promote development and at the same time decrease their "ecological footprint."[53] As we shall see, cities are using performance measurement systems that focus attention on the achievement of sustainability goals.

Chattanooga

Once a center of coke foundries and textile manufacturing—smokestack industries attracted by low-wage labor in the South—Chattanooga, Tennessee, in the 1960s was reputed to be the most polluted city in the United States. Today, it is a much different city. Chattanooga cleaned up the local environment and cast its future with sustainable development. The clean-up of the Tennessee River, bordered by industrial sites, was critical to the downtown's rebirth. The city also turned to a system of electric buses as a visible expression of the city's newfound livability.

Regional efforts in greater Chattanooga cross municipal boundary lines. Businesses and nongovernmental organizations took the lead in New Regionalism partnerships that developed the vision of a new and clean Chattanooga. The Chamber of Commerce provided the energy behind the Vision 2000 effort to identify sustainable development opportunities that could help change the city's national image. Nonprofit organizations took the lead in piecing together the Chattanooga Greenways, a seventy-five-mile network of parks and open space.[54] The city has a sustainability officer to oversee and coordinate the city's efforts and even an urban forester devoted to greening the city.

Austin

Austin, Texas, has utilized "Sustainable Community" performance indicators to measure the city's progress in areas such as air quality, energy and water conservation, and the reduced use of hazardous materials. The Austin city council set a target of purchasing 5 percent or more of the city's energy from renewable resources. The city also gives special priority to capital improvement projects that contribute to sustainability. City planners channel new development toward "smart growth zones" and away from areas lying above the local aquifer.[55] Austin offers fee waivers and other incentives to contractors who meet sustainability goals. The local utility gives customers a **Green Choice option**: utility customers can direct that the electricity used in their home be generated by wind, solar, and other renewable sources.

The Austin Energy Green Building Program rates new homes and commercial buildings according to the sustainability of their construction practices and materials. New homes are awarded one to five stars based on green features such as water and energy conservation, materials recycling, and indoor air quality. A 2007 Austin ordinance further requires that new homes be 65 percent more energy efficient than homes that were built to the then-current code.[56] The Green Building Program lowered the demand for energy during peak months and hours, reducing emissions from Austin Energy power plants and lessening the need to build new power-generating facilities.[57]

Boulder

Boulder, Colorado, mandates various green practices in new home construction, including evidence of energy efficiency and the use of recycled building materials. The city awards **Green Points** to builders and contractors for a wide variety of sustainable construction practices, including: permeable surfacing; water efficiency; roof overhangs that provide natural shading; passive solar heating; enhanced insulation; heat recovery in ventilation; the use of engineered lumber in a floor or roof; the use of local-source materials; and the employment of a green building consultant.[58] The city issues a building permit only *after* a project has earned a specified number of Green Points.

Similar to Austin, Boulder's municipal government relies on a system of statistical performance indicators to monitor environmental quality, to reduce its own energy and water consumption, and to increase the use of recycled materials and renewable energy sources. Partners for a Clean Environment (PACE) utilizes a nonintrusive, nonregulatory approach that seeks to educate business owners as to the variety of ways by which environmental goals can be achieved. A business can be certified as a "PACE partner" for having curbed energy consumption, solid waste, and the use of hazardous materials. Homeowners can also choose to have their electricity provided from wind and solar sources.

Portland (Oregon)

Portland, as we saw in Chapter 9, has gained international recognition for its Urban Growth Boundary and its efforts to promote infill and transit-oriented development. Portland's Comprehensive Plan sets the targets not just for reduced energy use and increased recycling efforts but also for social goals such as the construction of new units of multifamily housing. Portland planning also calls for a sizable reduction in carbon dioxide emissions as part of the city's contribution to the worldwide effort to combat global warming.

Solar panels on car parking lot, Arizona State University (2009): Green building construction codes can encourage the utilization of renewable energy. Copyright © Kevin Dooley and courtesy of Wikimedia Commons. htttp://commons.wikimedia.org/wiki/File:Solar_panels_on_car_parking.jpg.

Like Austin and Boulder, Portland utilizes a system of **sustainability benchmarks** to track just how well the city is doing in reducing pollution, promoting recycling, and providing citizens with a high quality of life. Portland uses **comparative performance measurement** to allow citizens to see just how well progress in Portland stacks up to that in similar cities.

Seattle

Seattle requires municipal agencies to prepare specific plans of action for the safe handling of hazardous wastes, the reduced generation of solid waste, and the conservation of energy and water. The city also has a policy of environmentally friendly purchasing. Seattle's Sustainable Indicators Project monitors progress and keep public pressure focused on the achievement of declared policy ends. The King County Benchmark Program and the extensive performance measurements reported by the Puget Sound Regional Council both add to the pressures to achieve sustainability goals.[59]

Seattle has gained national renown for the degree to which neighborhood dialogue, citizen organizations, and nonprofit groups play an integral role in the process of achieving sustainability goals. Citizen groups keep the pressure on government to

Green street-side swale, Seattle, 2008: By allowing for the capture of water runoff from abutting roadways, this low-lying green swale allows for natural, on-site filtration of water, minimizing the pollution that accompanies the underground piping and drainage of wastewater. Courtesy of the Environmental Protection Agency. http://commons.wikimedia.org/wiki/File:Streetside_swale_Seattle.jpg.

perform. A nonprofit organization, Sustainable Seattle, serves as the public's watchdog, criticizing public agencies when the performance indicators show that environmental goals are not being met.

A comprehensive plan, *Toward a Sustainable Seattle*, channels growth into a variety of mixed-use residential-commercial **urban villages** with the necessary densities to support neighborhood stores, mass transit, and walking.[60] Building codes and development regulation emphasize sustainable practices. The Street Edge Alternatives (SEA Street) program seeks to narrow the width of streets, eliminate curbs and gutters, and add trees and bordering green swales to increase storm-water retention, minimizing runoff, erosion, and stream pollution.[61]

Despite the environmental activism described above, cities in the United States generally lag behind cities in Europe, Canada, and East Asia when it comes to sustainable development.[62] But global networks are acting to change the situation, with local officials in the United States copying practices from abroad. Globalization also denotes the influence of supranational organizations. The United Nations, international environmental conferences, and various international nongovernmental organizations have all highlighted the importance of sustainable development. Even the International Olympics Committee has had an influence, with New York, Chicago, and other host-city hopefuls meeting the IOC's requirements for "green" development as part of their bids to host the games.

As the sustainability triangle denotes, cities cannot narrowly focus on environmental preservation at the price of decreasing the job and housing opportunities available to low-skill workers, newly arrived immigrants, and racial minorities. An inclusive sustainability agenda also requires cities to give special attention to the health consequences that pollution imposes on at-risk communities.[63]

Municipalities have begun to convert their municipal fleets from diesel to "cleaner" fuels—natural gas, hybrid electric, biodiesel, or possibly even hydrogen fuel cells—a transition that seeks to improve overall air quality and reduce the incidence of asthma attacks suffered by inner-city children who live and play in neighborhoods choked by diesel exhaust fumes.[64] Berkeley, California, is only one of a number of cities to switch trucks from diesel to cleaner-burning biodiesel (essentially vegetable oil) as part of the effort to reduce asthma.[65]

THE URBAN FUTURE AND THE "NEW NORMAL"

The prolonged economic recession of the early twenty-first century imposed great costs on cities and suburbs, exacerbating housing abandonment and numerous other urban problems. But even the eventual return to a growing economy will not solve long-term urban problems. Economic growth rates in the near future are unlikely to approach the level of the boom years of previous decades. There will be no sudden return to a prosperity that will solve urban problems. Instead, even in good years, cities will find that they are confronted by a **new normal** of slow growth rates, low investment returns, depressed housing markets, voter antitax sentiment, constricted intergovernmental assistance, and continuing budgetary difficulties. Demands for economic development will continue to dominate the local arena. City and suburban officials will face an exceedingly daunting task as they try to meet demands for job creation, downtown revitalization, neighborhood development, immigrant incorporation, improved schools and public services, fiscal moderation, and the protection of the natural environment.

In many ways, the urban crisis of the early twenty-first century looks quite unlike the urban crisis of the 1960s when a wave of riots swept cities and the core of big cities emptied as residents and businesses continued to flee to the suburbs. Gentrification has marked the rediscovery of many inner-city neighborhoods. Downtowns, too, have come back as a number of cities have found their place in a global economy. Still, despite these seeming indications of urban health, the problems of poverty, deindustrialization, sprawled development, and ghettoization remain. If anything, the capital mobility and the global competition for business serve to make the economic and fiscal position of cities even more tenuous than ever.

The challenge for urban leaders is to build viable political coalitions in support of practical policies that can ameliorate urban ills. A broad, overarching, national urban policy is no longer politically possible. Instead, urban leaders need to find workable change strategies that "fit" the political and economic realities of the United States in the twenty-first century.

NOTES

1. Atlanta BeltLine, Inc., "Atlanta BeltLine Overview" (2010), http://beltline.org/BeltLineBasics/BeltLineBasicsOverview/tabid/1691/Default.aspx.

2. Steven P. Erie, *Globalizing L.A.: Trade, Infrastructure, and Regional Development* (Stanford, CA: Stanford University Press, 2004), details the history of actions taken by Los Angeles decision makers in support of the city's and region's growth.

3. Evans Paull, "Vacant Properties, Tax Increment Financing, and What's Working Now," presented at the Reclaiming Vacant Properties conference, Cleveland, October 14, 2010; City of Dallas, Office of Economic Development, "Skillman Corridor TIF District," brochure, 2009, www.dallas-ecodev.org/SiteContent/66/documents/Incentives/TIFs/Skillman/skillman_marketing.pdf.

4. Robert G. Lehnen and Carlyn E. Johnson, "The Impact of Tax Increment Financing on School Districts: An Indiana Case Study," in *Tax Increment Financing and Economic Development: Uses, Structures, and Impact*, ed. Craig L. Johnson and Joyce Y. Man (Albany: State University of New York Press, 2001), 137–154.

5. Local taxes may have a considerable impact on a corporation's choice of locales within a metropolitan area, inasmuch as the corporation's access to suppliers, a qualified labor force, and markets is relatively the same throughout much of the metropolis. See Harold Wolman, "Local Economic Development Policy: What Explains the Divergence Between Policy Analysis and Political Behavior?" *Journal of Urban Affairs* 10, no. 1 (1988): 19–28.

6. Signe M. Rich, "How Important Is 'Quality of Life' in Location Decisions and Local Economic Development," in *Dilemmas of Urban Economic Development: Issues in Theory and Practice,* Urban Affairs Annual Review, vol. 47, ed. Richard D. Bingham and Robert Mier (Thousand Oaks, CA; Sage, 1997), 56–73; Dennis A. Rondinelli, James H. Johnson Jr., and John D. Kasarda, "The Changing Forces of Urban Economic Development: Globalization and City Competitiveness in the 21st Century," *Cityscape: Journal of Policy Development and Research* 3, no. 3 (1998): 85–89; Richard Florida, *The Rise of the Creative Class* (New York: Basic Books, 2002); idem, *Who's Your City: How the Creative Economy Is Making Where to Live the Most Important Decision of Your Life* (New York: Basic Books, 2008).

7. Kathryn A. Foster, *The Political Economy of Special-Purpose Government* (Washington, DC: Georgetown University Press, 1997), 103; David Ranney, *Global Decisions, Local Collisions: Urban Life in the New World Order* (Philadelphia: Temple University Press, 2003), 106–107, 111–118.

8. David L. Imbroscio, "Overcoming the Economic Dependence of Urban America," *Journal of Urban Affairs* 15 (1993): 173–190, discusses a number of these strategies.

9. "Racial Change in the Nation's Largest Cities: Evidence from the 2000 Census," report of the Brookings Institution Center on Urban and Metropolitan Policy, April 2001, www.brook.edu/es/urban/census/citygrowth.htm.

10. Ibid.

11. Alexandra Cole, "The 'Sleeping Giant' Shifts: Latinos and Orange County Politics," paper presented at the annual meeting of the American Political Science Association, Washington, DC, August 31–September 3, 2000.

12. In the 1998 congressional elections, the voting turnout rate was 32.8 percent for Hispanics as compared to 41.8 percent for African Americans and 47.4 percent for whites. See the U.S. Census Bureau, "Number of Hispanics Who Vote Up 'Sharply,' Census Bureau Reports," press release, August 29, 2000, www.census.gov/Press-Release/www/2000/cb00–139.html. See also Rodolfo O. de la Garza and Louis DeSipio, "Save the Baby, Change the Bathwater, and Scrub the Tub: Latino Electoral Participation after Twenty Years of Voting Rights Act Coverage," in *Pursuing Power: Latinos and the Political System*, ed. F. Chris Garcia (Notre Dame, IN: University of Notre Dame Press, 1997), 72–126.

13. Richard Benfield, "Newark's Mayor Cory Booker at Midpoint," *New York Times,* July 1, 2008; Elizabeth Dwoskin, "As Newark Rebuilds, Help from Beyond City Limits," *New York Times,* April 26, 2008. See also Andra Gillespie, "Losing and Winning: Cory Booker's Ascent to Newark's Mayoralty,"

in *Whose Black Politics? Post-Racial Black Leadership*, ed. Gillespie (New York: Routledge, 2009), 67–84.

14. Luke Mullins, "How Youngstown Is Tackling the Housing Crisis," *U.S. News and World Report*, December 15, 2008.

15. Roberto E. Villarreal, "The Politics of Mexican-American Empowerment," in *Latino Empowerment: Progress, Problems, and Prospects*, ed. Villarreal, Norma G. Hernandez, and Howard D. Neighbor (Westport, CT: Greenwood Press, 1988), 6.

16. Roberto E. Villarreal and Howard D. Neighbor, "Conclusion: An Overview of Mexican-American Political Empowerment," in Villarreal, Hernandez, and Neighbor, *Latino Empowerment*, 128.

17. Ali Modarres and Greg Andranovich, "Local Context for Understanding Poverty and Segregation," paper presented at the annual meeting of the Urban Affairs Association, Washington, DC, April 1, 2004.

18. Paula D. McClain and Steven C. Tauber, "Racial Minority Group Relations in a Multiracial Society," in *Governing American Cities: Inter-Ethnic Coalitions, Competition, and Conflict,* ed. Michael Jones-Correa (New York: Russell Sage Foundation, 2001), 111–136. For a description of the polarization between Cubans and African Americans in Miami, see Guillermo J. Grenier and Max Castro, "Blacks and Cubans in Miami: The Negative Consequences of the Cuban Enclave on Ethnic Relations," in ibid., 137–157.

19. Mark Baldassare, *California in the New Millennium: The Changing Social and Political Landscape* (Berkeley: University of California Press, 2000), 99–127. Other studies, however, argue that blacks and Latinos share a number of commonalities, that the two groups do not perceive each other as economic competitors, and that there may be a greater potential for a biracial or multiracial alliance than is commonly thought. See Matt A. Barreto, Benjamin F. Gonzalez, and Gabriel R. Sanchez, "Rainbow Coalition in the Golden State? Exposing Myths, Uncovering New Realities in Latino Attitudes towards Blacks," in *Black and Brown Los Angeles: A Contemporary Reader,* ed. Laura Pulido and Josh Kun (Berkeley: University of California Press, 2010).

20. Raphael J. Sonenshein and Susan H. Pinkus, "Latino Incorporation Reaches the Urban Summit: How Antonio Villaraigosa Won the 2005 Los Angeles Mayor's Race," *PS: Political Science and Politics* 38, no. 4 (2005): 713–721.

21. W. Avon Drake and Robert D. Holsworth, *Affirmative Action and the Stalled Quest for Black Progress* (Urbana and Chicago: University of Illinois Press, 1996), 71–79 and 120–125.

22. Mitchell F. Rice, "State and Local Government Set-Aside Programs, Disparity Studies, and Minority Business in the Post-Croson Era," *Journal of Urban Affairs* 15 (1993): 533. In its 1995 *Adarand v. Pena* decision, the Court struck a further blow against minority set-aside programs, applying the *Croson* logic to federal preference programs. Even federal set-aside requirements would be subject to strict scrutiny and must be narrowly tailored. See Mitchell Rice and Maurice Mongkuo, "Did Adarand Kill Minority Set-Asides?" *Public Administration Review* 58, no. 1 (January/February 1998): 82–86.

23. Rice, "State and Local Government Set-Aside Programs," 536–550; Neil Smelser, William Julius Wilson, and Faith Mitchell, eds., *America Becoming: Racial Trends and Their Consequences*, vol. 2 (Washington, DC: National Academic Press, 2001), 216–217; Heather Martin, Maureen Berner, and Frayda Bluestein, "Documenting Disparity in Minority Contracting: Legal Requirements and Recommendations for Policy Makers," *Public Administration Review* 67, no. 3 (May/June 2007): 511–520.

24. David L. Kirp, "Retreat into Legalism: The Little Rock School Desegregation Case in Historical Perspective," *PS: Political Science and Politics* (September 1997): 446.

25. Megan Twohey, "Desegregation Is Dead," *National Journal*, September 18, 1999, 2614–2619; Valerie G. Johnson, *Black Power in the Suburbs* (Albany: State University of New York Press, 2002), discusses the dramatic resegregation of schools in Prince George's County, outside of Washington, DC. African Americans constituted 24.5 percent of the school population when desegregation efforts began in 1973; by 2001, they were 75 percent of the Prince George's school population.

26. *Parents Involved in Community Schools v. Seattle School District No. 1* and *Meredith v. Jefferson County Board of Education*, 551 U.S. 701 (2007).

27. Susan Welch, Michael Combs, Lee Sigelman, and Timothy Bledsoe, "Race or Place? Emerging Public Perspectives on Urban Education," *PS: Political Science and Politics* (September 1997): 454–458.

28. Johnson, *Black Power in the Suburbs*, 119–121.

29. Edward J. Blakely and David L. Ames, "Changing Places: American Urban Planning Policy for the 1990s," *Journal of Urban Affairs* 14 (1992): 423. This was only one of a number of articles in the *Journal of Urban Affairs* special issue to call for a national urban policy. The prestigious Brookings Institution, a Washington "think tank," has also revived the call for a national urban policy. See Bruce Katz, "Enough of the Small Stuff! Toward a New Urban Agenda," *Brookings Review* 18, no. 3 (Summer 2000): 4–9.

30. Paul S. Grogan and Tony Proscio, *Comeback Cities: A Blueprint for Urban Neighborhood Revival* (Boulder, CO: Westview Press, 2000), 246–247.

31. Marshall Kaplan and Franklin James, eds., *The Future of National Urban Policy* (Durham, NC: Duke University Press, 1990).

32. Greenstein, "Universal and Targeted Programs to Relieving Poverty."

33. William Julius Wilson, *The Truly Disadvantaged* (Chicago: University of Chicago Press, 1981); idem, "Public-Policy Research and the Truly Disadvantaged." in *The Urban Underclass*, ed. Christopher Jencks and Paul E. Peterson (Washington, DC: Brookings Institution Press, 1991), 460–481. See also Robert Greenstein, "Universal and Targeted Programs to Relieving Poverty," 437–459 in ibid.

34. Theda Skocpol, "Targeting Within Universalism: Politically Viable Policies to Combat Poverty in the United States," in Jencks and Peterson, *The Urban Underclass*, 414.

35. Morton J. Schussheim, *Housing the Poor: Federal Housing Program for Low-income Families* (Washington, DC: Congressional Research Service, 1998), as cited by Charles J. Orlebeke, "The Evolution of Low-Income Housing Policy, 1949-1999," *Housing Policy Debate* 11, no. 2 (2000): 513–514. For a description of how the LIHTC works and its effect on housing investment, see Alex F. Schwartz, *Housing Politics in the United States*, 2d ed. (New York: Routledge, 2006), 103–124.

36. Kirk McClure, "The Low-Income Housing Tax Credit Program Goes Mainstream and Moves to the Suburbs," *Housing Policy Debate* 17, no. 3 (2006): 419–446. For the limits that even LIHTC faces as a tool for the geographic dispersion of subsidized housing, see Lance Freeman, "Siting Affordable Housing: Location and Neighborhood Trends of Low Income Housing Tax Credit Developments in the 1990s," a report of the Brookings Institution Center on Urban and Metropolitan Policy, Washington, DC, April 2004, www.brookings.edu/urban/publications/20040405_freeman.htm; idem, "Comment on McClure's 'The Low-Income Housing Tax Credit Program Goes Mainstream and Moves to the Suburbs,'" *Housing Policy Debate* 17, no. 3 (2006): 447–459; and David P. Varady, "Comment on McClure's 'The Low-Income Housing Tax Credit Program Goes Mainstream and Moves to the Suburbs,'" in ibid., 461–490.

37. The program is formally known as the Sustainable Communities Regional Planning Grant program.

38. Yonah Freemark, "HUD Unveils Winners of Sustainable Communities Awards," *Next American City*, October 15, 2010, http://americancity.org/columns/entry/2680/.

39. See, for example, the 2010 report of the Ohio Commission on Local Government Reform and Collaboration, "Building a Better Ohio: Creating Collaboration in Governance," www.morpc.org/pdf/Commission_Final_Report_Press_Quality.pdf.

40. Neal Peirce, "An Urban Agenda for the President," *Journal of Urban Affairs* 15 (1993): 457–467.

41. Ross Gittell and Avis Vidal, *Community Organizing: Building Social Capital as a Development Strategy* (Thousand Oaks, CA: Sage, 1998), esp. 33–56. Thad Williamson, David Imbroscio, and Gar Alperovitz, *Making a Place for Community: Local Democracy in a Global Era* (New York: Routledge, 2003), 213–235, review the potential and limitations of the CDC approach. Grogan and Proscio, *Comeback Cities*, 62–101 presents anecdotal evidence of CDC successes in cities across the country.

42. Grogan and Proscio, *Comeback Cities*, 94–95 and 248–253.

43. Douglas Farr, *Sustainable Urbanism: Urban Design with Nature* (Hoboken, NJ: Wiley, 2007).

44. "London Olympics 2012—Going for Green?" EurActive.Com, January 30, 2007, www.euractiv.com/en/sports/london-olympics-2012-going-green/article-161197; Global Forum for Sports and Environment, "New York City's 2012 Olympic Bid," (n.d.), www.g-forse.com/archive/news326_e.html; Nick Swift, "The Cities Bidding for the 2012 Olympics Have Learnt from the Salt Lake City Scandal," *City Mayors*, November 28, 2004, www.citymayors.com/sport/2012olympics_nov04.html; ICLEI-Local Governments for Sustainability, "ICLEI Joins The Climate Group and Chicago 2016 to Announce Olympic 'Green' Program," press release, June 25, 2008, www.icleiusa.org/news-events/press-room/press-releases/iclei-joins-the-climate-group-and-chicago-2016-to-announce-olympic-201cgreen201d-program.

45. For a discussion of the various land-use tools and other policies that governments can adopt to promote greater densities in development and mass transit, walking, and biking as alternatives to automobile use, see Timothy Beatley, *Green Urbanism: Learning from European Cities* (Washington, DC: Island Press, 2000), 29–106; and Robert Cervero, *The Transit Metropolis: A Global Inquiring* (Washington, DC: Island Press, 1998).

46. American Institute of Architects, "Green Building Policy in a Changing Economic Environment," 2009, 13, www.aia.org/aiaucmp/groups/aia/documents/document/aiab081617.pdf.

47. Allyson Wendt, "Cities Mandate LEED but Not Certification," *GreenSource*, July 30, 2008, http://greensource.construction.com/news/080730CitiesMandateLEED.asp; Margot Roosevelt, "L.A. and San Francisco Vie for Title of 'Greenest City,'" *Los Angeles Times*, April 22, 2008.

48. Elisabeth Rosenthal, "No Furnaces but Heat Aplenty in 'Passive Houses,'" *New York Times*, December 28, 2008.

49. For a discussion of rainwater catchment systems, green roofs, rain gardens, the use of natural and artificially constructed wetlands, and pervious alternatives to pavement, see: Raquel Pinderhughes, *Alternative Urban Futures: Planning for Sustainable Development in Cities throughout the Word* (Lanham, MD: Rowman and Littlefield, 2004), 38–46; and Christopher C. Boone and Ali Modarres, *City and Environment* (Philadelphia: Temple University Press, 2006), 101–106 and 124–126.

50. Ibid.

51. Cleveland City Planning Commission, "Reimagining a More Sustainable Cleveland" (2008), www.cudc.kent.edu/shrink/Images/reimagining_final_screen-res.pdf.

52. Except where otherwise noted, our description of the sustainability efforts of each of the five cities draws heavily on Kent E. Portney, *Taking Sustainable Cities Seriously: Economic Development, the Environment, and Quality of Life in American Cities* (Cambridge, MA: MIT Press, 2003), 181–219.

53. For a review of the concept of a city's "ecological footprint," see Peter Newman and Isabella Jennings, *Cities as Sustainable Ecosystems: Principles and Practices* (Washington, DC: Island Press, 2008), 80–91.

54. For a discussion of the importance of greenways to urban populations and to ecological systems, see: Boone and Modarres, *City and Environment*, 170–175; and Rob Jongman and Gloria Pungetti, eds., *Ecological Networks and Greenways: Concept, Design, Implementation* (Cambridge, UK, and New York: Cambridge University Press, 2004).

55. Beatley, *Green Urbanism*, 70–72.

56. C40 Cities, "Austin's Green Building Program Facilitates the Construction of Sustainable Buildings" (2008), www.c40cities.org/bestpractices/buildings/austin_standards.jsp.

57. American Council for an Energy Efficient Economy (ACEEE), *America's Best: Profiles of America's Leading Energy Efficiency Programs*, section on "Residential New Construction Energy Program, Green Building Program, Austin Energy," (n.d.), www.aceee.org/utility/5egrnbldgaustin.pdf.

58. See also Beatley, *Green Urbanism*, 320–321.

59. Donald Miller, "Developing and Employing Sustainability Indicators as a Principal Strategy in Planning: Experiences in the Puget Sound Urban Region of Washington State," in *Towards Sustainable Cities: East Asian, North American and European Perspectives on Managing Urban Regions,* ed. André Sorensen, Peter J. Marcotullio, and Jill Grant (Hampshire, UK: Ashgate, 2003), 112–131.

60. Beatley, *Green Urbanism*, 68–69; City of Seattle, Department of Design, Construction, and Land Use, "Urban Village Case Studies," March 2003, www.seattle.gov/dpd/stellent/groups/pan/@pan/@plan/@proj/documents/Web_Informational/dpd_001112.pdf.

61. Eran Ben-Joseph, *The Code of the City: Standards and the Hidden Language of Place Making* (Cambridge, MA: MIT Press, 2005), 122–123.

62. Beatley, *Green Urbanism*; Sorensen, Marcotullio, and Grant, eds., *Towards Sustainable Cities.*

63. Robert D. Bullard, *Dumping in Dixie: Race, Class, and Environmental Quality* (Boulder, CO: Westview Press, 2000).

64. Swati R. Prakash, "Beyond Dirty Diesels: Clean and Just Transportation in Northern Manhattan," in *Growing Smarter: Achieving Livable Communities, Environmental Justice, and Regional Equity*, ed. Robert D. Bullard (Cambridge, MA: MIT Press, 2007), 273–298; Pinderhughes, *Alternative Urban Futures*, 176–179; New York University Medical Center and School of Medicine, "Asthma Linked To Soot From Diesel Trucks In Bronx," *ScienceDaily*, October 30, 2006, www.sciencedaily.com/releases/2006/10/061017084420.htm.

65. Pinderhughes, *Alternative Urban Futures*, 178–179. Boone and Modarres, *City and Environment,* 106–114, review the potential advantages that biodiesel and other alternative fuels offer urban communities.

Name Index

Index

About the Authors

The late **Bernard H. Ross** was Professor Emeritus at the School of Public Affairs at The American University and directed the university's Master's of Public Administration Program and the Center for Urban Public Policy Analysis. Among his publications are *How Washington Works: The Executive's Guide to Government* (written with A. Lee Fritschler) and *Urban Management: A Guide to Information Sources.* Dr. Ross was instrumental in helping to organize the Council of the University Institutes for Urban Affairs, the forerunner of the present-day Urban Affairs Association.

Myron A. Levine, Professor of Urban Affairs at Wright State University, is the editor of Annual Editions: Urban Affairs and the author of Presidential Campaigns and Elections. His writings have appeared in the Journal of Urban Affairs, Urban Affairs Review, and Journal of the American Planning Association. He has received Fulbright awards for study in Amsterdam, Berlin, Bratislava, and Riga, and an NEH award for study in Paris. His research focuses on national urban policy, urban revitalization, and local government collaboration and consolidation.